SKIRMISH

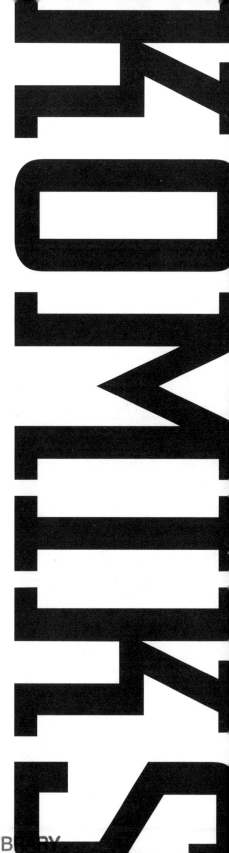

COMIC ART
IN RUSSIA

JOSÉ ALANIZ

University Press of Mississippi • Jackson

www.upress.state.ms.us

Designed by Peter D. Halverson

The University Press of Mississippi is a member of the Association of
American University Presses.

Copyright © 2010 by University Press of Mississippi
All rights reserved
Manufactured in the United States of America

First printing 2010

∞

Library of Congress Cataloging-in-Publication Data

Alaniz, José.
 Komiks : comic art in Russia / José Alaniz.
 p. cm.
 Includes bibliographical references and index.
 ISBN 978-1-60473-366-2 (cloth : alk. paper) 1. Comic books, strips,
etc.—Russia (Federation) 2. Cartoonists—Russia (Federation) I.
Title. II. Title: Comic art in Russia.
 NC1764.5.R8A43 2010
 741.59'47—dc22   2009027154

British Library Cataloging-in-Publication Data available

To the memory of two great women, sadly passed on:
Frances Till and Natalya Monastyrova;

and to two, to my great fortune, who are still with us:
Raquel Alaniz and Tiziana Bertolini

CONTENTS

ACKNOWLEDGMENTS

Portions of this study have appeared in different versions in *Ulbandus, Ante, Kinokultura*, the *International Journal of Comic Art*, the *Comics Journal*, *Khroniki Chedrika*, and the anthologies *Russian Children's Literature and Culture* and *Uncensored? Reinventing Humor and Satire in Post-Soviet Russia*. Research on this book profited immensely from a 2008 National Endowment for the Humanities-funded summer institute at the New York Public Library's Slavic and East European Collection, whose director, Edward Kasinec, proved a model of professionalism and collegiality. I would also like to thank an anonymous collector of Russian caricature and poster art in Prague for the chance to examine his materials in summer 2007. Irina Paperno at the University of California, Berkeley, got the first look in 1997 at what would become this project; without her support it may have gone no further. Others who contributed to my professional and personal development at Berkeley, the University of Texas at Austin, and the *Moscow Tribune* include Charles Ramírez-Berg, Robert Twombly, Anthony Vanchu, Frances Masiello, Eric Naiman, Linda Williams, Alexei Yurchak, Tomohiro Machiyama, and Anthony Luis. Of the University of Pittsburgh contingent, Volodya Padunov, Nancy Condee, and Helena Goscilo all pushed me along, in ways they may not have realized. Natasha Perova of *Glas* is my oldest and most-valued Moscow friend. My comics studies fellow travelers at the International Comic Arts Forum were the first to hear me try out much of this material; it has been greatly improved by their comments. Among these stalwarts, I single out Rusty Witek, Marc Singer, Charles Hatfield, Gene Kannenberg, Héctor Fernández-l'Hoeste, and Ana Merino. I bow my head low before the god-like John Lent. In Russia, I found a wonderful group of komiks artists, scholars, and supporters, without whom this project simply would not exist. Of special mention: Mikhail Sidlin, Zhora Litichevsky, Gosha Ostretsov,

Ilya Kitup, Andrei Ayoshin, Sergei Repyov, Dmitry Yakovlev, Khikhus, and all the staff at the KomMissia comics festival. No one helped me more than the great Misha Zaslavsky. For unflagging support and loyalty, though, none can compare to the illustrious Galya Diment. Indeed, all my colleagues at the University of Washington Department of Slavic Languages and Literatures have helped create an ideal environment for my work; none is more tireless than Shosh Westen. In particular I want to thank Bojan Belic and Katarzyna Dziwirek for their assistance with Serbian and Polish materials, respectively. Douglas Machle of Classics also helped with his Dutch skills. Seth Graham, time and again, has shown himself a great inspiration, consigliere, friend, and professional lodestar. Everything good in this book is owing to their influence; everything bad flows exclusively from me.

In this book I have used the United States Library of Congress transliteration system for the Russian language, except in cases where familiar names (Tolstoy, Dostoyevsky) might be rendered unfamiliar, and for readability (Litichevsky rather than Litichevskii). In the bibliography, I have adhered to the LOC system. Updates, corrections, and supplemental illustrations can be found at my blog at http://komiksoved23.blogspot.com/.

INTRODUCTION

KOMIKS AGONISTES

Those who grew up in the land of the Soviets will say that,
just as we didn't have sex, we didn't have comics.
—GULIAEV

Everyone knows that we are "gangsters, trampling on the
sacred name of art," that our works are "little pictures for
morons," that our muse is "a mad radioactive mutant."
—KHIKHUS

In December 2003, the exhibit *Apocalypse Today* (Apokalipsis sego dnia)
opened at the World of Art Museum (WAM) gallery in Moscow. Billed as
a modern revival of the sixteenth-century tradition of illustrated miniatures
produced by the Russian Orthodox Church, the show brought together thir-
teen artists' visions of the Book of Revelations. The works ranged from the
humor-laden reinventions of prophecy by Georgy "Zhora" Litichevsky; the
weightless, hallucinogenic sojourns of John to the higher realms, limned by
Alim Velitov; the fantasy stylings of Askold Akishin; the monumental ap-
paritions of Ilya Savchenkov; the faux naïve buffoonery of Pavel "Khikhus"
Sukhikh, among others. The religious theme linked the exhibit to the rising
interest in traditional culture among many post-Soviet Russians, but its medium announced it as very much a novelty, something few in the country
would have even considered art at all—for *Apocalypse Today* was among the
earliest gallery shows devoted solely to the ongoing renaissance in Russian
comic art.

3

It proved a breakthrough: in a country where comics often appear as short pieces or strips in children's magazines or advertisements, gallery visitors could view these biblically themed sequential narratives (some several pages long) and get a real sense of the medium's sophistication: its breadth of styles, diversity of designs, word/image meldings—as well as its links to past visual culture practices. After decades in the shadows, Russian comics were making their long-awaited debut.

Perhaps.

Yet, for all the attention generated by *Apocalypse Today* (some of the displayed works also appeared in WAM's celebrated art journal), its origins bore an object lesson for the optimists who saw a new dawn. Yegor Larichev, editor of the journal and initiator of the exhibit, told a reporter that he had intended to produce a film adaption of Revelations, but fell short on funding. As a secondary measure, he turned to comics, which he described as "close to film" (Malpas). Larichev, far from the only Russian cultural figure to see the medium as derivative of other, perhaps "higher" art forms,[1] saw *Apocalypse Today* as a sort of sketch, a stopgap, for his original vision, to give viewers an idea of what the real project (a filmed version) would look like.

Such, the reader will discover, have been the fortunes of this medium in the land of the Czars, the Soviets, and the Siloviki.[2]

The subject of this book, Russian comics, or *komiks*, belongs to an ancient world tradition of sequential narrative often combining word and image that entered its modern phase simultaneously with the rise of cinema (about 1895), but never enjoyed its popularity or, until recently, its estimation as an art form. In this as in so many other areas of life, the same things happened in Russia as in other parts of the world—only more so. From their origins in the religious icon-making and book-illustration tradition, to the immensely popular *lubok* or woodblock print of the seventeenth to twentieth centuries, to their vilification and marginalization under the Communists, to their economic struggles and Internet "migration" in the post-Soviet era, komiks have often borne the brunt of ideological change—burning in the summers of relative freedom, freezing in the hard winters of official disdain. As many Russians expressed about their own experiences, komiks never had a "normal life."

THE QUESTION OF MASS CULTURE

For nearly a century the comics medium repeatedly foundered in what Steven Lovell has called "the long and difficult history of modern Russian attempts to grapple with 'the popular'" (2005: 38). As elaborated in chapter 4, Russia—most acutely under the Soviets—struggled with mass culture (its seduction, its threat) to the extent that it has never existed as a stable concept.[3] Despite the ardent dreams of many, and even as the society altered so radically in the 1990s as to make possible an "enormous infusion of the lowbrow" (Barker: 36), even in the commodity-rich age of the post-Soviet *Homo consumptor*,[4] and—lest it go unremarked—no shortage of native talent, Russian comics *still* did not thrive.

"The situation for comics in Russia is, generally speaking, very strange," concluded the critic Ivan Kulikov, reviewing the first Russian comics festival in 2002. "In a short time the country has managed to acquire all forms of mass culture. Except comics!"

Russian comics artists, to their considerable befuddlement and pique, find themselves mired in a situation not unlike that of their contemporary French peers trying to inject a high art sensibility into BD. As described by Bart Beaty in *Unpopular Culture*: "Working in a field commonly derided as merely popular, but reaping few of the benefits that accrue to producers of genuinely popular culture, these artists are caught in a double bind" (2008: 15).

As mentioned, the same thing happens in Russia—only more so. An analogue to French groups such as l'Association, St. Petersburg's SPb. Nouvelle Graphiques (SPb.NG, which sees itself very much in the Franco-Belgian tradition) must contend with more than the usual difficulties faced by arts progressives everywhere, such as getting audiences to look beyond entrenched modes of perception and consumption, to possibilities beyond the mainstream. Russia *has* no mainstream. And as far as both the public and many comics artists themselves are concerned, it has no one-hundred-year, or fifty-year, or even twenty-year store of traditions, nor—thanks to the Soviets—no institutional memory of comics practice beyond occasional children's short stories. Therefore, SPb.NG, in addition to the ordinary financial hurdles (also worse in Russia), infrastructure issues (until recently much high-quality printing had to be done abroad), and rare opportunities to publish (there is no industry), must also contend with a broader culture that sees comics as suspect, contemptible, cheap, "popular" in the worst sense—a climate in which utterances such as this, from a 2005 theater review, remain routine: "The genre of this show is designated as 'theatrical comics.' On the one hand, that's good; comics are a reflection of modern life. On the other hand, are the creators of this concept implying something? Maybe they want to insult the audience? What could be more obtuse (*tupee*) than comics? And what could be more offensive than to call a parable 'comics'?" (Brzhezinskaia). To say the least, groups such as SPb.NG must operate in a semi-hostile environment, where comics have nowhere near the respect, social status, and cultural capital they enjoy in France. This, among so many other factors considered in this book, has shaped the practice, circulation, and aesthetics of Russian comics in ways unseen in the West.

DEFINITION AND METHODOLOGY

Echoing Joseph Witek in his landmark 1989 study *Comic Books as History* (and more recently sustained by Charles Hatfield in his 2005 *Alternative Comics: An Emerging Literature*), this study "presupposes that comic books as narratives and as cultural productions merit serious critical analysis" (Witek: 3). With the coming onto its own of American comics scholarship in the last twenty years, historical and theoretical studies of the form have abounded. Among the most insightful remain Ariel Dorfman and Armand Mattelart's Marxist *How to Read Donald Duck* (1971), David Kunzle's *History of the Comic Strip* (1973), Will Eisner's *Comics and Sequential Art* (1985), Witek's *Comic Books as History* (1989), Scott McCloud's *Understanding Comics* (1993), Robert C. Harvey's *The Art of the Comic Book: An Aesthetic History* (1996), and Annalisa Di Liddo's *Alan Moore: Comics as Performance, Fiction as Scalpel* (2009). These have added to older treatments of comics from communications and media studies (Marshall McLuhan), popular culture studies (Robert Warshow), and sociology, on top of a considerable body of European comics scholarship that has existed since the 1950s.

An important question at the outset of any such investigation pertains to definition: what counts as comics for the purposes of a given project? I take as my object of study that form of visual arts practice variously called comics, *fumetti, la bande dessinée,* manga, *tebeo, historieta*, and so forth, which the American theorist Scott McCloud defines as "juxtaposed pictorial and other images in deliberate sequence" (9). While one often sees an overlap with other closely related practices, I, following McCloud and others, privilege sequentiality as comics' primary mode of meaning-making.

This study also relies on McCloud's definition for its emphasis on distinguishing comics (often appearing, especially in Russia, as pictorial narratives) from single-panel and/or political cartoons and caricatures. (Almost all the works analyzed in this book appear in strip, album, web, or "comic book" form, not as single panels.) That said, I do not discount, as McCloud does, the cultural and historical construction of the category known as modern comics; thus I, following David Kunzle, see their proper emergence not in cave paintings or ancient Egyptian art but in the much more recent work of figures like Rodolphe Töpffer. (As discussed further on, many Russian artists adhere more closely to an ecumenical McCloudian scope, seeing comics in cave paintings.) The roots of Russian comics predate that era, and we do examine them; likewise, I discuss at some length the central role played by single-image, nonsequential caricature in the comics' development, particularly in chapters 1 and 2. In such cases I refer to this material as "comics-like," "proto-comics," or simply as cartoons.[5]

Furthermore, the deep interest many Russian artists have shown in blurring the (to them, illusory) word/image dichotomy forms a central concern in several portions of the study, as in my discussion of the Constructivists and the propaganda posters of the early Soviet era; as well as in the works of Ilya Kabakov, Elena Uzhinova, Vadim Rubtsov, the aforementioned SPb. Nouvelle Graphiques, and others. My analysis proceeds from the work of such scholars as W. J. T. Mitchell, Gene Kannenberg, and Charles Hatfield, who notes: "In comics word and image approach each other: words can be visually inflected, reading as pictures, while pictures can become as abstract and symbolic as words. In brief, the written text can function like images, and images like written text" (36).

These matters regarding an absolute definition or "essence" of comics (which have at times come to bedevil the online scholars forums and academic conferences of a still-emerging field) concern me less than arriving at a treatment of what I call in the text a "comics sensibility"—somewhat relatable to what the Russian writer Viktor Erofeyev sardonically called "the comics disease." In the absence of so much which Western comics artists take for granted in their practice (an industry, a mainstream, an "alternative") and very little in the way of Bourdieu's autonomous recognition or heteronymous remuneration, komiksisty have had to improvise, invent, and sustain a sense of themselves, their art and their fractured subculture. How this has affected their work—whether comics or comics-like—and how to interpret it: these have been the central concerns in my research and writing.

Throughout my task, I have taken as my lodestar the rigor, clarity, and systematic thinking of Thierry Groensteen—even if I have not always lived up to his high standards. Above all, I have tried to integrate his notion of comics as a system, made of disparate elements and devices that no single work need evoke comprehensively to retain the designation "comics." As he writes, "The comics system will be a conceptual frame in which all of the actualizations of the 'ninth art' can find their place and be thought of in relation to each other, taking into account their differences and their commonalities within the same medium" (20).

KOMIKS

A word on some important foreign terms employed in this book. The Russian *komiks* derives from the English "comics," and it is singular in number. One does also hear *"komiksy"* (which retains the English plural sense). In seeking to emphasize some notion of the cultural specificity of this medium, in my translation back to English I am keeping komiks as a singular to designate the art form in question. For the same reason, instead of terms like "comics creator" or "comics artist," I often employ such Russian terms as *"komiksmen," "komiksist," "komiksistka"* (feminine), and *"komiks-meiker."*

As I argue in part 2, at least some contemporary Russian comic art, despite the tidal wave of foreign influences coming in through films, televisions, and broadband connections, retains a sense of its own "Russianness." In a blatant move to legitimize and support that Otherness, that local identity, I am led, perhaps somewhat piningly but unapologetically, to call it komiks.

THE BOOK'S OUTLINE

I have divided this study into two parts. Chapters 1 through 4 cover the historical and sociocultural background of comics and proto-comics in Russia, from their roots in Orthodox Christian visual practices, through the prosperous period of the lubok, the experimental works of the prerevolutionary avant garde, to their Soviet-era semi-exile to the margins of culture, to the promise and catastrophes of the postsocialist era of predatory capitalism. The book then turns, in part 2, to its proper focus: close readings of individual works and/or artists, from a cultural studies perspective. These mine contemporary komiks for insights into how they reflect and shape attitudes regarding mass culture, globalization, nationalism, anti-Americanism, consumerism, and feminism in the post-Soviet era. I also examine the problematic status of autobiography in Russian comic art and the medium's contemporary status vis-à-vis other cultural practices, especially literature, art, and cinema.

This book traces the rise of komiks from the icon to the Internet. In a study of such ambit, we will leave many stories untold, or partly told, or mentioned in passing, or ignored. My goal (not dissimilar to what *Apocalypse Today* perhaps inadvertently managed) is to acquaint the reader with the enormous scope, diversity, and peculiarity of Russian comic art, especially of the contemporary period, at the same time providing a sense of the cultural conditions that led to its long troubled history and continue to affect its development in the twenty-first century. Finally, through my close readings in part 2, I assay a two-pronged task: to impart on the comics scholar or reader a portrait of this form's unique manifestations on Russian soil—while also demonstrating to the Russianists or Slavicists in the room komiks' particular suitability to address, reflect, reshape, and refract issues familiar (and some not so familiar) to Russian culture.

The following points are threaded through these pages. In whatever form they assumed, komiks

1. had to carve out a niche in a profoundly word-based culture that placed a strong emphasis on *literaturnost'* ("literariness");
2. partly due to their word/image combination often bore a trace of the foreign, degenerate and/or "mass" cultural;
3. consequently fell under the suspicious and jealous eye of the intelligentsia, becoming an art form adrift and available to many different movements, styles, and ideologies, but rarely grounded in its own industry or traditions.

In the early twenty-first century, komiks continues to negotiate these cultural preconceptions, to greater and lesser degrees of success. It poses a conundrum to many observers, in fact, why komiks endures in Russia, for the most part, as "the illegitimate child of 20th-century art" (Maksimova: 78).

Kulikov, in his festival review, cut to the core issue: "As an art form, comics are accessible. But are you prepared to make yourselves accessible to comics?" This study explores the history and cultural factors that influenced how Russians have and perhaps will continue to answer that question.

PART I

HISTORICAL

BACKGROUND

LUBOK AND THE PREREVOLUTIONARY ERA

THE ICON

The language of comics on Russian soil dates back to the country's earliest religious icon-making tradition, which is to say, to the roots of Christianity and thus of the nation itself.[1] According to Bruce Lincoln, "while frescoes and mosaics proclaimed the glory of God in Keiv's churches, paintings done on panels of well-seasoned alder, cypress, or lime (over which a layer of linen had been stretched and covered with several thin coats of gesso) became the windows through which the people of Rus entered the world of the spirit to receive the grace of God" (22).[2] Icons, having come to Rus (along with the new religion) by way of Byzantium in the tenth century, served both a religious (as objects of prayer and veneration) as well as an illustrative function: the severe, "transcendent" portraits of saints, the Madonna and the savior; heavenly scenes and biblical events, all brought to resplendent life before the eye of the illiterate believer a world he otherwise could only imagine.[3] Indeed, the power of the icon, which functioned according to its own "unearthly" representational schema,[4] exemplified early Russian culture's strong inclination toward the visual.[5]

So strong was this predilection, in fact, that icons in Russia took on supernatural characteristics far beyond their representational role; in this recently (and in many senses enduringly) pagan culture, they were venerated as manifestations of the divine in and of themselves, possessed of miraculous healing and protective powers. Peasants knew them as *bogi* ("gods"). They even substituted to a degree for a weakened political culture in the thirteenth and fourteenth centuries, a period when the Russians languished under the "Tatar yoke" of the conquering Mongols, while monastic icon-making flourished. As described by James Billington, "the omnipresent holy pictures provided an image of higher authority that helped compensate for the diminished stature of temporal princes. In Russia, the icon often came to represent in effect the supreme communal authority before which one swore oaths, resolved disputes, and marched into battle" (31). Since at least the thirteenth century, some icons included figures of saints in their margins, and, as in the Byzantine tradition, text identifying the subject.[6] Icons depicting the Last Judgment, following the formulae of frescoes and other large-scale works, also organize large numbers of figures in tiers about Christ pantakrator (e.g., Icon of the Last Judgment, Novgorod school, seventeenth century, in Rice: 72).

Sequential narratives, placing the same character in different temporal registers in the panel, are also not uncommon. Icons representing the story of St. Elias (Elijah) from the Novgorod and Northern schools (sixteenth century) typically show the saint being tended by an angel in the lower right, while in the upper portions of the image he is rising in glory on a chariot of fire, as his disciple strives to hold on to his mantle. The fiery chariot, incidentally, is often rendered as a red or yellow circle, in the manner of a graphic element, rather than "realistically."

This impulse toward longer-form narratives, deployed outright in panels, sees particular expression in the biographical (zhiteinyi) icons of saints. These feature a portrait of the subject, framed by a dozen or more incidents from his life along the margins, as in the hagiographic icon of the fourth-century Roman general St. Theodore (Fyodor) Stratelates, from the Novgorod school, early sixteenth century. These scenes, Rice reports, may have first introduced folkloristic motifs along with contemporary dress and other details (71). What also strikes the viewer of this work is the prominent role played by the fourteen sequential panels accompanied by text: not precisely "marginal," they are large enough to form a prominent and unified design feature of the work. Theodore's life—with its embrace of Christianity, various martyr's tortures, and crucifixion—unfolds chronologically in the panels, while his central portrait, holding the sword "symbolizing sovereign power" (Rice: 73), embodies his dignified, eternal presence. The beholder immediately takes in both the historical and the transcendent at once, then turns back and forth from the particular to the overarching in the course of contemplation.[7]

As icons develop through the medieval era and secular subjects start to appear, the turn to sequential narrative strategies comes to the fore in some works—as if the framing "incidents" of St. Theodore's portrait come to take over the center itself. This is especially marked in the Novgorod school's *Icon of the Battle Between the Men of Novgorod and the Men of Suzdal* (fifteenth century), Russia's earliest historical painting.[8] It depicts the siege of Novgorod by the army of Nikolai Bogoliubski in 1169, and the intercession of the city's icon of the Holy Virgin to aid in the city's defense (this is an icon about an icon). The artist has divided the action into three horizontal panels (most art historians call them "bands," "scenes," "planes," or "rows") with no "gutters," the first showing a procession carrying the icon to the Novgorod fortress or kremlin, over the Volkhov River (in an earlier moment, on the right, we see church elders bearing the icon out of the Church of the Savior, where it usually resides); the second shows the Suzdal army attacking the city, shooting arrows at the icon, which looms over the ramparts like a military banner; and the third depicting the battle itself, as the Novgorod army, led by the saints Boris, Gleb, Georgy, and Demetrius of Thessalonica, streams out of the main gate to clash with the besiegers, bodies lying at their feet. The work has dynamism and clarity of execution—one reads it "linearly," from the top down, but also appreciates its overall design, its "legendariness." To reinforce this unity of design, the wall of Novgorod stretches along the left side of the icon and over the two bottom panels, fusing the two moments of time into a continuum as well as underscoring the wall's height, its impregnability.

The "multi-incident" method enhanced the icon's capacity for conveying a historical and/or ideological message; it also, as Vera Likhacheva reminds us, points to the medieval approach to time, space, and representation adopted by Russian icon painters:

The coexistence on one panel of events pertaining to various times [raznovremennye sobytiia] relates to the icon's particular understanding of artistic space, whereby is represented not a restricted portion or small part of a real space, but a concept of space as limitless, ideal in length and scope.

In the case of Renaissance painting, an illusory space corresponds with the illusoriness of its representation of time. Here it is a moment that is being depicted. The viewer cannot penetrate the space shown him by the artist without crossing over into the moment which he has captured; concrete space is linked with concrete time. Whereas the icon is not tied to a concrete space, and therefore it does not represent a specific moment. Every object is conveyed "in general," as such; what is created is not the illusion of the object itself, but, as it were, its model. (30)

Likhacheva's contention as to the icon's "expansive" devices underscores its double-voiced nature, its capacity to represent time and space as both "here/now" and "everywhere/always." Its conventional approach to the object as not itself but a "model" obeying its own non-mimetic rules (i.e., a device), as well as its bringing together (in some cases blending) of image and explanatory text, would all have repercussions for the representational strategies of the later lubok, the direct antecedent of comics on Russian soil.[9]

THE PEOPLE'S PICTURES

С ним случай был: картиночек
Он сыну накупил,
Развешал их по стеночкам
И сам не меньше мальчика
Любил на них глядеть.

Once he bought his son
some little pictures,
Put them up on the walls,
And he himself, no less than his son,
Loved to look at them.

—NIKOLAI NEKRASOV, *WHO IS HAPPY IN RUSSIA?* (1873–1876)

To the extent it initially followed upon the icon—in propagating a religious message and as the object of worship—the first form of proto-comics in Russia emerged out of devotion to God. By the early seventeenth century, the *lubok* or woodblock print had secured an important place in the nation's visual culture as an expression of folk belief. In its simplest version, it was a painted wooden panel, though more typically the lubok was a cheaply made sheet (similar to European broadsheets, from which it probably originated) depicting religious scenes through crude drawings and textual captions. Though originally popular with the upper classes who could afford them, the prints slowly spread to the semiliterate peasantry—a process accelerated by Peter the Great's progressive reforms of the eighteenth century (under which imported Western prints replaced lubki among the well-off) and by copper printing introduced in the 1820s (which greatly increased their production).

Jeffrey Brooks notes that by the end of the eighteenth century *lubki* were "often the first printed materials to enter the homes of the common people" (63), who decorated their walls with them, particularly for holidays.[10] A steady secularization of subject continued through the eighteenth century; the lubok now depicted folk themes, fairy tales, and historical events (such as the War of 1812)[11] with accompanying text. There were also lubok almanacs and calendars. Even while mass-produced, lubki retained a primitive appearance and handicraft character; Brooks mentions that in Nikolskoye in the 1860s "a thousand self-trained women were employed . . . to hand-color the prints" (65), making each individual work unique. They were sold throughout the countryside by networks of wandering peddlers (ofeni), as well as in urban markets. By all accounts, the masses delighted in the simple "people's pictures" (narodnie kartinki), as some called them, associating the prints with festivity, humor, and diversion. As noted by Dmitry Rovinsky, a major nineteenth-century collector and scholar of the lubok: "Having firmly established themselves in the everyday life of the average Russian, the pictures decorated and prettified his humdrum existence (budni), while during folk holidays and fairs they made a discernible contribution towards the creation of a particularly festive atmosphere: free, somewhat informal, filled with laughter and a joyous apprehension of life" (11).

By the nineteenth century this carnival mood was in part sparked by "the association of popular prints and improper subjects" (Kelly 1998: 60), including bawdy or outright pornographic material (a topic explored at greater length in chapter 6). Another contributing factor was the Russian flair for "enlivening" the stories of the lubok through spoken commentary, as in the case of the *raeshniki*, showmen who incorporated the prints into their traveling peepshows (known as *rayok*) starting around 1830. As the viewer peeped into the box, the raeshnik "regaled them with salacious rhyming doggerel which purported to describe the pictures on view" though as often as not strayed far from the picture's content (Kelly 1998: 49). In any case, the lubok came increasingly to be considered (particularly by the upper classes, which now recoiled from them) as a commoner's medium, something by and for the masses. For some, this made it banal and vulgar, for others, endearingly "authentic."[12]

By the 1820s, the scholar I. M. Snegirov could declare the modest people's pictures a quasi-nostalgic repository of Russian heartland values: "[Lubki] serve as a manifestation of the national character (narodnost') in graphic art form; it contains material for studying the history of that Russian character . . . [I]t lumps together elements of our nation which themselves display the mind, spirit, beliefs, sentiments, world view, traditions and everyday life of the Russian people—in a word, it contains everything which constitutes the edification and the amusement of its life, its uniqueness, its past—which, by the ineluctable law of regeneration, repeats itself in the present day" (259). The lubok maintained this folk, downhome character even as it increasingly became a mass-produced item manufactured in urban centers, especially Moscow. Due partly to censorship decrees issued in 1839 and 1851 that ordered greater control over the prints' production; the advent of lithography; and the monopolistic practices of printer/publishers such as Ivan Sytin (himself a former peddler), by the twentieth century the "people's pictures" were made primarily in factories by large firms that had frozen out or appropriated the work of rural masters.

Further advances in printing, as well as illustrated periodicals, photographs, films, postcards, placards, and a general rise in literacy, contributed to the decline of the *lubok* in the early twentieth century. (Though lubki were put on display at the 1895 All-Russian Exhibition of Printing [Bowlt: 87].) The great surge of patriotic propaganda during World War I marked the last gasp of the traditional lubok as a mass medium in Russia, although in the two decades before the Bolshevik revolution it had great influence on avant-garde art (especially the Futurists and Neo-Primitivists), as discussed below.

WHAT IS LUBOK?

Since Snegirov launched the formal study of the lubok in the 1820s—to no small controversy among educated circles, who considered it beneath contempt—scholars have skirmished over several issues involved in the study of the subject. Avram Reitblat, reviewing the recent literature in 2001, notes that the very term "lubok" is problematic, since the historical record indicates that before Snegirov few people actually called the prints by that name. Instead, depending on the region and/or what they depicted, the prints went by poteshnie listy ("funny sheets"), Suzdalskie (from Suzdal), panki ("little panels"), bogatyry ("knights"), konnitsa (referring to figures on horseback), friazhkie ("Western European"), prazdniky ("holidays"), prostovik ("simple"), balagurnik ("joker," "jester"), satira ("satire"), Moskovskie kartiny ("Moscow pictures"), or simply listy ("sheets")—among a plethora of other names.

Snegirov himself called the prints "lubok" fully aware of the term's ambiguity: did it refer to the bark (lub) of the linden tree, from which he claimed peasants formed the wood blocks; or did it point to Moscow's Lubianka Street, where the sheets were printed and near which they were sold; or, indeed, to the wooden box in which the ofeni carried the prints for sale? Or did the word simply connote something "crude," "badly made," and "ramshackle," as it did in other contexts? Evidently, Boris Sokolov surmises, Snegirov simply picked one of the local names for the prints; already by the 1840s this had grown into a general term, handed down to the present day.[13] For his part, noted Brooks, the collector Dmitry Rovinsky seems to have named his 1881 book devoted to the subject *The Russian People's Pictures* (Russkie narodnie kartinki) precisely to get away from "lubok's" limited and negative associations (63).

Reitblat further argues that individual *lubkovedy* ("lubokologists") have focused too much on one or another aspect of lubok—technological advances, distribution networks, propaganda uses, subjects, intended audience, aesthetics, production methods—when only a unitary approach will yield a properly comprehensive picture. A certain fuzziness still adheres to the subject at hand: a 1997 collection of essays, *The World of the People's Pictures* (Mir narodnoi kartinki), featured essays on Indian, Brazilian, Mongolian, and other Asian popular prints in addition to Russian examples. Meanwhile, Reitblat laments, lubkovedy have largely yielded the study of lubochnie knizhki (lubok chapbooks or booklets) such as the Koren' Bible to folklorists, book specialists, and literary scholars.

Finally, even a minimal delving into the background and development of lubok demonstrates a great variety of styles and methods—engraving on wood, then copper; the turn to lithography and chromolithography; and the more artisanal approach of the risovannyi (drawn) lubok all had ramifications for the prints' look and subjects—yet today many scholars (especially, as we will see, comics scholars) tend to refer to the lubok as if it were one monolithic entity throughout its history.

CHIEF CHARACTERISTICS

In both form and content, lubok was a unique hybrid art. First, its interaction of word and image, notes the literary critic/semiotician Yurii Lotman, was not simply that of an illustration and explanatory caption, but more like a theme and its elaboration (razvertyvanie): "It is as if the caption 'plays up' (razygrivaet) the drawing, compelling the viewer to perceive it not as something static, but as an action" (484). This playful, dramatic quality of the lubok (along with its humor) encourages the reader/viewer to "enter into" the world of the story, to actively interpret it and not to regard it passively from "outside"—a reaction sometimes further encouraged by the marked departure of the caption text from the image.[14] This, according to Boris Sokolov, made the lubok a "Third Culture" combination of the graphic, textual, and dramatic arts, well tailored to narrative (195). A sort of "paper theater" as much as "paper icon," some lubki even framed the action with arches, footlights, and curtains, as in Mikhail Nekhoroshevskii's lubochniy chapbook *The Parable of the Prodigal Son* (nineteenth century).

The lubok's ludic characteristics further manifest themselves in its similarly humorous treatment of speech balloons[15] or scrolls (which some figures still held in their hands as late as the eighteenth century). Lotman chooses a well-known print of the Fool Farnos as illustration: it shows a cloud escaping his backside, with the inscription: "I let out some air (dukh) from my rump, so the mosquitoes I can lump" (484). The secular lubok, in short, presents its action with a marked conditionality that recall's Likhacheva's icon representing not the object but "as it were, its model." Compare this with Lotman's description of the lubok's nonmimetic approach to the image: "The representation of the scene produces a principally different artistic effect from a drawing which the viewer directly associates with some reality or other. In effect the representation of a representation, lubok creates a heightened degree of contingency, of conventionality (uslovnost'). An image that renders itself the sign of a sign transports the viewer into a peculiar, playful 'reality'" (483). This renders the "simple" print a complex, highly coded, interactive multimedia experience, tied to other aspects of the semiliterate peasant's world. Boris Dubin argues in his 1981 essay, "Towards a Poetics of the People's Pictures," that the secular lubok's representational strategies relate to the imagery and ambience of the holiday (at holiday time, revelers behave toward each other with a high degree of conditionality). Accordingly, in his Bakhtin-inflected account, the

The story of Lazarus from
The Bible of Vasily Koren',
known as the *Koren' Bible*
(1692–96).

lubok contains no "objective" speech; the characters "play themselves" (predstav-liaiutsia) (paraphrased in Reitblat 2001: 324).

Indeed, the phrase "play themselves" is not coincidental: the drama is enhanced by lubok's hieroglyphic nature: figures appear in recognizable dramatic poses for easy "reading," such as the oft-seen arms raised in panic in "Yaga Baba Fights the Corcodile" [*sic*] (eighteenth century); the swinging of sticks in panel after panel to beat drunkards in "The Great Head of Drunkenness" (mid-eighteenth century); and the Firebird with its characteristic outspread wings and beatific expression, seen in countless iterations up through the end of the nineteenth century. (In another, more repulsive example, the arc of vomit—whether from illness or, more often, drink—is rendered through particularly stylized conventions over the centuries.)[16] Furthermore, the many coded references in eighteenth-century works to Peter the Great (analyzed below) argue for the sophistication of lubok signifying practices, particularly when mobilized to evade the Czarist censor.

Another consequence of lubok's theatrical poetics is reflected in its treatment of time—in particular, through sequential narratives. Lotman agrees with Likhacheva that post-Renaissance painting largely abandoned narratival approaches in favor of more synchronic "freeze-frame" depictions, but the impulse to capture discreet moments as "stories in pictures," developed in the icon, was passed on to the lubok. Anna Nekrylova, in fact, links the lubok's dynamic, plot-driven strategies to the icon and, significantly, to comics[17]: "The desire to unite the entire course of events led to the breaking up of the sheet into panels (kadrirovka), whereby in each cell or conventionally designated frame were drawn different moments of the story, which allows the viewer, by means of transferring the gaze from one episode to the next, to 'read' the drawn text, as occurs when one views the border panels of hagiographic icons and modern comics" (13).

The lubok, in short, represents the first consistently realized expression of a comics language in Russia: it splits up the page into discreet, juxtaposed temporal units; brings together word and image—and, at times, sets them at odds; and also undermines the text/picture distinction through such schemes as the hieroglyphic "dramatic poses" of the figures, evincing Groensteen's "iconographic solidarity." Moreover, contrary to modern opinions about the reception of comics in Russia,[18] consumers themselves readily understood this sequential function of the lubok, as shown in Alexander Pushkin's 1830 short story "The Station Master":

Then he began to register my traveling passport, and I occupied myself with examining the pictures that adorned his humble but tidy abode. They illustrated the story of the Prodigal Son. In the first, a venerable old man, in a nightcap and dressing gown, was taking leave of the restless lad, who was hastily accepting his blessing and a bag of money. In the next picture, the dissolute conduct of the young man was depicted in vivid colors: he was represented sitting at table surrounded by false friends and shameless women. . . . Under each picture I read some suitable German verses. (190)

This episode in Pushkin's story illustrates the lubok's social context (a lowly stationmaster's house, decorated with the people's pictures), the ease with which one may casually read the sequential images and "suitable" text, pertaining to a recognizable story (in this case a parable). There is even registered the slight condescension of the narrator, a member of the gentry, toward the simple adornments of the lower-classes' "humble but neat" quarters, centering on the lubok.[19]

The Russian print's longest narrative expression came in the lubok-chapbook or people's engraved book (narodnaia gravirovannaia kniga)[20] such as the Bible of Vasily Koren', known as the *Koren' Bible* (1692–1696). This combined the approaches of illuminated manuscripts and icons for simplified versions of major biblical episodes on sheets sewn together into booklets. Some of these booklets, such as Alexei Rostovtsev's *Petra the Publican* (Petra-mytaria) (1740s), were made so as to unfold, harmonica-like, for display of the entire story on a wall—making them suitable for two functions: personal reading and group demonstration/explication: "[They were] read aloud to great numbers of people gathered in a hut, similar to how they would listen together to a fairy tale (even if some in the crowd could read)" (Sakovich: 128). The lubok-chapbook, in fact, was a direct forerunner of both the long-form narrative comic book and the poster in Russia.

A final point about the treatment of time in lubok poetics: as with the hagiographic icon, the viewer takes in the whole composition and retains this wider context (in her "peripheral vision," as it were) even as she reads its individual segments. This, along with the lubok's "conventionality" and word/image inter-action, blurs the temporal dimension: "The viewer perceives the drawing, in its turn, as pertaining not to some particular moment or other of the caption, but to its entirety" (Lotman: 491). This effect is achieved even in prints with only one nominal illustration:

Lubok artists, like the ancient Russian creators of illuminated manuscripts (knizhnie miniatiury) represented on the space of a sheet both the main episode and its result. Thus, for example, in pictures depicting [the folk hero] Ilya Muromets shooting his arrows at Solovei the Robber, two arrows are shown: one in the knight's tightly-drawn bow, the other in Solovei the Robber's eye. In actual fact this is one arrow, but by doubling it, the artist has recorded the beginning and end of its flight. Moreover, in the background of these same pictures, we often see depicted the outcome of the encounter: Ilya Muromets mounted atop his knight's steed, on his way to Kiev, the defeated Solovei the Robber strapped to his stirrups. (Nekrylova: 13)

In reading the lubok, we are distinguishing between discreet moments (the only way narrative can unfold), but we are also in a sense "unifying" these contrasting moments into one structurally related composition in which time goes backward or forward, or in any order the reader/viewer's eye wishes to go. The addition of text further complicated this signifying practice, at times "bringing the picture to life," at others contradicting it. The doubly two-fold nature of the lubok (its paradoxical treatment of time, and its word/image combination), its easy read-ability as well as its capacity for sardonic subtlety, would appeal to artists given to smooth narratives and politically subversive sleight-of-hand. That the form only "played at" meaning did nothing to dull its sharp satirical barbs in a context of state censorship.

THE USES OF THE PEOPLE'S PICTURES

In technique and printing, lubki throughout the centuries tended to lag behind the prints of William Hogarth and other artists of Western Europe, but they re-tained a wicked satirical edge—and not rarely, a veiled political message. Though loved by "the people," authorities of various sorts in Russia tended to view them with suspicion. As early as 1674 the Russian Orthodox Church drafted decrees against "paper icons" and what it then called "German (foreign) sheets" that "cor-rupted the image of the savior." The Orthodox especially feared and railed against prints disseminated by the Old Believers (schismatics who had broken from the church over the Patriarch Nikon's reforms in the mid-seventeenth century). Under the Czar Peter's (1682–1725) Westernizing reforms, secular subjects in the people's print proliferated, and the government itself (as well as its opponents) made liberal use of the form to propagandize.

Owing to the difficulty of regulating the easily made lubki, the Russian state would periodically address the best way to monitor and if possible censor subversive images. This it did in 1804, 1839 (when it decreed that all images must bear a stamp of origin), 1848, and most decisively, 1851. The latter law, drafted by Dmitry Bludov, head of the Second Section of the czar's chancellery, ordered all previously existing printing plates destroyed, the better to prevent reproduction of nonapproved old messages and to control the content of new approved ones. The law's effect, however, proved mostly commercial: folk artisans and smaller lubok producers went out of business, while entrepreneurs like Petr Sharapov cornered the publishing market with superior resources, and production of lubki moved to factories in cities. As Rovinsky mourned, "so ended the uncensored people's pictures."[21] Yet even then, regulating the message of the lubok proved no easy task, particularly given the coded imagery so often used by artists.

Several satirical eighteenth-century works, for example, attacked Peter's reforms through stealthy Aesopian strategies. One widely reproduced print slyly mocked Peter himself as the bewhiskered "Cat of Kazan," while others ridiculed his Enlightenment-era attempts to modernize the country; for example, the emancipation of women led to reactionary lubki depicting their abuse (Kunzle: 252–54), while the Westernizing edict to shave beards sparked "The Barber Wants to Cut Off the Old Believer's Beard" (Norris: 38). Rovinsky interpreted "Baba Yaga Rides Forth to Fight the Corcodile" [sic], another topical early eighteenth-century print, as a lampoon on Peter's marital strife, with a tiny ship beneath the "crocodile" signifying the czar's passion for the navy; his wife, Catherine, as the folk witch Baba Yaga; and a bottle of spirits showing the couple's drinking habits.[22]

Of the "revenge on Peter" series (attributed to the Old Believers or other groups resistant to the reformist czar), none achieved as much popularity as "The Burial of the Cat by the Mice," released in at least three versions in the first half of the eighteenth century. These depict the funeral procession of the "Kazan cat" by up to sixty-six mice, each named after regions of Russia, some playing musical instruments (music at funerals had only been allowed since 1698), with satirical text. Some versions of the work stretched out over several normal-sized sheets; Rovinsky exhaustively catalogs the innumerable clues that identify the cat as Peter and the mice as the relieved Russian people, freed from their Westernizing despot to return to traditional life (139–48).[23]

Wartime lubki offer another example of the medium's satirical bent, as in Ivan Terebenev's 1812 "Russians Teaching Napoleon to Dance": the invading emperor's humiliating defeat is crowned by his being forced to perform a recognizably Russian dance, to the whip of a peasant. An example from World War I, "So You Want to Be Napoleon" by Ivan Sytin, evokes both the shaving motif of "The

1.2. *The Burial of the Cat by the Mice*, lubok, first half of the eighteenth century.

Barber Wants to Cut Off the Old Believer's Beard" and the strong xenophobic stance of this genre. In a series of five panels, the towering Kaiser Wilhelm is brutally transformed into "Napoleon"—by having his mustache and head shaved, feet lopped off, and arm broken. The "before and after" effect capitalizes on the lubok's sequential narrative strategies.

The drawn (risovannyi) lubok, a particular form adapted by Old Believer communities from the printed type (as well as icons and book illustration), made especially trenchant use of separate panels for purposes of contrast. Several, such as "Attributes of the Divine Service And Symbols Used by Old-Believers and the Official Orthodox" (1880s), depict the differences—sometimes slight—in the two denominations' rituals, with a decorative column or gutter between them. The viewer is clearly meant to compare the two rather similar scenes precisely in search of the (critical) differences and arrive at the proper ideological conclusions. The Old Believers, as noted by E. I. Itkina, saw in the lubok a particularly effective, "visually clear" (nagliadnyi) means of spreading their religious messages (7), while their artisanal production methods and closed distribution networks allowed them to long elude the censors.[24] The "cross-gutter" comparison, as we will see, became a standard technique in Soviet anticapitalist propaganda during the twentieth century.

As a form of kitsch, the lubok borrowed iconography, personages, and plots from bourgeois culture, but refashioned them into a "primitive" and insolent amusement for the masses. The prints, along with their clarifying (or, as it were, obfuscating) text, often of a satirical nature, combined words and pictures in some ways not dissimilar to those of illustrations on the editorial pages of major periodicals of the European west. As a popular form, the lubok mirrored the mass appeal of cartoons elsewhere—though the semiliterate, Orthodox audience of Russia called for a different approach much closer to theater, rhyming verse, and the carnival. Finally, by illustrating and elaborating on scenes from favorite stories, Bible passages, or historical events, the lubok was inextricably tied to other media; in this too, like modern comics elsewhere, it was a hybrid form.

1.3. *Attributes of the Divine Service And Symbols Used by Old-Believers and the Official Orthodox*, Old Believer lubok, late nineteenth century.

The patriotic fervor stirred up by Russia's disastrous war against Japan (1904–1905) and World War I proved the last gasp for the lubok as a mass medium. It eventually gave way to rising literacy rates and more "impressive" technologies like radio, cinema, and the placard, but the "crude" lubok made an indelible stamp on the comics style of future generations. It was precisely to this "hand-made," primitive, and above all indigenous quality of the lubok that the Russian avant-garde would turn to create a new style of art for the twentieth century.

THE WORLD OF ART AND IVAN BILIBIN

With the turn of the twentieth century, the lubok's nationalist "authenticity" would appeal to Russian artists eager to reject or reshape European modernism and draw inspiration from home-grown forms. Two major art movements of the prerevolutionary period made use of the lubok in this way, to varying degrees: Alexander Benois and Sergei Diaghilev's World of Art (Mir iskusstva) and the Russian Futurists.

Inspired by the philosophy of Sergei Soloviev, and embodying some of the highest aspirations of Russia's fin-de-siècle Silver Age, the St. Petersburg-based World of Art straddled the border between old and new, East and West, fine and applied art, high culture and commerce—laying the foundation for the much more radical avant-garde. Uniting disparate artists, poets, and literary critics, the movement proclaimed a new era in Russian art, one that fed off European culture but ceded nothing to it. The *World of Art* journal, started in 1898, was the first Russian publication to focus such close attention on the quality of printing, design, and the relationship of text to illustration, celebrating beauty of a decidedly urbane, aristocratic stripe. In seeking to build bridges between European modernism and ancient Russian traditions, the World of Art brought lubok-inspired painters such as Viktor Vasnetsov and, in 1906, the graphic artist Ivan Bilibin to the front ranks of art.[25] Albeit polished up and "idealized," the people's pictures would no longer be reflexively thought of as a peasant, folk, or mass-produced form unsuitable for cultured Russians; the World of Art was the first group to incorporate Russian popular printing into a serious arts practice.

The direct link between the lubok and Russian graphic art and comics of the twentieth century is Bilibin, book illustrator, caricaturist, set designer, and amateur ethnographer, who joined the World of Art in 1906. In search of "classical" Russian culture to revive and reshape for the new era, artists like Bilibin conducted excursions to the provinces and incorporated what they found there—peasant architecture, embroidery designs, the lubok—into their work. At the same time, the cosmopolitan Bilibin was heavily influenced by Art Nouveau (he had studied in Munich, though briefly, in 1898) and deeply admired the German satirical journal *Simplicissimus* (a tremendous inspiration to a generation of Russian caricaturists; see below). The result was a "softening" and "mainstreaming" of the lubok's more crude edges, while often retaining its compositions, for an idealized image of traditional Russian (especially medieval) culture, brought to life in illustrated books of fairy tales, epic heroes, maidens, and castles.[26]

Bilibin's most "lubok-like" mature style appears in his 1910 illustrations to Pushkin's *The Golden Cockerel:* not only do the drawn lines have a "roughness" evocative of a print, but the elaborately adorned horses assume stylized poses lifted from the lubok. Bilibin's series of postcard illustrations (early 1900s) featuring men and women in traditional dress, animals, and other subjects, integrated old-style Russian text in familiar ways, as well. A 1905 postcard, "The Bird of Paradise Alkonost," is extremely suggestive of lubok; the picture contains a caption, a scroll of text held up by the figure, and even speech emanating from its mouth.[27]

While Bilibin's style did not alter much throughout his career, after 1910 it reflects a closer link to Byzantine and Russian icon-making, but the lubok-like compositions, flattened space and "handicraft character" remain. Though by 1915 the World of Art movement had passed its moment, accused of having descended into philistinism and "academicism," its various members soon to be scattered by the Revolution, the group proved a crucial bridge between the old Russian popular printmaking culture and the dizzying experiments of the emerging avant-garde. In the graphic arts, none embodied that cross-over ethos as did Bilibin.[28]

THE RUSSIAN FUTURISTS

In contrast to other national Futurist movements of the early twentieth century which promoted a total break with the past, the Russian Futurist and Neo-Primitivist artists we will consider, such as Aleksei Kruchenykh, Olga Rozanova, and Mikhail Larionov, hearkened back to the tradition of lubok and older medieval forms to impart on their works an amateurish, hand-made, and decidedly

1.4. *War*, chapbook by Olga Rozanova and Alexei Kruchenykh, 1916.

"non-European" look. As E. F. Kovtun writes, "In contrast to their Western col-leagues, Russian artists had close at hand, at home, a living stratum of peasant art, preserved, from which their own art received a direct impetus. It was not neces-sary to travel, like Gauguin, to Tahiti; it was enough to go to the Viatsky or Tula region to encounter the deeply-laid, at times even archaic traditions of the people's art" (1989: 95). Thus the Futurists looked to the indigenous lubok—rather than the Western cartoon—for their primitivist and Cubo-Futurist graphic works.[29] In 1912, they brought the lubok and the Russian proto-comics form to the front ranks of the high art movement with their experimental lithographic works *The World Backwards* (Mirskontsa), *Old-Time Love* (Starinnaia liubov), and *A Game in Hell* (Igra v Adu) (over the next four years, they produced over fifty publications in all). These collaborative, cheaply produced chapbooks challenged what they saw as the more effete aestheticism of the World of Art; Kruchenykh and the young Vladimir Mayakovsky sought to produce "anti-books" with which to undermine common stereotypes of perception.[30] Many, like Mayakovsky, were poets as well as artists, and saw their task as dissolving the artificial borders between text and image; they were "artists working in a textual medium" (Degot 2000: 18). Responding to these works in 1913, the critic Sergei Bobrov noted, "the analogous aspirations of both poem and drawing and the explanation of the poem by means of the drawing are realized not by literary, but by painterly means" (quoted in Gurianova: 97).

Indeed, the illustrated poems of *Mirskontsa* and its sister publications represent a new attempt to combine words and images; the handwritten texts change their character from page to page, getting entangled with the primitivist drawings of

Rozanova and Larionov in blots and bursts of color. As with the lubok, the coloring often crosses the contours of the drawings and the paint varies minutely from copy to copy, giving each book the uniqueness of an original; this is especially evident in Larionov's illustration for Kruchenykh's poem "Pomada." In many cases the text itself becomes the illustration, as in Rozanova and Kruchenykh's *War* (1916), a book of anti–World War I woodblock prints. "With Horror He Recalls the Ones He Himself Saw Crucified Upside-down by the Germans" combines the text indissolubly with the illustrated atrocity for a horrific effect, made only more so by the naïve style.

The Futurists created a type of lithography in which words and images worked in intimate closeness; one could not simply remove one or the other from the page without destroying the work's total meaning. (This would have a tremendous influence on future Russian artists, such as the Constructivists, who also dynamically combined text and visuals.) In trying to find the ancient "organic unity" of word and picture on the printed page, the artists of this circle reimagined the lubok, infusing it with a distinct aesthetic sensibility. Through their experimentation with different media (ink, crayon, pastel, collage) they expanded the possibilities of the medium.

Among the most radical of these experiments with text and image, Kruchenykh, Vasily Kamensky, and K. M. Zdanevich's anti-book *1918* (1917) employs a full-fledged hieroglyphic style in their so-called ferro-concrete poems. Here the words swerve and twist along textual landscapes, unfolding in quasi-plots. Kamensky's "Sun (a lubok)" from the same album, explicitly harkens back to its predecessors in Russian printmaking, while boldly pushing their compositional and narrative capacities to the edge of abstraction—and beyond.

"The urge to restore to the word and the image their lost primordial purity" (Petrova and Markade: 136) led the Futurists to provocative creations, to a new language that was both ancient, "primordial," and thoroughly modern, groundbreaking. No less a personage than the collector Sergei Tretiakov struggled, in fact, to adequately describe the effect of these works, with their shock of the new/old, had on him: "No, these are not poems. These are drawings; the graphics predominate, but graphics-in-letters (bukvennyi), bearing with them (as accompaniment) the sensation of sounds, outgrowths of associations linked with speech noises" (quoted in Kovtun: 75). The Futurists rechristened the "contemporary lubok" (sevodniashnyi lubok) as an icon of modernism—spectacularly so—just as the traditional form was dying out—along with the ancien régime of the Romanov dynasty.

THE SATIRICAL JOURNAL

While Russia (owing in part to more severe censorship under the czars) did not have as long a pedigree of satirical caricature and cartoons as other European powers,[31] we can at least briefly mention some of the highlights before the watershed year of 1905, when the number of illustrated satirical publications exploded.

The politically subversive sensibility seen in the anti-Peter lubki of the eighteenth century lived on in the work of such artists as Alexei Venetsianov (who started the first satirical journal in Russia at the start of the eighteenth century) and Terebenev with his anti-Napoleon prints. By midcentury the first regularly published humor journal, *Eralash* ("Jumble"), appeared, though it soon fell victim to the upsurge in censorship in the wake of the revolutionary turmoil in France. The year 1859 saw the most important satirical journal of the century, *Iskra* ("The Spark"), which described itself as "the doleful chronicle of the amusing and dark sides of Russian life," followed in 1862 by another periodical of politically inflected caricature, *Gudok* ("The Whistle"). One of the most popular caricaturists of the era, Alexander Lebedev, published his work in such journals as *Strekoza* ("Dragonfly," 1875), *Oskolki* ("Fragments," 1891), and others.[32] In 1896 the premiere of Albert Langen's German weekly *Simplicissimus* had an incalculable impact on Russian cartoonists.

Satirical works were also widely used in the turn-of the-century yellow press: "Drawings lampooning local officials or commenting sardonically on the city's social problems or simply illustrating the day's stories were daily features" in such down-market fare as *Peterburgskii listok*, which specialized in chronicling the waves of "hooliganism" engulfing the city (Neuberger: 17). An especially sadistic drawing from December 31, 1903, for example, shows a "Petersburg-style" stabbing (in the back) that delights in wide-eyed, cartoony gore (41). A more realistic illustration, "Drunkenness Among Children in Petersburg" (March 20, 1914), employs a sequential technique to contrast besodden boys with a girl rescued from their fate by "some old auntie or grandma" (183).[33]

The 1905 Revolution and its aftermath saw a burst of caricature and satirical journals as a result of the stark changes in the nation's political life. In the wake of the violent crackdown against protesters in St. Petersburg in January (an event known as "Bloody Sunday"), Czar Nicholas II was forced to concede some of his powers in the form of the October Manifesto, which promised greater civic rights and freedoms, including freedom of speech. Publishers seized on the reforms and new journals poured forth—309 from 1905 to 1907, as compared to 89 for the whole of the nineteenth century (Bowlt: 111). And it was not only a matter of quantity; some of the greatest works of Russian caricature appeared in this era; renowned artists such as Boris Kustodiev, Dobuzhinsky, Bilibin, and Valentin Serov vented forth their indignation at the state in morbid expressionistic works full of marauding skeletons, piles of corpses, grotesque politicians, and soldiers. In one the most striking images, "October Idyll" (1905), Dobuzhinsky showed a huge splotch of blood against a wall and sidewalk, with a child's doll, a shoe, and a pair of glasses strewn on a city street.[34]

The short-lived journal *Zhupel* ("The Bugbear," 1905–1906) proved one the most notorious and oft-confiscated by the censor, despite the new free speech law. It published two of the boldest satirical drawings aimed at the czar himself: Bilibin's "Donkey (Equus Asinus), 1/20th Life-Size," which showed an ass surrounded by czarist emblems (this caused the journal to be shut down and got Bilibin arrested); and Zinovii Gzhebin's "Werewolf Eagle, or Internal and Foreign Policy," which right-side-up depicts the state coat of arms with its double-headed eagle—but when turned upside-down reveals a portrait of the sovereign's bare rear end.

Cartoonists also quickly learned how to make their points more subtly and evade the censor; they "constantly expanded their territory and their targets of attack, demolishing one obstacle after another as they went, thriving on censorship" (King and Porter: 18). At times, these artists made use of the "cross-gutter" comparison and sequential properties of juxtaposed panels observed in the Old Believers and wartime lubki. The first issue of *Zritel* ("The Spectator") responded to a legal restriction on openly depicting the 1905 disorder by placing a frame of soldiers' feet marching next to another frame of civilians' feet, fleeing. The wordless art followed the letter of the law, while the meaning, read "across" the panels, was clear.

Such politicized aesthetic strategies, honed over centuries in the indigenous lubok, reinvigorated by the Futurists and satirical cartoonists, would carry over into the dawn of the Soviet era—and transform Russia's comics heritage in new, exciting, and tragic ways.[35]

2

COMICS DURING THE SOVIET ERA

REVOLUTION

The Bolsheviks, led initially by Vladimir Ilyich Lenin, sought a radical break with the traditions of the past as well as with the capitalist West, and launched a bold refashioning of what they saw as backward Russian society into a modern industrialized state grounded on Marxist principles.[1] As a result, the seventy-year Soviet domination of Russia inaugurated by the Communist revolution of November 7, 1917 (new style), proved on the whole disruptive to the development of comics as an art form, consigning it to the margins of culture. Contrary to popular perceptions of comics (or their absence) under communism, however, we should view this as the beginning, not the end, of the story.

Almost from the moment they wrested the country from the provisional government of Alexander Kerensky, the Soviets set off a wide-ranging propaganda war aimed at winning over the populace to the new order and discrediting the old regime (parts of which were still fighting the Reds in a civil war). As the historian Victoria Bonnell noted, for the Bolsheviks the issue was "not only the seizure of power but the seizure of meaning" (1). The new state embarked on a mammoth campaign to destroy the old czarist emblems of the Romanov Dynasty (toppling statues, destroying churches, assassinating the former czar himself along with his family) and erecting its own symbols (the hammer and sickle, the heroic proletariat, the emancipated woman).[2] This campaign encompassed all available means, from the old (posters, public speeches, gazettes) to the new (cinema, radio, street reenactments of history). Censorship was for the most part lifted, and artists of various persuasions were encouraged to pursue their most radical visions. In so doing, the Soviets in the first decade of the revolution unleashed an unparalleled

31

era of social and artistic experimentation. As Richard Stites notes: "A whole array of new symbols and rituals were introduced and infused with anti-capitalism,
the collective spirit, atheism, and machine worship. Bolshevik artists and propa-
gandists went to the people with a culture for the people and in doing so they
tried to combine the new with the old, self-consciously infusing circus, fairbooth,
lubok, folk ditties, songs and dances with revolutionary content" (1992: 39). Few
images better captured this spirit than Dmitry Moor's iconic 1920 poster *Have
You Volunteered?* which depicts a Soviet army soldier in blazing red, rifle in hand,
pointing at the viewer with a steely gaze, challenging him to join up and fight the
Whites. Behind him stands a factory (also burning red), its smokestacks belching
black—emblem of the new state's industrial might. Moor's poster repackages the
old tropes of bravery, patriotism, and masculinity with the promise of a brave,
new, electrified world.[3]

In short, visual culture formed a central front in the war of ideas. The turbulent condition of the arts in Russia after 1917, the emergence of proletarian culture
as seen in such leftist groups as the Proletcult,[4] and the continuation of projects
from the prerevolutionary Silver Age all saw themselves reflected in the diversity
of the comics and proto-comics language which survived into this time of great
innovation. In this process, the dynamic visual strategies of the lubok, both in its
traditional form and as reimagined by the Futurists, held strong appeal for its ef-
ficacy as a mass medium. But, as noted, the lubok also represented a vestige of the
old world the Soviets increasingly sought to expunge.

One arts movement from that era of particular interest, due to its focus on
the interaction of word and image, is the Constructivists. This loose association
of artists and theorists (chief among them Vladimir Tatlin and the husband/wife
team of Alexander Rodchenko and Varvara Stepanova) valorized the new values
of utility, functionality, and the machine. As "artist-engineers," they emphasized
industrial materials (metal and glass), architectural forms, and pragmatic objects,
all intended to bring art out of the museums and into everyday life.[5]

Yet by the end of the first Soviet decade, with Lenin dead, the country de-
pleted, and the New Economic Policy (NEP)[6] undermining (as some saw it) the
hardcore principles of War Communism, the state began clamping down on free
expression, particularly on the avant-garde—which it now accused of bourgeois
obtuseness and "formalism." Starting in earnest in the 1930s, with Joseph Stalin
having eliminated his rivals, consolidated power, cancelled NEP, and launched the
first Five Year Plan of crash industrialization, Soviet policies on the arts looked inward, casting an intolerant gaze on anything that bore traces of Western-type mass
culture and, during the cold war, America. Comics, broadly speaking, fell victim
to this political outlook; no comic book industry as such ever developed in the
Soviet era.

Yet it would be wrong to label Russian "comicsophobia" an exclusively "top-down" phenomenon. Especially after 1931, Soviet edicts on reading, children's upbringing, and "foreignness" in their main points coincided with the preferences and prejudices of Russian literary culture.[7]

To the extent they pondered the question, the word/image interaction of comics indeed struck many educated Russians—reared on nineteenth-century classic authors—as "alien," simplistic, and an impediment to "real" reading. (This attitude, as we shall see, remains alive to the present day.) The historical context is also relevant; the elimination of illiteracy in the first decades of Soviet power and the creation of an educated populace was one of the state's major tasks. Certain "weighty" literary works (Tolstoy, Gorky) were valued far more highly than other "lightweights." The sort of mass-culture product represented by comics simply struck educators and ordinary Russians as antithetical to this mission.[8] Moreover, as noted in our discussion of the prerevolutionary lubok, the small Russian intellectual class, or intelligentsia, had a long tradition of viewing popular culture or art meant chiefly for diversion and/or profit as suspect, even morally hazardous. (The Russian masses, eagerly consuming lubki and lubochnaia literatura in the nineteenth century, of course viewed the matter differently.)

In short, the upper-class antipathy to the lubok attached to modern comics; Soviet ideology and censorship practices enforced that posture as state policy.[9] As Stephen Lovell has argued in *The Russian Reading Revolution*, both the leadership and the ordinary citizen contributed to the emergence in this period of a powerful "Soviet reading myth"—a self-image of Russians as "the most active readers in the world" (samyi chitaiushchii narod v mire). At best, then, comics were something to grow out of; at worst, they were a mind-numbing capitalist diversion and impediment to learning. Mostly, they were absent. In general, comics culture as understood in the West remained a marginal phenomenon, particularly as the Soviet Union under Stalin developed into a full-fledged authoritarian state in the twentieth century. (As we will see, this ideological stance had consequences both economic—the lack of a comics industry—and aesthetic—the relative paucity of word balloons and sound effects in such Soviet-era comics and strips as did exist. Presumably, those comics devices seemed too identifiably "Western.")[10]

However, the comics language did survive, even in the official sphere. At times it even prospered. This tended to happen during moments of national crisis, when aspects of the culture normally submerged or marginalized (such as pseudo-capitalism or religion) were revived out of existential necessity, as during World War II. But even in quieter times, examples of a Soviet comics style never fully disappeared from the satirical and children's press, nor from the propaganda and advertising poster. In addition, during the postwar era there arose an underground of artists, the Non-Conformists, viewing banned foreign works and producing their own, though with little chance of ever seeing them published or exhibited; some were punished for their activities. A subset of this group, the Conceptualists, incorporated comics techniques as a not-infrequent element of their work, partly due to comics' "subversive" cachet in mainstream Soviet culture.

The history of Russian comics under the Soviet regime thus falls into three main parts: the Revolutionary Era (1917–1934), Socialist Realism (1934–mid-1980s), and, parallel with the latter, the Non-Conformists (1960s–1980s). Furthermore, this being an age of schism, when Russian culture was split in two, we will also note the work of comics artists of the diaspora—the "Whites" who fled the Red Communists during and after the Revolution. These figures in some cases made enormous contributions to the comics cultures of other countries (e.g., Yugoslavia), while comics in the USSR remained, by comparison, a "stalled medium."

This was the general picture until the ascension of reformist Communist Party general secretary Mikhail Gorbachev in 1985 and his policy of Perestroika, when comics finally shuffled off their customary shackles—though not the age-old prejudices adhering to the form. This chapter provides (can only provide) a schematic survey, filling in some of that long, colorful, often tragic, history.

THE REVOLUTIONARY POSTER

The first, most explicit and for a time most wide-ranging application of comics techniques in the Soviet era appeared in the crucial mass medium of the poster—the direct descendant of the satirical journals of the 1905 generation as well as the lubki of World War I; in fact, many artists, such as the renowned Moor, formed living links to the older traditions.

The poster or *plakat* (as advertisement, as public service announcement, as breaking news vehicle) became a major tool for the Bolsheviks to spread information far, wide, and in a form they could control. Capitalizing, as the icon-makers had done, on Russian culture's penchant for the visual, the producers of posters could cast their message more cost-effectively than film, more quickly than newspapers, more lastingly than radio or the telegraph, all while making an emotionally engaged appeal to the eye. Between 1919 and 1922, over 7.5 million posters, postcards, and lubok pictures were distributed, while in 1920 alone the state publishing house Gosizdat released more than 3.2 million copies of 75 different posters (Bonnell: 5).[11] The need for a modern, progressive, and "dialectical" design of these visual materials was met by new art groups eager to serve the revolution, in particular the Constructivists.[12]

But the plakat, as noted by several scholars and Sovietologists, did much more than disseminate news or showcase modern art techniques. It played a critical role in explaining, visualizing, and shaping a new civilization, Bolshevism, at a time

2.1. *Every Blow of the Hammer is a Blow Against the Enemy!*, propaganda poster by Viktor Deni, 1920.

when its symbols, culture, and "look" were still nascent and very much in flux and when vast swathes of its population could not, or could barely, read. Calling the plakaty "the continuation of politics by visual means," Klaus Waschik and Nina Baburina argue they helped to produce the unprecedented "reality" they depicted: "The poster . . . became a space in which the visual model of this civilization was created, a space which became its proving ground, its picture exhibit. Along with the illustrated children's book, it was called upon to inculcate representations of the new society into people's consciousness. In this sense the Soviet poster met one of the greatest communications challenges of the 20th century" (85).[13] This does not mean that the process of "inculcation" flowed smoothly. For one thing, poster artists (plakatisty) had to invent novel imagery, metaphors, and slogans (or at least revamp old ones), often at a feverish pace, with little consistent guidance from above. The initial overseer of plakat production, the State Publishing House (GIZ) demanded only that artists adhere to chief principles of clarity, simplicity, directness, and accessibility[14]—though the vagueness of such terms led to a great diversity of styles in the early posters: realism, Suprematism, allegory, Constructivism, satire, lubok.

Above all, and especially during War Communism, the leadership wanted eye-catching, compelling works that exalted the saints and demonized the enemies of the new society. The plakat, thought uniquely suited to such a task, was indeed elevated to star status among the arts. As Commissar of Education Anatoly Lunacharsky wrote in 1924: "The masters of 'great' art, too, not only can but must take up agitational art, for his results will often turn out not worse but better, than a master of the literary, theatrical, painting, musical, etc., agit piece. A great honor to the master painter who manages to create a vivid poster!" (quoted in Waschik and Baburina: 87).

We can see the variety of artists' responses to such calls through a comparison of some well-known early posters. Viktor Deni's 1920 *Every Blow of the Hammer is a Blow Against the Enemy!* depicts a proletariat smith hammering away at an anvil; instead of "sparks" this produces bullets showering an astonished, bewhiskered man in czarist general's dress. Deni's work clearly follows the strategies of

2.2. *One Must Work with a Rifle Nearby*, poster by Vladimir Lebedev, 1920.

the satirical press, with its easily recognizable "types," cartoony effects, and Manichaean worldview.

Indeed, many early plakatisty simply applied the techniques of prerevolutionary caricature or redressed entire compositions to address the new Soviet conditions. Nikolai Kochergin's 1920 *Capital and Co.*, for example, shows a pyramid-like structure allegorizing the world economic order: priests, petty merchants, et cetera, form the bottom tier; military officers and lackeys the middle; the leering Clemenceau, Wilson, and Lloyd George near the top; and looming over all a repulsively fat Jabba the Hutt–like creature representing capital, its royal robe spread out to swathe the others. All sit on a huge pile of moneybags. "This is the bourgeoisie's 'icon,'" growls the accompanying poem by the proletarian poet Demian Bedny. "Here are all the pillars of their law." Kochergin's piece is a direct reinterpretation of Alexei Radakov's 1917 *The Autocratic Order*, which puts the czar at the top of the pyramid and the proletariat ("You work!") at the bottom. Radakov's work, in turn, recrafts a 1901 lithograph, *The Pyramid*, by Nikolai Lokhov (the first Social Democrat print).[15] The Soviet poster artists were tapping the familiarity of popular imagery for new goals.

The avant-garde posters evince another strategy. The Leningrad artist Vladimir Lebedev's 1920 *One Must Work with a Rifle Nearby* (Rabotat' nado vintovka riadom) adheres much more to the strategies seen in the Futurist anti-books, especially in its blurring of drawing and text. The words "work" (rabotat') and "must" (nado) follow the line of an iconic, faceless proletariat's arm as he saws a board, a rifle intersecting it to form an X. Bright primary colors, particularly red for the worker's shirt, identify the poster's Suprematist leanings. The height of this approach was reached by El Lissitzky's noted 1920 *Beat the Whites with a Red Wedge*, in which text and geometric shapes dynamically clash (a visual correlative to the ongoing Civil War).

Over time plakatisty incorporated photography in their works. Rodchenko, among other things, pioneered the use of dynamic photos for advertisements, as seen in his famous 1925 poster for the Lengiz Bookstore: the stylized word "books" (knigi) seems to burst directly from the mouth of model Lily Brik. Later, photo-montage plakaty such as those of Gustav Klutsis became synonymous with the era of the first five-year plan of the late 1920s and early 1930s.[16] Some series, like the agitational "poster newspapers," combined caricature and photos.

But whatever the style or technique, plakatisty relied on clearly recognizable, politically approved imagery, motifs, and character "types" such as the fat, top-hatted capitalist; the venal, often drunken priest; the stalwart worker; the emancipated woman. They also drew Lenin and other leaders. In the 1930s the exemplary "shock worker" Alexei Stakhanov became a staple of posters, as well as several other media. Viktor Deni, responsible for popularizing many of these types, captured the appeal of this strategy in his celebrated 1920 *Comrade Lenin Cleanses the Earth of Scum*. This shows a "cartoony" behatted Lenin astride the globe, sweeping smaller figures off the planet: a priest, a capitalist with a money-bag, and two crowned regents.[17] Demonstrating its utility for different themes, Deni would reuse this "sweeping" motif during the war against rising bureaucratism, in his 1931 *Red-tape Monger, Bureaucrat, Saboteur, Out of the Soviet!*, which depicts the named (and labeled) parties, along with a "Loafer," being swept out a window by a titanic pair of red hands. The stylized, allegorical economy of these works clearly derives from the satirical press.

Despite their continuities with the past, the posters were theorized and celebrated as something new, and particularly Soviet. V. S. Zemenkov, writing in 1930, argued, "the compact, concrete image—this is how the Soviet poster defeats the often extreme symbolism and conventionality of the bourgeois and petty bourgeois intelligentsia's satire" (38). Similarly, El Lissitzky contrasted the plakaty's innovations with the Western illustrative approach (in which, he opined, image only *illustrates* text): "As opposed to the Americans, our posters were created not so as to be quickly caught by the eye from a rushing car, but for reading and explication up close" (57). However, Lissitzky's celebration of the poster's complexity (with its swipe at the West) clashed with the view of a poster production official, who in 1931 wrote, "the eye of the peasant finds it easiest to comprehend the lubok and gets lost in the details of the usual 'city' poster" (Bonnell: 111).

Whatever the innovations of the Civil War–era plakatisty, it is telling that their White opponents resorted to much the same techniques: clear, eye-grabbing imagery, a communication of the urgency of victory, and demonization of the Reds. White posters depicted their enemies as reptiles, sadistic brutes, and trolls. An anti-Semitic 1919 poster, *Peace and Freedom in Sovdepya*, capitalizes on the widespread belief that the Communists were a power-hungry Jewish cabal. The unknown artist shows Leon Trotsky, at that time head of the Red army, as a mammoth red devil wearing spectacles and a gold chain with a red star shaped like the Star of David. He (it) sits atop the Kremlin walls, dripping blood from its hands and feet, overseeing a mountain of skulls as Chinese troops execute a prisoner and shovel remains.

Others proved no less direct: *Retribution* (1918–1920) depicts Lenin and his followers being driven by an archangel and the White army down to the pit of hell. A central composition shows a cavern in flames, where the Communists cower before demons, a huge snake-like monster, and an enthroned Satan. The bottom tier shows five panels of varied tortures, for "lies," "betrayal," and so forth. In its religious iconography and form the poster recalls the hagiographic icon, as well as the three-tiered narrative approach of the Novgorod school's *Icon of the Battle Between the Men of Novgorod and the Men of Suzdal* (mentioned in the previous chapter). In addition, the artist makes use of a well-known lubok motif, the humorous, semi-sadistic depiction of hell's torments as punishment for a life badly lived; see, for example the 1882 poster *Drunkenness and its Horrible Consequences*, in which the anonymous artist shows a drunkard carousing and trouble making for eight panels before landing at the center of the composition, in a fiery cave very similar to that which greets Lenin's entourage.

Of whichever political stripe, in short, plakatisty made use of the poster's iconographic economy and visual impact to great effect. Of particular interest to comics scholars, however, is to what extent these artists participated in and invoked a comics language (particularly sequentiality) in crafting their works and to what degree a viewer relied on a grasp of this language to understand and appreciate their message. The answer is: from the Soviet plakat's beginnings the use of recognizable comics devices—chief among them the use of multiple panels for contrast or narrative development—was a standard part of the poster maker's toolbox.

Clearly an inheritance of the Old Believer icon, lubok, and satirical press, the comparative or "transformational" potential of the gutter was routinely exploited for "us/them," "then/now," and other ideological point scoring effects. Moor's 1919 *The Czarist Regiments and the Red Army* exemplifies this formula: on the left panel (caption: "What they fought for before"), a detachment of White soldiers defend fat capitalists with moneybags, the enthroned sovereign, a cross-thumping priest, and banners proclaiming "slavery," "pogroms," and other evils. On the right panel ("What they're fighting for now"): army men, sailors, and ordinary peasants march forward, while in the distance behind them loom factories, modern buildings, a multi-hued sun, and flags declaring "Freedom," "Bread," "Emancipated Labor," "Science," and so forth. An antireligious 1925 poster *Kopeck by kopeck . . .* by Dmitry Melnikov utilizes the gutter for a similar contrast. The top caption reads: "Kopeck by kopeck the church took from the peasantry its trappings—gold and silver," over an image of a circular fortress-like city with a church at its center, "open for business," as peasants crowd in and around to make

2.3. *1917–1920*, poster by unknown artist from Gomel, 1920.

their humble offerings. The bottom panel shows the fortress now closed, black-robed priests ringed around the church full of treasure, as peasants slowly starve outside the walls. The lower caption reads: "Why have you become a black camp? Everyone must give to the peasants, who are dying of hunger."

Other uses of the gutter proved more "aspirational" or "transfigurative," as seen in a 1920 work by an unknown artist from Gomel. On the left panel, with the year 1917 over it, appears a tiny striding worker carrying a rifle, a sledgehammer, and a red banner. Towering over him, reaching up to the very clouds, are the White generals Kornilov, Kaledin, and Dutov. The next panel, with the year 1920 over it, shows the worker grown enormous, so that he now dwarfs the Whites and unceremoniously kicks them out of frame. "Long live the power of the Soviets!" his banner proclaims. The poster demonstrates a deep understanding of the gutter's transformative nature, as directly over the interpanel space, the artist has placed the hyphen—the linguistic mark that signifies the proletariat's meteoric evolution from the years 1917 to 1920. It is almost as if the gutter itself represents a third "panel" with its own caption; like the hyphen, the white space denotes "change."

At the same time, another aspect of this poster represents a departure from most Western comics conventions, at least of dialogue. The words "Death to [White general] Vrangel" seem to emanate from the vanquished generals as they abandon the scene. It makes no sense, of course, for the Whites to disparage one of their own; the declamation is clearly meant as an additional agitational message by the plakatist. But the placement of the message (below the huge worker's boot, as if he will stomp on it) and the stylized letters ("receding" toward the enemy) muddles the delivery for most modern readers, who would probably take it as dialogue from the generals.

Another striking divergence, in this case from the usual "left-right" direction of reading, appears in a 1919 work from another unknown artist, from Petrograd. Written across the top portion of a two-panel composition, the message declares,

"Worker! Only by breaking the chains of darkness will you come to socialism."
An iconic sun also extends across both panels, blazing bright in one, obscured by
clouds in the other. But the arrangement of the action is not what most contemporary Western readers would expect: the worker, along with his family, greets
the sun in the left or "first" panel, while in the "second," right-hand panel, he lan-
guishes alone in chains. Strictly speaking, this order reverses and contradicts that
of the written message.[18]

However elaborated, the "cross-gutter split reality" technique was employed
from the time of the Civil War and remained part of the propaganda arsenal, deployed for various uses, through seven decades of Communist rule. (And as we
shall see, it was not limited to posters.) The "enemy"—Whites, illiteracy, the capitalist West—would change, but the approach remained consistent. Waschik and
Baburina relate the device, in fact, to a distinctly Russian "bipolar" view of the
world: "As a fundamental way of thinking, in which one's own positive qualities
(pozitivnost') are demonstrated through a direct comparison with negative alternatives (one's own defects, the world of capital, etc.), it offers insight into the ways
of self-identification in the Soviet utopia: by distancing oneself from the other
(capitalist) world and entering one of ideal, exemplary and indistinct forms, in
the final analysis one is forced, through the poster's confrontation with this world,
into a position of perpetually searching for proof and comparisons" (185).[19] It bears
repeating, however, that such approaches were not confined to the Soviets. For example, the White poster *What Did the Bolsheviks Promise the People, and What
Did They Deliver?* (1920) provides not one comparison, but three. To appropriate
illustrations arranged in three tiers of two panels each, the captions read: "They
promised freedom . . . they gave executions. They promised bread . . . they gave
famine. They promised order and a peaceful life . . . they gave war." As this and
some of the previously mentioned works show, plakatisty all along the political
spectrum had mastered another important principle of the multipanel composition: its ability to convey narratival action, even on a very "micro" level (i.e., Mc-
Cloud's "moment-to-moment" transitions). In short, they applied the sequential
capacities of the form toward storytelling.

Again, Moor provides a striking example: his 1925 *The Soviet Turnip* unfolds
over five descending, plakat-wide panels, as a group of humorously drawn coun-
terrevolutionary figures (and their pets) strive to pull a turnip out of the ground.
Their great efforts (they form a tug-of-war line, as a hare, a frog, and a crow look
on) receive a cruel reward: in the last panel the mammoth head of a Red army soldier, wearing a budyonovka or peaked hat (the "turnip"), emerges from the earth
and blows them away with his breath: "They all flew away, hard did they fall / The
Soviet turnip had punished them all." Moor and other artists in the first decade
of the Soviet experiment routinely used such sequential techniques to depict both
"momentary" actions (the unmasking of an enemy, the production of goods) and

2.4. *There is the Metro!*, poster by Deni and Dolgorukov, 1935.

longer-form narratives. A good example of the latter: Radakov's 1920 *The Life of the Illiterate / The Life of the Literate*, which uses two tiers of four panels each, with captions, to contrast the alternate paths and very different fates of its two heroes (the first suffers numerous tragedies, the second succeeds in life and dies contented).

Another use of this progressive panel technique, in *There is the Metro!* (Est' metro!, 1935), dispenses with conventional narrative altogether in favor of a more baldly ideological message. The photomontage by Deni and Dolgorukov, celebrating the 1934 construction of the Moscow subway, unspools over three tiers, and opens with the bombastic line "There are no fortresses which the Bolsheviks could not capture" across the top. The first and third panels' "establishing shots" show views of Moscow buildings. Overlaid on these panels, dominating them, is a snapshot of Joseph Stalin; the montage juxtaposition leads to the implication that Stalin is somehow responsible for that cityscape—it "emanates" from him. The second tier, made up of one large panel, shows a map of the city over which strides a mass of people at a sharp diagonal (they seem to pour forth out of the third panel above). The first metro line, in bright red, stretches over the map. One man holds a banner proclaiming, "Long live our great Stalin!" Another man, who looks somewhat like Stalin, leads the people as this tier's largest figure; this gives the impression that the great leader has "descended" from his lofty, totemic position in the first tier to walk among his subjects. Finally, the final tier—the most dynamic—first shows a shot of a dark tunnel, followed by another panel of a metro train (the train has "burst forth" from the tunnel). The finale: the bright-red message "There is the Metro!" glares over two panels depicting a station escalator and the exterior of the new station.

As I have tried to show by this lengthy exegesis, the poster is quite complex in its unfolding, its design building up a remarkable anticipation which its climax relieves. The semiotics of the work lead to an indisputable ideological conclusion: the great civilization of Bolshevism, made possible by the god-like benefactor and father figure Stalin, has led to this exciting scientific and cultural achievement. The poster is a stirring relic of the triumphalist 1930s, its power underscored by skillful progression of panels to guide the eye.[20]

If plakatisty all along the political spectrum made use of the "cross-gutter" device for various purposes, another comics-like convention, represented speech, turns up much more rarely. Rodchenko's Lengiz advertisement, mentioned above, is perhaps the most famous instance from the early Soviet era (so famous, in fact, it was adapted as the cover art by the Glasgow rock group Franz Ferdinand for their 2005 album *You Could Have It So Much Better*). But other devices, first and foremost the variation of panel shape, were common. Maria Nesterova-Berzina's *Work like Daria Garmash!* (1946), for example, frames its portrait of the exemplary collective farm tractor-driver in stylized "panels" formed by elaborately woven "wheat."

A more somber work, Nikolai Ushin's *Neglected Children are Attracted to the Street, Which Turns Them Into Homeless Children* (1927), manipulates text and panels to catalog the evils which lead to one of the worst social ills of the NEP era. As with *There is the Metro!*, the poster's design leads the eye to an inescapable conclusion: a portrait of two street urchins "produced" by the conditions described (though instead of anticipation, this work conjures up a sense of inexorability and disgrace).

This short excursus through the early Soviet poster has given the reader some idea of the medium's versatility, made possible in part by its affinity to comics techniques such as sequentiality, cross-gutter contrast, and the variation of panel shape. Though this study concerns itself mostly with issues of aesthetics, the popular reception of these 1920s and 1930s plakaty certainly meant a good deal to the fledgling state. Valentin Kataev's 1932 production novel *Time Forward!*, about a Socialist team competition to break the world record in cement mixing, offers at least a sense of that reception. Several scenes feature the production and hanging up of the posters by the artist Soldatova in the industrial city Magnitogorsk, in an attempt to motivate the team:

A multitude of placards had been nailed over the gates:
"Loafers and idlers are strictly forbidden to enter here."
"Smoking is strictly forbidden. Comrade, throw away your cigarette. For violation the fine is 3 rubl. And immediate court action."
"Give us the seventh and eighth batteries by the first of September."
And so forth.
The placards were generously decorated with symbolical drawings in garish colors. Here were: a smoking cigarette the size of a factory chimney; a hellish

*broom which was sweeping out the loafer; a three-story airplane of amazing
construction, with the figures 7 and 8 on its wings; and a snub-nosed tramp in a
checkered cap, with the propeller stuck into an altogether unfitting place. (23)*

When the Magnitogorsk team is upstaged by their rivals from Kharkov, Soldatova
uses her posters to humiliate them through satire:

*Beside the tortoise, the nag and the bicycle, Shura Soldatova was nailing a new
placard with a brick: by a rope, the Kharkovites were pulling a large galosh
in which sat Khanumov with his tyubeteika [Uzbek cap], Yermakov with his
necktie on, and the bare-footed Ishchenko. The red utopian sun illuminated the
antediluvian landscape around the galosh. The galosh had lost its dull significance. The overshoe had become a metaphor.*
    Under the galosh was written in large blue letters:
    "The Kharkovites are towing our concrete men!"
    *"The Kharkovites have set unheard-of tempos. They poured three hundred
and six mixtures in one shift, breaking the world's record, while we are sitting
in a galosh!*
    "Shame on you, comrades!" (34)²¹

Interestingly, Kataev's plakatist makes posters that refer back to previous works
(reflecting the fortunes of the competition); she too invokes a type of sequentiality and continuity along with the satirical techniques. One particular style of
poster, however, made the most elaborate use of all the aforementioned methods,
producing the first fully realized comics works of the era, in the process becoming
an indelible part of early Soviet visual culture.

THE ROSTA "WINDOWS"

During the difficult period of War Communism (1918–1921), the Russian Telegraph Agency (ROSTA) introduced a dynamic new type of communications device which fully exploited the sequential language of comics to spread breaking
news, propagate against class enemies, and educate the semiliterate on the expectations of the new state. These slapdash works, often executed in stencil, combined
iconographic imagery with rhyming stanzas in series of four to twelve or more
posters in sequence, and hung on windows in several cities and towns (though
rarely in the countryside). "ROSTA satirical windows" (okna satiry ROSTA), as
they came to be known, informed the masses of political developments and the
progress of the ongoing Civil War; raged against the enemy Whites and capitalist exploiters; and reminded the populace to boil water, practice good hygiene,
and stamp out alcoholism. While humorous and cartoony, the windows bore a

"laughter with menace" (smekh s ugrozoi), wrote the literary critic Osip Brik (8), which made them decidedly not (or not exclusively) for children; as a purely native form of comics, they owed much to both the bawdy lubok and rayok verse.

According to Waschik and Baburina, the immediate precursor to ROSTA windows was a 1919 series of twelve posters depicting the workers' rise to consciousness after the revolution through pictures and captions. A key poster in this series, *Once Upon a Time There Lived the Bourgeoisie*, depicts its action in eight numbered panels, through the course of which a peasant is relieved of his blindfold, "sees the truth" about the Bolshevik cause, joins the Red army and vanquishes the capitalists, eventually taking their place at a restaurant table. While the artist Mikhail Cheremnykh invented the ROSTA window, other artists (Ivan Maliutin, Vladimir Lebedev, and especially Vladimir Mayakovsky) contributed to what became an essentially collective style.

The Moscow ROSTA artists produced windows collaboratively, through a stencil technique that allowed for quick turnaround and, through dissemination of the stencils, mass reproduction in remote locations—at least until the originals wore out (according to Semenyuk, they lasted up to 150 passes).[22] Using these methods, and working in crowded, unheated rooms in winter, a team could put out scores of windows a day, addressing the latest events. As Mayakovsky recalled years later: "A machine-like speed was demanded of us; it would often happen that a report of some victory at the front would come in by telegraph—and 40 minutes to an hour later, the news would be hanging out in the street, in the form of a colorful poster" (83).

More so than with any other mass medium, the narratival possibilities of sequential panels were at the heart of the windows' style, from early in their development. Petr Kerzhentsev, a ROSTA official who oversaw their production, commented, "At first the posters were drawn in the form of pages from a journal. Later we began to move toward full narratives, unfolding sequentially in 4–8 drawings, organically related and unified. This group of drawings on one theme soon became typical for the satirical windows" (4). Writing on a 1968 poster exhibit, Anna Chistiakova also noted their comics-like qualities (without using that word): "The articulation of a basic theme into several episodes made it possible to show the successive development of events. The interrelationship of discreet images, the graphic clarity of the image/text combination, the commanding resonance of their percussive endings, led to the posters' unity and expressive vividness" (8).[23] From their debut the posters proved a hit, with street crowds gathering around each new release, necessitating more frequent postings per week (Kerzhentsev: 4).

Cheremnykh's *Window No. 522* (1920) typifies the form's strategies and bipolar worldview. The first panel shows a saluting White officer and his superior, to the caption: "What do White generals order their officers to fight for?" A large question mark (a common windows device, used to open a theme) hovers over the superior's head. Subsequent panels detail the answer: the Whites fight for the czar (drunk), the fatherland (fat capitalist with moneybags), for the faith (fat priest with moneybag). In contrast, panel five depicts a Red army soldier and large question mark, with the caption, "And what does a Red officer fight for?" Answer, in the final panel: "He has a different faith; the commune calls the Red officer to fight for the happiness of all humanity," with a picture of the soldier standing guard over the globe, swathed in a red banner.

Even more than the single-image posters, the pictographic windows rely on *tipazh*, the reduction of social "types" to their most basic recognizable essence. This, combined with its other devices, makes for a unique visual language, a synthesis of old and new:

The lubok may have been a very powerful source for the ROSTA windows, but it was not the only one: they also tapped the tradition of political cartoons, the devices of cinema, and they bore the stylistic influence of cubism as well. As a result, there formed a structural-visual (strukturno-obraznaia) system whose basis was the multi-paneled development of a narrative and the image-symbol as a particular species of artistic typification. Elements of this system, image-symbols streamlined (svedennye) down to pictograms, subsequently became well-established components of the graphic language of propaganda art: the smith by his anvil, the red bayonet, the red hand, the globe, the "column of demonstrators" motif, the red banner. (Waschik and Baburina: 204)[24]

Even more so than Cheremnykh, Vladimir Mayakovsky pushed the windows' hieroglyphic reductionism to the edge of abstraction. An important Futurist poet, playwright, and "anti-book-maker" before the revolution, his predilection for combining rhymed verse with narrative was already evident in such World War I–era lubki as *The Rough, Red-Haired German* (1914). (Two panels: peasant brings down German zeppelin with a pike, wife sews him pants from the remains.) In the windows, he pushed the dissolution of text/image into a novel linguistic realm. As Brik wrote:

Mayakovsky's posters are remarkable in their primitivism, their laconism, their absence of superfluous details and parts. They are almost ideograms—concepts conveyed not through words but pictures. Interestingly, in the course of his work Mayakovsky indeed put together something like an ideogram dictionary for himself. So that, for example, a large number of the posters included the phrase "What is to be done?" And then they would provide the answer. This question—"What is to be done?"—was always hieroglyphically represented by Mayakovsky by one and the same picture: the head of a worker in profile, staring at a big question mark. (9)

Through such techniques, a 1921 public service announcement warning against the dangers of cholera becomes a humorous if disturbing journey to a surreal world. *ROSTA Window No. 274* begins, against a black background, with a rotund red figure (nearly featureless, on "quivering" legs) vomiting brown sludge, out of which emerges a green question mark. "What should you do to avoid getting sick with cholera?" reads the caption. Mayakovsky flouts realistic perspective and preserves the lubok's iconic "shorthand" for vomit—its trajectory and splash pattern look much as they did in eighteenth- and nineteenth-century prints.

The next several panels detail the various steps to avoid infection (keep clean, build a public bathhouse, maintain water purity). Yet a mood of paranoia pervades the work: in panel two an ominous larger-than-life, red hand descends from above to admonish, "It's not enough just to look after yourself," while in panel nine a giant silhouette physically grabs a citizen by the arm, keeping him from filling his cup in a stream. The prohibition "Don't drink untreated water" emerges from the "Big Brother" silhouette's lips. The citizen is clearly startled by the encounter; his cap falls. Panel seven shows another disconcerting image to go with its innocuous caption, "Careful not to let dirt fall in your water": a medium close-up of a figure caught in mid-drink, the cup almost at his lips. The water contains black swirls (germs, abstracted to flourishes of ink) and a huge fly sits on the rim. The wide-eyed figure, mouth agape, stares directly at the viewer, as if in shock. The effect is one of a spotlight suddenly shone on some dark corner (the background is black), to expose a criminal in the act. Even the fly looks back with its three dots for eyes and nose. In the climactic eleventh and twelfth panels, "cholera" appears as a blue, crescent-like miasma floating in the air, driving panicked citizens to the "free inoculation" point, with wide-open doors.

Rosta Window No. 274 limns a society obsessed with impurity, control, and surveillance, a dawning police state. Moreover, its rhetoric and mis-en-scene seem oddly biblical, with imagery of plagues, moral obligation, conformity to rules, and smoke-belching factories that recall churches or temples. (To underscore this, the final panel, showing the inoculation center where the frightened citizen flees, has window panes that resemble crosses.)[25] For all that, the windows' "laughter with menace" suffuses the work, even self-consciously so: panel eleven shows citizens driven to flee by the news of a cholera outbreak; their information sources include a ROSTA window hanging on a wall. These verbal/visual devices, which Mayakovsky uses frequently, constitute his own vernacular, a universe of association and rhyming commentary on the new Soviet society.

The Moscow ROSTA posters often transcend their agitprop, "state-building" function to touch on the paradoxes and pitfalls of Bolshevism, even if "only" humorously, obliquely. While in content they resemble the kinoagitki[26] filling Soviet screens[27] at the time, the windows' perceived crudity, "lack of seriousness" and accessibility—all heightened by their comics-like visual/verbal blend and penchant for sequential narrative—proved an asset for their penetrating social satire.[28]

Conversely, the Petrograd posters of Lebedev, Vladimir Kozlinsky et al. transcend their communications role by giving full expression to Cubist, Suprematist, and Constructivist influences. Anything but crude, these windows were often produced as linocuts, not stencils (in full spectrum color schemes that abstract the figure to its most basic components) and mostly eschewed narrative in favor of a single large image. These avant-garde leanings made the Petrograd posters more monumental—and for some, less viewer-friendly. Nicoletta Misler characterizes the differences as in part due to the varying conditions in the two cities: "The Moscow windows were, perhaps, more subservient to the everyday exigencies of the new government (the capital moved from Petrograd to Moscow in March 1918), responding more to ideological newsflashes than to aesthetic considerations, whereas the Petrograd ones tended to express more general themes of propaganda and, therefore, manifested a greater emphasis on formal experiment" (73). Soviet critics picked up on these contrasts, describing the color in the Petrograd posters as more subtle, expressive, and varied, likening the works to paintings (Chistiakova: 10), and, tellingly, seeking to downplay their lubok roots: "One cannot but see the link to the lubok, but this a link in the sense of continuity or organic growth, like the connection between soil and the tree that grows out of it" (Kovtun 1998: 4). Rather, their debt to the avant-garde Suprematist movement of Kazimir Malevich is stressed.[29]

Along with the aforementioned *One Must Work with a Rifle Nearby*, Lebedev's 1920 *The Red Army and Navy Defending Russia's Borders* exemplifies the Petrograd style: austere, iconic in its use of figures broken down to geometric shapes, more varied in its colors, and less responsive to current events. (Juxtapose Lebedev's use of the "sweeping motif" in his 1920 *Workman Sweeping Criminal Elements Out of the Republic* to Deni's for a striking comparison.) Kozlinsky's 1920–1921 two-panel engraving *Holiday Attire: Then and Now* more closely resembles the satire-driven Moscow windows, though its figures too are more abstracted and somber. In general, the Petrograd windows display little of the "laughter with menace" so vital to Mayakovsky and his cohort.

The era of the ROSTA windows lasted until about 1930, when other mass media and ideological change made them politically passé. The turn away from narrative in posters doomed the Moscow windows, while their Petrograd colleagues suffered for their avant-garde ties; the Communists now called on illustrators to render iconic imagery of recognizable proletarian "types" (industrial worker, kolkhoz farmer, and so forth) and reject the "old, primitive" lubok style. By the 1930s, with Stalin firmly in control, no less a luminary than Moor castigated the "peasant poster" as a relic of the prerevolutionary bourgeois past (and his own; see Bonnell: 107).

The year 1931 saw the founding of the Union of Revolutionary Poster Workers (ORRP), with Moor as its director. This short-lived association (it closed in 1932) sought to further centralize control over the plakatisty and their message, but throughout its existence was plagued by low morale, infighting, and complaints from the state about the flagging quality of the works.[30] These problems continued even after ORRP was subsumed under the Moscow Regional Union of Soviet Artists (MOSKhKh), where the poster artists section received little respect from those who saw themselves as practicing "real" art (Waschik and Baburina: 254).

The fate of plakaty, sadly, mirrored that of the other arts; from 1934 they had to adhere to strict standards of realism, closely follow party edicts on style and content, and pay dearly for deviations (past, present, imagined) from state orthodoxy. To cite but three examples from the 1930s: Lebedev was personally attacked in the pages of *Pravda*, the party newspaper, for "formalism"; Klutsis was arrested and executed during the purges; Mayakovsky committed suicide, some claim over his disillusionment with the Revolution. For his part, Moor played an important role in training the next generation of poster artists and satirists (including the Kukryniksy) as a professor at the Higher Art and Technical Studios (VkhUTEMAS).

Born of the tumult and hardship of War Communism, the ROSTA windows did not survive much beyond the first decade of the Soviet state.[31] Yet they contributed immensely to defining its "look"—which is to say, the visual culture of Bolshevism, and further, to the dynamic techniques of the propaganda poster throughout the world. As Brik observed, they served as a model for art at the service of power: "Not only in propaganda, but in the artistic-political sphere as well, the ROSTA windows played a huge role. These satirical posters posed the question regarding the participation of artists in the political life of the country. It became clear that to participate in the proletarian revolution did not just mean to be inspired by its topicality, but to actually, through one's work, assist in the struggle against its enemies and build socialism" (9). Early Soviet poster art, especially the windows, had another effect and an additional legacy: as Kovtun noted, it served as the de-facto satirical press at a time when caricature was not yet being used for political purposes (1968: 3). In this way, the windows served as a vital link between several traditions: the lubok, the avant-garde, and the next generation of Russian visual satirists. The rise in the 1920s of the Soviet satirical journals, with their liberal use of comics techniques, is in large measure owed to the style and innovations of the posters and ROSTA windows. It is to this period that we now turn.

THE SATIRICAL JOURNALS

"Caricature concedes nothing to other forms of art in its artistic-agitational significance," wrote Boris Nikiforov (9) in the catalog for a major exhibit of the form in 1932. By then, the heyday of the early Soviet satirical journals—an era whose like would never be seen again in the USSR—had mostly passed, victim of the same changing political winds that so compromised the plakaty. But Nikiforov's comment reflects the high regard (as well as suspicion) in which satirical cartoons and strips were held, even by luminaries of the state leadership.[32]

While satire and humor journals had never completely disappeared, prerevolutionary censorship, then the severe disruptions of the revolution and civil war, had drawn popular attention to other matters.[33] The state, as noted, put its mass media efforts into areas such as the cinema and posters. But as the austerity of War Communism eased in 1921, the *Pravda* journalist Mikhail Koltsov could write—employing the new politically correct language—of the zeitgeist's need for "journals of a light and dynamic type: literary, illustrated, satirical, conceding nothing to the bourgeoisie in their form and liveliness, but bringing into this form a red antidote to their yellow poison" (quoted in Belaia and Skorokhodov: 441).

The explosion of Soviet satirical journals that soon followed thus represented a compromise between mass taste and Bolshevik ideology. They entertained as they inculcated party dogma. All the same, ironically, this new, massively popular satirical press owed its origins largely to NEP, the policy which reintroduced quasi-capitalism as a boost to the floundering Communist economy—leading to public/private investment in the press. Of course, this did not keep the journals from railing against the emerging business class of "Nepmen" and speculators in the 1920s.

Within three years, scores of new publications had launched, taking over a role which the ROSTA windows had mostly had to themselves since 1919. Though they soon displaced the windows in the public's imagination, the "thin journals"[34] derived a vital spark from their predecessors' visual techniques and sensibility: "The experience of the revolutionary poster and the ROSTA satirical posters, themselves having absorbed the traditions of the Russian lubok, helped the thin journals find their own particular forms for presenting sociopolitical material, to make it visually clear, accessible and biting. The eye-catching, rhymed headings; topics split up into series of pictures; dynamic drawings gradually developing the theme—all this found excellent application in the thin journal. No wonder Mayakovsky considered the ROSTA windows 'the ancestors of all Soviet satirical journals'" (Belaia and Skorokhodov: 444). Many of these journals began life as supplements to newspapers. To name only some of the most important: *Smekhach* (later *Chudak*, launched 1923), supplement to *Trud*; *Prozhektor* (The Projector, 1923), supplement to *Izvestia*; *Krasnaia Niva* (The Red Niva, 1923), supplement to *Pravda*; and *Krokodil* (The Crocodile, 1922), supplement to *The Worker* (from 1932, *Pravda*). Another major satirical journal launched independently: *Bezbozhnik* (The Atheist, 1923), a monthly devoted to withering attacks on religion.[35] All of these periodicals took on the task of ridiculing the vestiges of prerevolutionary culture (greedy merchants, prostitutes, priests) and exposing the shortcomings of Soviet society (bungling bureaucrats, drunkards, homelessness).[36]

The journals, by hiring many of the artists who had worked on the ROSTA windows, carried through on their forerunners' "laughter with menace" and employed their devices, for example, short sequential pictures unfolding to sadistically funny rhymed verse—the revival of rayok by way of Mayakovsky.[37] The new illustrated periodicals also served as the training ground for the next generation of Soviet caricaturists, including Ivan Semenov, Boris Efimov, Yulii Ganf, the Kukryniksy group, and Konstantin Rotov. In their hands, the windows' general depiction of social conditions took on a more specific, personalized cast. Still recognizable as types, the fat capitalists, Red army soldiers, and emancipated women now spoke, did more. In some of the longer sequential narratives (up to a full page), the approach was dramaturgical, dialogue-driven. Finally, responding to Koltsov's calls for "liveliness" in form, the journals emphasized visually dynamic design, large-format illustrations, caricature, photoreportage. Though not a satire journal, Koltsov's own *Ogonyok* adopted a "show, don't tell" policy (Belaia and Skorokhodov: 443).

The most popular and long-lived of the new Soviet satirical journals, *Krokodil*, fully exploited caricature and strips to define a sensibility. Under founding editor Konstantin Eremeev and second editor Nikolai Smirnov, its humor had a cynical edge, reflecting a worldview that looked on foreign exploiters and domestic shirkers with a jaundiced eye. A well-known 1925 Konstantin Eliseev cartoon[38] shows a minuscule citizen looking up at a gigantic bureaucrat at his desk, who booms, "How many times have I told you to come back tomorrow, and you always show up today!"[39]

From early on *Krokodil*'s approach—on the side of the "little man" against power, be it for or against Soviet orthodoxy—won it a loyal following. (That it began as the supplement to a newspaper aimed at workers also helped.) Various sections of the journal were devoted to dispatches, drawings, and letters from readers themselves (which often dealt with corruption, social ills, and the like), making it a more "communal" read. *Krokodil* also published more foreign cartoons (e.g., from *Simplicissimus*) than any other journal. Within six months of its August 1922 launch, *Krokodil*'s circulation shot up to 150,000, an unheard-of figure for such a publication (Stykalin and Kremenskaia: 183).

As noted, the Soviets at first supported (or ignored) the satire journals' mission, provided they attacked class enemies. One critic, writing in 1930, outlined the basic requirement: "If the artist is able within one or another *tipazh* to properly reveal the character's class essence and within this same image provide a sufficiently vivid evaluation [of that essence], then this, of course, is a sign of the image's dialectical construction" (Nikiforov: 13). And, indeed, the journals did support the general goals of the revolution. Many of them sincerely took up the satirist's task to reveal, simplify, and bring down to earth the new ideas overtaking the culture. In a 1923 editorial, "On Soviet Caricature," the publishers of *Prozhektor* wrote: "[Soviet revolutionary caricature] deciphers in lines of ink what at times seems not quite clear in words. It is in the best sense propagandistic, even when it doesn't want to be" (Belaia and Skorokhodov: 446).

As with the ROSTA windows, comics devices and iconography formed a large part of the caricaturists' repertoire. The posters' familiar use of the gutter (for contrast and "transformation") appears, for example, in Ivan Maliutin's *An Old Fairy Tale, or a New Fact of Life* (*Krokodil* no. 2, January 1927, 4). A citizen drops in on a government office for some business, only to discover an arctic cave populated by snowmen who "make him feel as cold as in an ice house." But when, in the next panel, he produces a "magical" note from an influential uncle, a "miracle" takes place: the ice all melts, leaving an efficient staff eager to serve the man, all smiles. A two-panel assault on corruption. Rotov similarly employs the gutter, though for more optimistic ends, in a 1934 diptych. The first panel shows a well-dressed woman holding flowers, on some stairs. The second shows the same woman dressed as a worker, with a pick-axe, on an underground ladder. "Who is this attractive Muscovite, who in six month's time will be walking down into a metro station?" the caption asks. "The same one who today is descending its shafts!" (Avramskii: 22). Rotov lauds the brave new equality of women through a cross-gutter, reverse-chronology transfiguration.

Rotov seems to have used the widest array of classic comics iconography the most consistently, in *Krokodil* and other publications. "It's Like This Every Night!" (*Krokodil* no. 9, March 1927, 4) portrays a group of drunken louts keeping an entire building awake with their obnoxious singing. In a three-tier design, the drunks appear in the middle, while the *upravdom* (building manager) in a separate panel complains, "Comrades! It's four o'clock in the morning! Can't you be quiet? The building residents can't sleep!" The besotted "name day celebrant" responds: "They ca-a-an't? Oh, poor things! We've gotta help 'em. C'mon, guys, let's belt out a lullaby!" Rotov uses every imaginable device to convey the loud noise: the drunkards' poses banging on things, lines emanating from their mouths, and long, twisting musical notes that stretch into the other tiers' panels above and below, to torment the building residents.

Another Rotov piece, the single-panel "Communal Living" (Budni obshche-zhitiia, from *Krokodil* no. 8, February 1927, 12) is a virtual cornucopia of techniques familiar to readers of George Herriman, Rudolph Dirks, and Billy DeBeck. To depict the chaos and open war that erupts in a crowded communal kitchen, Rotov throws in speed lines; "pain stars"; broken lines connecting a character's eyes to the subject of his vision; a stylized smoke-filled explosion. One figure even bears a strong resemblance to Barney Google.[40]

Speech balloons appear in the 1920s, though rarely (Rotov and Ivan Semenov seem to draw them the most often). The Soviets tended to prefer captions for dialogue. When balloons do get used, they disproportionately adhere to strangers or "others" of one sort or another. A 1929 caricature by Mikhail Khrapkovsky, "A Foreigner in Moscow," shows an obese, derby-wearing figure smoking a cigar (all signs he hails from a capitalist country), who notes a passing Red army man. In a thought balloon (shaped like a modern speech bubble), we see the front page of the British newspaper *Daily Mail*, with a "barbaric" bearded man standing in front of it. The caption reads, "Capitalist: It seems like he [the Red army man] is much more dangerous than we imagined!" (Manuil'sky and Nikiforov: 31). Apparently, the bubble bore a tinge of foreignness (Americanness?) for some Soviet cartoonists.

Finally, as mentioned, sequential narratives (from two panels to page-long shorts) show up routinely in the 1920s satirical press. Those who made the most of the technique include Boris Antonovsky, to portray the progressive decay of buildings and to chronicle the adventures of the simple-minded Evlampii Nad'kin, and Semenov.

The 1920s were an unprecedented time in all of Russian history; its relative freedoms and support for experimentation could not last. To wit: as the curtain began to fall on the age of the fellow traveler,[41] the Soviet leadership increasingly took note of the journals' unruly expression and "over-eagerness" to point out social ills. As one critic wrote: "The daily feuilletons . . . screaming about outrages and disorder, are dangerous. Like drops of water hollowing out a stone, they drip onto the brain of the reader and inevitably drive him to ask, 'Will these disgraces ever end?' and 'is the party fully committed to eliminating these outrages?'" (Skorokhodov: 467). By 1927, the chorus of complaints had built up to where no less an organ than the party's Central Committee published the resolution, "On the Satirical-Humor Journals," which in no uncertain terms attacked *Krokodil* and its cohorts for not fulfilling their role to expose retrograde elements or attack class enemies here and abroad, and for orienting itself to "bourgeois" tastes (Stykalin and Kremenskaia: 23).

By the end of the 1920s, further attacks by leftist organizations such as RAPP (the Russian Association of Proletarian Writers); paper shortages; censorship; the end of NEP and party efforts to reduce "parallelism" (i.e., too many journals), among other factors, all reduced the satirical press to a husk of its former self. Journals scaled back, merged, then closed down by the score. Those left had to operate in a drastically restricted playing field, with only party enemies left as legitimate targets for satire, and even then in a more "muzzled" tone. By 1933, *Krokodil* was the only major unionwide satirical journal left, with a circulation of 500,000. (Though it was now published under the supervision of *Pravda*, the Communist Party newspaper.)[42]

The devastation did not stop there. As was occurring with the poster artists (and indeed throughout the culture), many fell victim to the Stalinist repressions that began in earnest in the 1930s. In 1940 Rotov was arrested and sentenced to eight years in a concentration camp. Koltsov, a major figure in establishing the satirical press and at one point editor of *Krokodil*, was arrested in 1938, and later executed.[43] By then the brief golden age of Soviet caricature had long ended.

THE AVANT-GARDE BOOK AND CHILDREN'S PRESS

Comics techniques found their way into other spheres of Soviet culture, including *knizhnoe iskusstvo* (book art), a form which attracted some of the shining lights of Russian modernism. Like their Cubo-Futurist predecessors in the Silver Age, poets and artists of the new society sought to reinvent the book—in large measure by filling the imagined gap between words and images. Many were attracted to the children's book for its openness to radical experimentation and its potential to shape the first generation of the "new Soviet man" (Novy sovetskii chelovek). Among the many notable children's books of the era[44] (whose content can be guessed from their titles): *Alphabet* by Lebedev (1925); *Children and Lenin* by Klutsis (1924); *How the Capitalists Are Armed* by V. Zhukov and Maria Siniakova-Urechina (1931). This brief survey will focus on two major figures and their comics-like contributions to early Soviet book design.

The Suprematist El Lissitzky, whose arts practice privileged "transcendent" forms, extended Kamensky's prerevolutionary "concrete poems" to a new level of abstraction, as seen in the aforementioned *Beat the Whites with a Red Wedge*. Lissitzky takes this "hieroglyphic" approach in a longer-form narrative direction in his children's booklet *About Two Squares* (1922), a sequential (anti-) narrative that depicts two eponymous shapes—one red, one black—colliding, shattering, and resettling amid "energetically" shifting text. The effect of this "story-in-language"[45] is almost like watching some sort of spiritualized astronomical event, best described by Lissitzky himself: "Build a book like a body moving in space and time, like a dynamic relief in which every page is a surface carrying shapes, and every turn of a page a new crossing to a new stage of a single structure" (quoted in Railing: 37).

In his 1929 essay "The Book from the Point of View of Visual Perception is the Visual Book," Lissitzky models his new "visual language" on the ideogram and hieroglyph. Indeed, like others at this time, he fetishizes them:

We stand on the threshold of a book form in which the image plays the primary role and the text a secondary role. . . . We know two kinds of typeface: the sign for general understanding, the ideogram (today in China) and the sign for sound, the letter. The progress of the letter compared to the ideogram is relative.

The ideogram is international. This means: if a Russian, a German or an American learns the signs (pictures) for understanding, he can read to himself in Chinese or Egyptian without having to learn to speak these languages, since language and letter are two different things. For example, for the meaning of "good" and "evil," Japanese ideograms have many different nuances which aural speech does not. Visual speech is richer than aural speech. This is an advantage which the book, assembled out of letters, has lost. Therefore, it seems to me, the future form of the book will be plastic-visual. (56)

In addition to the word/image blending, *Story About Two Squares* utilizes juxtaposed sequential imagery to "animate" its geometric figures and build a considerable tension. One critic even noted the work "might . . . be mistaken for a *false* comic strip" (Bois and Hubert: 120, emphasis in original)—false because it undermines narratival linearity and unity even as it constructs it "like the residue of an animated film from which the best moments have been excerpted" (119).[46] The book, Bois goes on to argue, could be read as an allegory for the quandary faced by antirepresentational artists like the Suprematists, for whom, "in a revolutionary period, it is impossible to eliminate the signified" (117).[47]

The Futurists, too, experimented with the Soviet book. Ever versatile, the "poet laureate of the Revolution," Vladimir Mayakovsky, also contributed to this art, as he had to posters and the satirical journals (one gets the impression the man was everywhere and did everything in the 1920s).[48] His 1919 *Soviet Alphabet* combined drawings and humorous verse into a booklet of lithographs he printed himself and distributed to Red army soldiers. Yurii Rozhkov adapted Mayakovsky's 1923 poem "To the Workers of Kursk, Who Extracted the First Ore" as an extraordinary fifty-page photomontage in 1924. We might also describe it as a "word montage"; the images and text fly and jumble with exceptional energy—Rozhkov reenergized Larionov and the primitivists' "anti-book" aesthetic with photography and printing techniques. Klutsis's 1925 photomontage illustrations to another Mayakovsky poem, *Vladimir Ilyich Lenin*, are notable for their depictions of the great leader with text emanating from his mouth[49] (Lenin had died in 1924; this work among others served as both commemoration and "resurrection" of the state's founder).

Mayakovsky's most sustained post-ROSTA contributions to Russian comics art were his illustrated booklets included as inserts to newspapers like *Krasnaia Nov'* in the early to mid-1920s. With titles such as *Story About a Deserter Who Set Himself Up Pretty Well . . .* (1921) and *Neither Folk-healers, Nor God, Nor God's Servants Will Help Us* (1923), these four- to fourteen-page narratives mostly showed printed verse below the pictures, with an occasional line of dialogue emanating from a figure's mouth. The stories transferred the windows' agitational methods to a book format, necessitating a longer-form sequential organization,

2.5. From *Away With Home Brew!*, a neo-lubok booklet by Vladimir Mayakovsky, 1923.

more complex characters and situations, and an alignment of the plot to the rhythms of page-turning.

Away With Home Brew! (1923) combines rhymed verse in a faux peasant key and lubok-like imagery for the tale of a woman who drives an entire village drunk with her vodka. (Addressing rampant drunkenness was a major Soviet policy concern.) In the last two pages, Mayakovsky "resolves" the story through a montage strategy of diametrically opposed pages in sequence. The penultimate page shows three pictures: villagers drinking from a huge bottle (held by a giant hand), their settlement in ruins, and a drunkard's silhouette before a cackling priest, an old landowner, and a White Cossack soldier: "Yes, our enemies broke into a smile" (Mayakovsky: 223). The next page banishes that nightmarish scenario through a larger picture of a powerfully built Bolshevik seizing both the woman and another peasant; their bottles drop and break. A smaller, closing image depicts two silhouettes holding up a banner with the date of the Revolution: October 25 (old style), beyond which a sun rises: "Drive away those who offer drink / Drive away those who imbibe . . . Only he who is healthy is a bulwark for the peasantry; / Only thanks to them will the commune blossom" (225).

Mayakovsky's neo-lubok booklets offer a tantalizing hint of what direction Soviet comics might have gone if allowed to develop. As the reader has already surmised, however, the avant-garde books (including those for children) succumbed to the same forces driving the USSR toward totalitarian control of the arts by the end of the 1920s. By the late 1930s, book design had returned to less "experimental" paradigms; the same applied to the form and content of children's literature.

One can see the stark changes by comparing works from the first decade of Soviet power to Vladimir Konashevich's 1937 children's book *What a Scatterbrain* (Vot takoi rasseiannyi). The story, about a middle-aged man with a severe lack of focus on everyday matters, unfolds through simple drawings that mostly echo the text; lines like "On his way out, instead of his hat / He put on the frying pan" is accompanied by an image showing him doing exactly that. The emphasis is now on clarity, directness, a lack of tension between text (primary) and illustration (supporting the text). Conversely, in Mayakovsky's booklets the words and images interact much more organically; as in the lubok tradition, his stylized drawings ironicize and "enliven" the text, at times openly contradicting it. Very little of this survives the 1920s.

Despite the imposition of a new realist aesthetic in the early years of Stalin's rule, the children's press retained some limited freedom of expression into the 1930s.[50] Chief among these journals were *Murzilka* (1924), *Pioneer* (1924), and Nikolai Oleinikov's *Yozh* (Hedgehog, but also an acronym for "Monthly Journal," 1928) and *Chizh* (Siskin, but also "Very Interesting Journal," 1930) in Leningrad. In addition to publishing some of the most important writers of the era—Daniil Kharms and other absurdists of the OBERIUTy group, Kornei Chukovsky, Samuil Marshak—these journals were the first to feature the comics-like adventures of continuing characters. *Yozh's Makar the Fierce* (illustrated by Boris Antonovsky and others) told humorous adventures through "action-to-action" panel progressions. The accompanying captions stretch underneath the gap separating the pictures, facilitating a more dynamic "flow" of the (usually thrilling) narrative. One critic noted that Oleinikov "did not disparage the narrative form thought up by the authors: an unfolding series of pictures unified by a developing plot" (Moskin).

Boris Malakhovsky's *Smart Masha* in *Chizh* (often written by Kharms) dealt with the young heroine's brilliantly simple solutions to complex problems and her interactions with a local boy, "stupid Vitia." In *How Smart Masha Tidied Up the Garden* (*Chizh*, November 1936, back cover), Masha attaches a rake to Vitia's tricycle, so while he "works" she can "have a bit of rest." The story unfolds in a three-panel composition (problem, idea, solution), with the final "punch-line" frame twice as large as the others: Vitia raking (with an obliviously blissful expression), Masha on a bench studiously reading a book. (Everyone's happy.) Though—with the exception of *Murzilka*—most of these publications ceased by World War II, a number of characters popularized by the early Soviet children's press would be revived and revamped in the postwar era.

SOCIALIST REALISM

The dizzying array of creative activity in Soviet Russia came to an inauspicious halt with Stalin's consolidation of power by the late 1920s, the subsequent disenfranchisement of the avant-garde[51] and the attacks on "formalism" in the arts.[52] The change was codified in 1932 with the party's outlawing of the numerous cultural groups and the resolution "On the Restructuring of Literary Organizations." This formally introduced the term Socialist Realism, later defined[53] at the 1934 First All-Union Congress of Soviet Writers as "the basic method of Soviet literature . . . . [D]emand[ing] of the artist the truthful, historically concrete representation of reality in its revolutionary development" (Kenez: 157), with its goal "the creation of works of high artistic significance, saturated with the heroic struggle of the world proletariat and with the grandeur of the victory of Socialism" (Struve: 256). A straightforward, unadorned, mimetic style would replace—under penalty of state sanction—the formal experimentation of the previous decade. Furthermore, the arts were now officially branded organs of government propaganda and, as such, must adhere to its message.[54]

Secretary of the Central Committee of the Communist Party Andrei Zhdanov, in his address to the congress, made it clear the new Soviet order would have little tolerance for material that smacked of Western capitalist art, which he derided: "Characteristic of the decadence and decay of the bourgeois culture are the orgies of mysticism and superstition, the passion for pornography. The 'celebrities' of bourgeois literature—of the bourgeois literature which has sold its pen to capital—are now thieves, police sleuths, prostitutes, hooligans" (11). In the drive for ideological and aesthetic unity,[55] the mass-culture products of the capitalist world (pulp literature, including comics) were definitively forbidden, their poisonous subject matter and degraded forms to be avoided by right-thinking Soviet artists. From the 1930s on—with NEP annulled; alternative voices eliminated; the first five-year plan launched; and the implementation of absolute dictatorship under Stalin—no Russian artist who valued his career would openly advocate a Western-style comics culture. In short, the landscape had changed too much.

The effects of resurgent conservatism, Socialist Realism, and the Great Terror of the 1930s we have to some extent already discussed: posters retreated even further away from ROSTA window-style narratives in favor of iconic single-image representations; modernist styles disallowed in books; the satirical and children's press muzzled; artists persecuted. Discussing the work of the by-then preeminent cartoonist of the USSR, the historian Mikhail Zlatkovsky succinctly characterized the prosaic mission of caricaturists by the end of the decade: "In his drawings Boris Efimov achieved the main goal put to Soviet artists: the representation of the enemy in as repulsive a form as possible. . . . For Soviet propaganda there existed no nuances or distinctions: the satirist paints them one after another in the same black hue. In his gallery, standing single-file: a White general, American bankers, English industrialists and fascist leaders" (208).

THE DIASPORA

We now turn briefly to survey the comics and comics-like work of those whom the Soviets drove out of Russia in or after 1917. Left in the revolution's wake to carry on their lives and creative work all over the world, this disparate group of artists constituted a separate branch of Russian comics in exile, even if their contributions to the form were scattered or incorporated into other countries' traditions.

Among the older cadre of artists who could not reconcile themselves, at least initially, to the revolution and emigrated—Mikhail Larionov, Natalia Goncharova, Ivan Bilibin—was the important plakatist Alexander Apsit, who had contributed mightily to the construction of early Soviet symbols (such as the blacksmith figure). He fled to his native Latvia in 1921.

A major portion of the Russian diaspora settled in Serbia and had a great impact on its comics culture; many of these artists belonged to the 1930s "Belgrade Circle," which pioneered the industry in what was then the Kingdom of Serbs, Croats, and Slovenes. In the decade before World War II, artists such as Djordje (Yurii) Lobachev (*Bloodied Inheritance, The Bandit Stanko*); Nikolai Tishchenko (*Funny Things Happening to Detective X-9*); Nikolai Navojev (*Black Wings on Amazon Island, Tarzanetta*); Konstantin Kuznetsov (*Czar Peter the Great*); Sergei Solovyov (*The Cossacks*) and Ivan Shenshin (*The Good Soldier Schweik*) exemplified a style of Russian comics under Western pulp influences; they owe a particular stylistic debt to Alex Raymond, Hal Foster, Burne Hogarth, and other adventure strip artists.[56] Many of these komiksisty published in the first and most important comics magazine, *Mika Mis*, launched in 1936 by another Russian émigré, Alexander Ivkovic.

Needless to say, one finds little of the lubok or ROSTA windows in these works. A 1938 episode from Navoyev and Branka Vidica's *The Little Sailor* (Mali moreplovac) features a wild jungle adventure, in which a femme fatale vanquishes her rival with an arrow through the heart. The eye-patch-clad hero intones, "I will have my bitter revenge," only to see a black panther maul the villainess before his eyes. "The beast beat me to the punch," he utters. The drawings enhance the thrills through low-angle compositions that emphasize depth, frequent shifts in point of view, and gruesome mis-en-scene. Kuznetsov takes a more polished, "literary" approach in his adaptation of Alexander Pushkin's *The Queen of Spades* (1940): characters speak in more elevated phrases such as "declaration of love," while the lush art recreates the costumes, drawing rooms, and boudoirs of nineteenth-century St. Petersburg.[57]

The comics artist and historian Zdravko Zupan notes that the Russians' contributions proved vital to making Belgrade one of the most active centers of comics production in Europe by the end of the 1930s: "Serbian comics never before and never again attained such heights of self-expression and authenticity, such narrative and graphic contributions to European and world comics" (93). Tragically, history in the guise of World War II and the postwar order caught up with these artists: as a result of the 1944 Communist occupation of Yugoslavia, Shenshin was executed, Kuznetsov fled to America, others were displaced. Lobachev was deported and eventually returned to Leningrad. (Of the émigrés in Yugoslavia, he alone lived to see a new generation of comics artists emerge in Russia in the 1980s, as we discuss in the next chapter.)

Another Russian exile saw a kinder fate. The caricaturist Mariamne Davydoff, of noble birth (an ancestor had married Peter the Great), illustrated her memoirs with watercolors of prerevolutionary life in the provinces. After moving to Paris in the 1920s, she reconstructed that lost era from memory: details such as the patterns of wallpaper, the likenesses of visitors, the architecture of buildings on her former estate. She also reproduces the social divisions that contributed to the outbreak of revolution: in the family's private chapel, the servants are segregated (Davydoff: 14–15). For the most part, however, her account treats turn-of-the-century Russia as a sort of paradise ruined by the Bolsheviks (she had intended the work as a legacy to her descendants).

Published decades after the author's death in 1961, the memoirs do not attempt a strong integration of visual and verbal. Rather stagy—Davydoff uses an "invisible fourth wall" arrangement and idealized, stiffly posed figures—the work's genteel images of Christmas celebrations and dances nonetheless underscore the author's desire to recapture and *show* the country she would never see again.

This puts her in the company of other twentieth-century Russian exiles remembering their homeland, particularly Vladimir Nabokov, whose own *Speak Memory: An Autobiography Revisited* (1966) tries to do in words what Davydoff assays through an image/text strategy. While not a comics artist or cartoonist, Nabokov expressed a lifelong affection for American strips and mined them for material: the phrase "tiger tea" from Herriman's *Krazy Kat*, references to the *New Yorker* cartoonist Otto Soglow, and so on.

Clarence Brown even ascribes a "bdesque" sensibility to his writing, which evinces "slight traces of sequential pictorial narrative" (251). In an explicit example, the 1938 novel *Invitation to a Beheading* contains an elaborate description of an eight-panel comics work representing the hero's escape from prison.

In an odd overlap of worlds, the teenage Nabokov had taken drawing lessons from Mstislav Dobuzhinsky, the important prerevolutionary satirist mentioned in chapter 1. (The teacher called the student the worst he ever had.) Brown argues that the artist's emphasis on drawing from memory contributed to Nabokov the writer's "fetish for precise description and his high esteem for those people who do not move through the world in a half-somnolent state but actually see their surroundings" (252). Brown, himself a cartoonist, pushes his bdesque thesis a bit far, but vision—*how* one sees the world—does play a critical role in Nabokov's oeuvre. One "flawed" way of seeing and representing the world, kitsch, along with the related Russian idea of *poshlost'*, flows from the author's fixation on seeing. A form of self-satisfied banality, for Nabokov poshlost' finds its reflection in Norman Rockwell–type advertisements and other cheap, sentimentalized propaganda that robs life of its complexity and detail. One would presume mass-culture products such as comics would fall into this rubric for the aristocratic Nabokov, yet he qualifies their inclusion: "by poshlust[58]-literature I do not mean the kind of thing which is termed 'pulp' or which in England used to go by the name 'penny dreadfuls' and in Russia under that of 'yellow literature.' Obvious trash, curiously enough, contains a wholesome ingredient, readily appreciated by children and simple souls. Superman is undoubtedly poshlust, but it is poshlust in such a mild, unpretentious form that it is not worthwhile talking about" (1959: 68). Nabokov's curiously backhanded compliment to comics, represented by Superman, as "obvious trash" that nonetheless contains a "wholesome ingredient" appreciable by "children and simple souls," seems to betray mixed feelings. As kitsch, comics may contribute to "the ongoing dumbing-down and debasement of humanity" (Erofeev: 447), but (perhaps due to his affection for the form) he also realizes that even a "simplistic" drawing (even a stroke in a drawing) potentially contains worlds, that it can denote an archly sophisticated view on reality. But only those of "simple soul," whose vision has not grown encrusted by habit or societal preconceptions, can apprehend it.[59] On the other hand, Nabokov's dismissal of Golden Age Superman as harmless fluff "not worthwhile talking about" hardly constitutes a ringing endorsement.[60]

In any case, much of the author's work depicts people who, tragi-comically, do not "see" what lies before them. In his 1957 novel *Pnin*, Nabokov uses (intriguingly) a *New Yorker*–type cartoon to convey the eponymous lead character's visual illiteracy. Not only can the Russian emigré not accept the physical impossibility of the "deserted island" gag ("So small island, moreover with palm, cannot exist in so small area"), he is flummoxed by comics grammar:

> "Now, you look at the picture. So this is the mariner, and this is the pussy, and this is a rather wistful mermaid hanging around, and now look at the puffs right above the sailor and the pussy."
>
> "Atomic bomb explosion," said Pnin sadly.
>
> "No, not at all. It is something much funnier. You see, these round puffs are supposed to be the projections of their thoughts . . . The sailor imagines the mermaid as having a pair of legs, and the cat imagines her as all fish." (60–61)

In not understanding the cartoon's pictoriographic signs (the thought balloons), Pnin is responding like a cultured Russian, whose logocentrism "blinds" him to other kinds of (visual) language.[61] It is a miniature portrait of the intelligentsia's distaste and incomprehension of comic art, made all the more poignant by its displacement to the novel's setting in America. (When it came to comics, twentieth-century Russia was—broadly speaking—a nation of Pnins, with or without the Soviets' enforcement.)

Another major figure of the Russian comics diaspora is its most controversial: Vincent Krassousky, an émigré to France who worked on the pro-Nazi children's journal *La Téméraire* during the German occupation of World War II. A veteran White soldier possessed of "an intense, visceral hatred of the Russians,"[62] his recurring character Vica (a Popeye-type sailor) mocked and excoriated England, America, the Bolsheviks, and "Jewish conspiracies." Krassousky—who may have been mentally deranged—was tried after the war and sentenced to a year in prison.

Among the children of Russian émigrés who have gone on to careers in comics and illustration, we can include the Americans Boris Artsybashev (son of the important turn-of-the-century Russian novelist Mikhail Artsybashev) and Jerry Robinson, creator of Robin and the Joker for DC Comics; and the Chilean writer Alejandro Jodorowsky.

WWII AND BEYOND

Adolf Hitler's German army invaded the Soviet Union on June 21, 1941. Operation Barbarossa envisioned complete defeat of the Russians by the end of the year, but such did not occur; the conflict between the Nazis and the USSR, what Russians refer to as the Great Patriotic War (Velikaia Otechestvennaia Voina), lasted until the Allies' victory in May 1945.[63] As had occurred during World War I and the Civil War, with the outbreak of hostilities the leadership turned to posters to mobilize the population against the enemy. The accelerated production methods also returned; Iraklii Toidze's iconic placard *The Motherland Calls* (the most famous Russian poster ever made) papered public spaces within days of the German advance. The state even revived the comics-like "windows," this time produced by TASS (Telegraph Agency of the Soviet Union, the successor to ROSTA),[64] and now utilizing more advanced printing technology.

The TASS windows recycled imagery from the earlier conflicts' propaganda: brave, handsome Red army soldiers; animalistic Germans; the "sweeping" motif. In many cases, it was the same artists doing the recycling. The older artists (Moor, Deni, Cheremnykh, Efimov) along with the younger generation (the Kukryniksy, Viktor Ivanov) tapped the narrative capacities of the comics medium as well, to demonize the Nazis and agitate for greater sacrifices. Bonnell argues this revival of what she calls the "lubok style" in posters "most likely . . . was thought to provide an easy means of communication with a broad strata of the population, especially those in the countryside" (222).[65]

The satirical posters of the prolific trio Kukryniksy became an inextricable part of Soviet World War II visual culture. Their collective pseudonym, derived from their names (Mikhail **Ku**prianov, Porfiry **Kry**lov, and **Nik**olai Sokolov), underscored their collective ethos, practiced since the mid-1920s in *Krokodil* and other publications. In their World War II posters they unleashed their full satirical arsenal against Hitler, often employing a two-panel "before/after" technique, for example, Germans troops triumphantly approaching Moscow, then retreating in terror and humiliation. In their *TASS Window No. 747: Fritz's Caftan* (1940s), a German soldier evades the Red army's artillery barrage for two panels, until the finale, when a bomb rips him to pieces—sadistically reflected in rhyming verse by Samuil Marshak: "Like a flock of birds the shrapnel flies / And with it Fritz takes to the skies!"

While other World War II poster artists did not use comics techniques as extensively, some did imply sequence through self-referentiality. Leonid Golovanov's *We'll Make It All the Way to Berlin!* (Doidem do Berlina!, 1944), which shows a fresh-faced young recruit donning his boots, appears on the wall behind the *same* soldier beaming and displaying his medals in *Glory to the Red Army!* (Krasnoi armii—slava!, 1946). Plakatisty also referenced each other in their intertextual propaganda efforts: Nikolai Zhukov's *Hit Them 'Til They're Dead!* (Bei nasmert'!, 1944), depicts a furious machine-gunner firing away; hanging on a brick wall behind him: Viktor Koretskii's *Red Army Warrior, Save Us!* (Voin krasnoi armii—spasi!, 1942), showing a Russian woman and her child threatened by an unseen Nazi's bayonet. The town in flames in the distance, coupled with the Koretskii poster, come to represent a projection of the soldier's inner feelings; like thought balloons, they represent the reasons why he fights so desperately. Zhukov's work comments both on the righteousness of the Soviets' cause as well as the effectiveness of their propaganda.[66]

With the close of World War II, the USSR took to the mammoth task of rebuilding. In the realm of the arts, this regrettably meant reining in the freedoms granted during the conflict and reasserting the primacy of Socialist Realism. Spearheaded once more by Central Committee secretary Andrei Zhdanov (hence known as the Zhdanovshchina), this retrenchment began in earnest in 1946, with an attack on the satirical writer Mikhail Zoshchenko and the poet Anna Akhmatova.[67] Along with the charges came a renewed suspicion of foreigners and "rootless cosmopolitans" (a code word for Jews), culminating in the infamous "Doctor's Plot" purges of the early 1950s. (Only Stalin's death in 1953 kept the cost in lives relatively low.)

To its discredit, *Krokodil* contributed many anti-Semitic caricatures to the "cosmopolitanism" campaign—though this did not prevent a new wave of censure for

2.6. "The words and the deeds of the American butchers" by Yulii Ganf (*Krokodil*, 1953).

its "low level of quality" in the form of party resolutions "On the Journal *Krokodil*" (1948) and "On the Shortcomings of the Journal *Krokodil* and Measures for Its Improvement" (1951). Even with the post-Stalin Thaw, which loosened restrictions on expression in literature and film, target opportunities for satirical caricaturists remained few; as Zlatkovsky notes, "The repressive political satire that had formed by the beginning of the 1950s had only one function: the struggle with the enemies of the socialist regime, both abroad and on the home front" (13).

The tone grew more confrontational as the cold war deepened. Aside from their grotesque depiction of Western politicians; emphasis on American militarism, racism, and class inequities[68]; and lionization of Soviet technological feats (e.g., Sputnik), caricaturists made much use of the two-panel "us/them" technique, often effecting a "metaphorical" transformation across the gutter. Yulii Ganf's cover to *Krokodil* no. 2 (January 1953) shows, in its top panel, a weeping politician at a podium, shedding tears as he delivers a speech. The caption says, "The words . . ." The politician has an oddly elongated torso, which stretches down across the gutter into the bottom panel, where it becomes the handle of a gigantic axe stuck upright on a tiny island marked "Longana"; the island holds only a military base or camp encircled in barbed wire.[69] The politician's tears, which also drop into the bottom panel, have become blood splattering the axe blade. The caption reads ". . . and the deeds of the American butchers." Ganf's image extends the "supernatural" quality of the Old Believer lubki to the materialist cold war, retaining the power of its gutter to depict—indeed, catalyze—change. The gap between "us and them" grows so massive across that ideological space between panels, as to constitute a sort of secular "magic."

As argued by Waschik and Baburina: "The bi-polar design found its best accord ever with the worldview predominant in the Cold War era . . . This dialectical method, which demonstrated the horrors of a negative milieu side by side with a positive one, managed to secure in the consciousness of the viewer a representation not only of the 'happiness of socialism' but also of the 'horrors of capitalism.' In this way it proved that the viewer was extraordinarily fortunate not to live in a 'bourgeois nightmare'" (184). Posters also tapped the technique to give explicit (if grotesque) lessons in Marxist exchange value. Ivan Semenov's 1953 poster *The Goal of Capitalism is Always the Same* organizes a sequential series of panels depicting human suffering as a result of imperialist policies. Their blood, sweat, and labor drips down below the panels, where a fat capitalist stretches out his hands to catch the drops, now transformed into gold coins.[70] The Kukryniksy make the same point in even more direct fashion in a 1966 cartoon composed of a large dollar sign superimposed over dead Vietnamese women and children in the top panel, with their blood dripping down to the bottom panel and turning into gold coins. The dollar sign is actually made up of one elongated arm with a hand at each end: the top hand holds a bomb over the dead civilians, the bottom hand catches the money. "The left hand knows what the right hand is getting," says the caption.[71]

Most postwar "cross-gutter" diptych cartoons did not treat violence so explicitly, instead using the technique for endless variations on the "us/them" theme. Koretskii's popular *The Path of a Talent . . . Make Way for the Talented!* (Doroga talanta . . . dorogu talantam, 1948) combines the method with socialist realist sentimentality. The left panel presents a destitute young man with a violin, trundling the nighttime streets of an American city, downcast and unemployed. The caption reads, "In capitalist countries." The right panel shows another young man performing a violin solo before an accompanying orchestra in a symphony hall, to the caption, "In socialist countries."[72]

The Path of a Talent exemplifies Soviet strategies for agitation (designed to appeal to the emotions) versus propaganda (the detailed, logical proof of the superiority of Marxism): no explanation is provided for the differences in the young men's fates; their expressions and material conditions suffice to convince. Neither do we receive clarity on how precisely blood "becomes" gold in the hands of capitalists; the images merely require the viewer to make a connection between the two and draw the right (horrified) conclusion. The differences between agitation and propaganda became the subject of cold war study for American scholars seeking to understand the Soviet threat; they devoted a number of works to caricature.[73] The nuances between agitation and propaganda had long been noted by the Soviets (including Lenin), who respected the power of cartoons and posters as agitational media; even in the age of cinema and television, the poster and caricature remained vibrant parts of Soviet visual culture.[74]

But not all Russian uses of the comics language were, in the broad sense, propaganda. In a fascinating echo of "duck and cover" an ocean away, the Soviets published informational comics booklets on atomic war, chemical attacks, and the procedures for what to do in their aftermath. The color booklets, released up until the 1970s, detail through sequential panels and text the delivery of nuclear bombs (by B-52, ICBM); the stages of a nuclear explosion; expressionless citizens in gas masks against postapocalyptic landscapes, blandly following orders, lining up, tending to the wounded, showering. These works have nowhere near the energy of the ROSTA or TASS windows (they evidently were not made by caricaturists): the figures seem blandly docile and bizarrely calm, given the Armageddon-like setting. As one post-Soviet publisher put it, "The pictures show a fantasy world, an anti-utopia that would result from a nuclear attack."[75] If nothing else, these booklets demonstrate that comics not intended as humorous or for children did exist in the Soviet Union.

All the same, the Russian mind in the postwar era continued to regard comics as, at best, light entertainment for kids. It was therefore no surprise to find short comics stories in *Veselie Kartinki* (Merry Pictures, 1956), a major new children's journal cofounded by Ivan Semenov, the veteran *Krokodil* caricaturist and poster artist. The first issue baldly declared its continuity with the great 1920s and 1930s traditions of Oleinikov's *Chizh* and *Yozh*: on the cover stride such beloved classic characters as Smart Masha, Stupid Vitia, Makar the Fierce, and Buratino.

Semenov's work in *Veselie Kartinki* is among his best, and represents the purest example of narrative-driven comics in this period.[76] His series *The Incredible Adventures of the Famed Traveler Petia Ryzhik and His Loyal Friends Mik and Muk* strongly recalls Hergé's *Tintin*, with an overt ideological bent; the youth Petia[77] and his friends travel all over the world (and to the moon), encountering class foes (usually Americans) and friends (third-world peoples). The stories always end with the vanquishing of the former, though never in any overly violent way.

Although the earlier stories unfold in a combination of pictures, captions, and occasional word balloons, by the mid-1960s Semenov often divides his pages in up to twelve panels and makes free use of word balloons with no captions. In one 1964 episode, the boy Petia (dressed similarly to the Young Pioneers youth group, only with a red hat instead of a kerchief) and his two dogs explore a cave, in which they make remarkable discoveries: primitive wall drawings; magnetic ore; a new kind of yellow petroleum; and, most intriguing, a dragon (in a silent six-panel sequence, the unflappable Petia lassoes the creature and drags him out of a whirlpool). All ends happily: the dragon leads them out of the cave and receives free housing and "three meals a day" at the zoo. Petia's other discoveries are lauded by archeologists and geologists. The tale (similar to the first episode of the 1960s animated series *Cheburashka* in its "happy zoo" theme) conveys—somewhat bizarrely, perhaps—the Soviet values of teamwork, fearlessness, embrace of the other, and a benevolent state providing for the needs of all, to the extent that a creature torn from its home would give up its freedom to live in a caged environment!

A more strident tale appears in a 1964 book adapting episodes from *Veselie Kartinki*. Told in pictures with captions, the story involves a somewhat petulant

2.7. *Pavlik Morozov, a diafilm by V. Gubaryov and R. Stolyarov, 1959.*

Petia constructing a kite, which spirits the adventurous trio to an "imperialist colony" in Africa. Petia brings disorder (and an angry crocodile) to a nearby military base (the soldiers' helmets bear dollar signs), then befriends some village boys. There suddenly appears "a wicked man with a whip," in cowboy hat—the obese plantation owner, telling the newcomers to stop interfering with the "black-skins'" work. Petia, without fear, proposes to the capitalist that he try out a new machine that will raise a "heavy weight," improving efficiency on the plantation. He ties the kite to the man's belt, and he promptly rises up into the air, astonished. A strong wind carries him "somewhere to the sea" (kuda-to v more), and Petia, Mik, and Muk engage in a native dance with spears and elaborate head-dresses; "Later, Petia taught his friends a Russian dance." Semenov's Petia stories operate on the level of anecdotes: they bifurcate the world into black and white (in this case, literally), reveling in their own improbability and naïve faith in Communism.[78]

A popular character, Petia also appeared in diafilms (film strips), another medium which dabbled in comics iconography. These stories on slides could be watched individually or projected for an audience. They could be accompanied by music or recorded commentary, or one could simply read the captions aloud. Subjects went well beyond children's stories, to include science lessons, historical topics, and government propaganda. In the 1960s, several diafilm series were devoted to outer-space-related material, especially Yurii Gagarin's first manned space flight in 1961.

A more controversial subject appears in the 1959 diafilm *Pavlik Morozov* by V. Gubarev and R. Stoliarov. This tells the story, in fifty consecutive panels with captions, of the (in)famous young pioneer who denounced his family to the Soviets in 1932 and was martyred in a revenge killing.[79] Like many historical-subject diafilms, this one has painted art in a Socialist Realist style, which portrays the villainous family members in perpetual dark tones, while the heroic Pavlik often appears with a halo-like nimbus about his head. A middle ground between books and cinema (or if you will an electric version of the rayok), the diafilm offers yet more proof of the text/image/sequentiality method's prevalence in postwar Soviet visual culture. A number of cartoon diafilms, in fact, were adapted from animated films as well as comics material in *Veselie Kartinki*.

Yet another example from children's literature: the so-called *knizhka-raskladu-shka* or "fold-out book." Similar to pop-up books, these often-short works could come in unconventional shapes, and opened up accordion style for hands-on reading or play. (The raskladushki harken back both to the experimental constructivist children's books of the 1920s as well as people's print works like the *Koren' Bible*, which also folded open for display on a wall.) *Ai da ia!* (Way to Go, Me!, 1961) by L. Gamburger typifies the form's strategies of sequentiality, juxtaposition, and dialogue in captions: an overly confident puppy ("I'm brave!") scares off a menagerie of animals—including a lion and an elephant—with his aggressive barks and bites, until a goose boxes his ears ("Ma-a-ma! . . ." he screams). Depending on how one manipulates the book, the raskladushka functions as a diafilm-like series of consecutive pictures and text, or as a juxtaposed pictorial narrative, but in any case the role played by sequentiality is key.

As the promise of the post-Stalin Thaw receded into the emerging Stagnation Era of the 1960s and 1970s under Leonid Brezhnev, the confrontation with the free world settled into a steady drumbeat of vituperation. The environment for a Western-style comics culture thus had little chance of taking hold; if anything, prejudice against American mass culture deepened[80] (as we discuss in the next section).

Nonetheless, the 1960s saw a flowering of "alternative" caricature from a new generation that venerated *Krokodil*, yet chose to strike out in its own direction. Appearing in such youth-oriented periodicals as *Smena* and *Literaturnaia Gazeta*, the new cartoonists favored "universal," timeless themes, and thus eschewed the standard "types" familiar to readers since the 1920s; cave dwellers and everymen took the place of bureaucrats. (They also for the most part eschewed text.) Much of this "unofficial" caricature, which ignored the decades-old propaganda mission of the form, went unpublished, but what did came to be associated with the "12 Chairs Club" artists: Oleg Tesler, Andrei Nekrasov, Igor Vorobev, among others (Zlatkovsky: 288–89).

As a result of the postwar European order in the 1960s, Russians could enjoy satirical journals imported from the other Soviet bloc countries. A number
of these featured comics, including *Szpilki* (Poland), *Dikobraz* (Czechoslovakia),
and *Ludas Matyi* (Hungary). The literary journal *Inostrannaia literatura* (Foreign
Literature) reported in a 1965 article on an Italian conference devoted to comics.
Another landmark of sorts was reached in 1961, when the Mexican cartoonist Rius
(Eduardo del Rio), became the first foreign cartoonist to publish his work in the
government newspaper *Izvestia*. In addition, the popular Russian journal *Science
and Life* (Nauka i Zhizn') reprinted French children's comics, while the U.S. Department of State's propaganda journal *Amerika* (distributed in the USSR) would
feature occasional stories on comics, such as a major piece in 1966.[81] The exchanges occasionally went both ways; Viacheslav Kotenochkin published his popular
comics *Nu Pogodi* ("Just You Wait," even more famous as a 1970s animated series)
in the Bulgarian magazine *Daga*.

The lubok also made a minor comeback under Soviet auspices, as seen in prints
by Iu. Ivanov and L. Rakov, such as *He Who Comes to Us with a Sword Will Die by
That Sword. Russia Stands and Will Stand by This* (1969). This pairs the famous
saying by thirteenth-century prince Alexander Nevsky with an "antiquated" image of a medieval knight and Soviet soldier facing down the viewer together. The
official artist Viktor Penzin opened his studio Sovetskii lubok in 1982 to advance
the production and study of contemporary lubki. He described their pedigree:
"The Russian lubok, ROSTA windows, TASS windows, the agitposter, the Soviet lubok. They are like the five fingers of one hand" (Penzin). The artist's lubok
works seem an odd but intriguing amalgam of old and new: Soviet cosmonauts,
Jesus Christ, and the Cat of Kazan are revisualized in the familiar woodblock style
of the eighteenth and nineteenth centuries.

But by far the most consistently accessible (Western) comics in the Soviet
Union appeared in the French Communist Party journal *Pif Gadget*[82] and the collections of Danish Communist caricaturist Herluf Bidstrup[83] (both freely available from the 1960s, due to their left-wing cachet).

SOVIET ANTI-COMICS ATTITUDES

Still, the popular associations of the word *komiksy* in this period were not with
works by Bidstrup and Penzin or journals like *Pif Gadget*. Much more common
were persistent denunciations of the form as mind-numbing, even dangerous,
bourgeois mass culture.[84]

The cultural critic Isaak Lapitsky devotes a scant four pages to comics in his
ideological travelogue *In the Shadow of Skyscrapers* (V teni neboskrebov, 1958),
but his comments are damning—part of a sustained cold war attack on the barbarity of American culture.[85] Visiting an American bookstore, he is astonished to

see customers foregoing "the classics" for twirling stands of brightly hued comics, which he argues "call for no great mental exertion"; with their "primitively-colored" or black-and-white drawings they divert readers with stories of easy money, casual crime, and nationalist characters such as Superman, "who, of course, is a white 100-percent American defending the country against black people, Indians, communists and foreigners" (126).[86] The free market, he concludes, has produced predatory values in children's entertainment: "The heroes of [American] comics are not miners, welders, mechanics, engineers, farmers, tractor drivers. They're successful gangsters, cunning business men or police officers who manage to carry a profitable operation in the 'black market' in Europe or Asia and get rich in one day or smuggle out of there some priceless work of art and become millionaires in a flash. Judging by the comics, life is only for such people" (Lapitsky: 128). Comics, Lapitsky adds, "inculcate a hatred of people and implant a cult of violence and sadism." He cites the case of John Graham, who in 1955 blew up a United Airlines flight and killed forty-three passengers in order to cover up the murder of his mother for the insurance money. Graham, apparently, "read a lot of comics" (128). Lapitsky's sociological analysis goes no deeper—nor would his Soviet reader expect it to, since he is merely expressing an ingrained Russian preconception about the medium (and the United States). The book goes so far as to print a picture of a little boy brandishing a two-by-four at a woman, presumably his mother, with the caption, "This little chap hasn't started reading detective novels yet. But he already knows all about comics" (127).

For the most part, then, the party line on comic books labeled them pseudo-literature for eroded capitalist minds that needed pictures to follow the story. The stories themselves only polluted those minds with lies, immorality, and bourgeois propaganda. This view is upheld even by more perceptive critics than Lapitsky, such as Alexander Kukarkin. Well acquainted with the Western culture industry, he addressed the medium in numerous books and essays in the late-Soviet era, even praising such figures as Milton Caniff and Charles Schulz. This did not prevent him from attacking, like Lapitsky, the superheroes he saw on movie screens: "There is nothing human about these supermen from space: they have the most primitive sensibilities and emotional needs (zaprosy), and they completely lack an inner world (dukhovnyi mir). Strong muscles and fists—that's all they have" (1985: 298).[87] In a vigorous response to a 1966 *Amerika* essay ("In Defense of Superheroes"), he argues: "Comics do not at all represent 'a world where good triumphs over evil'—more often it's the other way around; the heroes in the majority of comics do more than just 'carry weapons'—they constantly use them (including napalm)" (1977: 73).

Also like Lapitsky, Kukarkin turns to the most hysterical voices in the U.S. comics wars for evidence of the form's malign nature, including testimony from the 1954 Senate Subcommittee on Juvenile Delinquency hearings chaired by Estes

Kefauver. (He claims they led to "no practical result.") Essentially following the arguments of Ariel Dorfman and Armand Mattelart, he sees comics in the West as an instrument of imperialist propaganda, whether deployed to promote Pentagon policy in Asia (*Steve Canyon*), whip up anti-Soviet paranoia (*Agent X-9*), or celebrate violence and fascism (*Diabolik, Hessa*).[88]

For Kukarkin, echoing Zhdanov and other party pronouncements, this seems the bottom line:

The Soviet Union, with all its keen desire for cultural contact with other peoples, is not inclined—and quite naturally so—to promote the penetration of pseudo-culture[89] with its cult of violence and sex; neither is it inclined to permit a discriminatory disproportion in the exchange of cultural values.[90] Soviet people, who stand for the sovereign equality and complete independence of all countries in world politics and the democratization of international relations as a matter of principle, are convinced of the necessity for erecting insuperable barriers in the path of phenomena of this kind, including ideological phenomena, which places some states in a privileged position and others in a dependent one. When there is no possibility of imposing direct domination, the temptation arises to resort to methods of cultural enslavement. (1979: 366)

Very much embracing such notions, the Soviet leadership to its last gasp kept the comics medium at arm's length, particularly where it touched on the rearing of its youngest citizens (which is to say, at all times). This had an effect on aesthetics; as we have seen, with a few exceptions such as Ivan Semenov, those who did produce comics material largely avoided word balloons, sound effects, and other "American" devices until late in the Stagnation era. Content, too, reflected party decrees on proper types, the antagonism of the outside world, and the moral superiority of socialism, as it had since the 1930s.

By the last decade of Soviet power, the attitude toward Western comics (shared by the government and most ordinary Russians) had ossified into pronouncements like this: "They mainly show adventures using violence and weapons and do not pursue the objective of moral edification. The badly executed drawings foster bad taste and with its elements of adventure and militarism the primitive content produces a defective system of values, ideals and conceptions. The Western comic strip entertains but does not educate the younger generation. Recent Soviet children's publications show attempts to use comic strips devoid of the negative features inherent in the Western comic strips" (Mansurov: 153). N. S. Mansurov's 1986 report, "Children's Publications in the Soviet Union," written in response to an international survey on children's literature, draws on the party resolutions of the 1930s to describe the primary criteria for children's book illustration: the artist must contribute to the formation of positive attitudes, be informative, and inculcate party values. As such, the drawings must appear in a "realistic/representational form" and have "good artistic taste," since "children perceive everything directly, in a concrete manner, believing that every stylized feature of a drawing must exist in nature." Above all, Soviet artists were to avoid "leading the child away from reality" and to emphasize that "the drawing belongs to the current Soviet era" (149).[91] Socialist Realist children's literature would permit no more than 50 percent of each page to be covered by illustration, and that only for very young readers, so that they might better understand the text; for older children who could already think "abstractly," the percentage of space allotted for pictures plummeted to 10 percent.[92] Finally, ideology was overt; drawings could never provoke doubt in the grand magnanimity of the USSR: "Soviet publications for children show drawings of weapons mainly as a means of protecting the motherland from an attacking enemy" (150). Children's periodicals, *Murzilka* and *Veselie Kartinki* (Merry Pictures) chief among them, with their "primarily functional" art, contained various kids' activities, stories derived from fairy tales, informative articles and games, but only occasionally was a comic strip allowed. And although "psychologically, a comic strip appeals to readers in that it leaves much room for conjectures and speculations . . . for participation with the author and artist" (153), all the same "Soviet periodicals for children rarely bring in more then [*sic*] one story in pictures since it is believed that they must not dominate in the magazines" (155). Furthermore, Mansurov noted, this "relatively new form" of children's illustration "cannot be applied to works of fiction" (154). Comics thus played a limited role in late-Soviet children's magazines. In 1980, Mansurov reported, *Murzilka* published four "stories in pictures" featuring animals, while in 1982 it saw fit to publish only one (154). "The Happy Little People on BAM" (Veselie chelovechki na BAMe) by Sergei Ivanov and Sergei Tiunin (*Murzilka* no. 5, May 1982, 9–12) tells a simple story of "the happy little people's" encounter with the animals of the Siberian taiga while traveling on the Baikal-Amur Magistral' railway. Led astray by a paranoid crow, a family of bears tries to wreck the "little people's" train by rolling a giant snowball onto it. However, the would-be saboteurs end up trapped inside the snow boulder as it rolls down in front of the train. But the "little people" (along with a human conductor) kindly free them from the snow, musical instruments are produced, and everyone has a nice dance party in the taiga. In the conclusion, the crafty crow joins the train ride, to work as a crowing rooster: "I've decided to mend my ways!" she declares (12). The story underscore's Mansurov's description of the approach to comics in children's periodicals as "above all, do no harm." The "good" characters form a collective majority (and seem rather undifferentiated), while only the "bad" crow bears any traits of individuality (she mispronounces words and has a reputation as a manipulator). The bear family wavers between these two poles. The story also shares the Mansurov report's trepidation about the depiction of evil, a counter to Western "sensationalist" works: "Illustrations can

2.8. From "The Happy Little People on BAM," by Sergei Ivanov and Sergei Tiunin (*Murzilka*, 1982). "This is how good they are!" says the crow mistress.

substantially alter children's attitude to moral values if evil is presented beautifully . . . Illustrations of evil must not evoke sympathy among children but should help them realize what evil would mean" (151). Hence the crow's "unattractive" appearance and malapropisms—as well as her eventual reform.[93]

Straightforward and "universal" as it may seem, however, "The Happy Little People on BAM" bears ideological traces of its era. The crafty crow sees herself as the "mistress" (khoziaika) of the forest, which motivates her to keep the outsiders away, through violence if necessary. Though "evil," her sabotage is basically an attempt to stave off human(oid) encroachment and keep the taiga for the animals. The story and its utopian conclusion thus operate as an allegory for the development of Siberia in the name of progress, "misguided" nativist resistance notwithstanding—indeed as a subtle attack on the rising environmentalist movements of the late-Soviet era (many of them operating in Siberia).[94] The two largest panels in the story reinforce this reading. The first shows the crow describing the vile hidden intentions behind the "little people's" appearance: in her speech balloon, the words "This is how good they are!" illustrate a monstrous anthropomorphic train on the hunt for forest animals to catch with its nets and mechanical arms (10). The second of the largest panels, on the concluding page, puts the lie to the crow's vision: the "little people" and animals joyously dance to the music of a tuba, cymbals, drum, and balalaika. The first panel is shown up as "propagandistic" through the device of the speech balloon; the second is "objective" truth, due to the absence of any "attribution"—this happy ending is simply the way things are. The "false" and "true" panels' similarity in size subtly suggests the comparison, not unlike the "us/them" caricatures of the satirical journals and posters. In this respect, *Murzilka's* story fulfills the major tasks of Soviet children's literature, according to Mansurov: "inculcating in children valuable civic qualities like collectivism, optimism, the love of their motherland . . . explaining to them what is good and what is bad and what moral standards exist in the socialist society" (147). This, then, is what "respectable" Soviet comics looked like.

THE NONCONFORMISTS

The final milieu we will examine in this survey is the least scrutinized, particularly from a comics studies perspective. Unofficial or Non-Conformist art as a loosely defined movement emerged in the late 1950s and early 1960s in reaction both to Socialist Realism as a state policy and the lack of opportunities to publish/exhibit for those shut out of the officially backed Artists' Union.[95] Viktor Ivanov's works, for example, came to exemplify the Severe Style, which dispensed with politics in favor of more personal and "pessimistic" subject matter (Brown 1989: 20). The Moscow artist Eli Belyutin ran an informal studio pursuing abstract expressionism during the Thaw era, which led to his involvement in the notorious Manezh exhibition scandal of 1962, when Nikita Krushchev himself publically berated the artists for their "formalism" and "amorality" (Sjeklocha and Mead: 94–95). Another important milestone was Yevgeny Rukhin and Oskar Rabin's "Bulldozer Exhibit" of September 15, 1974, when the police and KGB forcibly broke up an open-air show of unofficial paintings in southwestern Moscow, using water cannons and bulldozers. (The subsequent outcry led to more rights for unofficial artists.) A subset of the Nonconformists, the Moscow Conceptualists, formed in the late 1960s and early 1970s. Through a strategy of appropriation, "counterfeiting," and "emptying out" of the predominant Socialist Realist imagery and rhetoric, this group exposed the ideological roots of Soviet culture precisely by reproducing its forms all too well. This was especially true of Sots-Art, an approach related to Pop Art, which took the familiar slogans and visual culture of the USSR as raw material for their subversive, quasi-nostalgic visions (much as Andy Warhol used Campbell soup cans). Other groups, such as Mukhomor (Toadstool), AptArt, and Medicinal Hermeneutics, followed conceptualist principles in their own directions. For the Moscow Conceptualists—whose ranks include the installationist Ilya Kabakov, multimedia jokesters Vitaly Komar and Alexander Melamid, and the poet-artist Dmitry Prigov—the discursive practices and iconography of Soviet culture served as fodder for ironic reproduction, reappropriation, recycling, and redirection. As noted by Elizabeth Sussman, Sots-Art "inscribed itself in a reflection of the banal, the quotidian, as signifiers of the social. It defined itself as an underground practice situated between mass culture and the avant-garde" (64). In these works of "total quotation," language and visual images lost all link to their referents; the conceptualist works to meticulously reproduce their codes, so as to subvert their ideological underpinnings from within. This proved especially appealing in Russia during its late-Communist phase, when, as noted by Mikhail Epstein, the country was "spiritually and materially poor but rich in ideology" (2002: 224). It should come as no surprise that comics, an officially "suspicious" medium, held considerable appeal for artists themselves engaged in unofficial, underground creative work. Furthermore, as an "international" language, comics attracted a movement that saw itself as reconnecting with global trends in art from behind the Iron Curtain. Indeed, a large segment of the Non-Conformists taps comics (even if only in a few works), while Sots-Artists in particular often quote comics sources ala Lichtenstein. (This became especially true once many Moscow Conceptualists emigrated to the West starting in the 1970s.) Yuri Albert, for example, appropriates the Pop-Art master himself in *I'm Not Lichtenstein* (1990), done as a blown-up panel from a comic strip: a blonde tells her companion, "Why, Yuri, darling this painting is a *masterpiece*!" to which he replies, "Thank's dear—but it's a shame I'm not *Lichtenstein*!" (emphasis and errors in the original). Another canvas, *I'm Not Baselitz* (1986), is an upside-down portrait of Ivan Semenov's character Karandash (Pencil) from *Veselie Kartinki*. Several works by Pavel Pivovarov incorporate text and image, such as his series *Plan for the Everyday Objects of a Lonely Man* (1975), while Leonid Sokov's *Salvo of the Aurora* (1984) features a scatological sound effect, *khuiak* ("fuck"), emanating from the cannon of the famed cruiser. Vadim Zakharov uses captions in sequential photographs documenting his performance art, as in *I Know Any Resistance to Elephants Is Useless. Elephants Hinder Our Life* (1982), and word balloons in works such as *B-Ua* (1986). Grisha Bruskin's monumental *Fundamental Lexicon* (1987), made up of over thirty smaller paintings, evokes an iconostasis, according to Brown, of contemporary Soviet types (1989: 96). Finally, Alexander Kosolapov frequently quotes Western popular culture iconography. In *Thwip* (1985), Spiderman interrupts a revolutionary strategy meeting at which Lenin, Stalin, and Mickey Mouse are present—superheroes, cartoon characters, and Soviet leaders share the same mythological plane.[96] Oddly, Russian art critics, even after the collapse of the Soviet Union, would tend to read these comics allusions and techniques as "naïve." For example, Ekaterina Degot notes that Pavel Pepperstein, in work influenced by book illustration, displays "a specific 'children's discourse' as a sphere of individual, private psychedelics" (1995: 96), while Konstantin Zvezdochotov has mastered the "lower echelons of the Soviet 'agitational folklore': kitsch posters for civil defense and safety, newspapers—the entire sphere of the naïveté of Socialist Realism" (1995: 202). Yet as we have seen from our survey of posters and caricature, they were anything but naïve.

The conceptualist best known in the West—and one of the most-renowned Russian artists of the twentieth and twenty-first centuries—Ilya Kabakov uses pictorial narrative techniques extensively in his albums, paintings, and installations. No art critics, to my knowledge, have called them comics,[97] instead describing his *Ten Characters* album series (1971–1974) as "narrat[ions] in words and pictures" viewed in a "quasi-theatrical" way or "recount[ings] through text and drawings" using a "trivial visual language."[98] Other critics, like Degot, point out that "the genre of the 'picture with a text' is one of the most important for Kabakov" (1995: 62), describing it as a representation with "commentary" about the object (even if they have a "non-sequitur" relationship).[99] Also, most critics cite Kabakov's background as a children's book illustrator for having shaped his disarmingly "naïve" blend of words and images.

Of particular importance to this discussion is the role played by the verbal in Russian art. As elaborated by Margarita Tupitsyn, visual art was subservient to the word in the sense that, whether explicating the Bible or party dogma, the "visualization of verbal concepts" had historically formed a central concern for Russian artists. This proved especially pronounced in the Revolutionary era, when "every image in a poster was accompanied by a slogan and every photograph or montage printed in a magazine was followed by an explanatory phrase or a short narrative" (304). Like prerevolutionary artists such as Larionov, the Soviet Conceptualists sought to visualize the verbal (even if parodically) by incorporating "low" forms of culture into their work (lubok and Soviet propaganda, respectively). Thus, the Conceptualists "fulfilled the course of linguistic intrusion laid down by the early avant-garde" (304).[100] For Kabakov this finds expression not only through the word/image combination and sequential panel techniques, but also through his fixation on narrative.[101] His maddeningly complex installations integrate textual explanations and elaborations, character background, and self-referential commentary (including illustrated plans for the exhibits themselves) to recreate fully realized Soviet spaces such as communal apartments, kitchens, public toilets, and so forth. In this the albums have played a central role, as they, among other things, visualize parts of the story not physically reproducible (such as a city's entire population flying through the air). But they also add a vital, voyeuristic intimacy. Like the installations of which they form a part, the albums bring Kabakov's novelistic discourse to vibrant life through the interactive process of reading. A "hybrid" art, the albums partake of literature, fine arts, cinematography, and drama for a highly "personalized" aesthetic experience. As Kabakov, speaking as one of his creations, "The Person Who Describes His Life Through Characters," explains: "The main feature of the 'albums' is that the viewer himself may turn the pages. Besides the physical contact with the page and the possibility to dispose of one's time as one pleases while looking, one gets a particular impression from turning the pages which makes the 'albums' like temporal types of art. A special experience of time derives from the expectation of things to come, like plot, denouement, finale, repetition, rhythm, etc." (Kabakov 1989: 35). At the same time, Kabakov disappoints those conventional expectations of storytelling; these are fractured narratives, or as Wallach calls them, "models of conceptual narrative, narrative as investigation and deconstruction" (55). The first *Ten Characters* album, *Sitting-in-the-Closet Primakov*, is among the more conventional-seeming, as its panels

2.9. From *The Flying Komarov*, part of the *Ten Characters* album series by Ilya Kabakov, 1971–1974.

depict—through the lead figure's subjective gaze—a steady progression away from his closet, family, apartment, city, land, and up into the sky, to nothingness. While some of the accompanying captions make "sense" (all-black panels: "In the closet"; "A strong wind is blowing"), others appear nonsensical (all-white representing the sky: "Fresh carrots."). While comparable in some respects to the extreme "reverse tracking shots" seen in Winsor McCay's *Little Number in Slumberland*, the effect ultimately disorients and confounds a unified meaning—and yet the reader/viewer still is compelled to make the text/image combination arrive at some sort of coherent message. The sixth *Ten Characters* album, *The Flying Komarov*, likewise conveys a plot of sorts, albeit an absurd one. In thirty-two pages, we see Komarov decide to join the masses of people flying up into the air, forming intricate patterns, having tea (their furniture floats, too), hanging onto the wings of passing airplanes. Eventually, they all disappear, "and soon it is impossible to see anything but ordinary birds in the air." Like all the image portions of the albums, it ends with a blank page. *The Flying Komarov*'s pictures seem to carry through on a strong sequential line, but the work as a whole self-consciously flouts such a "naïve" reading; this is made clear in the comments of other fictional characters with which the albums conclude. When we recall that the captions are themselves comments from the friends or relatives of the artist-character which produced the album (each album is the product of a different fictional character), they take on an oddly dubious quality. Though the text appears to follow the drawings slavishly, these are mere interpretations, others' opinions and readings, contingent, subjective, and open to challenge. When we reread them in this light, the supposed one-to-one correspondence between text and image breaks down. For example, a picture captioned, "Or, 'HAVING GATHERED A FEW BIRDS' into a team, some quickly rush about in the pure cool wind, turning their faces toward the hot sun" (emphasis in the original) appears to portray exactly that, but further scrutiny yields some problems: why is the sun referred to in the text not in the picture? how can we tell there's a "cool wind?" is the floating couple relaxing—or dead? A million different captions to this picture would focus on a million different things; we can therefore trust no caption—or picture—no matter how well they seem to "fit" together. While to a casual reader *The Flying Komarov* resembles the absurdism of Daniil Kharms (and this is not a "wrong" reading, either), Kabakov's work further comments on legibility itself.

Mikhail Epstein reads the albums with this hermeneutic in mind, arguing Kabakov reinvents the lubok as a postmodern genre: "In the traditional lubok, image and word supplement each other. This constitutes its felicitous totality of meaning. Kabakov's totality, however, is no longer completely felicitous, because there can be no real totality in a world in which centrifugal artistic forces split this totality into parts, while centripetal political forces violently unite the separated parts" (2002: 319). "Kabakov's neo-lubok perverts the logic of the lubok genre by inverting or suspending the correspondence between word and image" (2002: 322).[102] We should keep in mind that the albums are not an incidental practice of the installationist Kabakov; they predate the installations, sometimes by decades, and formed a crucial breakthrough for the artist. Here his "modernist obsession with ultimate truths is caught in the postmodernist quicksand of shifting meaning" (Wallach: 56). The sequential, visual/verbal strategies of the "neo-lubok" (i.e., the comics language) are themselves central to that insight.[103] Until the Perestroika era, both Non-Conformist art and comics as an expressive medium remained officially in the shadows, though late-Soviet cultural politics were such that each survived in its own niche. Perhaps the most notable incident of the comics language's association with open resistance to the regime took place during the *"Metropol"* affair" of 1979. The illegal samizdat literary anthology, published clandestinely by Viktor Erofeev, Yevgeny Popov, and Vasilii Aksionov, featured "Fetters" (Puty) a poem by Genrikh Sapgir with illustrations by Anatoly Brusilovsky. The surreal drawings show human-like figures escaping from various bonds. Along with the stanzas, they are ordered sequentially, recalling Mayakovsky's agitational books— though here the text/graphics strategy expounds a hallucinatory tale, as the figures slip the fetters of oppression: "To break your bonds is to experience birth anew. / Only he is born who breaks free" (826).[104]

The subversive cachet of comics-like work—to the extent that it was perceived so by the authorities—led to the 1983 arrest and imprisonment of the caricaturist Vyacheslav "Slava" Sysoev[105] on the ludicrous charge of disseminating pornography. He served two years in a labor camp. Others, such as Efrosinia Kersnovskaia, Nadezhda Borovaia, and Leonid Lamm, used pictorial narrative techniques to recount their experiences in the camps. For his part, Konstatin Rotov, the *Krokodil* caricaturist, did not overtly address his incarceration, but simply returned to work upon release. A younger generation of artists, active in the last decade of the Soviet Union, avoided such complications.

Georgy "Zhora" Litichevsky, the most avid practitioner of comics in the late-Soviet era, channeled his affection for French comics journals like *Pif Gadget* into wryly humorous stories projected for friends through slide shows or distributed through samizdat in the early 1980s.[106] (I address Litichevsky's work in chapter 5.)

The final manifestation of late-Soviet pseudo-comics I wish to address did not belong to the "unofficial" sphere as such, though it had much in common with the Conceptualists in approach and spirit. Alexander Brodsky and Ilya Utkin, both graduates of the Moscow Institute of Architecture, began winning international competitions for their impossible building designs in the late 1970s, thus garnering state support and launching the so-called Paper Architecture (Bumazhnaia Arkhitektura) movement. With antecedents in both the eighteenth-century fanciful works of Giovanbattista Piranesi and doomed Soviet monumental projects (such as Boris Iofan's unrealized Palace of the Soviets), the Paper Architects set down their grandest fanciful visions in otherworldly settings, often breaking up the page into panels and accompanying (sometimes obtuse or illegible) text, producing "hybrid architectural-narrative" works (Nesbitt). See, for example, their *Crystal Palace* (1982). Brodsky and Utkin do more than design fantastical structures—they evoke a time and space which the reader traverses as a traveler crosses the ocean to reach an island in the thee-panel *Diomede I* (1989), on foot, via a viaduct just below the water's surface.

As Russians approached the end of their own seven-decade journey across the ocean that was Communism, a new climate of reform descended on their exhausted country. Perestroika, with its promise of free expression and economic opportunity, raised hopes that a real comics industry might at last come together. Only time would tell if such optimism reflected real possibilities or something more akin to one of Brodsky and Utkin's paper dreams.

THE REBIRTH OF RUSSIAN COMICS

PERESTROIKA AND THE "FIRST WAVE" OF KOMIKS

When the fifty-four-year-old Mikhail Gorbachev—the first Communist Party general secretary born after the Revolution—assumed power in March 1985, few predicted the depth of change the Soviet Union would undergo in six short years, leading to its collapse and the restoration of Russia as a quasi-capitalist, quasi-democratic country. Gorbachev's policies of a new engagement with the West, ending the disastrous military venture in Afghanistan, economic reform, and loosening of censorship transformed Soviet society and opened vast new opportunities for (sub) cultural activities long suppressed. The era of Perestroika ("restructuring"), for the first time in six decades, offered comics the chance to come in from the cold.

Soviet publishing reaped the rewards—and bore the brunt—of Glasnost ("openness"), Gorbachev's radical new policy of free expression in the media. Hitherto taboo topics—including criticism of the party—were now permitted, the better to rejuvenate the culture, face up to the mistakes of the past, and build a more transparent society.[1] Nothing like this had been seen since the 1920s. To this end, from 1986 onward the Soviet press and book market was increasingly liberalized; the first cooperative publishers appeared in 1987, and by 1990 almost a tenth of all books were produced by nonstate publishers.[2] Following global norms, these presses favored consumer demand over ideological prescription. And the Russian readership made its desires clear: at first the forbidden works of the past (Nabokov, Solzhenitsyn) and, as the decade wore on, "trash" (Western genre fiction, self-help). As Lovell noted, "The Soviet people was rather more concerned to develop a mass culture than to plug the many gaps in its knowledge of high culture" (76).

KOM

In any case, almost immediately after their implementation, Perestroika and Glas-nost led to the beginnings of a Russian comics industry, which took root through the efforts of a young staff artist at a popular entertainment weekly, *Vecherniaia Moskva* (Evening Moscow). In September 1988, Sergei Kapranov,[3] a lifelong dab-bler in comics, approached the *VM* editor-in-chief Alexander Lisin for permission to found a "Komiks Klub" of artists and to introduce comics stories to the maga-zine. Lisin agreed, and an invitation to artists soon appeared in the weekly.

This announcement attracted trained artists, rank amateurs, closet comics fans, and the curious. The club started meeting on Thursdays at the *VM* offices. KOM, the first collective of Russian artists convened to produce comics works, would eventually include Askold Akishin,[4] Dmitry Spivak, Andrei Snegirov, Andrei Ayoshin, Alexei Kapninsky, Igor Kolgarev,[5] Yury Zhigunov, Sasha Egorov, Mikhail Zaslavsky, Ilya Voronin, Konstantin Yavorsky, Ilya Savchenkov, Yury Pronin, Olga Kozlenkova, Alexei Iorsh, Alim Velitov, and the oldest, Vladimir Spiridov.[6]

KOM material began appearing in late 1988, within the pages of the maga-zine and as supplements. The stories ranged from short gag strips to three-page narratives. Some featured continuing characters such as Bovik (a trouble-making kid) and Barik (a puppy). Though some of the works were "kid-friendly," and all were humorous, many seized the spirit of Glasnost to deal with adult themes, mock social institutions like the family (Kolgarev's "Hearth and Home"), or ad-dress "problematic" areas such as alcoholism, the superiority of Western consumer products (Savchenkov's "Gum Made in the USA"), and AIDS (Sviridov's "The Golden Lie"). A casual attitude to sex also figures in some of this material, as seen in Kolgarev's "The Little Fish," in which two fishermen (inadvertently) undress a nubile snorkeler by hooking her bikini. In content and form, these early KOM works reflected a more Westernized approach to sequential storytelling. And by Soviet standards, they were indeed rather bold.

Savchenkov's "The Kids" (Malchiki) pushes the sociopolitical critique further than most. In eight brisk panels, the artist tackles class differences in a supposedly classless society. Marinka and an unnamed boy are playing in a sandbox, when the stylish Vadim appears. A privileged son of the nomenklatura, he shows off the extravagant presents his father has brought him from France: a jacket and a walk-man. He boasts of the new videocassettes his family received, and invites Marinka to come watch them. She accepts, leaving the other boy to exclaim, "But Marina, what about our sand castle . . . ?" Walking off with Vadim, she replies, "Ah . . . you're boring!" The boy then attacks Vadim, who calls out, "Papa-a-a!" The final panel shows the unnamed boy, despondent, at his own doorstep before his father. Holding him by the scruff is Vadim's father, his pin-striped suit and black hat de-

noting a member of the party's top ranks. "Your son will never grow up to be a real Soviet man!" he says.[7]

The initial response to KOM's comics stories was, to say the least, mixed. While "young people" proved very supportive, an "older" segment of readers vented their outrage in virulent letters, noted Lisin: "*Vecherniaia Moskva*, having sheltered KOM, was accused of reviving 'alien socialist realism,' bourgeois 'mass art'; indulging in primitivism and even 'Americanism.' Our longtime subscribers, reared on the beneficent masterpieces of Socialist Realism, demanded that we immediately put a stop to the club's activities, give it no more space 'in the crowded pages of the newspaper'; otherwise, they threatened to cut off relations with *VM*." Despite the vitriol, Lisin continued supporting Kapranov's KOM venture, and the "club" grew. With the Perestroika reforms in full flower by the late 1980s, the collective joined Fotofilm press[8] and reorganized itself as an independent studio, which Kapranov envisioned as made up of two departments: "Western," headed by Dmitry Spivak, and "Give Soviet Comics" (daesh' sovetskii komiks), with a more "social" mission (Barmina).

Kapranov also promoted the new studio and comics as an art form in the press. Like Lisin's letter writers, articles on KOM from that period reveal Soviet biases against the medium, but also a curiosity about this alien fruit imported to Russia from the decadent West. Many also struggle to define the term; G. Ananov calls comics "bookified cinema or cinematized books" (khizhnoe kino ili kinoshnye knizhki), but also seems to have been among the first to put the word "komiksist" in print (*Vecherniaia Moskva*, 1990). Elsewhere Ananov calls them, facetiously, an "overseas wonder . . . Something trashy, base, far removed from art, a peculiar surrogate of literature" ("Znakomtes'," 1990). Natalia Barmina starts her piece by stating, "There were two things we didn't have in my childhood: chewing gum and comics. Someone long ago, and apparently forever, decided for us that gum was unhealthy, and comics were good-for-nothing bourgeois art." Most articles made reference to Spiderman, Batman, Superman, and/or Mickey Mouse. Barmina provides a warning to racketeers: there's no money in comics.

For his part, Kapranov defended comics as "no surrogate, but an interesting and original art" (Ananov 1990, "Znakomtes'"); defined them as "the unfolding of plot in pictures," interpreted cave paintings, and ancient Egyptian hieroglyphs as a form of comics (Barmina); and declared, "We would like for comics to get well-grafted onto the tree of Russian culture" (Ananov 1990, "Znakomtes'"). He added that KOM would proceed on an "author-based" schedule, rather than a mass production model; this meant they would publish occasional *sborniki* (collections of work) rather than regular journals. (This would have an impact on the future of the studio, as we will see.)

The independent KOM comics studio formally debuted with a book presentation held at the Central Children's Movie Theater on November 30, 1990.[9] The studio presented its first four sborniki for sale: *KOM O.K.* (a collection of works previously published in *VM*); *Breakthrough* (Proryv),[10] military-themed comics; *Nekropolis*, horror, a highly unusual genre in Russia at this time[11]; and *KOM-pani-ia* (COM-pany), described by Kapranov as "the most commercial" (Ivanova).[12]

Kapranov later declared the well-attended event a success, culturally and commercially, telling a journalist: "In a few days we sold the lion's share of our print runs.[13] We see now that people in our country are no less interested in comics than people abroad" (Ivanova). Still, the evening's venue and comics' long association with children's literature (especially in Russia) made for a bit of a clash of worlds. A picture published in *VM* the next day underscored the problem: it showed a little girl puzzling over a copy of the adult-oriented *Breakthrough*.

The night's most poignant episode occurred when KOM komiksisty Misha Zaslavsky and Yury Zhigunov approached a prominent figure in attendance: Yury Lobachev, the veteran artist of the 1930s Yugoslav Golden Age. As Zaslavsky later described the meeting: "Our talk with Lobachev left Yury and me in a state of slight shock. . . . You can easily understand our feelings if you take into account the enormous information vacuum regarding comics which existed throughout the history of the USSR. The genre itself was forbidden, and information about it came through in microscopic doses and in extremely distorted form. That evening, for the first time, we managed to talk with a world-class professional" (2003). Lobachev's presence at KOM's public debut closed a circle in Russian comics' tortured history; the exiled master had lived to see the art form take root once more in his native soil. By the time he died in 2002, komiks would experience still more triumph—and disappointment.

In its five years of existence, KOM released some sixteen collections and graphic novels, in such diverse genres as fantasy, humor, horror, adaptations of classic and sci-fi literature, war, neo-lubok, and erotica. Zaslavsky notes that despite their often stark differences in style and orientation, all the artists developed close bonds: "The eternal conflict between the upholders of 'mainstream' and 'alternative' was not in evidence. The Americanists did not charge the Europeanists with elitism, the Europeanists did not disdain the Americanists for their vulgarity" (2003).[14] We should note that none of KOM's sborniki proved commercially successful, and only a handful broke even. But the Perestroika era's hothouse conditions for comics publishing—state subsidies, print runs running as high as 100,000, a rising media profile for komiksisty—largely smoothed over such troubling signs. Kapranov's "author-based" model of production was working—for the time being.

If the commercial picture looked somewhat disappointing, on the cultural front comics in Russia had never had it better. In "The Myth of Comics," his introduction to *KOM O.K.*, Lisin captured the euphoria over the medium's long-delayed "arrival"—if not for the society at large, then certainly for those who venerated the form and could now practice it openly. He at one point recites the long

list of alleged comics crimes: their celebration of sex, violence, drugs; their role in
imperialist propaganda; primitive interpretations of the classics; anti-Sovietism.
Then the essay pivots with these lines:

*Today, when we are torturously freeing ourselves from the living legacy of the
Proletkult aesthetic, from the political barriers (nagromozhdeniia) of the "Cold
War," the time has come, at last, to dismantle this myth (just as scores of other
ideological chimeras await their reckoning) that separates us from global civilization, from the real, living world, with its sufferings and joys, its humanity
and cruelty, its hope and innumerable contradictions.*

*It's time, at last, to understand, that no medium in and of itself is guilty of
the ends for which it's been used.*

Any genre, any art form can serve for the good or the harm of humanity.

There follows another list: of comics manifestations through history (like Kapranov, Lisin sees comics on cave walls). The essay mentions Lascaux, William Hogarth, Egyptian pictograms, lubki, ROSTA windows, Bidstrup, concluding with
the modern form of the "graphic narrative genre." He ends with the fervent declaration, "But it seems enough has been said to finally rehabilitate comics as an art
form and to heartily congratulate those who, loving and fostering this genre in its
best incarnation, enrich our contemporary spiritual perception and understanding
of the world."

Lisin's manifesto, with its use of the politically charged term "rehabilitate" (victims of the purges were "rehabilitated," their good names restored) reflects the
enormity for him of comics' reappearance in the Russian landscape; it signifies
and concretizes the larger changes afoot. The introduction to *KOM-paniia* echoes
the point, albeit in more joking fashion, by alluding to the chronic shortages of
consumer and food items in the late-Soviet era:

*"What's going on here?" you ask. "There's no sausage, there's no eggs, no sprats
in oil, no Dutch cheese. But we have comics?"*

*"Precisely so, comrade. And the members of Moscow's comics studio KOM
believe that once comics have appeared, sausage will show up too. Because comics
are culture. And as they say, everything begins with culture."*[5]

The works in KOM's publications vary from a page to book-length and were
made with the intent of showcasing the comics medium's variety and narrative
capacities. As Kapranov noted, "We were like any artists. We wanted to succeed,
first of all. Secondly, we wanted comics, as we understood them, to be recognized
and valued as such" (2006). Only secondarily do they attempt any sort of overt
political critique, preferring to mock Soviet society in general. Others simply tap

3.1. From *The Joke*, an homage to the lubok, by Alexei Kapninsky [A. Sfinktr], November 1990.

genres not often seen in the USSR, such as horror, dystopia,[16] and Western-style science fiction, in adaptations of H. G. Welles (*The Wonderful Visit* by Kolgarev); Ray Bradbury ("Usher 3" by Akishin, "The Foghorn" by Zhigunov), Harry Harrison ("At Last, The True History of Frankenstein" by Akishin); Ronald Chetwynd-Hayes; and Robert Sheckley.[17] Most bold (or brazen) from a Russian perspective are adaptations or outright parodies of classic Russian literature: "Tatiana's Dream" by O. Kreizi, based on Pushkin's *Evgeny Onegin* and Igor Belov's "A Lethargic Sleep" in which the nineteenth-century author Nikolai Gogol returns from the "dead" (due to a mistaken burial), only to have his friends call him an impostor and drive him off.[18]

Still other KOM artists make explicit links to the Russian roots of komiks. The introduction to *KOM-positsiia* provides a brief history of the lubok and concludes, "The young artists presenting their work in these pages have tried to unite in them two essentially related genres: traditional Western comics and the ancient Russian lubok."

Not all succeed as well as A. Sfinktr's[19] *The Joke* (Shutka), which pays direct homage to the lubok, in effect creating a self-reflexive blend of traditional and modern graphic narrative. Its look immediately recalls an eighteenth-century woodblock print, with crudely drawn types in period dress: Balakirev, the vulgar dwarf; the irritating romantic Uber-Hofmarschall Liebenwalde; and his resplendent beloved, Natasha Lopukhinskaia. The artist presents his story in the "stagy" manner of the lubki, through frontal compositions and visible theater wings, and even duplicates the rudimentary colorings of old-style prints, in which the hues bleed out of the figures.

Subtitled "A scene from a composition by a hack writer of Russian trifles" (pikulia), the simple story captures the old-time bawdiness of popular prints, too: Balakirev, suffering from diarrhea, witnesses the annoying Liebenwalde ("la-la-la-triu-liu-liu . . .") discover the spring's first strawberry. The fop places his hat over it and skips off to find his love, so as to surprise her with this gift. But Balakirev has other plans. Bent on avenging himself for a previous slight, the dwarf squats with a beatific expression, his buttocks just off-panel. "This is going to be my best joke," he grins, re-covering the soiled strawberry with his master's tri-corn. The inevitable happens: Liebenwalde invites his "goddess" to raise the hat, she discovers the steaming mound ("pfui-pfui" she sniffs). Comically, Natasha's angry insults are cut off mid-panel as she thunders off: "You, sir are a shi—." The final panel shows all three "actors" bowing onstage to the reader. "Modernized" in form, the spirit of lubok breathed again.[20]

Savchenkov pays an homage to another part of komiks' wayward patrimony in his "Red Army Men and Comics," a two-page spread (doubling as an ad for KOM) that knowingly mimics the look of a Socialist Realist poster circa 1940. Only instead of celebrating the soldiers' ideological purity or love of the motherland, the "plakat" shows them obsessively devoted to comics—especially those about themselves. "Comics hit the bull's eye!" says the commander of an artillery detachment. "Dear komiksisty," another writes in a letter, "please make more comics about us."

Other KOM artists treat Soviet subjects with varying degrees of respect, from Akishin's hagiographic portrait of World War II marshall Georgy Zhukov[21] to Yavorsky's "Pioneers," a sexually explicit depiction of students playing hooky from school. Other komiksisty completely ignore the Soviet context, unless they are constructing some sort of elaborate allegory about it. This might be one way to interpret Kolgarev's bizarre *War with the Snowmen* (1992), which utilizes various zombie-movie tropes (woods, remote shack, helpless humans) to tell its demented story of a snowpeople revolt. The "monsters" eventually fall victim to their weakness: an obsession with carrots. Unusually, Kolgarev's art is printed against a black background that bleeds to the end of the page, lending an even more (absurdly) disturbing mood.

Two stand-out KOM artists—and with Nikolai Maslov the komiksisty best known in the West—were also among its most prolific. Akishin's stark black-and-white line work, comparable to that of the Argentine artists Carlos Sampayo and Alberto Breccia, as well as the Italian Sergio Toppi, suits his preferred material (adaptations of Lovecraft, Poe, and other horror masters), though he also produced

3.2. *A Chronicle of Military Actions,*
Askold Akishin's adaptation of Erich
Maria Remarque's *All Quiet on the
Western Front,* 1990.

humorous strips. *A Chronicle of Military Actions*, his 1990 version of Erich Maria Remarque's *All Quiet on the Western Front*, follows the doomed characters through atrocity after atrocity, graphically portrayed, with an existential laconism. His adaptation (with Zaslavsky) of Mikhail Bulgakov's *The Master and Margarita* (1992–1993, published in France in 2004), renders the complex multiperiod story in fragments, depicting 1930s Moscow and Pontius Pilate's Palestine in radically different styles. After difficulties finding work in the early post-Soviet era, Akishin settled into illustration work, producing occasional comics stories.[22]

Zhigunov, the one KOM artist to achieve international stature in the 1990s, showcases his early strengths as a young komiksist in the realist style, while still evincing the anarchic humor of the KOM strips, in "The Magical Power of Art." The three-page story shows a film actor playing Hitler, who performs his role too well. His inspiring rhetoric ("Deutschland uber alles!") and magnetic delivery overwhelm the film crew, who in the final panel give the Fascist salute and scream, "Heil!" Zhigunov snidely comments on the expressive power of the comics language (as well as Soviet-era denunciations of it as veiled propaganda) by depicting "Hitler's" utterances through pictures in speech balloons. Though the reader does not know the actor's exact words in these panels, his audience reacts, "Magnificent . . . magnificent . . ." "The Magical Power of Art" reflects on the hieroglyphic nature of the medium, as well as its denotative advantages; in this work, an actor playing Hitler looks and moves exactly like Hitler, making the story's punchline more "plausible." Zhigunov dealt with the difficult post-Soviet market for comics after the USSR's collapse by avoiding it altogether, and launched a career in Belgium. His success with *The Letters of Krivtsov* (1995) led to the espionage series *Alpha* with Pascal Renard and Mythic.

KOM had other notable releases in its brief history: *Ryby* (Fish 1990), a digest; *Shtuka-Driuka* (Thingamajig 1991) children's material; *Sem' moikh "ia"* (My Seven "I's," 1991), a surreal photomontage novel by Kapranov and Elena Dobrovol'skaia; *Ofenia*[23] (The Peddler) Vol. 1 (1991) and Vol. 2 (1992), fairy tales; *Reanimator*

3.3. "The Magical Power of Art," by Yury Zhigunov, 1990.

(1992), horror and sci-fi; *Galago* (1993), a joint venture with the Swedish journal of the same name, this presents Swedish comics in Russian translation. By 1991, the economic climate for publishing in the Soviet Union was affecting Fotofilm's finances, and its resources would prove inadequate to compete under the new free-market conditions.[24]

TEMA

Though KOM was the only studio exclusively devoted to komiks production in the late-Soviet era, others did work in this field as well. Vladimir Sakov's Moscow-based Tema primarily made animated cartoons for commercials, but also published a number of comics albums with extraordinary print runs (as high as 500,000). These brought the firm virtually no revenue, but allowed its staff to indulge in a childhood dream of working in comics. Moreover, because Tema did not require healthy comics sales to survive, it too followed an "author-based" production model.

Formed in 1989, Tema exemplified the precipitous development of the Russian comics scene. Its works, when they managed to see print, often appeared in handsome hardcover editions with glossy paper that meticulously reproduced the wide range of colors and paints used in the originals. (Tema albums had uniformly better printing and production values than KOM's, but appeared less frequently.)²⁵ Tema distinguished itself metaphysically as well, through pursuing a "spiritual" mission beyond the dissemination of comics on Russian soil. Based on an Eastern-derived martial arts philosophy they dubbed *lentiai* ("lazybones"), the group stressed a communal approach to comics making. Considering all forms of interaction a "dialogue," the collective collaborated on most comics projects in creative "jam sessions," downplaying individual achievement. As Sakov explained: "Two people might be drawing a picture, two who can draw, and five who stand beside them, who can't draw, who are interfering with them. But they're not interfering, they're simply creating a different situation. If we were alone, we'd think up one thing. But with these others around, we draw not what they tell us, but it acts on our work, on our brains, even if it's an annoyance. Our emotions fall onto the page. And in the end, whose work is it? We say, 'it's ours'" (1997). Sakov's collective (about ten artists) emerged from the break-up of other animation studios; several of them trained as animators at VGIK. This lends much of their works the action-driven sensibility of short animated cartoons. The material, while often humorous, irreverent, and fantastical, deals with decidedly mature themes such as war, mendacity, and despair. This is seen most vividly in Alexei Lukyanchikov's *The Crew* (Ekipazh, 1992),²⁶ a surreal story—or rather, unrelated episodes—of two crash-landed pilots trying to find an "enemy" who never appears. Lost in the woods, they end up mistakenly shooting at imagined hostile forces and at each other, until they stumble on a mysterious "sect" of experimenters living in the space "between the extremes of enemies and friends." Lukyanchikov combines Joseph Heller and the contemporary Russian satirist Viktor Pelevin with a stylized underground comix sensibility; the egg-shaped pilots look absurd in their goggles and exaggerated armaments, while their dialogue recalls Samuel Beckett:

"So where are you going? . . ."
"To our guys . . ."
"I'm going to the enemy . . . Are we going the right way?"
"We're going the way the map says . . ."
"Okay, we made it!" (29, ellipses in original)

Lukyanchikov also experiments with comics iconography, giving thought balloons a ridiculously mimetic "heaviness," and —*Wizard of Oz*–like—portraying the experimenter's world in color (though the pilots remain in black and white).[27] Slight and "silly," by its last panel *The Crew* assumes the trappings of a profound fable on masculine violence and paranoia.

Sakov's own work has more literary roots and, perhaps for that reason, a consequent wordiness. While Lukyanchikov's story recalls the "universal" parables of the 1960s "12 Chairs" school of satirists, Sakov's series of graphic novels, *The Adventures of Captain Donki* (Prikliucheniia kapitana Donki, 1990), mounts a more direct critique of late-Soviet culture, particularly the absurdities and injustices wrought by economic reform. In this respect, Sakov's work continues the time-honored Russian literary theme of the "little man and the state."

Donki features a cynical if pure policeman's picaresque adventures in a modern-day Heaven and Hell of decidedly Slavic cast. Sakov parodies Dante (even in his hero's name) to mock the oddities and chaos of contemporary life in Russia. The plot involves a scheme by Lucifer to have Donki steal a piece of evidence to use as *kompromat* (blackmail material) against God. At the same time, Sisyphus leads a mass revolt against Lucifer's rule. Other figures include Charon, Tantalus, and Death, each bemusedly fulfilling their function through a morass of arcane rules and red tape.

Signs of Perestroika's confounding changes are everywhere. In part 1, Donki is given a tour of Hell by Lucifer, who proudly points out the corrupt practices of his realm: U.S. dollars obtain the damned special treatment in the form of jacuzzis to boil in, while those without money burn the old-fashioned way (Sakov 1990, 10). Paradise turns out little better, with the Apostle Paul running it like an all-seeing enforcer; the entire afterlife is a maze of bureaucracy, byzantine laws, warring authorities, zealous tax collectors, state surveillance, and palace intrigue, with the simple soul always trapped in between. Sakov's at times overly rendered art, reminiscent of Sergio Aragones, transmits the lunacy of the next world, modeled all too closely on 1980s Russia.

As Perestroika wound down and Gorbachev started losing his grip on the ever-accelerating reforms, other presses and studios published comics. Among the most important were Pilot in Moscow, Komiks in Nizhnii Novgorod, Mukha in Ufa, and, in other Soviet republics, Klips in Riga, Latvia and ASAT in Tashkent, Uzbekistan. In addition, the Leningrad House of Satire and Humor released two issues of *Komiks Review* (1989 and 1990), reprinting classic American series such as *Rip Kirby*, *Flash Gordon*, *Hagar the Horrible*, and *Conan the Barbarian*, as well as works by Hugo Pratt in Russian translation. It introduced a comics genre virtually unknown in Russia, the western.

Perestroika proved fair and foul for the medium. It leap-frogged from state-sanctioned marginality to a cutting-edge artistic novelty, from humble children's strip to adult graphic novels, virtually overnight. Veterans of that heady period, which produced the "First Wave" of Russian comics, told of how they could feel the air buzzing with possibility. But as the end of the USSR neared, the signs were less encouraging.

Comics did not capture the attention of the public in the way Kapranov had hoped; it did not prove so easy to "rehabilitate" Russian comics with the mere wave of an editorial hand, as Lisin believed, though the relative affordability of publishing in the late 1980s and early 1990s did usher in a period of relative prosperity for komiksisty. While governmental strictures on the form eased and ulti-mately shriveled with Perestroika, the realities of an increasingly liberalized mar-ket driven by consumer demand took their toll on KOM and other practitioners trying to build a comics industry.

Zaslavsky, besides a komiksist the preeminent historian of komiks, came to call the late Perestroika era the beginning of Russian comics' Wild Age. With the im-minent collapse of Communism in Russia, it was about to get a lot wilder.

RUSSIAN COMICS' SECOND WAVE

The years from 1991 to the present proved among the most exhilarating, groundbreaking, and frustrating of all in the medium's checkered history. Despite the launching of festivals and journals, the rise of an active online community and publications abroad, efforts to establish a working industry repeatedly came to naught. Still, the "Second Wave" komiks subculture in contemporary Russia brings together an array of talent, diversity, and professionalism never before seen. Much disaffection remains, but the road to today's gains was not easily paved, as shown in this chapter's overview.

COLLAPSE

Surveying the landscape for Russian comics in the mid-1990s, Sakov made a succinct, penetrating assessment:

With Gorbachev, the monopoly of publishing houses came down and new possibilities opened. Then when the dollar became the main thing, it got to be dependent on money. We had been able to produce quality comics, we even lived off the comics for a while, we offered our work to foreign publishers, but then the situation got worse. Today the main publishers do not want comics. Once we came out with editions of one million, but now other offers were deemed more profitable for publishers, other things which did not need such good paper, which could be done on cheap paper. There came other things, too, foreign materials, serials, adventures, and we got kicked out of our own market, while we couldn't break into the foreign market. (Sakov 1996)[1]

Such, in short, was the situation not only for comics but for many other areas of Russian culture after the collapse of Communist rule. This had been hastened in August 1991 by a disastrous coup attempt of reactionary forces against a vacationing Mikhail Gorbachev. These putschists, known as the Vosmerka (Group of Eight) and nominally led by Vice President Gennady Anayev, sought a rollback of the liberal reforms and return to Brezhnevite single-party rule. But after a half decade of relative freedom, an opening up to the West, and an astonishingly precipitous realignment of the Soviet bloc countries in 1989, the Soviet people would no longer tolerate going back to the way things were.

Led by the charismatic, recently elected president of the Russian Republic, Boris Yeltsin, they took to the streets of Moscow to face down tanks and riot police sent to cow them into submission.[2] Yeltsin electrified crowds at the White House (the Supreme Soviet building), which became a symbol of resistance, the army refused to fire on civilians, and within seventy-two hours the putsch imploded—taking the last shreds of the Communist Party's credibility with it. Gorbachev returned from his brief house arrest, but the USSR as a viable state was doomed; on December 25, 1991, the hammer and sickle flew over the Kremlin for the last time. In its place went up the tricolor banner of the new Russian federation. The other fourteen constituent republics became individual countries.

The Perestroika reforms had led to the death, after seventy-four years, of the Soviet Union. The country, in the writer Viktor Pelevin's phrase, "improved so much that it ceased to exist" (3), achieving a sort of socioeconomic Nirvana. Euphoria seized Russians with the disintegration of the state and creation of a new order: free-market democracy under Yeltsin. An era of prosperity, transparency and Western-style civilization beckoned.

What actually took place came as a profound shock. With state subsidies and price controls eliminated, economic security vanished. Inflation soared, the ruble's value crashed, pensions went unpaid or long delayed, unemployment grew, the value of life savings evaporated.

The news, sandwiched between the pornography and scandal sheets at the kiosks, was uniformly bad: a sharp spike in mafia violence; the theft of former state assets by corrupt bureaucrats and "oligarchs"; uncouth "New Russians" flaunting their ill-gotten wealth; squalor and despair in the provinces; homelessness, rising drug use, and AIDS in the cities; a new war in the breakaway region of Chechnya; high school girls whose greatest ambition was to become prostitutes; skinheads, punks, and neo-Nazis running lose; a drunk President Yeltsin humiliating the country before foreign heads of state.[3]

On the cultural front, Russian film, television, literature, and art faced near collapse as foreign product rushed in to dominate the new market. For a period in the early to mid-nineties, one could ride the Moscow metro and see most passengers reading Agatha Christie or Danielle Steel paperbacks,[4] get off and walk on streets blaring Queen or Ace of Base, enter a cinema to watch a third-rate American action movie full of sex and violence[5] (while munching a Mars or Snickers bar), and return home to watch television soap operas from Mexico or the United States, with almost all the commercials peddling foreign wares.[6] What Russian representations did emerge reflected a dystopian outlook, wrote Eliot Borenstein: "Russian popular culture was heavily invested in portraying a dangerous, violent, and cynical postsocialist world" (2008: x).[7]

Welcome to post-Soviet Russia: violent, insecure, valueless, coarse, apocalyptic.[8]

As alluded to by Sakov, in such conditions, the nascent comics industry was assaulted on multiple fronts: skyrocketing publishing and transportation costs made presses risk-averse—and comics were hardly a sure thing; foreign titles with the advantage of brand recognition and lower per-unit production costs were flooding the market; other media such as television, video games, cinema, music, genre fiction, and videocassettes competed for scarce entertainment rubles (or dollars, the unofficial currency).

In short, komiks' rebirth was strangled in its cradle; Perestroika-era hopes for a true comics culture on a Western model came crashing down. Fotofilm, squeezed for resources, first shut down KOM in 1992, then itself went bankrupt. Kapranov tried to continue his venture independently, then with the Tema studio, but found no backers; KOM dissolved. Its last publications appeared in 1993. Tema, on somewhat surer footing as an animation studio, nonetheless cut back on comics production in the leaner times. Scores of komiksisty, now out of work, turned to illustration, animation, advertising, or anything they could to survive, and went back to making comics as a hobby, or for the rare publication.[9] Zhigunov, as mentioned, wisely departed for Western Europe. (Kapranov himself would eventually return to his roots as a musician and promoter with the rock group Van Gogh's Ears.)[10] Only Snegirov managed to keep working regularly in comics, thanks to the popularity of his children's character Keshka, for the weekly *Sem'ia* (The Family). KOM published a collection of Keshka strips in 1993, one of its last releases.

It wasn't merely the dismal career outlook that dismayed komiksisty. Outraged, they had to look on as overseas "licensed product" quickly swallowed up their tiny market. To add insult to injury, the sort of foreign comics making it into the kiosks were not the classics reprinted in *Komiks Review*, but (in their opinion) the same sort of third-rate pulp being dumped onto Russian TV screens and movie theaters. As the komiksist Alim Velitov noted, "After the fall of the iron curtain, Western culture poured into our country. But, out of the huge world of comics, the only thing that broke through to us was the paltry *Mickey Mouse*. The untold riches of comics culture just lay out there, beyond our reach" (1999).[11]

Moreover, there still existed a branding problem. Much did not survive the downfall of the Soviets—but the popular Russian prejudice against comics did just fine. Once vilified outright by the state, now they were merely considered trash, beneath the contempt of any educated person. As initial hopes for a 1990s economic miracle cruelly deteriorated into mafia violence, hyperinflation, and "decadence," comics—in a kind of ideological afterimage—continued to be seen as an alien, specifically Western, affront to Russian literary culture.

Kapranov had seen all of this in the 1980s, but now mostly out of the business, he had no way to change public perceptions: "We produced some outstanding fairy tales in comics form, and you would think parents would have wanted to buy them for their children. Screw that! They're thinking: 'Why should I turn my kid into an idiot?' The kid takes a look at it: there's no Mickey Mouse, no [Soviet animated series] *Just You Wait!*—so that means this isn't comics, it's just some crap or other. Because there's no comics culture here" (Velitov 1999). Alexei Dvoryankin, director of the Lin Art Studio and BigAnt Comics, confirmed that Russians had such a low opinion of the medium that, even when they bought comics, they somehow saw them as something else. In 2002 he wrote:

Comics are sold openly, print-runs are growing, and illustrated stories about beloved Disney characters are enthusiastically purchased. It might even seem that the genre has finally been accepted and valued in Russia, but it isn't so. When children buy comics about Mickey Mouse, Donald Duck, and Uncle Scrooge, their parents don't give a thought to the fact that they are buying comics. Most of them could not clearly answer the question as to what made them buy the comics, because the question itself would be a revelation to them. For they didn't buy comics, they bought illustrated stories based on the plots of their child's favorite weekly cartoon series. They wanted to make the kid happy, and maybe to carve out some free time for themselves with the help of the comics. This is why the current popularity of comics is not the popularity of a genre, but of famous animated and movie characters or brands. It is no accident that all of the comics on the market today are a form of printed support for the Western film industry, and are bought only because their protagonists are so well known from films. (Maksimova: 87–88)

For his part, Kapninsky could only utter in disgust: "We just need to wait 40 years, for people of the older generation to die off. That's how long it'll take to build a comics culture in this country. That's the only way" (2005).

In 1997, Sakov estimated that firms actively producing comics work in Russia numbered no more than fifteen. Yet for his more philosophical, lentiaia-practicing collective, this had its advantages: "[In the West], there is an industry. The industry dictates a defined set of rules. Here, no rules. Everyone draws what he saw somewhere, sometime. He relies on his own roots, or serves whatever god he has in his head. Here we're more in the vein of artists. We don't have comics literacy."

"Thank god we don't make money on this," added Lukyanchikov. "We're like children. We play" (Sakov 1997).

4.1. *Blaster*, one of many a comics series which lasted only one issue in the turbulent post-Soviet economy, 1995.

As we will see, the vexing question of whether Russia has (or could develop) a bonafide comics industry would over time come to dominate forums and discussions about the medium, especially among komiksisty themselves.

THE 1990S: "THE NEW UNDERGROUND"

In any case, despite popular prejudice, financial instability, and infrastructure limitations, a good deal of native comics works did see print in the first post-Soviet decade. Komiksmeny lent their skills to animation departments, the wildly popular music video industry, advertisers, politicians,[12] and any venture whereby they might make a living in the brutal new market economy.

At the same time, critics like Mikhail Sidlin at *Nezavisimaia Gazeta* championed the form in occasional articles, while the Moscow-based collector Anna Chukhlebova organized an exhibit at the Belgian Comic Strip Center in Brussels in 1995. This featured work by Akishin, Sakov, Irina Rudakova, Lukyanchikov, Sergei Yakutovich, and Maxim Radayev (Brouns).[13] While Russian visual culture—due to the influx of foreign films, advertising, and magazines—popularized comics iconography,[14] komiks themselves developed along three,[15] somewhat overlapping lines: the would-be Mainstream, made up of those publishers (marginally

4.2. "They Got Him," by Alexei Nikanorov (*Mukha*, 1993), addressed alcoholism with sardonic humor.

successful at best) who struggled to establish a comics culture and industry; the Independents or WebKomiks, produced by komiksisty mostly on a freelance basis for publication in journals, or more often, on the Internet; and ArtKomiks, appearing in galleries and elite art publications, usually done in an ironic or neo-conceptualist vein. (The latter is best represented by the work of Zhora Litichevsky and Gosha Ostretsov, the subjects of chapter 5.)

Most of the early attempts to establish ongoing comics journals failed after only a few issues, many after only one. Among these were: *Veles* (Yekaterinburg, 1993–94), original and translated works of adventure, fantasy, notable as the first publication of Konstantin Komardin; *The Legend of Fantom* (St. Petersburg, 1993), adventure, cancelled after first issue; *Mishka* (Moscow, 1994), children's comics, lasted no more than three issues; *The Watermelon* (Ulyanovsk, 1994), children's comics, one issue; *Blaster* (Moscow, 1995), adventure/fantasy, one issue.

The many failed ventures make all the more extraordinary the success of *Mukha* (The Fly), an anthology journal published by Vitaly Mukhametzyanov, from Ufa.[16] It actually began publication in January 1991 (before the collapse of the USSR) and lasted, with interruptions, until 1995. *Mukha* represented native Russian comics in their most commercialized, mainstream form. Printed on cheap newsprint that nonetheless captured full-color, at times painted art by Ruslan Suleimanov, Oleg Khalimov, Andrei Abramov, Alexei Nikanorov, Vadim Rubtsov, and others, the journal featured a variety of genres and styles, from horror, humor, and children's tales to classics adaptations (issue #11, 1993, features Bulgakov's *The Fatal Eggs*).

Mukha lifted much of its presentation and format, including bombastic lettering styles and exaggerated sound effects, from Western—especially American—comics, though with a more "hand-made" aesthetic. The journal was at its most derivative in continuing series such as *A Nightmare of Forgotten Epochs* by Abramov (whose adventures of the bearded warrior Perun essentially aped the style and content of *Conan the Barbarian* in its Thomas/Buscema incarnation) and *Star Patrol* by Suleimanov, in which the main characters, Steve and Ted Mitchell of San Francisco, battle the mad Professor Randall and his space pirates. *The Portrait*, a humorous horror series by Rubtsov, guest-stars Freddie Kruger from the *Nightmare on Elm Street* and Jason from the *Friday the 13th* series. Other continuing stories, such as Rubtsov's *School of Mages*, mix broad humor and fantasy, in a painted style reminiscent of Richard Corben. In some respects, these works strongly resemble those of the Belgrade Circle of Russia émigré artists from the 1930s.

Though genre material predominated, some stories touched on the chaos and inverted values of post-Soviet Russia. "They Got Him" (Pobrali 1993) by Nikanorov tells a cynically inverted tale of a well-dressed professional man with a suitcase who stumbles upon a dilapidated town. He soon notices that everyone is drunk. The police, too, have been indulging, and when they see the newcomer they immediately arrest him "for sobriety." It turns out the town has outlawed the avoidance of alcohol (even a pensioner is forced to engage in a drunken brawl by the cops, who ignore his "exemption certificate"). At the police station, another man tries to excuse his sobriety to the duty officer, saying he had to celebrate his son's name day, and begs, "Just please don't report me to my boss!"

Finally, the stranger, who has resisted orders to imbibe, is strapped to a chair by the policeman and "cured" by a "doctor" who forces liquor down his throat. Now completely soused, the red-faced stranger clamors, "Petrovich! Pour me a full one!" as the doctor nods and says, "Quite a law-abiding youngster he turned out to be! Makes an old man happy!" Emerging from the "medical endrunkening station,"[17] the stranger passes by a man in a hat and trench coat, who proposes, "Hey, man, you need some mineral water? I got it, cheap!" "They Got Him," subtitled "A Comics Utopia," uses its *Outer Limits* premise (or perhaps Nikolai

Gogol's *Dead Souls* is more apt) to skewer the enduring problems of alcoholism and corruption in the 1990s.[18]

Mukha's regular nonstory features fostered an imagined community of regular fans: a letters page of fan mail, which included reader illustrations of favorite *Mukha* characters; "news columns" informing the reader about upcoming attractions in the magazine, written in an informal, even chummy tone; articles on the comics creators themselves, and drawing advice from the artists. Many issues feature the journal's "mascot," a stylized fly, in brief, textless anecdotal adventures; in issue #12, the fly horseshoes a steel flea in a tale reminiscent of Nikolai Leskov's 1881 novella *Levsha* (Lefty).

Besides the comics journal, Mukhametzyanov's studio also released *sborniki* of comics works, including some for export, in English. Later issues of the journal showcased collaborations with the Tema studio and features on the rock group Alisa. By to some extent mimicking imported periodicals like *Jurassic Park*, *Indiana Jones*, and *Mickey Mouse*, *Mukha* sought to break into the commercial market with stories designed for mass consumption along a mainstream Western paradigm. But inflation, infrequent distribution, and publishing costs (problems that plagued most independent publishers) finally doomed it after five years—a very long time in the Russian market.[19]

Besides journals, some publishers in the 1990s elected to brave the same roiling waters that had consumed KOM by releasing original graphic novels. Among these were *Andrei Brius* by Kir Bulychev and Petr Severtsov (ABLAD 1993), a science fiction/adventure story; Kapranov's *Kneklik: Buy a Shrink* (Moscow: ARTKOMIKS 1996), experimental; and Kapninsky's neo-lubok history *The First Russian Princes* (Terra 1997). Irina Rudakova's "How-to" children's books *Granny Kumi's Lessons*, which use sequential comics techniques, also appeared.

Other *komiksisty*, utilizing copy machines (access to which was a novelty in Russia), pursued a do-it-yourself ethic. Such was the path of Moscow artist Ilya Kitup, whose comics zine *Kitup's Own Propeller Comics Monthly* appeared sporadically and in small editions (about one hundred) through the mid-1990s. Kitup's early nineties stories rarely extend more than a page, telling short absurdist narratives in a percussive rhythm. (They owe much to the 1930s poet and comics writer Daniil Kharms, discussed in chapter 2.) Continuing characters such as Misha and Grisha argue, make up, or discuss banalities—sometimes in coarse language—in the space of six or seven panels, with usually no narrative resolution. Other stories eschew narrative completely, as in the recurring "A Nightmare," which closes several issues.

Kitup continued publishing *Propeller* after he moved to Berlin in 1997, and that same year he wrote the introduction to a section on Russian comics in the Slovene anthology *Stripburek: Comics from behind the Rusty Iron Curtain*. A komiks pessimist, he saw no future at all for the medium in Russia, and explained his choice to

4.3. "The Only True Guide to Russia: Hidden Secrets Revealed, Fact 3," by Ilya Kitup (*Propeller*, 1998).

always write his comics in English: "Because no one would read it in [my] home-land" (1997: 66). From Western Europe, Kitup continued to cast aspersions on his mother country; "The Only True Guide to Russia: Hidden Secrets Revealed, Fact 3" mocked its descent into economic ruin and chaos in the late nineties (1998). But his work also grew in girth; the four-page "Skew Power: A Novel" (1997) indeed seems Tolstoyan compared to his previous six-panel quick-shots. This tells the story of the "skews" (cross-eyed people), a persecuted minority whose lust for power leads to a ruthless coup d'état. They in turn are eventually toppled by the "one-eyed forces." Kitup does not stray far from his moral: the futility of resistance.[20]

Other artists such as Litichevsky, Daniil Filippov, the Serb Alexander Zograf, and the Italian Carlomaria Pilloni made "guest appearances" in *Propeller*. The late Filippov's comics work experimented with "automatic writing" for its antinarratives; as the artist explained to me, he would draw while listening to the radio, and this would largely determine the random content of the piece (1996). For example, his continuing series *Research of Text* delights in disjuncts between image and caption/dialogue, in a style more "free-flowing" even than Kabakov's conceptualist albums: in a panel showing a person being carried off to surgery (or the morgue), a character says, "I showed my translation to my instructor" (1994). This refusal of a unified meaning creates a fractured, contradictory narrative; it seems as if critical parts of the plot, which would resolve the contradictions, are simply missing. And yet each panel (and individual episode) has just enough in common with its neighbor as to strongly *suggest* a meaning.

Writing from his perspective in the mid-1990s—truly the "Dark Ages" for the medium—Kitup noted that the "tradition [of self-published Russian comics] could be called 'underground' if there were an underground. In fact, the 'underground' means nothing more than the small number of the readers of *Propeller*" (1997: 67). As we've already seen, there was more going on than that. There certainly seemed no shortage of komiksisty producing work, printing, and distributing it however they could. Studios such as Tema, for example, regularly received unsolicited submissions. One self-published work, *The New Adventures of Uncle Lenin* by O. Kushnirev and M. Olenev, came to me through the most unorthodox of channels. While riding the Moscow metro in 1997, I happened to strike up a conversation with a stranger. When I told him about my interest in komiks, he produced a copy of the work (he was the artist), quickly autographed it, gave it to me, and got off at his stop.

KOMIKS JOURNALS AT THE NEW MILLENNIUM

At the turn of the twentieth century, the new, post-Internet model of mainstream komiks production—with its advantages and disadvantages—was represented by a variety of journals which, while they enjoyed no more success than their post-Soviet predecessors, greatly improved production values to a Western level of quality. (Whether the art and stories were any better was a separate matter.) These years also saw attempts to better target product to niche markets, to make komiks more relevant to a changing Russian culture (one more attuned to material acquisition), and to use them in more pedagogically "appropriate" ways—in short, for inculcating values. Russians, fast building a new consumer society, wanted their money's worth, even in so marginal an area as komiks. The goals outlined above may sound contradictory—and indeed, Russian comics in this era became both more kid-friendly (*Magnificent Adventures*) and unabashedly coarse (*Novy Komiks*). And then there were the publicity stunts; witness the uproar over Katya Metelitsa, Valery Kachayev, and Igor Sapozhkov's *Anna Karenina by Leo Tolstoy*, a 2000 "graphic novel" which set that classic tale in the "New Russians'" world of strip clubs, sushi bars, and flowing cocaine (as discussed in chapter 6). Whatever else one may say of it, it was, thanks to a sensation-hungry mass media, the komiks work *everybody* had heard of.

Launched by a psychologist, Dmitry Smirnov, in 1999, *Magnificent Adventures* targeted adolescents with its "cheerful illustrated stories" of a closely knit group of 20-somethings visiting exotic locales (to ski, snorkel, skydive); uttering words trendy among the young, such as "Wow" (vau); and enjoying Moscow in expensive cars, chic cafes, and posh apartments (sort of a Petia Ryzhik meets *Friends*). Money was no object, but the group's ambitions seemed somewhat uniform: to a

4.4. *Komikser* appeared in 1999. Its West European "art comics" sensibility may have led to its cancellation after one issue.

person, they dreamed of working as models or on television. In short, they are all beautiful, rich narcissists with lots of toys.

One story, "Skiing Mayhem," depicts Ryzhyi (echo of Petia Ryzhik, indeed!) and Dimych skiing bare-chested and dressing as a bear and a snowman in a convoluted scheme to find a hidden present for Marina's birthday. Whoever finds it will receive a kiss from Marina and get "to dance with her all evening!" (3). This last plot point underscores an intriguing aspect of *Magnificent Adventures:* despite the youthful, hypermodern milieu, it remains curiously Soviet in its staid (non-) depiction of sex. The women make no comment on the men's handsome exposed torsos, while Ryzhyi's playful attempt to peek in on the girls in a bathhouse is coyly rebuffed with a ladle to the face (23). It is a bright, shining, G-rated world. The series does introduce other novelties, most interestingly in the figure of Webik, a smart and computer savvy friend who happens to use a wheelchair. Well aware of comics' potential to shape the outlook of the young, Smirnov promotes a "self-positive" image of the new Russia that one might dub "Capitalist Realism."[21]

Another journal reached out to a more narrow demographic with a darker view of the world; perhaps as a consequence, it lasted only one issue. *Komikser* appealed to a comics-literate readership in the West European mold.[22] Though an anthology made up of very short pieces (like many such Russian collections of the past), the journal featured some of the best veterans of the KOM era (Velitov, Ak-ishin, Snegirov, Lukyanchikov) and introduced some exciting new works (this was one of the first publications of Elena Uzhinova's adult-themed stories), all with the best printing and paper most of these komiksisty had ever seen.

The pieces varied from Lenin parodies to fairy tale parodies to autobiography, but they all assumed a level of sophistication in the reader hitherto rarely observed in Russian comics publications. Sasha Egorov's "Good Night, Kiddies" captures *Komikser*'s arch sensibility: Cheburashka, the popular 1960s children's animated cartoon character (who resembles a mouse with large ears), sits at a table, scowl-ingly pondering, "Prices have gotten totally out of hand! How'm I gonna make some dough . . ." He catches sight of his old friend, Crocodile Gena (trustingly watching TV) and has an inspiration; the final panel shows Cheburashka on the street, eagerly hawking boots and bags made from crocodile leather.

The final turn-of-the-century komiks publisher I will examine cast the widest net in terms of audience appeal and arguably bottled a workable formula—though in the end it too fell victim to another hazard of the post-Soviet marketplace. Rus-sian Comics Corporation (RKK), a short-lived Moscow firm headed by Vladimir Komarov, a former television producer, released series that combined *Komikser*'s cynicism with *Magnificent Adventures*' commodity fetishism and trendy look, try-ing unabashedly to give the people what they wanted. In interviews with the press and with myself, Komarov—a voluble, fast-talking man—radiated an intense de-sire to promote comics as a legitimate, if mass, art, and sought to professionalize their production to the level of what he observed abroad—while keeping them uniquely Russian: "Our task is to enter world culture. We can't license *Batman* and then resell it abroad. I'm creating Russian comics with Russian characters. Original ones. And with stories that will interest only us!" (Kulikov 2001).

Komarev professed no sentimentality about comics' "debilitating" effect on elite Russian culture; he saw his job as in part to dismantle the old traditions and put money-making new forms in their place. His rhetoric also tended toward a heady mix of messianism, populism, nationalism, and hedonism:

We want to put into circulation characters of mass culture. So as to create on the societal level an intense emotional exchange. We absolutely need them, these characters, and the ones we do have we can count on one hand. Brother[23] . . . *And that's it. As for comics, we need to produce them by the thousands. . . . I am creating an absolutely mass product. We have a social obligation to give the people what they need. And what brings them pleasure. Foreign licensed prod-ucts have that drive. But they don't reflect our Russian realities. (Kulikov 2001)*

RKK's offerings, released starting in 2001, certainly reflected the new Russia in form and content. They also spared no expense: oversized, with glossy paper, computer

4.5. *Nesmeiana*, with line art by Askold Akishin, represented RKK's strategy of mass-culture entertainment combined with post-Soviet values and pop culture.

lettering and coloring, and no ads, these comics appeared far more the "quality" product than the shoe-string-budget *Mukha*. One could imagine the nouveau riche (or those aspiring to join them) buying something like this for their kids.

Cracking open the pages of *Nesmeiana*, those kids would find a world very similar to what they were already seeing on television, in advertisements, at school. Billed as its heroine's "unbelievable and at the same time absolutely realistic adventures, full of love and a personal struggle against treachery, hypocrisy and human wickedness," the series follows the blonde bombshell ingenue from Siberia, Nesmeiana, in the urban jungle of Moscow, where almost everyone she meets schemes to exploit her beauty for their own base ends. Still, she always does the right thing and retains her heartland faith in people—until they cross the line.

In "The Last Swallow," featured in the second issue, Nesmeiana meets Adelle, a grocery store clerk who somehow also happens to be a producer on the reality show *The Last Swallow*. She urgently needs a model for an ad campaign. Soon the two women have jetted in to the tropical island of Po-Go, where Adelle tries to frame our heroine for the theft of the show's grand prize: "three lemons" (tri limonka), that is, three million dollars. The story is nothing if not topical; capitalizing on the fad for reality shows in post-Soviet Russia, it bares the devices, stage management, and sexism of such programs: retakes and "cheat shots" of "spontaneous" scenes; a woman contestant told to look attractive even as she forces herself to eat worms. When introduced to the beautiful Nesmeiana, the director's only comment: "Ha! The main thing is that the ass look hot on camera, everything else will work itself out" (10). Crystallizing the chief values in vogue, Adelle shoots Nesmeiana in a bikini, sprawled on a pile of money. Message received.

For all that, the heroine never utters a cynical or disrespectful word to anyone; she only lies and uses violence when needed, so as to escape confinement and catch the back-stabbing Adelle. But when she acts, Nesmeiana does so swiftly and remorselessly. Like her fairy tale namesake, a princess who never smiles, she is resolute, principled, and poker-faced (and an undercover secret service agent, to boot). The series fulfills Komarov's mission to provide readers with Russian populist heroes they can believe in: strong but good-hearted, who know right from wrong, will safeguard their friends, and show no mercy to the enemy. To cement the connection to the *Brother* films, the story ends with the astonished director, Bodrov,[24] wishing he had filmed Nesmeiana's daring exploit. He even knows what the title would be: *Sister*.

RKK's other major series aimed at adolescents keeps the cynicism but drops the heartland values; *Dimych and Timych*, written by Komarov, Elena Voronovich, and others, with art in its later issues by the renowned komiksist Andrei "Drew" Tkalenko, might best be described as *Austin Powers* meets *Bill and Ted's Excellent Adventure*. The two eponymous heroes (a computer nerd and a would-be rapper) delight in hacking, downloading Internet porn ("Turkish titties!"), ogling women in elevators, smoking pot, and coming up with hare-brained schemes to meet celebrities. The series traffics in offensive parodies of the latter: "Dimych and Timych Rescue Pritney Poops" showcases cartoonish versions of the husband-and-wife pop duo Alla Pugacheva and Kirill Kirkorov,[25] making below-the-belt assertions about her weight and age (she was twice as old as her husband) and his talent (he proposes to simply sing and dance to whatever Westerners are doing).

But the journal loves to skewer Americans most of all; tired of competing with them, the pop stars hatch a plan to kidnap Pritney Poops (i.e., Britney Spears)—dressed as Islamic terrorists. "The Westerners will get scared," says Pervacheva's producer, "and stop coming here" (5). Another story, "Dimych and Timych Save the World," features Kadum, another Muslim terrorist who forces the lads to hack into the Pentagon and the Russian Ministry of Defense, bringing both world powers to their knees. Using an extremely offensive phrase[26] meaning, roughly, "We're fucked," a helpless President Bush can only mutter, "*Eto pizdets*, like you say in Russia" (15).[27]

Unapologetically pleasure-seeking and randy, Dimych and Timych's "unmagnificent adventures" certainly struck a chord with the swaggering zeitgeist of the early Putin era. RKK's products walked a fine line: they married handsome packaging with pulpy trash (a formula perfected by Metelitsa and colleagues and the makers of *Novy Komiks*), excoriating the new Western excesses while at the same time reveling in them. Lamentably, the excesses of the corrupt economy did in the publisher. As with many fly-by-night concerns in the 1990s, RKK apparently turned out to be a money-laundering front: "[RKK] only existed because, well . . . Of course, this wasn't registered anywhere. Basically, this was a group of people who needed a place to put their money, say $100,000, and they put it in this 'company.' They decided to get into the business of children's comics. In the course of a year, they spent all the money, the corporation shut down, the director ran off, and he didn't leave a forwarding number" (Zaslavsky 2004). In this sense, Dimych, Timych, and Nesmeiana's employers reflected their era all too well.

THE SCHOLARS TAKE NOTE

The late 1990s' production advances and professionalization of komiks should not, of course, be construed as a sign of their acceptance by cultured Russians as a whole. If anything, the slicker package only made them more despicable for some. A 2002 *Izvestia* article, for example, noted that comics "were always associated with American culture, and brought to mind images of Batman, shining skyscrapers, dark-skinned youths listening to rap, graffiti-covered walls. But it seems comics, slowly but surely, have started to sprout here as well" (Kubeeva). Note the vaguely xenophobic, even racist imagery, the approach of some overseas menace, its roots seeping into Russian soil, spreading urban decay.

Komiks' growing profile in this era did get the attention of Russian scholars, who for the first time turned to a serious study of the form. Among the first to take note was the film journal *Kinovedcheskie Zapiski* (Cinema Studies Notes), which in 1996 published excerpts and summaries of two essays from the Hungarian journal *Filmvilág*, on Winsor McCay and the links between cinema and comics.

The first Russian scholarly work to treat comics on its own terms—minus the ideological attacks of Kukarkin, Nedelin, or Lapitsky—was Viktor Erofeyev's 1995 essay "Comics and the Comics Disease." This proved a landmark for several reasons, first and foremost Erofeyev's cachet among the intelligentsia as a respected literary critic, novelist, and coeditor of the "unofficial" 1979 *Metropol'* anthology, which led to state repercussions against him and his collaborators (discussed in chapter 2).[28] Furthermore, as the son of a Soviet diplomat who had lived in France (and experienced its bande dessinée culture firsthand), Erofeyev could speak with considerable authority about comics as a global phenomenon, rather than mere ideological propaganda or mass-culture dreck (not that he shies away from those labels, either). Finally, while he was at last bringing them the attention they merited on the cultural landscape, Erofeyev does not "celebrate" comics in some overweening promotional vein. Rather, he does the medium the service, for the first time in the Russian language, of subjecting it to a rigorous but balanced aesthetic critique. However riddled with historical errors and wrong-headed one might consider the essay,[29] "Comics and the Comics Disease" does treat the medium as—before anything else—an artistic practice like any other, and a decidedly modern one, at that.

Erofeyev guides his reader through the background of comics (more cave paintings; Rudolph Dirks; the "castration" of the Comics Code; underground comix; the 1967 Louvre exhibit), at several points relating the foreign material to such native Russian expressions as the lubok and Kornei Chukovsky's work. He marvels, "Of all the countries in the world, it is Russia that holds the record for holding comics at bay the longest. One hundred years of comics (the ninth art!) just passed her by. . . . The most comics-esque region of the world turned its back on comics" (23). He castigates Russian intellectuals, the "most conservative" element in cultural matters, who in their disdain for the form, marched in lock-step with the Soviets. He also credits comics' influence on Russian postmodernism, via Pop Art. At the same time, Erofeyev sees comics—a spawn of the "garbage dump" of the other Arts—primarily as evidence for the flattening-out of human experience in modernity. Like the anecdote, the television, or other popular media, comics relies on and perpetuates stereotyped representations of reality. He concludes: "No single art form so precisely conveys the ongoing dumbing-down and debasement of humanity as does comics. . . . Comics simply reflected—to recite Herbert Marcuse—the demolition of multi-dimensional man and his transition to one-dimensional man, his psychological diminution to a few simple desires. Comics is the mirror to man's collapse, the cheery pictures that accompany our own decomposition" (36).

Erofeyev does not "blame" comics in any sort of moralistic way for this; on the contrary, he applauds their "rabid" nature when and if they *do* cause societal harm—as, he seems to argue, real art should. Judging from this essay, Erofeyev knew nothing about what was happening in the contemporary comics scene of his own country, so we can only imagine what he would have made of the "stereotyped" representations of *Mukha* or KOM. But his exposition on the subject must have made at least a few think twice about this shadowy corner of Russian culture.

All the same, as pointed out by Zaslavsky, to this day most discussions of the genre in Russia are held in almost total ignorance of its history, aesthetics, and acceptance (even veneration) in other parts of the world.[30] This explains why, when scholarly discourse on comics proliferated in the post-Soviet era, it often centered on comics' "effect" on children: either as harmful (foreign) influence or potentially useful pedagogical tool.

With this in mind, in 2002 the journal *Narodnoe obrazovanie* (National Education) organized a roundtable of educators, child experts, literary critics, and publishers to discuss the current state of comics in Russia. The speakers' presentations ran the familiar gamut from chauvinist to pragmatic to utopian. All the speakers recognized the fact that comics' visibility in post-Soviet Russian culture had been growing (though too slowly to be called a "boom"), and that educators would have to face up to the genre's presence in the lives of young people. Yet almost none of the (nonpublisher) participants questioned the presumption of comics as solely a children's genre; the idea of this as an adult-oriented medium or, indeed, as a legitimate literary form exemplified by the graphic novels of Europe, Japan, and the United States, seemed alien.

By and large this has to do with the newness and still-exotic aura of post-Soviet comics, the most popular of which remained Western imports of such well-known personages as Mickey Mouse, Donald Duck, and Spiderman. As the pedagogue Svetlana Maksimova noted: "Russia's relationship with comics is quite culturally specific: *a priori*, people distrust them as somehow detrimental, lacking in value and possessed of a horribly destructive influence on the just-forming personality of the child; they underestimate them, ignore them. . . . [W]e don't distinguish between the form and content of comics, the wheat and the chaff" (75). Similarly, Irina Arzamtseva, a specialist in children's literature at Moscow State Pedagogical University, gave the medium its due, despite reservations:

The world of comics has its own style, authorial schools of thought, changing fashions, and its own slang. It is a subcultural niche that is forming before our eyes. And it cannot be ignored.

Moreover, we must not underestimate the potential of comics. It is well known that comics are actively being used in advertising. Why do advertisers like comics? Because they are an excellent means of transmitting information into people's consciousness. What sort of information it is is another matter. For now, comics are saturated with light, entertaining information. But they are capable of exerting an influence on a person's consciousness, perhaps even to a greater degree than literature, although the influence of comics is cruder and more straightforward. And their influence applies primarily to the consciousness of those who are not accustomed to or fond of reading books. (Maksimova: 77–78)

The more skeptical pronouncements on the genre came from the editor and pedagogue Alexander Kniazhitsky of the Moscow Institute of Open Education, who singled out imported Western comics for their potentially harmful effect on the young:

It seems to me that comics, like any other mass-art phenomenon, often discredit themselves. They are guilty of bad taste, and they refute themselves merely by virtue of their execution. Also, insofar as comics in Russia are a new phenomenon, by definition they cannot yet be good. Only that which is well-understood and assimilated can be good. Comics in Russia are not yet understood, and are even farther from being assimilated. There are no traditions, schools, or internationally recognized artists. There are not enough real professionals, much less geniuses. It is still premature to speak of an actual comics industry. The lion's share of comics published in Russia are licensed American products, excessive exposure to which is ruinous to the minds of the adolescent generation. We do not yet have a sense of the direction in which Russian comics will develop. (Maksimova: 82, my emphasis)

Coming to the defense of comics, the pedagogue Viktor Guruzhalov praised the form's capacities to stimulate learning through its combination of words and pictures, which appeal to the child on an emotional level. He also chided both the idealist and alarmist positions, adding:

It is somewhat ridiculous to demand that a genre solve such global challenges as those faced by the educational system, just as it is ridiculous to view comics as the source of all that system's troubles. . . .

To speak about comics as a threat to the spiritual and mental world of children, or to national security, only underscores the fact that something is not right in our system of education. That children are retreating from the real world into comics, computers, etc. is in fact not an indicator of their popularity and influence, but a sign of our pedagogical weaknesses. If a child prefers a pile of comics to actual interaction with teachers and parents, it is not the comics that are at issue, but the teachers and parents, who cannot or do not want to find a common language with the child. (Maksimova: 81)

As these excerpts show, the roundtable discussion reflected a level of respect for comics (whether in a positive or negative sense) nothing short of remarkable, given historical treatments of the topic in Russia. However, if "Comics in Education" showed how much things had changed in this regard, a curious postscript to the conference revealed to what extent—in some quarters—nothing had changed at all.

One of the participants, Natalia Markova, withdrew from the roundtable under awkward circumstances. Markova, a sociologist, served as director of Barrier, a research center at the Institute of Socioeconomic Problems of the Population (ISEPN), under the Russian Academy of Sciences. In preparation for the roundtable, Markova submitted a draft of her comments, which the organizers felt compelled to show the other panel members for their review. The respondents, including Zaslavsky, faulted the draft for its historical inaccuracies and poor arguments.

I find it enormously difficult to properly excerpt this draft for my reader, as nothing I highlight will properly convey the article's profoundly hysterical, paranoid, xenophobic, borderline psychotic comicsophobia. It might help to know that Barrier vigorously advocates for closer ties between the state and the Ortho-dox Church, which it considers the foundation of Russian civilization, and mobilizes its scientific resources to that end. The center also has a history of condemning the mass media for their destructive effect on families and tends to see the hand of the West behind what it considers harmful influences on Russian children (e.g., Disney movies).

All the same, curiously, the heart of Markova's article is not a Christian appeal but a move right out of the atheistic Soviets' playbook: that all art is ideological. Citing hentai, adult comics, and Fascist comics from occupied France and Frederic Wertham, she implicates the genre in what "scientists" have identified as a plan by which countries "commit suicide," helped along by dark international forces. Some of Markova's denunciations of "bestial comics" (vzbesenye komiksy) sound familiar from debates about media representations and children, such as: "I ask you: can anyone, seriously and with complete responsibility, affirm that a child raised on merry pictures from the magazine of the same name from the 1980s and a child who has studied blood-stained and erotic comics, will possess similar inner worlds and commit the exact same acts in critical life situations? Can any such specialists be found?" But from there, Markova, for most observers, goes straight over the top. She, for example, can hardly bring herself to pronounce the name of the very thing she condemns: "In Soviet times, children's journals did not avoid merry pictures (one doesn't want to call them comics—a revolting word, like a wet rat)." And on pictorial narratives in Soviet-era journals: "These 'comics' didn't frighten anyone. Roundtables with serious, busy people didn't need to be convened concerning comics or ABC primers in *Veselie Kartinki*."

It is not so much that she descends into self-parody as that she occasionally drifts slightly out of it, as in her xenophobic rant about the new komiks:

It would be a mistake to think that [Russian comics] are emerging on their own, like Lysenko's wheat on mistletoe[31]—that, as they're saying, a real demand has arisen. Just a year ago we had two comics publishers [sic], and now we have 15 [sic]. A Guild of Comics Publishers has instantaneously formed. Before they could even blink their eyes, there appeared the first comics festival in Russia: KomMissia, where they gathered all the Russian artists who have even the tiniest bit to do with comics. Let's ask ourselves some reasonable questions. Given that our market (inert when it comes to comics) promised no advances, who provided the money for these expensive events? Which of our nation's smooth operators was tempted into this business, knowing full well the characteristic Russian attitude toward comics ("bubble gum for morons")? Who brought the artists together? Who's actively firing up the market with the help of a reliable mover of the product, the promotion from the festival, opinions expressed in the press? (Our roundtable, incidentally, is also to a certain extent popularizing comics.)

We can answer this question easily. What's being published are exclusively American licensed products [sic!]: Rovesnik *(Coeval),* Ded Moroz *(Father Frost),* Gen¹³, Fantastic Four, Spiderman, X-Men. *Practically all the comics advertised on the internet are American product, made in the destructive style of the 1950s. . . . What are Russian comics? Alas, they are Russian only in language.*

Markova concludes her four-and-a-half-page screed with the assertion that comics unfailingly lead to

The cultivation of criminal behavior.
The cultivation of sexual perversion.
The discrediting of classical literature.
The substitution of real historical facts by false ones . . .
What can we do? (Kak zhe byt'?) In my view, we have a great opportunity to expose, stop, boycott. We must call upon parents not to buy new comics. The bestial comics are fatally dangerous for the spiritual and physical health of the nation.

It was perhaps inevitable: a *Dimych and Timych* backlash. But what makes this episode more than a laughing matter is that Markova is not some fringe figure; she represents a sizable constituency and runs a major scientific center funded by the government. That government, its constituency, and the population in general have in turn grown more conservative and restively anti-West in the Putin/Medvedev era (as demonstrated by public reaction to the 2008 conflict with Georgia).

This is why what happened next turned the incident into a real fiasco. Somehow, Markova's letter wound up in the hands of Khikhus, the cofounder of the KomMissia Comics Festival (the first of its kind in Russia, discussed below). Incensed, he, sometime around September 25, 2002, posted it on the Internet without Markova's permission; it soon accumulated scores of profane mocking comments from the online community of komiksisty. She quickly acquired a nickname: "the wet rat." The komiksmen Daniil Kuzmichov, a big presence in these forums, whipped the feeding frenzy with posts such as, "Come, come, come. Why are you all talking like that. Just because a person is a dumb, uneducated, laughable obscurantist, and just because she 'needs a man'—well, that's still no reason to get personal! Am I right?" (2002).

Things got worse. Soon after the letter's unauthorized posting Markova wrote Alexei Kushnir, editor of *Narodnoe Obrazovanie,* the journal which had organized the roundtable:

My interview for the round table on comics has turned into a detective thriller. This is a letter that appeared on my website's forum on 9/25/02:

"Hello.

"Pardon me, Miss Markova, is it to your pen that the article on comics and wet rats belongs? I'm asking because I just don't understand at all how a person who claims to be 'educated' can possibly bring forth into the world such complete and utter nonsense." Albert Alien.

For Markova the theft of the letter, the coarseness of the comments, and the missive from Mr. "Alien" not only confirmed the worst about the nascent Russian comics industry and what she now called a "fictional" roundtable, it made her fear for her life: "Now that the criminal essence of these intellectual 'comics specialists'—the participants in the 'round table,' none of whom I knew before—has been shown as plain as day, I refuse to take part in this publicity stunt for the producers of comics . . . This demonstrates the seamy criminal underside of the new comics. Furthermore, this now concerns my own personal safety! I am forced to turn to the proper authorities." This farce had serious consequences; it nearly led to the cancellation of the roundtable— *"Narodnoe obrazovanie* is a serious scientific journal, it doesn't need scandals," Zaslavsky told me[32]—and given comics' troubled history in Russia, it could ill afford to risk baiting ideological power structures. As it turned out, the blow to the medium's scarce credibility was contained. Markova posted the article and letter online, to no great response; today chuckles over "the wet rat" incident occasionally resurface in the komiks chat forums. A clash of civilizations, truly decades in the making.

KOMIKSOLYOT AND THE INTERNET AGE

As the first post-Soviet decade came to a close, Russia started to feel some sense of returning "normalcy." After the chaos and economic mismanagement of the Yeltsin era, President Vladimir Putin's administration, launched in January 2000, restored stability and national pride (thus was the widespread perception). The near opposite of Yeltsin, who was rumored to have gone through bouts of depression and binge drinking, Putin was all business: a tee-totaler, a Judo enthusiast, and a man of action. A former KGB officer, he had the clear-eyed sense of mission to bring about (or simply the good fortune to arrive during) resource-rich Russia's emergence as a major petro-state. As government coffers swelled with oil money, citizens enjoyed a rising standard of living, especially in the cities. Such was the master narrative.

Putin's reign, of course, had its dark side: the continuation of a second brutal war in the breakaway province of Chechnya; terrorist attacks tied to that conflict; the mismanagement of the *Kursk* submarine disaster; a reigning-in of press freedoms, to the extent that the twenty-first-century Russian mass media essentially functions as a pro-government propaganda arm; the squelching of the in any case tiny political opposition; increasing confrontation with the West as Russia assert-ed its newfound strength. The nation was Westernizing but also falling back on its superpower habits.

Though it occurred in the echo chambers of academia and online forums, the Markova case to some extent betrays the reactionary, quasi-Soviet biases of the Putin era. As the twenty-first century dawned, most Russians' enduring percep-tion of komiks was that of disposable, contemptible, possibly dangerous, "foreign" trash ("Markova-lite," so to speak). Yet, particularly among the young, this atti-tude was slowly yielding to a more nuanced appreciation of the medium's mass-culture pleasures.

Comics primarily appeared, much as they had in the Perestroika era, in three-to-four-page stories in journals. Only now those journals had a much wider am-bit,[33] appealing to gamers, skateboarders, and other youth groups, as well as to an emerging base of comics fans. These journals, such as *Khuligan* (Hooligan), *Len-tiai* (Lazybones), *Fantom, Ptyutch, Navigator igravogo mira* (Player's World Navi-gator), *Mega-geim, Molotok* (the Hammer), *Yes!, Ded Moroz, Klassnyi Zhurnal*,[34] and several others took on the task of creating "imagined communities": they would inform a given group of the latest (mostly Western) trends relevant to its subculture, but they also educated that group as to how to *be* that subculture. In this sense, comics were part of a much larger process of neoliberal mass-culture globalization.

But by 1999, the paper-and-ink version of komiks, in a very real sense, was sim-ply not where the action was anymore. As the Markova affair also made plain, a new agent had entered the field, whose effect would transform the medium in Russia: the Internet. We can in fact trace that transformation—and what has come to be known as the "Second Wave" of Russian comics—to the January 30, 1999, uploading of Andrei Ayoshin's Web site *Komiksolyot* ("Comic-opter"), a vast clearinghouse, encyclopedia, and gallery of komiks art. Here the reader could find not only stories to suit every taste (crude genre material, humor, erotica, Manga, photocomics, flash comics, Christian, literary adaptations, KOM-era material), but also reportage, news updates, work solicitations, interviews, and, critically, an interactive forum.[35]

KOM veteran Ayoshin, in collaboration with Web master Andrei Zhukov, di-vided the site's comics offerings into categories: Adventure, Fantasy, Manga, Fairy Tales, Classics and Remakes, Retro, Occult and Horror, Anti-Utopia, Punk, Hu-mor. It gave new life to Soviet and early post-Soviet works many had not seen, or not seen for years, from *Mukha*, Tema, Pilot, and KOM. It also rescued lost classics from oblivion, such as Akishin's unpublished *Chronicles of Military Ac-tions* and Zhigunov's graphic novel *Adam* (which had still been in preparation when KOM closed). *Komiksolyot* was one of the first venues to publish work in a relatively new genre, Cyberpunk. In all, Ayoshin's site contains almost twenty years of material.[36] As Zaslavsky noted, "through his scanner passed 1,000 pages of the genre's fate in the post-Soviet era" (Zaslavsky 2002). Ayoshin also did the right thing. In a significant gesture, he flouted the rampant piracy of intellectual property in Russia by obtaining publication rights from each creator.

Komiksolyot also proved a useful resource for those who make and study komiks. It regularly posted advice on production, drawing, and information on comics industries and festivals abroad, as well as fan art, artists' galleries, and critical texts (some uploaded by visitors). The site's *Chronology of Russian Comics 1988–2001* was the first of its kind, and despite some inaccuracies, served (and doubtless will serve) as a crucial reference on that period for Russian comics scholars.

Finally, the site played a vital role, especially for those outside Moscow and St. Petersburg, in creating and shaping the modern komiks community—which is primarily Internet based.[37] In 1996, when I first started studying Russian komiks, I noted that many of the artists I met had never heard of each other, even those that lived in the same cities. Now, in the first decade of the new century, they had a vibrant—at times raucous—online presence, largely driven by passionate men and women in their teens and twenties, where artists from all across the country's eleven time zones communicated, argued with, and supported one another on a daily basis. These contacts led to meet-ups, trade associations, arts collectives, festivals. Nothing short of a revolution: the Internet not only closed the "Wild Age" of Russian comics; it not only spawned the Second Wave of Russian comics; the Internet *saved* Russian comics.

The problem, however, is that in too many ways, the Internet *is* Russian comics. One might deem it a bizarre parody of the culture's devotion to the ideational, the ineffable, and the abstract, but today komiks exists overwhelmingly in the more "spiritual" electrons-and-pixels realm of the World Wide Web. Alas, the Web giveth, the Web taketh away. A vicious circle developed: in an economy where few comics publishers could even get a toehold, komiksmeny simply elected to go from "underground" to online. With so much free content on the Internet, print publishers proved even more reluctant to finance large-scale projects or series, and continued to cede much of the domestic market to foreign translations of Marvel and Disney.

In August 2005, *Komiksolyot* ran out of server space, and now functions as a forum, reference source, and "floating museum," in Ayoshin's phrase (2008). He feels no need to revive or update the site, as many others devoted to komiks have followed in its wake: comics.com.ua; Amin' Comics; many devoted to manga, as well as the homepages of comics publishers and importers. The year 2009 saw the launch of an important new Web journal devoted to comics, the *Chedrik Chronicles* (Khroniki Chedrika), under editor Alexander Kunin.[38] Yet another popular site became a key destination for komiksisty in the early twenty-first century: kommissia.ru, homepage of the first Russian comics festival.

KOMMISSIA

With *Komiksolyot* and the increasing professionalization of the form, komiks were starting the new century in better condition than anyone could have predicted ten years before. Though there still did not exist a viable Russian comics industry, interest had reached enough of a critical mass that on October 7, 2001, representatives from half a dozen publishers (including Smirnov of BETMIRS; Dvoryankin of BigAnt Comics; and Komarov of RKK) met to form the Guild of Russian Comics Publishers (GIK). Those assembled came to the same sober conclusion: "The Russian audience does not adequately understand what 'comics' means; for this reason, it is absolutely necessary to break the stereotype that has arisen of comics as a product that demands little intellectual effort, that is 'pulpy trash' and that is alien to the Russian reader" (Bunkin).

Toward this, GIK outlined a strategy based on mutual cooperation to create a market for comics in Russia, improve their image, and establish the genre as an independent product for consumers of literature. More specifically, they agreed to advertise in one another's publications and Web sites, prepare an annual anthology of comics published by guild members, and work toward the development of a PR campaign. Eduard Bessmertnyi of BigAnt Comics was elected the first president of GIK. This was an important first step in the establishment of an industry.[39]

Another step was taken a few months later, when the contacts and collaborations fostered by Internet forums like *Komiksolyot* led to the launch of the first annual Russian comics festival. KomMissia[40] took place in February 1–3, 2002, at the Zverevsky Center of Contemporary Art in Moscow. Over eighty artists took part in exhibitions and competed for prizes, GIK publishers[41] presented their wares, several journals served as sponsors, and press coverage was good. No event of this magnitude had taken place in Russia since the KOM presentation of 1990, and this event exceeded its predecessor by every measure.

KomMissia was the brainchild of Pavel Sukhikh (a.k.a. Khikhus), former editor of *Fantom* (a youth-oriented sci-fi/fantasy magazine), and his partner Natalia Monastyrova, literary editor at *Fantom* and general director of the ad firm Creagen.[42] A longtime comics practitioner, Khikhus was also an impresario, a businessman, and the founder of the studio/artist's agency People of the Dead Fish (Lyudi mertvoi ryby) or LMR.[43] Representing a new, post-KOM sensibility, Khikhus became the face of komiks' "Second Wave": youngish (born in 1968); exotic (he sports dreadlocks); cosmopolitan (he lived in Denmark and other West European countries, and he spoke English); knowledgeable about the comics scenes in France and Japan; adept at all aspects of production, from creation to computer processing to printing to promotion.

His address to visitors in the first festival catalog resonated with the aspirations of countless frustrated komiksisty through the decades: "Well, finally! It's

4.6. The cover to the 2005 KomMissia Festival catalog.

happened! Comics in Russia have stopped being an overseas wonder, like eggplant caviar. The times have changed, to where the question, 'Do you have comics?' no longer provokes the amazement of the kiosk-vendor. Now we can confidently ask, '*Which* comics do you have?' without the risk of being taken for an idiot. And this is good" (Khikhus 2002, emphasis in the original). A tireless promoter of komiks in all media, Khikhus's name and profile quickly became associated with the medium in Russia. The festival became a regular event of the spring arts season, receiving heavy press coverage. KomMissia grew exponentially every year, attracting up to four hundred artists and thousands of visitors as it moved first to the Sakharov Museum and Community Center[44] in 2003, and then to the M'ars Gallery in 2004–2008. International guests have included Chantal Montelier, Moebius, and Erik Arnoux (all France); Joe Pinelli (Belgium); the Fabrique de Fanzine group (Switzerland); Tomáš Prokůpek (Czech Republic); and Giuseppe Palumbo (Italy).[45]

André-Marc Delocque-Fourcaud, director of the Angouleme Comics Festival (and grandson of the famous Russian art collector Sergei Shchukin), also attended. The festival gained extra notoriety among Russians due to the participation of the renowned writer and playwright Lyudmilla Petrushevskaya in 2005 and 2006. Comics works from all over the world have been exhibited at KomMissia, whose sponsors have included Motorola, Wacom, Raiffeisen Bank, Scrabble, numerous Russian ad firms, several national embassies, and MTV Russia.

The festival catalogs, along with an LMR anthology published concurrently, became a yearly showcase of komiks work. And though visitors came to the event from as far away as the Russian Far East, Khikhus sought to bring KomMissia to the provinces, through tours of the prize-winning competition works[46] to St. Petersburg, Kaliningrad, Novosibirsk, Yakutsk, and Khabarovsk. Finally, in a country with vast gaps in its comics knowledge, Khikhus and his staff envisioned an important educational role for KomMissia. He explained: "I often go to Western festivals, but over there it's usually like this: people come, they have a look at the works, then they buy an album of comics that they like and ask the author for an autograph. But in our case, the festival is not just a way of seeing the creative work of Russian and foreign komiksisty, but a chance to learn something" (Ruban). To that end, KomMissia organized lectures, workshops, film screenings, and master classes by both local talent and international experts. Some of these included the historian Alexander Bychkov (Bulgaria); the scriptwriter Santiago Garcia (Spain); the Russian BD expert Mikhail Khachaturov; and the *Stripburger* editor Ivan Mitrevski (Slovenia).[47] Khikhus's comment, however, does touch on a perennial weakness of the festival, from a Western perspective: it has a very limited commercial role—some say to its and the medium's detriment. KomMissia had a galvanizing effect: November 2005 saw the launching of the Ninth World Festival in Kiev, Ukraine, the first event of its kind devoted to comics there[48]; and a second major komiks festival, Boomfest, debuted in St. Petersburg in September 2007.

MCCLOUD AND MAKAROVS

The komiksist Xatchett's KomMissia 2005 master class[49] provided a good example of how these sorts of events operate at KomMissia. The creator of the adventure/funny animal series *Mercs*, and with Bogdan, the self-published *Skunk and Ocelot*, Xatchett lived in the United States and Canada, and now worked in Moscow as, among other things, a storyboard artist. Like Zaslavsky, he knew the American comics industry and fan culture, but belonged to a younger, post-Soviet generation for whom its products—via the Internet—were far more accessible, if not always understood. His personal tastes veered more toward Drew Hayes and Wildstorm, though in his talk he made clear that the cultural reception of superheroes in Russia is a thorny issue: "The same image means different things to different people. When Americans see Superman flying through the air, they think, 'Oh, freedom, truth, justice, the American way.' When we see him flying through the air, we think, 'That looks stupid' or 'How come he's horizontal?' or 'Down with American imperialism!' or whatever. For them superheroes have 50+ years of baggage that they just don't have for us." (Still, this does not by any means signify that young Russians don't embrace American pop culture—and not just ironically. The word "Tarantino" wove its way throughout Xatchett's lecture, issuing reverently from the lips of both speaker and audience.)

Well versed in McCloud and Eisner, and peppering his talk with references to Western works like *Maus, The Authority* and *Poison Elves* (all of which remain untranslated into Russian, at least legally), Xatchett tried to bring the crowd to a more sophisticated, theoretically-grounded understanding of comics, at one point relating the form to the work of Kazimir Malevich. But the audience, which included many amateurs, gravitated to more nuts-and-bolts issues, like criteria for distinguishing "good" from "bad" work; whether one should use "voice-over" captions; and whether artists should research props or "just draw them however you want."

"When we're making our comics, we're creating a whole world," Xatchett insisted. This could mean that if a character is using a pistol, the komiksist might just have to learn everything about that pistol, and reproduce it with unimpeachable accuracy, down to the model and caliber. (He cited the manga artist Akihiro Ito as the paradigm for such a detail-driven approach.)

"Nobody gives a damn about that. No reader's gonna care," objected the komiksist Slava Makarov (whose last name, oddly enough, is a famous Russian brand of pistol).

THE QUESTION OF WORDS AND DEEDS

In an attempt to free komiks from its negative associations of the past, some have called for renaming and "rebranding" the genre; after experimenting with other terms,[50] Khikhus proposed "drawn stories" (risovannye istorii) which perhaps doesn't have the same ring as Petrushevskaya's neologism, "ristoriia"—from *risovat'* (to draw) and *istoriia* (story). The event's official name was KomMissia 2005: The Moscow International Festival of Drawn Stories, which does not flow trippingly from the Russian tongue. But this insistence on a separate term reflected the organizers' drive to change negative stereotypes about the "funny" medium. "Our motto says it best," Khikhus remarked repeatedly. "'Some artists' stories just don't fit into one picture.'"

KomMissia 2005 had a multilingual theme as well: "fanjin"—an amalgam of the English "fanzine" and the Japanese *dojinshi* (a genre that mixes fan fiction and original alternative material in small print runs). "We wanted to highlight the fact that both these forms of comics expression are *samizdat* (self-publishing)," explained Khikhus. "An artist, without being tied down to the demands of a publisher, produces his own work and his own vision, and then distributes it himself. This process, which goes on around the world, just captures the spirit of what this art form is all about" (2005).

4.7. Khikhus at the 2005 KomMissia festival. Photo by José Alaniz.

The term "fanjin" was born during roundtable discussions at the 2004 Kom-Missia. Apart from the neologism's "global" links, Khikhus and Monastyrova felt they could best "legitimize" the discredited, "foreign" idea of comics by associating it with the familiar Russian concept of samizdat, the Soviet-era underground practice of circulating dissident tracts and stories in manuscript form. (They made no mention of Soviet komiksisty like Kabakov, Sysoev, and Litichevsky, who had done the same thing twenty years or more before, or Ilya Kitup, who was doing it in the early 1990s.)

While the political edge of the word "samizdat" does not apply to post-Soviet comics (these artists will not be sent to the gulag for self-publishing their work), Khikhus insisted that Russian komiksisty were involved in a revolution: despite the lack of a developed industry, they would make komiks socially acceptable by getting their work out there every way they can—on the Web, in small-circulation photocopies, art galleries, soft-porn mags, and the like. He has admonished them: "Every komiksist has a right to publish and be published. He has this right in his hands. Therefore, dear esteemed artists, scriptwriters and simply those not indifferent to the fate of Russian comics, we urge you: *publish your work yourselves.* Let people read you, see you, discuss you, curse you and praise you. Give your work away or sell it, but publish and get yourselves published, don't begrudge your efforts and very modest means when it comes to this" (2004, emphasis in original).[51]

With the 2005 show, KomMissia organized a regular "trade fair" for samizdat and the independent press, in which up to a dozen komiksisty put up their works for sale. But every year its results proved disappointing. For all the media coverage, and Khikhus's exhortations, KomMissia has had a very limited impact on the actual buying and selling of komiks; its commercial activity is tepid.[52] The situation got so obviously bad that in 2006 the komiksist and caricaturist Sergei Repyov posted a short missive, "Sad Thoughts About Samizdat" on his *zhzh* page:

Today, "Samizdat" is the publication of one's own beloved self without the least hope not only of earning money, but of even meeting expenses. In the best scenario, it's a means of promoting oneself, that is, of creating a sort of paper portfolio.

At this KomMissia in particular, practically no one was buying samizdat. There was a very small group of fans; there were friends of the artists for whom it would have felt awkward not to shell out some money; there was a whole crowd of artists for whom it wasn't at all awkward not to shell out any money; and there were visitors to the exhibit, whose attitude to samizdat resembled that which a rabbit might have for a heavy machine gun.

As a result, out of 100 copies of my collection Blabber at the Bar Counter *(Tryop za barnoi stoikoi), the first day of the festival I sold 12, and the second I sold four. The rest remained the personal property of the author, and more than likely, will little by little be given away. It was a good thing that this undertaking didn't require a heavy financial investment.*

Repyov went on to say that others did suffer real economic pain from printing too many copies, or expensive copies that were of very high quality, only to see them go unbought. Cutting the price, selling at cost, sweet-talking passersby, begging, nothing seemed to work. The ones who invested the greatest care and resources into their works got burned the most. He concluded: "Of course, it's nice to hold in your hands a solidly printed color album of your comics, it's very inspiring, and so forth, but such a venture is really, really expensive (2000–3000 u.e.)[53] and it'll take you decades to sell off your stock. Alas . . . alas . . ." (2006). Repyov, not one to suffer phoniness lightly, was calling the "fanzinshi"/samizdat philosophy a sham—a rich country idea that did not work in Russia.

THE QUESTION OF MANGA IN RUSSIA

In encouraging his peers to self-publish, Khikhus pointed to the example of Japan's "doujinshi" culture, which he claimed formed a significant part of the market there. Knowing his audience, he did not pick that model at random.

Manga had hardly appeared on Russia's cultural radar screen until the mid-1990s. The first legal—as opposed to pirated—Japanese anime films on videocassette (*The Legend of Prince Arislan, Akira, Ghost Ship*) appeared only in 1998, although Moscow's television channel 2x2 had broadcast such fare as *Sailor Moon* and *Transformers* much earlier. In the late-Soviet era, the state's Channel I showed 1970s classics like *Puss'n boots* and *Grave of the Fireflies*.

Manga decisively entered the Russian cultural scene by the late 1990s, its popularity especially among the young fueled by televised anime such as the *Pokemon* series and—as with Russian comics in general—the rise of the Internet. Yet even in the darkest days of the Stagnation era, manga had seeped into the country in diplomats' mail pouches and travelers' luggage. Snegirov, for example, had a friend whose mother worked in Moscow's Japanese trade office, and she brought home samples. At the first KomMissia in 2002, Snegirov noticed some examples of manga in the exhibit. But he was shocked just two years later at how completely the manga style had established itself in Russian comics culture.

By 2005, the style was so popular it made the "fanzinshi" theme appealing to Khikhus and Monastyrova. The Japanese manga-ka Hayami Rasenjin attended and gave a lecture for the second year in a row. The festival's grand prize winner, Ekaterina Balashova (a.k.a. Berenica), also received the prize for "Best Manga" from the Japanese embassy in Moscow. The first Manga exhibit, "Komiks vs. Manga," took place in Yekaterinburg in 2000. Another show, of Osamu Tezuka's work, was held in 2007 in St. Petersburg, under the auspices of that city's comics festival, Boomfest.

Aside from innumerable Web sites, the sweeping interest in manga and anime has taken nonvirtual form in clubs throughout the country, where (as in other parts of the world) young people congregate to discuss Japanese culture, show off their latest work, study the Japanese language, watch films, and practice martial arts.[54]

The first such group, R.An.Ma, formed in 1996. Konstantin Dubkov, a manga-ka from the provincial city of Yekaterinburg, helped organize one of two such clubs there, with up to 150 members.[55] The premiere anime event, the All-Russian Festival of Japanese Animation, first took place in 2000 in the southern city of Voronezh, while in 1999 Boris Ivanov published *Introduction to Japanese Animation*, which has become a prized object for many Russian animators. (The Japanese scholar Motoi Kawao calls Ivanov the leading Russian expert on anime.)[56]

One can easily see the manga/anime influence throughout post-Soviet Russian visual culture: in the 2004 Timur Bekmambetov film *Night Watch* (a major Hollywood-style Russian "blockbuster"); videos by the pop singer Glyuk'oza; in countless advertisements; in magazines aimed at young people such as Khikhus's *Fantom, Gameland*, and *Anime Guide*; and in the 2005 Pavel Khakhizov film *Manga*. In addition to innumerable "scanlations" (illegal translations) of classic manga available online, in 2006 Sakura Press released the first legal Russian translation of a Japanese manga work, Rumiko Takahashi's *Ranma ½* (Ranma-and-a-half). Each two-hundred-page, small format volume comes complete with *omake* explaining Japanese vocabulary, suffixes in names, and terms of address; the history of Japanese manga; biographical information on the author; and other useful cultural information. Meanwhile, Egmont Russia had been publishing the Italian manga journal *W.I.T.C.H.* with art by, among others, Giada Perissinotto, since 2003. As for Russian comics, the Moscow-based Edvans Press began publishing a manga journal for young girls, *Yula*, in 2004. By 2006 three publishers specialized in manga: Sakura Press, Fabrika komiksov (importer of Matsuri Akino's *Pet Shop of Horrors*), and Neomanga.

Many komiks reflected a manga influence in the early 2000s, particularly the work of "Second Wave" artists Konstantin Komardin, Xatchett, Tatka, and Dubkov. The popular Bogdan published *Nika*, the first Russian manga series, in the journal *Klassnij Zhurnal* in 1999. A collected works volume, *Nika Vol 1: The Magical Book*, appeared in 2002. A "remastered" version, along with *Nika Vol. 2: The Dragon of Desire*, followed in August 2008.[57]

Nika tells the story of the eponymous heroine, a high school loner and martial arts prodigy who discovers that her daydreams about a magical fairy tale world of sorcerers, trolls, and satyrs are real. Bestowed with a sorcerous lineage as mistress of a magical book, she must defend it against an evil mage who intends to use the tome's power to extend his realm into "our" reality. He temporarily succeeds, transforming Moscow into a medieval nightmare of gothic architecture and gargoyles.

Bogdan's novel comes off as a delirious fusion of East and West: it uses the same devices, cartoonish stylized expressions, sound effects, and dynamism of Japanese manga, while retaining a strong Russian sensibility. For one thing, it contains far more dialogue and exposition than conventional fantasy/adventure manga; speech balloons at times crowd out the characters. That "talkiness" allows for some funny wordplay (Nika's right-hand man is named Brys', the sound one makes to shoo away a cat—which leads to awkward double-takes with another major character, a cat) and sly references to Russian fairy tales (the evil sorcerer Kashei recalls Khoshchei the Deathless, which Nika herself sarcastically points out). Also, unlike most manga, *Nika* is colored on computer, and at only thirty-three pages, volume one is far shorter than the typical Japanese product. Finally, this and subsequent episodes underscore that Bogdan takes only the style and grammar of manga for his epic; the sensibility, literary flair, culturemes, and ethnicity of characters in the work is decidedly un-Japanese. *Nika* is a Russian adult fairy tale in a manga bottle.

Other Russian manga-ka take a different approach, reproducing not only the style but the racial identity of Japanese pop culture, while playing with the formulae in other ways. Such is the approach of Sato Kai (Alexandra Tyuleneva) for her story "Metro," in which the characters are all Asian and the setting looks like Tokyo. The prize-winning Berenica, conversely, hews closer to Bogdan's middle course, combining manga and Western fairy tales, though her art is painted. In fact, for some, "Beyond the Rain" might not resemble manga at all.[58]

Liminal cases like Berenica's fueled debates at KomMissia 2005 over the exact definition of "the manga style." As Mitrevski noted, "Manga is like Chinese food. It's never the same in any country, but everywhere they still call it manga."[59]

THE QUESTION "WHAT IS KOMIKS?"

Nor, of course, am I going to analyze all the modern axioms
laid down by Russian boys on that subject, all of them based on
European hypotheses; for what is only an hypothesis there, becomes at once an axiom with a Russian boy, and not only with the
boys but, I suppose, also with their professors, for Russian professors are quite often just the same Russian boys.
—DOSTOEVSKY

In his essay "Birth of the Russian Intelligentsia," Isaiah Berlin describes early-modern Russia as a backward society split into three jagged shards: an authoritarian czarist government intent mainly on preserving its stranglehold on power; a vast sea of peasants living out their miserable lives in appalling ignorance, poverty, and religious devotion; and tiny islands of what (in a later historical moment and milieu) we would term a "cultural elite." Only Peter the Great's violent opening up of his "window to the West" inaugurated the slow, painful, ongoing transformation of Russia—which would come to dominate one-sixth of the earth's land mass— into something not-quite Asian, not-quite European.

A large part of this process, Berlin notes, involved the manic, ad hoc assimilation and implementation of concepts which in other countries had never gone beyond the realm of the mental: "You must conceive, therefore, of an astonishingly impressionable society with an unheard of capacity for absorbing ideas—ideas which might waft across, in the most casual fashion, because someone brought back a book or collection from Paris (or because some audacious bookseller had smuggled them in); because someone attended the lectures of a neo-Hegelian in Berlin, or had made friends with Schelling, or had met an English missionary with strange ideas" (125). This penchant for practicing a distorted version of what someone far away only preached, would lead not only to Russia's most excruciating—often tragic—social experiments (Communism), but to its greatest literary-artistic achievements as well. I hazard to say that something of this "national trait" appears at first glance in komiks, manifesting itself in all their vibrancy and heterogeneity. Many komiksmeny, who access foreign work online, and some of whom travel abroad, actively emulate the forms, genres, and look of Western and Japanese comics, at times—as per Markova's accusation—adding nothing to it but the Russian language. The "national style" in komiks has been described as "a vinaigrette" (Dubkov), no style at all (Snegirov), a DJ remix of other national styles (Lukyanchikov).[60]

Something of this informs Zaslavsky's opinion: "Komiks' specific characteristic is that it has no unified style, to which someone could point to and say, 'That's the Russian comics style.' Ilya Kitup was exposed to American comics, while Andrei Snegirov saw Belgian comics like *Tintin*, someone else saw *Pif*. Today there's a big interest in manga. So Russian comics is very eclectic. This might be its particular feature" (2004).[61] Another characteristic, about which the specialists on the 2002 *Narodnoe obrazovanie* roundtable reached consensus, was that as a "predominantly verbal" culture, Russia would produce comics that were more verbal than visual. This predilection might even explain the text-privileging Russians' "discomfort" with comics, they suggested (echoing some of the old Soviet arguments). This is the familiar literaturnost', the narratival impulse in Russian art, against which some in the avant-garde grappled (Malevich) and others embraced (Kabakov). "Our theory is that Russian comics are first of all based on text, not drawing," Khikhus told me in 2004.[62]

Mitrevski, further, speculates that the Russian resistance to comics stems from an aversion to "Westernized" blendings of word and picture which predate the Soviets, harkening back to Orthodox prohibitions against graven images in general (as we examined in chapter 1). Mitrevski extends this line of thinking to explain why even the devout Christian komiksmen Igor Kolgaryov, whose New Testament adaptations in his *Amin' Komiks* unironically seek to spread the word of God, met with resistance from Orthodox Church authorities.[63]

Modern Russians' response to komiks (to say nothing of comics) coincides with the cultural critic Dragan Kujundzic's postcolonialist reading of a Moscow McDonald's "picture menu," which foregrounds its whiff of linguistic and cultural "contamination." Besides flashing such monstrous terms as "Dvoinoi Mak" and "Chizburger" in bright colors, the menu affronts Russian "text-based" purity because it "does not even require *any* linguistic competence, since you may order simply by pointing to the picture" (emphasis in the original).[64] Komiksmeny swim in the current of what they take for granted as a "text-based" culture modeled on literary values still extant from the nineteenth century, if not earlier.[65]

The only amendment I would offer to this position, as I understand it, is that exceptions to "literature-based" komiks come easily to mind, from throughout the history of the form. Certainly komiks have primarily been used to tell stories, but quite often they have done so exclusive through sequential pictorial imagery. Wordless komiks appear too often to discount as anomalies.[66] A large contingent of komiksisty have indeed tried to go beyond literaturnost' to a more art-oriented approach: the KomMissia 2008 special jury prize winner Spinoza, many of the SPb. Nouvelles Graphiques artists from St. Petersburg, even born storytellers Elena Uzhinova and Askold Akishin impart on their work a rich expressionism—one does not "read" them so much as "take them in."

For all that, the gold standard remains solid storytelling in a mainstream European vein, hence "drawn stories." For some, in fact, to fail at this is to fail at the medium. Khikhus has complained about the lowering quality of komiks' scriptwriting; in the catalog to KomMissia 2008 (which ended in acrimony), he wrote his fellow komiksisty:

No, really, how long will you keep your characters pointlessly suffering for three pages and then jumping out a window on the fourth? Bo-o-o-ring! If you have nothing to say, go to a museum, paint. . . . But if you want to be a komiksist, be so nice as to come up with a story. *If you can't do it yourself, find a scriptwriter. Or do your own adaptation of a literary classic. Show your unique vision of a plot that everyone already knows. . . . So, here's some advice for you: before sitting down to draw, imagine that you're about to film a movie that will be seen by thousands of people.[67] Think through your plot, bring it to life, and finally, discuss it with your friends. (2008, my emphasis)*

The storytelling imperative, however, must contend with the realities of the Russian marketplace, which allows for komiks primarily in magazines, often in no more than four-page bursts. This leads to an emphasis on humorous or anecdotal pieces in an episodic vein. ("It's impossible to make short but attractive and interesting adventure comics" in the three-page format of the magazines, Khikhus says.)[68] Perhaps in compensation, some komiks sport a garish, ultra-manufactured look. Many artists use devices such as Wacom tablets and computer lettering software to create slick genre material, including erotica, science fiction, and action adventure for the rare publisher who will put it in print. The apogee of this approach is *Ten': The Hero and Death*, a 2005 series from Progulka press, a sci-fi/fantasy story done in a mid-1990s Image style, complete with absurdly muscled men, outlandishly proportioned women, and lots of exclamation points.

Furthermore, the vast majority of Russian comics studiously avoid political commentary, and there seem to be very few komiksisty doing autobiographical work. This, along with art "enhanced" on computer, led Mitrevksi to identify a disjunct between Russian artists' avowed antiauthority stance (imported along with the pop culture they're consuming) and the predominantly corporate style of their comics.

"In that sense the Russians are a little strange," Mitrevski said. "In the West, to be 'alternative' or 'underground' means you reject the slickness of the mainstream corporate product, and create something more personal, with your own hands. But here they go straight for all the hi-tech, slick computer software first, especially the young people. It all tends to look overdone, overproduced, flashy. They just love to push all the buttons, try everything at once. They talk about being 'alternative,' but they basically end up aping a lot of Western and Japanese genre material" (2005).

In many ways, this is the direct result of three factors: komiks' continued reliance on the Internet as a publishing venue; the worldwide computer revolution in comics production, which hit Russian comics just as they were emerging from their Soviet semi-coma; and, as mentioned, the inescapable presence of American pop culture in post-Soviet Russia. Some of the more adept komiksisty embrace the U.S. cultural hegemony even as they mock it through clever parody. Alexei Lipatov sends-up superheroes in his *Stalin vs. Hitler* (2000), a demented recreation of World War II which cannot be appreciated without a thorough absorption of *both* generic conventions spawned by Bronze Age Marvel Comics *and* twentieth-century Soviet history.

Another parodist, Alexander Remizov, delights in puncturing the pretensions and illogic of American genre films by injecting them with a dose of Russo-Soviet realia. His "How to Forget Everything" (2008) lampoons the sci-fi thriller *Total Recall* (d. Paul Verhoeven, 1990). It shows Quaid (Arnold Schwarzenegger), the hero trying to remember his past, eluding his pursuers, until he stumbles on some drunks. They advise him, proffering a bottle, "In order to remember everything, first you have to . . . forget everything!" (ellipses in original). The next several panels show a bleary and unshaven Quaid waking up at the landing to his apartment, before his houserobed wife. When he can't remember her name, she berates him as an alcoholic who has ruined her life. The final panel depicts Quaid's shadowy pursuers deciding they can give up their chase; "ancient methods" have worked better than their memory-erasing technology. While based on a foreign work, Remizov's parody grounds itself in familiar Russian situations and visual culturemes, especially the dilapidated landing of a multistory Soviet-era apartment building (including the unmistakable design of it trash chute).

Modern Russian comics, then, are typically short, humorous narratives produced or processed on computer, with allusions to American or Japanese pop culture, usually irreverent; occasionally they will allude to Russo-Soviet history with the same sardonic sneer. This to some degree fulfills Zhora Litichevsky's axiom that comics, especially given their seventy-year semi-suppression under Communism in Russia, are "naturally subversive" (1996). And yet, this narrows the compass of comics much too severely. It essentially affirms the old specious link between komiks and humor. And it leaves little room for works that steer clear of humor and irony altogether. The lack of Russian publication for such "serious," politically engaged comics as Nikolai Maslov's autobiography (the subject of chapter 7) and Mikhail Zaslavky/Askold Akishin's adaptation of Bulgakov's *The Master and Margarita* (both were published initially in France) speaks to that prejudice.

THE QUESTION OF AN INDUSTRY

A subculture has formed, authors scattered throughout the country
and the world have met, started to create their own studios, associations and even presses. I'm happy to note that there have been
successful [Russian] projects, both here and abroad. In stores, separate shelves of "drawn stories" material are slowly but surely getting established. These shelves, though still disorganized, already
hold a pretty representative selection of comics, BD and manga.
Taking all this into account, in a couple of years these shelves will
turn into full-scale store sections.

—KHIKHUS

With that and similar declarations, Khikhus, the clown prince and PR ideologue
of Russian comics, has buoyed his fellows to greater achievement since 2002. In
countless interviews before a mass media hungry for the exotic, he appears as the
dreadlocked, goateed, smiling figurehead of a growing movement on the cusp of
breaking out into a full-fledged industry.

But more than twenty years after KOM's first tentative publications, it still
had not happened. Every year, with greater urgency (and frustration) the question
hovers in the air: will a viable domestic industry ever come together, beyond some
scattered publications, some annual festivals, and a plethora of Web sites? In the
Soviet "dark ages," komiksisty produced "for the drawer." Today, in a crony capitalist post-Soviet Russia given over to consumerism, it seems artists are drawing
mainly for the homepage, or for each other.

Worse, the explosion of komiks on the Web, through such venues as *Komiksolyot*, etc., has expanded their reach, but at the same time further ghetto-ized the
form into what is popularly perceived as a cult, youth-driven activity for those
with fast Internet connections, mobile phones, Web savvy, and of course, money.
While that description does fit a lot of young people in the urban centers, it leaves
behind many more—millions more—who barely scrape by on the average national salary of 600 dollars a month.

By 2005 komiks had become something not unlike eighteenth and early
nineteenth-century Russian literature: an elite pastime of the connected, privileged, lettered, Western oriented, and relatively affluent, which left the masses in
the cold. This matters, because in a Putin–Medvedev era of reasserted hard-line
values, it has become increasingly problematic to be perceived as "not Russian
enough."[69]

In short, the "industry question" has drawn a long shadow over KomMissia.

Almost all the comics market in Russia is product oriented to children or
youth (manga has made some inroads in recent years among young girls). In 2006

the most successful publisher—enjoying a 70 percent market share with its seventeen journals, for a total monthly circulation of over a million—was the Danish firm Egmont, which publishes *Mickey Mouse*, *Winnie the Pooh*, *Tom and Jerry*, and similar titles.[70] Praim-Evroznak, publisher of *Shrek*, *Hellboy*, *Terminator*, *Superman*, multiple *Star Wars* titles, and more, came in second; while Komiks Press was third with *X-Men*, *Spiderman*, *Fantastic Four*, *The Simpsons* (total monthly circulation: 500,000). Rounding out the top four: Rovesnik, which publishes, among others, *Scooby Doo* and *Gen[13]* (Styshneva).

This list immediately recalls Dvoryankin's observation that in Russia, when parents buy comics for their children they don't perceive them as comics, but as an extension of a film or TV show. That fact underscores one of the main hurdles for domestic producers: they must compete against a well-financed arsenal of globally recognized brands; as happened throughout the 1990s, they are routinely outgunned and outspent on advertising.

As Kuzmichov told his KomMissia 2005 lecture audience:

We have to compete with a foreign industry that developed over many, many years, and now it's come here and swallowed up everything with superior resources, brand recognition, cheaper production costs. It costs them far less per page to translate Spiderman *and sell it to an audience that's already been conditioned by the films, than for Russian artists to make something new from scratch and then have to go out, with no resources, and find and win over an audience. What's more, we don't always have the best product to sell. We've got artists that can't write and writers that can't draw. (2005)*

The cost structure is indeed very different for the publishers of imports or "licensed products," which in 2006 went for fifteen to twenty dollars a page. Manga rights cost even less, about ten to twenty dollars (Styshneva). As noted by Zaslavsky, editor in chief of the domestic publisher Edvans Press: "Naturally, these licensed products are cheaper. The production cost for [imports] is maybe about $20 a page, plus the translation. As for us, we have to come up with scripts, art, everything from scratch, so our production costs are different" (2004).[71]

All the same, this does not mean all licensed products will succeed if the Russian importer has a faulty market strategy. The worst failure of this sort was suffered by Nitusov Press in 2004. Director Yevgeny Nitusov had committed to producing elegant, expensive hardcover albums in the French format: chiefly translations of French titles such as Régis Loisel's *Peter Pan* and the *Golden City* series by Daniel Pecqueur and Nicolas Delfin, but also some Russian material like Elena Shcherbinovskaia and Sergei Gavrish's *Secret of the White She-Wolf* (2003) and Konstantin Komardin's popular cyberpunk novella *Site-o-polis* (2004). Nitusov stayed committed right up until he went out of business. (At KomMissia 2005

Nitusov told me, "We had some setbacks, but we have learned our lessons and we plan on trying again with a better business plan.")[72]

The consensus among competitors (and komiksisty) was that Nitusov approached the market impulsively, releasing his albums all at once, without proper publicity, without localizing them to the Russian market, printing too many of them and, crucially, pricing them beyond the reach of most consumers. (In many ways, Nitusov's "plan" resembled the anarchically optimistic publishing practices of the KOM era—minus the state subsidies.) "The calque from the European model did not justify itself commercially," said one of Nitusov's rivals, in the driest of understatements.[73]

But even with the best business model, domestic comics producers must deal with the major problems of distribution and marketing. Khikhus's "shelves of drawn stories" had simply not materialized in most bookstores. So, comics works—including some meant for an adult reader—wound up in the children's literature departments, where they led to some parental complaints. (This is one of the reasons Khikhus prefers to sell his own works over the Internet.) Much more significant is having to deal with outright corruption in getting one's product to consumers. If in the first years of Perestroika publishers struggled with the enduring Soviet image of comics as "pseudo-literature," a new hurdle, one much more banal, has emerged to take its place.[74] As explained by Zaslavsky:

> *The main stumbling block is the current press distribution system. A publisher, releasing a new journal in the periodicals market, must pay an "entry fee" to whatever distribution network he uses. The prices are very high. The glossies, tabloids and newspapers can pay to enter the networks, since their expenses towards "marketing services" are covered by their advertising revenue. But those publications that contain little advertising live on sales. Comics belongs to the second category. All the same, the distributors don't differentiate between types of publication. The price is the same for all. So, comics end up having to compete not with each other, but with the glossies,* Playboy, *and the yellow press.*[75]

Even worse, firms must contend with the sort of dirty tricks that have become all too common in the cut-throat world of Russian publishing. In 2004 Antonina Larina, financial director of Edvans Press (which publishes the children's comics monthly *Just You Wait!*), told me that some Moscow news kiosks refused to carry her product because they had been bribed by the better-off competition. Similar problems crop up with nationwide distribution, which remains a nightmare in Russia. Still, *Just You Wait!* managed a print run of 40,000 copies, many going out to subscribers; while its sister title *Yula* (Russian manga aimed at young girls) printed 20,000 before it had to cut back in 2007–2008. These were the longest-lived domestic publications on the market in 2009.[76]

4.8. *Just You Wait!*, based a popular animated series from the 1970s, represents Edvans Press' attempts to compete against imported product with native Russian brands.

Neither magazine strayed beyond the safe and predictable, but they were entirely Russian-made, reflecting a cultural specificity which the imported products could not match. They too followed a brand strategy, with established Russian properties. *Just You Wait!* published stories about a hare and wolf team by Alexander Kurliansky and Alexei Kotenochkin, based on an enormously popular Soviet animated cartoon from the 1960s and 1970s; and the long-running adventures of Keshka the cat by Andrei and Natalya Snegirov. Zaslavsky is adamant that only by laying the groundwork for an industry today—based on competitive mainstream product—will Russian comics have a future beyond their current marginal status in the market and the culture.[77]

One way to get around the marketing and distribution problems would be to open specialized shops catering to comics readers, allowing for product categorizations, assortment by genre, national tradition, and the like. No such shops exist; the closest to this model is Pangloss, a Moscow bookstore[78] of French-language literature with a large selection of bande dessinée and some Russian works, where a new version of the "Komiks Klub" convened starting in 2008.[79]

The plight of Russia's nascent comics industry makes KomMissia a cheerleading section with no team on the field (or at best, a poorly equipped one); the festival functions fundamentally differently from its Western analogues, which serve primarily as trade fairs and promotional events for their national industries. The Russian fest, conversely, tries both to showcase what an industry *would* look like, and also to fill the gap in domestic publications through its catalogs, anthologies, and exhibits. All this gives it a rather surreal Brigadoon-like quality. KomMissia is a showpiece in a void—the tip of the iceberg without the iceberg.

The situation recalls the cultural critic Mikhail Epstein's description of the Russian *prezentatsiia*, a ubiquitous 1990s variation on the Potemkin village:

This word was assimilated from English ("presentation") in, approximately, 1990–91 to denote the ceremony of an official opening of some public institution. In spite of the fact that Russia grows poorer and continues to crumble from day to day, such festive presentations are now widely fashionable. . . . The overwhelming majority of these businesses and associations collapse within several weeks or months, leaving no memory of themselves other than their dazzling presentation. None of the cheerful participants at such lavish events, marked by long speeches, caviar, brandy and oysters, would attest that the object of their presentation will survive even until the following morning, but most are fully satisfied by their inclusion in today's presentation and by the anticipation of more in days to come. (1995: 32)

In this *prezentatsiia* sense, the country does have a comics industry: one dominated by foreign translations; with concerns that sprout and vanish like wild Russian mushrooms[80]; with festivals and trade shows nearly void of domestic publications. Despite all this, of course, Russian komiksmeny, their publishers and readers harbor a profound devotion to this medium (something I have witnessed myself)—year after year, the party goes on, and everyone hopes for the best.

There does, however, exist a KomMissia backlash.

For some critics of the festival, it does nothing for komiks, and was never designed to do anything but benefit a select few. Its "positive media profile" is just TV footage of some twenty-somethings drinking, smoking, and gabbing on their cell phones in front of pretty pictures. Oleg Semenyuk, comics writer, collector, editor of *Sport* magazine, and former editor at RKK, broke from KomMissia after its first two years, concluding: "This is just a *tusovka*, a get-together. It's always the same people, drinking together, partying together, awarding prizes to each other, year in, year out.[81] It's clear from reading their comics that they don't know how to make them, how to design a page. It's all just so they can see themselves on television and get free advertising for their commercial projects. Nobody cares that the comics are terrible" (2005). When I bring up such critiques to Khikhus, he sighs like a man who's heard it all before. "We've got hundreds of people coming now, from all over the world," he told me. "It's gone way beyond what Oleg imagines. And, yeah, this does get comics out there, it makes it into something cool, not childish. We've got links now with the Lodz Festival, with Angoulême; right after this we're exhibiting work in Kiev. We've grown into a serious festival" (2005).[82]

This is true, but the annual feel-good vibe provided by KomMissia, as well as its cultural programming and guests, no longer satisfy a segment of komiks professionals (and would-be pros) who see it as no substitute for an actual industry. Sometimes their frustration at waiting twenty years spills over into acrimony and full-scale verbal warfare,[83] though most working komiksisty restrict themselves to appreciating Khikhus's PR efforts but recognizing his hype as hype—much of it self-promotional, intentionally or not:

His thing is to make a lot of noise about comics, but the problem is that there's no money in that, just noise. Of course, he attracts a lot of attention to himself. He's very famous. People who have no connection to comics will recognize Khikhus, they'll say, "Oh, yeah, he's the number one comics artist in Russia!" But he's not any kind of number one. He's just a loudspeaker for comics. He screams a lot about comics, that's why he's so visible. . . . But this is not business, it's not work, it's not organizing a comics industry. It's promotion of a certain kind of comics. But I can't say that Khikhus is the principal comics artist. He's an effective promoter, but we need to construct an actual market. (Ayoshin 2006)[84]

Others, while not contemptuous of KomMissia, no longer have any faith in it as a catalyst for change. Tkalenko, the renowned komiksist, noted:

Khikhus himself has already understood that, alas, you can't do anything with the "comics industry" in this particular country. Its beginnings fell apart and came to nothing. And if, in the early 2000s, you could still see some representatives from the publishers at KomMissia, nowadays there's pretty much no one[85]. . . . Everyone's just got his own personal work assignments; there's nothing bad about that, it's normal. I, too, am worried more about whether I'll personally find a publisher than about "the situation for the country's comics industry and whether comics will ever become popular here." Life's too short. (Alaniz 2008: 853)

KomMissia does serve another valuable purpose besides promotion: its catalog and Web site serve as a publishing venue for many otherwise unknown artists from throughout the country—but here, too, there are complaints. The four-page limit restricts those with ambitions toward longer narrative—the same problem they face in the magazines. (The festival ameliorates this somewhat by linking its Web site to full-length versions of longer works.) And of course, each comics festival only comes once a year.

Those able to pool their resources, such as LMR, put out self-published anthologies and one-shots tied to book fairs or promotional events, such as *The Trojan Rabbit* (part of the 2006 Territoriia Contemporary Art festival in Moscow) and *City Stories I* (2006), a bilingual joint project between Russian and Polish

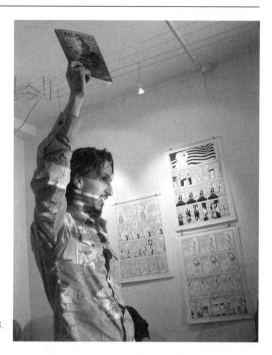

4.9. Alim Velitov holds up the People of the Dead Fish (LMR) anthology at KomMissia 2008. Photo by José Alaniz.

artists organized by the International Comics Festival in Lodz. While significant, well-made works, these all represent stopgap, unsatisfying alternatives to regular publication, their contribution toward an industry virtually nil.

Tkalenko, with scriptwriter Elena Voronovich, made the most of the situation, releasing the dystopian series *Bitch* (Sterva) in ten- to twenty-page batches, which appeared in the LMR anthology, his personal Web site and whatever venue for long-form narratives he could find. Expanding on concepts from Boris and Arkady Strugatsky's classic sci-fi novel *Roadside Picnic* (1971, source of Andrei Tarkovsky's 1979 film *Stalker*), *Bitch* involves an emotionally wounded heroine, a Stalker, who wanders a postapocalyptic Moscow turned metaphysical Zone left behind by an alien visitation. It combines the philosophical foreboding of the Strugatskys' vision with action-adventure set-pieces, ultraviolence, and an antiauthoritarian critique all-too applicable to contemporary Russia.[86] *Bitch* would reside not uncomfortably as a title in DC's Vertigo imprint, but in its own country it must wander a different kind of purgatorial Zone.

Xatchett and Bogdan prefer to laugh about their nonindustry in their ongoing strip and comics *Skunk and Ocelot*. A series called *Insectarium* shows the two heroes musing on various types of allegorical insects: "publishers" (most of them extinct or endangered) and "quasi-fans." In strip No. 8, Skunk prods a "komiksist" in the grass. He describes him to his friend: "Laureate of three exhibits in hangars, four festivals in cramped apartments, possessor of a prize in something-nobody-

4.10. The dystopian series *Bitch* by Andrei "Drew" Tkalenko and Elena Voronovich, expands on the work of Soviet sci-fi authors Boris and Arkady Strugatsky.

will-ever-see, a creature highly respected in narrow circles!" Ocelot replies, "Wow! But, like, why doesn't he put up a fight?" Skunk keeps prodding, and answers, "He's starved to death" (19).

With few reliable venues to publish, komiksisty turned to many nontraditional areas for work. Some projects involved online gaming, online porn, mobile phone content (especially porn), and expensive erotic glossies such as *Moulin Rouge.* The airline Aeroflot published a children's magazine, *Junior,* which included Ayoshin and Snegirov's comics, among others. Some of the most lucrative jobs were for the advertising industry, whose interest in comics steadily rose in the 2000s. Most advertisers tapping the form early on worked with foreign companies: Head and Shoulders, Tide, Konika, Dirol. An especially elaborate Nike campaign gave out comics booklets made by LMR along with a line of backpacks. (They knew the strategy was working when they saw customers holding on to the booklets rather than throwing them away, as they did with brochures.) The campaign produced 120,000 booklets (Styshneva). In a 2006 promotion with the drug manufacturer Narodnye lekarstva, Bogdan produced a comics adventure story, *The Gams* (Gamsy), about a superhero team that derives its powers from chewing kids' vitamins.

Apart from storyboarding, komiksisty engaged in film-related ventures such as promotional tie-ins and adaptations, including the Taganrog artist Roman Surzhenko's version (with Vladimir Sakhnov) of the historical epic *1617: A Chronicle of the Time of Troubles* (d. Vladimir Khotinenko, 2007).[87] Additionally, movie producers sometimes turned to comics sequences as cost-saving measures: Ayoshin's work appeared as a "flashback" sequence in *It Doesn't Hurt to Dream* (Mechtat' ne

4.11. "Cum to Daddy," by Otto
(*Razchlenyonka*, 2007), defined the
"alternative" anti-corporate model
of komiks.

vredno, d. Yevgeny Lavrentiev, 2005), while Alim Velitov's comics graced the comedy thriller *Happy Birthday, Lola!* (d. Vladimir Shchegolkov, 2001).

Yet another, more unusual, line of work involves what we might call "vanity" projects. These include comics commissioned by the wealthy for their children as birthday gifts and the like (often for fabulous sums). A perhaps more socially conscious example is *The Story of a Real Man* (2006), an adaptation by Yevgeny Gusev of the 1946 Boris Polevoi novel about a real World War II ace, Alexei Mares'ev, who lost his legs in combat but returned to the air to fight on.[88] The cultural fund in Mares'ev's name, headed by his son Viktor Mares'ev, planned to release the work in schools. "This is a new way, a modern way, to reach young kids with the important stories and figures from our history," Mares'ev told me in 2007.

An auspicious blend of comics and high finance, the LinArt Design Studio's supplement to the year-end accounting book of Zenit Bank (by Andrei Ross and Sergei Gavrish) won first place in the Print Ad category at the 2003 Moscow International Festival of Advertising.[89] Remarkably, Zenit chose to forego the common stereotypes of comics for the project. Noted the journalist Dina Yusupova: "At first the LinArt artists thought up superheroes, like Rubleman and Euroman, but the bankers asked for a straight story about a businessman who achieved success by using the services of the bank." Conversely, LMR decorated the offices of an investment company, depicting employees as superheroes (Yusupova: 2).

The lack of an industry has spawned another perennial question, often broached at KomMissia: with no defined Russian comics mainstream, what does it mean aesthetically and politically to follow an alternative practice? Some answer is provided by Pegas Komiks, an independent company formed in 2005 by artists and enthusiasts, whose low-budget, desktop-published anthology series *Pegas* (Pegasus) features a mix of fantasy and humor pieces, mostly with an unpolished "amateur" look. Snegirov's work has also appeared in the anthology.

A stand-out *Pegas* contribution, if for nothing else than its transcendent coarseness, is *The Man-Mold* (Chelovek-litoi) by Roman Safarov. Combining parody of *A Clockwork Orange* and Mikhail Bulgakov's *Heart of a Dog* with toilet humor, it tells the story of a ruthless, foul-mouthed midget petty criminal chosen for an experiment to rehabilitate him into a law-abiding citizen. His genitals and anus are surgically removed by the sexually perverse head of the experiment, Professor E. B. Obezobrazov (the family name suggests "ugly" or "disgraceful," while his first and middle initials spell out "fuck"), thus he becomes the Man-Mold. Needless to say, the experiment ends in failure and disaster; our hero more than ever wants to cause havoc. Obsessed with restoring his lost penis, Man-Mold swears vengeance on the professor. Safarov's little opus (two episodes in five pages) knows no bounds of taste or propriety: shit and fart gags, bestiality, sexual perversions of all stripes, graphic violence. Yet the biggest transgression involves the Russian taboo against *nenormativnaia leksika* or foul language—a taboo Safranov's criminal underground antihero breaks with abandon.

Man-Mold would fit quite easily in another "alternative" anthology project, *Razchlenyonka* ("Dismembered Bodies"), spearheaded by the outspoken artist Daniil Kuzmichov and the caricaturist and Krokodil veteran Sergei Repyov. Kuzmichov broke with KomMissia after the 2005 festival (a choice opinion about Khikhus: "He is a shit."). An ardent blogger, and creator of the pirate-adventure series *Thursday's People*, Kuzmichov has a mythic standing among disgruntled factions who chafe under the would-be industry's corporate, clean image of comics.[90] Released in fall 2007, *Razchlenyonka* is the apogee—or nadir—of Russian comics freed from (self-) censorship, conventional morality or the need to be "beautiful." Its contributors, including Lumbricus, Repyov, Kuzmichov, Otto, Grif, Piton, Tania O, Okhotnik and Saville, and Velitov, wallow in depictions of deviant sex and outré violence. Otto's "Cum to Daddy," for example, is a twisted western about a woman fellating her father before shooting his brains out— through his anus (23). Repyov's lubok-like "Life Goes On," meanwhile, centers on a woman whose sexual fulfillment involves repeated dismemberment and "resewing up" at the hospital.

Needless to say, the *Razchlenyonka* style won't be decorating the interiors of Moscow investment firms in the foreseeable future. These independent published works (along with the plethora of adults-only material online, such as Iorsh's *Shitmonster*) do little to advance the industry, but their demented and nonconformist visions certainly propel the art form—and in directions many Russians would never have contemplated when the Soviet Union fell.

Another alternative approach to komiks emerged early in the new century in St. Petersburg, by reputation the liberal "creative" counterpart to Moscow's brute mercantilism. Formed in 2005, SPb. Nouvelles Graphiques united seven young artists with art school, design, and animation backgrounds (most had worked at

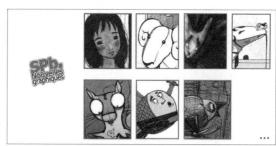

4.12. Advertisement for
SPb. Nouvelles Graphiques'
A Fairy Tale . . . ?, 2005.

the Melnitsa Animation studio): Re-I (Lyudmilla Steblianko); Namida (Anastasia
Vasil'eva); Roma Sokolov; Ilya Maximov; Yozh; El'ru; and Tatka (Tatiana Pogro-
movskaya-Glazyrina). Most have won prizes at KomMissia, including the Grand
Prize for Namida at the 2003 festival. Rendered in an "arthouse" style, their works
follow the Franco-Belgian tradition, especially l'Association. Reflecting their animation background, narrative is often downplayed in their short stories in favor of
visual flair, mood, and lyricism (as in the work of Tema's Lukyanchikov, another
animator).[91]

A Fairy Tale? (2005) displays the group's collaborative ethos and avant-garde
sensibility. Conceived by Re-I, the book splits its story about an imaginative lovelorn cellist into seven chapters or "movements," each handled by one of the artists.
While engaged in advancing the plot (and having to adhere to a "happy ending"
rule), within his/her own aesthetic fiefdom each artist could invent and extrapo-
late at will. This makes *A Fairy Tale?* a disorienting but enthralling experience to
read: each komiksist has a distinctive style, with concomitantly radical shifts in
mood, the characters' appearance, and the reality in which they live. In one chapter, the girl's stuffed toy "friends" look cute and docile, in another dark and menacing. The coauthorship strategy produces a multiperspectival but unitary world,
recalling the reader to the subjectivity of perception. The group has gone on to
publish the themed anthology *Napoleon Is Always Happy* (2006) and the fanzine
ChPKh.[92]

SPb. Nouvelles Graphiques first came together in a 2005 exhibit curated by
Dmitry Yakovlev at the mediathéque of the French Cultural Institute in St. Pe-
tersburg (the show proved so popular it was continued at a city café, Quo Vadis).
Yakovlev went on to found the Komiks Boom International Festival of Drawn
Stories (or Boomfest, as it is popularly known), the second event of its kind in
Russia, which launched in September 2007.

Boomfest 2007 was organized very differently from KomMissia: month-long
exhibits in six locations throughout town showcased work by Osamu Tezuka
(his 1954 version of Dostoyevsky's *Crime and Punishment*); the Finns Tove and
Lars Jansson's classic *Moomintroll* strip; KomMissia winners; Norway's Tor Aerlig
and Lene Ask; and several other artists from Canada, the Balkans, and Germany.

Another exhibit focused on the history of Swiss comics, including Rodolphe Töpffer and Matthias Gnehm. Taking advantage of the September weather, some works were displayed on stands in city parks and streets.

The festival's last three days concentrated lectures, master classes, performances, and film screenings at the Anna Akhmatova Museum and the Sheremetev Garden. Guests included André-Marc Delocque-Fourcaud; Kristiina Kolehmainen, head of Serieteket, the Swedish comics library in Stockholm; Olga Davtyan, instructor at St. Petersburg's Smolny Institute, the rare Russian instructor who has taught a course on French and Russian comics; and Khikhus. The festival also held a digital comics competition through *ZhZh*. Contestants produced work reflecting the theme, "Stories of the City." The top-ten stories were selected through an Internet vote and a professional jury, and displayed in the last ten days of the festival. The top-three winners were Elena Uzhinova, Andrei "Drew" Tkalenko (both Moscow), and Elena Komarkevich (St. Petersburg).

Boomfest sponsors included several European consulates, the firms Wacom, Coreldraw, Lunokhod-1, the *St. Petersburg Times*, *Afisha*, and others. According to statistics compiled by the festival, over five thousand visitors took part in the event, of which about 50 percent were between the ages of sixteen and thirty. Guests for Boomfest 2 in September 2008 included the French graphic novelist David B., the American artist Gary Baseman, and the English journalist and publisher Paul Gravett. An exhibit on the 1990s journal *Mukha* took place. Noted Boomfest's catalog: "We are certain that, with the help of educational and enlightening programs, Russian society will come to agree that comics, like literature, painting and film, is its own independent form in art" (3).

BREAD AND PASTRIES

This is fucked up . . .
I don't have a single reason to love this shitty world.
But for some reason I love it anyway.
—TISHCHENKOV, *THE CAT*

A weighty, expensive hardback from the trendy Artemy Lebedev studio, Oleg Tishchenkov's *The Cat* appeared in time to go on sale at KomMissia VII in 2008. The collection of one-page dialogues between an unnamed man and his cat follows no particular order or thematic line: in a typical post-Soviet apartment, the two discuss the weather, the motion of water in a tub, insomnia, walking along ledges. They are frank exchanges between men in a modern vernacular which, while not as coarse as *The Man-Mold* (nothing is as coarse as *The Man-Mold*), comfortably incorporates profanity.

Two aspects of Tishchenkov's work strike me as representative of komiks as it approaches the second decade of the twenty-first century. Firstly, this is the sort of witty, adult-oriented, lumpen-philosophical entertainment at which many in the genre excel. In any country it would deserve a wide readership. Secondly, its price: a wince-inducing 1,450 rubles ($60) at the KomMissia book stall, putting it well out of the price range of many at the festival—yet it hardly belonged in the same league as the 2006 collected edition of Evrosenia Kersnovskaya's works, *How Much Is a Man Worth?* at 6,747 rubles ($281) or Mikhail Zlatkovsky's 2006 illustrated history *Russian Caricature* at 8,000 rubles ($333).[93] *The Cat*, in other words, was another significant comics publication oriented to the wealthy, few of whom have much interest in comics. Its natural audience, meanwhile, makes do with Internet scans, infrequent publications, and resentment that things aren't getting better.

The "historical" portion of this study, now coming to a close, has tried to show how Russian comics arrived at such predicaments. Marginalized from their earliest forms by a class which equated the Word with civilization and the "people's pictures" with trash; attacked by the Soviets for its whiff of bourgeois, American mass culture; dismissed and exiled to the net by a capitalist petro-state which saw little use for such impecunious, "semiliterate" scribbles. Yet all along komiks survived, at times out in the open (the lubok publisher Sytin was a wealthy man), at others in the interstices of Russian culture (the imprisoned Sysoev). Mostly, though, they occupied a sort of middle ground, comics in all but name—ROSTA windows, *Veselie Kartinki*, propaganda booklets—before exposure to imports doomed komiksisty to bottom-feeding in their own market. At the same time, comics are everywhere in contemporary Russia for those who look; to cite one example: the ubiquitous "Preved" youth movement's emblem, the altered John Lurie painting *Bear Surprise*, which shows a bear with its paws in the air disturbing a couple *in flagrante delicto*, its speech balloon declaring, "Preved!"[94]

But, at the same time that comics are everywhere, komiks are nowhere—or almost nowhere. The bitterness over the failed industry, slow development of the art form, its semi-exile to the online realm, leads to occasional eruptions, anger, blind lashing out—as seen immediately after KomMissia 2008. Widespread dissatisfaction over the judging was all it took to uncork a seething cauldron of recriminations and vitriol, which boiled over for weeks on the Internet forums—Khikhus on one side, Zaslavsky on the other.

The riven komiks world at that point found its inadvertent allegory in *The Cat*, as Tishchenkov's everyman bitterly drowns his sorrows over some setback. "Why are you doing this!" says the cat, trying to pep-talk his friend. "Of course I understand you, but come on, you know you never realized what they needed and how they think. They're just totally different beasts!" The man grabs the feline by the neck, and growls, "Listen here, 'beast'! You better shut your trap, or I'll castrate you!"

Russian readers are indeed "totally different beasts," and komiksisty are still figuring out how to reach them—those who have not given up in disgust. This is why artists like Akishin, Uzhinova, Litichevsky, Ayoshin, Velitov, the SPb. Nouvelles Graphiques group, Khikhus, Nikolai Maslov, and others, spanning generations and styles, who continue to produce works regardless of remuneration, for sheer devotion to the medium—offer an important model for komiks' sustained development as an art form. (An industry, of course, is another matter.)

A May 26, 2008, post on his *zhzh* page by the KOM veteran Iorsh captures what I mean. In a response to the pop singer Dima Bilan's win at the 2008 Eurovision Song Contest (with *Never Let You Go*), Iorsh produced a retreaded ROSTA window, complete with a fat, top-hatted bourgeois holding Bilan in his palm, rhyming couplets, and mobilized masses. The plot is the classic formula of consciousness-raising, only in this case the goal of *partiinost'* or party spirit is replaced with an anticorporate message: the hero Mitya flouts MTV drivel, becomes a turntable DJ and drives the bourgeois popsters out of town. The lyrics (minus the rhyme):

The Burzhuis sponsor all these Bilans
and we don't have enough for drums!

Today with him skates [professional skater Yevgeny] Plyushchenko,
Tomorrow he'll sing at some banquet with [Ukrainian President Viktor]
Yushchenko.

How can we avoid letting the bourgeois plague
Enslave our hearts and minds?

Proletariats, don't delay for a moment
Master a hand instrument

Or take your place behind a turntable
So techno will destroy the bourgeois crap.

Go make your proletarian dances
Don't give the "pops" the tiniest chances!

The final panel shows a crowd holding a banner that reads, "Down with depressing shit!" Iorsh's mini-tirade drinks deep of komiks' traditions for an all-

4.13. Untitled Mitya comics by Iorsh, 2008.

too contemporary protest. No appreciation of the piece, despite the post-Soviet theme, is complete without knowledge of its 1920s antecedents; the ghost of Mayakovsky nods. Such allusive and complex works (ironic and at the same time "serious") combat enduring prejudices against the form as *nizkoprobnyi* or base; they also carve out a niche (specific references, themes, and look) for the indigenous art of komiks within world comics culture—even while, as mentioned, that local specificity remains under threat from globalization, U.S. cultural imperialism, and other realities.

In a 2003 *Ogonyok* interview, the artist Ilya Falkovsky noted that modern komiks material runs the gamut from *Dimych and Timych* to mythological adventures to the "taboo zones of human consciousness: scatology, drugs, porn, fights between rappers and skinheads" (Arkhangel'skii: 48). He celebrated the opening of a permanent komiks installation at the Tretyakov Gallery's Krimsky Val branch in Moscow, which he touted as a major step up in cultural respectability for a long-ignored and maligned form. But then Falkovsky, like some in Russia, takes things a bit too far, overselling comics as a way to "work through" the trauma of the 9-11 attacks: "They're their own sort of therapy: with the help of comics on 'tragic themes,' we can relieve pathological sensations. Through this means, the comics reader can perceive both terror and unmotivated cruelty with a lower level of personal involvement. Komiks, it turns turn out, can heal too" (Arkhangel'skii: 49). Not that comics, like all great art and literature, can't be "used" to widen one's views of life, et cetera, but Falkovsky's discourse strikes me as an echo of the belief in the Russian Orthodox icon's miraculous powers of healing.[95] It would help komiks more, it seems to me, for komiksisty to avoid the all-too Russian penchant for the messianic and utopian, which in the opinion of Erofeyev has ruined much otherwise decent Russian literature.[96]

At the same time, after all those generations spent in the cultural wilderness, komiksisty should certainly not sell komiks short. Kuzmichov, at KomMissia 2005, began his talk before an adoring crowd with something that rattled me: "Let's remember that we, komiksisty, are not baking bread. We're baking pastries."

Again, I have nothing against pastries, and komiks certainly should be in the business of providing pleasure—even harmless diversion—to their readers. But pleasure is a manifold concept, extending from escapism to juvenile scatology to memoir, to political tracts and metaphysical discourse, from (a handy example) *Dimych and Timych* to *Keshka* to *Research of Text*, from Khikhus's Eastern-philosophy-derived comix to SPb. Nouvelles Graphiques' aestheticism to Iorsh's rants to Maslov's somber autobiographical works, to many other possibilities. "Pastries" doesn't quite seem to convey that scope.

When it comes to komiks and what to think of them, Russians have never found what they call the *zolotaia seredina*, the "golden" middle ground. Instead, they have trampled, excoriated, scorned, and misunderstood them. The next several chapters of this study, devoted to case studies spanning the late- and post-Soviet eras, will attempt to demonstrate that Russians might do better simply to accept, appreciate, and enjoy komiks as a wayward part of their artistic patrimony, and welcome them home.

The 13th Book of the Revelations of John, by Ilya Savchenkov, part of the 2003 *Apocalypse Today* show.

Icon of St. Elias, the Novgorod School, sixteenth century.

Icon of the Battle Between the Men of Novgorod and the Men of Suzdal, the Novgorod School, fifteenth century.

Yaga Baba Fights the Corcodile [sic], eighteenth-century lubok.

October Idyll, by Mstislav Dobuzhinsky, 1905.

The Soviet Turnip, poster by Dmitry Moor, 1925.

Rosta Window No. 274, by Vladimir Mayakovsky, 1921.

"How Smart Masha Tidied up the Garden," by Boris Malakhovsky and Daniil Kharms (Chizh, November 1936).

TASS Window No. 747: Fritz's Caftan, poster by KuKryNiksy, 1940s.

Hit Them 'Til They're Dead! poster by Nikolai Zhukov, 1944.

The Incredible Adventures of the Famed
Traveler Petia Ryzhik and his Loyal Friends
Mik and Muk, by Ivan Semenov (Merry
Pictures, 1964).

Advertisement for KOM publications,
1991. Art by Yury Zhigunov.

The Crew, an existentialist parody of militarism by Alexei Lukyanchikov, 1992.

Satan shows the different ways to burn (or boil) in hell in Vladimir Sakov's The Adventures of Captain Donki, 1990.

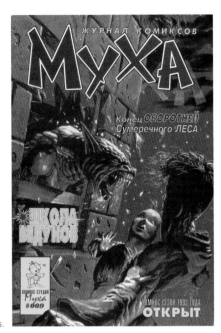

Mukha (The Fly), the most successful comics anthology series of the 1990s.

Nika, the first Russian manga series, by Bogdan, 2002.

Litichevsky before his canvas *Muhammad Ali in the Russian Forest*, 2005.

From *In Process* by Ostretsov (a joint exhibit with Litichevsky), 2005.

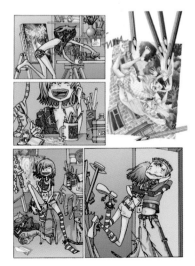

"Angel, Don't Be Sad," by Natalya Bronnikova, 2004.

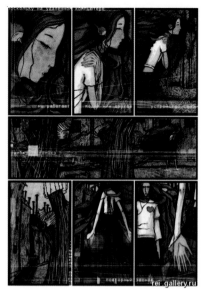

"Menia.net," by Re-I, 2004.

Love and the modern Russian woman:
"I Want," by Uzhinova, 2007.

PART II

CLOSE READINGS

ARTKOMIKS IN THE MUSEUM

Judging by these works, comics has become for us the most
important of the arts. In any event, practically all the participants touch on this genre, offering full-blown parodies
of young people's photo novels (in the case of Lyudmila
Gorlova), or little autobiographical stories with attempts at
philosophy (in the case of Georgy Litichevsky), or absurdist agit-prop in the spirit of the ROSTA Windows (Georgy
Ostretsov) . . .
—MOIST

Writing on the 2003 group exhibit "Viewing Area" at Moscow's Central
House of the Artist, Vladimir Moist betrays the bemusement of some Russian art critics toward the significant trend of comics appropriation in the
post-Soviet era. His sardonic phrase "for us the most important of the arts"
mocks a well-known utterance attributed to Lenin, "cinema is for us the most
important of the arts." (Recall that the KOM publication *KOM-paniia* had
made the same pun in 1988 and had thrown in a drawing of Lenin reading
comics to boot.) Similarly, the *Kultura* critic Konstantin Bokhorov, assessing
the 2007 KomMissia Festival, comes off as both perturbed and contemptuous: he calls his review "A Modern Day Balagan," referring to a traditional
form of Russian low farce or traveling circus show—though today the word
connotes a chaotic mess. The walls of the M'ars Gallery seem to him an inappropriate venue for a comics show. Citing Clement Greenberg and Ro-
land Barthes, Bokhorov lectures the reader on the derivative nature of low
art. He concludes, "My diagnosis: there is no mystery to comics; it is pornographically obvious. Pornographically, because contemporary graphic art has
achieved an absolute consubstantiality (tozhdestvennost') with reality. Today
that reality is the commercialization of life."

We see here that even the rarefied Russian art scene (in recent years infused with cash by the nouveau riche) retains a whiff of Soviet-era disdain for comics as a "bourgeois" pseudo-art form that destroys minds and souls. Yet since the early 1990s, with the new possibilities for exhibition and foreign influence, Russian modern artists experimented with, and in some cases embraced, comics iconography, "mainstreaming" it in a way the Nonconformists could not have done in the late-Soviet period. ArtKomiks (a label not all these artists would accept) forms a mostly separate branch of comics practice in contemporary Russia which privileges exhibition over publication. This was now another tool, another color, available to the Russian palette after the collapse of the USSR, noted Andrei Erofeyev, director of the Novel Trends department at the New Tretyakov Modern Art Gallery: "Although the genre of comics was not at all an invention of Russia, well, naturally, many Russian artists have fallen under the charm of [its] foreign imagery. In Russia today, the culture of comics is only picking up speed. It is greedily swallowing up all possible Western images: from American pop academicism of flying patriotic 'spidermen' to European expressionistic comics existentialism" (Kravtsova: 91). Erofeyev raised eyebrows by including the works of such comics-inspired artists as Georgy "Zhora" Litichevsky, Georgy "Gosha" Ostretsov, the Blue Noses group (Alexander Shaburov and Vyacheslav Mizin), and Ilya Kabakov in the Tretyakov's permanent exhibit of contemporary art. (Notably, he feels no discomfort referring to Kabakov's conceptualist albums, also in the exhibition, as "comics.") But this was simply affirming the new "comics-friendly" landscape of Russian art. From its first inroads in Perestroika (e.g., a display of Yevgeny Zhilinsky's artwork from his comics adaptation of the film *Assa* at the First Biennale of Contemporary Art in Leningrad in 1990), the medium or its devices appeared in, among others, the work of performance artist and transvestite Vladislav Mamyshev-Monroe: photocomics albums recorded his wordless adventures dressed up as various characters, communicating through mime and gesture. In 2003 his photocollage project *Dindin ou Saint-Paparazzi* featured the artist in the role of a Tintin-like personage (complete with cowlick and stuffed dog Snowy). Lyudmilla Gorlova participated in this 1990s trend as well, with her photonovels *Happy End* and *How I Love*. In 2006 she executed Pop-Art works for her show *Hidden Threat*. The PG Group (Ilya Falkovsky, Alexei Katalin, and Boris Spiridonov) incorporated comics, video, film, and installation for their scatological and scandalous depictions of teenagers, skinheads, criminal acts, drug use, and petty terrorism.

The artists Leonid Tishkov represents yet another longtime practitioner of a comics-like art. A physician and poet, since the 1980s he has produced multimedia series centered on his "Dabloids" mythology of creatures shaped as feet, stomachs, and other internal organs. Many prints utilize speech balloons and sequential narrative strategies. Finally, the 1980s New Wave of young artists pursuing visions based on popular iconography—rock, fashion, comics—came onto its own in the

5.1. *A Fairy Tale* by the PG group (2003) parodies the illustrations of Ivan Bilibin for its depiction of punks, drug addicts, and skinheads.

1990s in the practice of Litichevsky, Sergei Anufriev, Andrei Royter, Daniil Filippov, Pavel Pepperstein, Nikita Alekseev, and Ostretsov.[1]

Indeed, comics—as ArtKomiks—had gained more acceptance in the art world than at newsstands and bookstores in the decade and a half since the Soviet collapse (resistant critics notwithstanding).[2] This interest in the form culminated in the 2004–2005 exhibit *Bubble: Comics in Contemporary Art* at Moscow's Guelman Gallery. Promoted as an opportunity for artists to experiment with "comics in the absence of comics" (given the medium's relative rarity in Russia), the show featured work by Litichevsky, Ostretsov, the Blue Noses, the PG group, Zoya Cherkasskaya, Mamyshev-Monroe, and others.

In his artist's statement to *Bubbles*, Litichevsky described the situation for Art-Komiks in the post-Soviet era:

We cannot ignore the fact that, before anything else, comics is a complex and somewhat alien phenomenon for Russia. And if in America the comics medium was elevated to an elite status by Roy Lichtenstein as early as the 1960s, in Russia it is looked upon with derision to this day. Precisely for this reason Russian artists working in the comics style find themselves in a dual position: they ironicize traditional comics, engaging in its deconstruction—while nevertheless, at the same time, inculcating comics into their audience, propagandizing for it. This constitutes the chief difference of our position from that of the West: however freely and casually we ourselves may deal with comics, we must simultaneously convey our conviction that comics [itself] is a phenomenon worthy of attention. (Litichevsky and Ostretsov 2004)

ArtKomiks artists—heirs to the Sots-Art movement of the late-Soviet era—work in a cultural milieu preconditioned to view comics exclusively through the prism of Pop Art, a situation which cuts both ways. Can one, in Russia, ever say something unironically "serious" through the comics form (as one can in France, Japan, the United States . . .)? As Ostretsov has noted: "In the Russian tradition a different artistic language, that of conceptualism, took root, so comics, a somewhat 'alien,' exotic, colorful, mass culture form, inevitably polemicizes with the profound, rather heavy-handed conceptualist approach, which is oriented more towards text (as opposed to the simple exclamations of comics)" (ibid.).

ArtKomiks had to carve out its own space within the conceptualist sphere for the medium to go beyond humor (though not beyond irony), while retaining its subversive edge.

THE "QUINTESSENTIALLY RUSSIAN" COMICS OF ZHORA LITICHEVSKY

I was making comics before I knew they existed in nature.
—LITICHEVSKY

Born in 1956, Georgy "Zhora" Litichevsky trained as a historian of the ancient world[3] and as an artist and has exhibited frequently in the Moscow and European art scenes.[4] He has been drawing humorous comics in a crude, naïve style since childhood.[5] Like other unpublished komiksisty in the Soviet era, he shared his work with friends. In 1993, he became a founding editorial board member of the influential *Arts Journal* (Khudozhestvenniy zhurnal), where he continues to publish his satirical comics work, which sometimes mocks the Moscow art scene itself. A series about a pair of prostitutes who take in a filthy homeless man first appeared there and was later turned into a parodic calendar[6] as part of a 1995 XL Gallery exhibit *Impropriety, or The Erotic in Comics*.

In the 1990s his comics appeared in the youth-oriented magazine *Ptyutch* and in other publications, but Litichevsky's practice was much more about taking his work into "the real world" through enlargement, applied art, performance, and other means. His self-invented "Slide Comics"—drawn directly onto transparency film and projected onto walls—proved a way of displaying his work at secret gatherings in the 1970s and 1980s, when publication was not possible, but it also blew up comics into a spectacle meant for mass consumption. Slide comics nostalgically recalled the "dia-films" most Soviet children grew up with—even as they parodied the form with more sophisticated subject matter. His "Lecture on the Spider," for example, consists of over seventy slides detailing the confrontation between a lecturer and an anthropomorphic insect family. To a staccato-like rhythm which Litichevsky played up through commentary (like a rayoshnik), visions of the metaphysical "spider" fill the wall-screen: spider sun, sea-spider-snake, spider-guitar, spider-goat, spider-earth—all variations of Steve Ditko's design for the Spiderman costume. The "spider" comes to dominate the universe. One may imagine the guffaws provoked by such works, given that in the Soviet era Spiderman

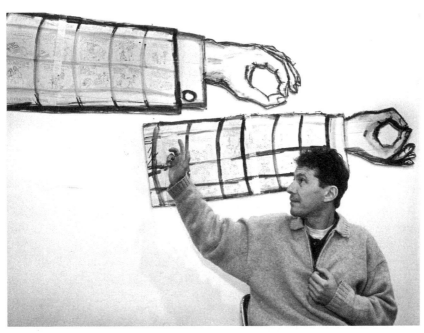

5.2. Georgy "Zhora" Litichevsky before his "monumental" exhibit *Impropriety, or The Erotic in Comics*, 1995.

amounted to a sort of "forbidden fruit" and marker of Western decadence (recall Kukarkin's views on the genre).

Litichevsky's comics have appeared in other nontraditional settings (beaches, parks, theatrical stages) and media (linen, cardboard, papier-mâché, painting), all oriented toward integrating them into everyday life and/or other arts practices.[7] For the 1993 action *The Horror of Emptiness*, for example, he set out pages of his comics along the stairs leading into the large Rossia Movie Theater in central Moscow. Passersby were encouraged to read them, walking up or down the steps. Comics also appear in his elaborate performance art, frequently based on ancient Roman or other classical sources, which combine paper costumes, loud music, pyrotechnic lighting, video, and absurdist poetry. In 2005, Litichevsky opened a group exhibit,[8] Madame Korobochka, at Moscow's Dom Cultural Center with an hour-long multimedia performance that included elements of screechingly loud acid rock, Euripides, pitchforks, cardboard boxes stacked to serve as a video projection screen, inflatable animals, duck-shaped life-preservers, comics, green mummies, and scatological phrases screamed above the din.

Even in the relatively traditional setting of the gallery, Litichevsky's ArtKomiks appear as oversized murals, or "leap" off the canvas as characters in cardboard cutouts which mill about the space, or flicker in short films, or attain monolithic status. With Ostretsov, he launched the theory of "Total Comics," which seeks to create monumental works out of the marginalized medium. In his 1995 *Impropriety*, for example, he placed the comics inside two huge cartoon arms in coat sleeves. His 2006 *Militiaman* series of paintings makes each canvas a separate panel: the policemen meditate and perform yoga, seeming to move from work to work. In 2007, Litichevsky returned to his roots, so to speak, with the "exhibit/self-portrait" *Eternal Student.* He set himself the task of re-creating the many comics scribbles from his student notebooks, long lost, in oversized form. He meticulously depicted the texture and look of notebook paper, including its lines, along with the drawings in marker and colored pen—a Lichtensteinian exercise in zero-degree reproduction and nostalgia.

As noted by the exhibit's press release: "Whatever [Litichevsky] has done, it has all been a form of comics; in fact, he himself is perceived as some kind of comics character, his own species of 'comics-man' (komiks-chelovek)." This point is crucial: as a continuation of his art practice, Litichevsky embodies a "comics persona" not unlike the post-Soviet performance art self-inventions of Mamyshev-Monroe, the conceptualist poet Dmitry Prigov or the Actionist Oleg Kulik. This too represents an attempt to "bring comics to the people."

For all the elite, cosmopolitan posturings of Litichevsky's Russian modern art milieu (where he is a long-recognized figure), I will argue that this artist adheres to the most "quintessentially Russian" of komiks practices. Litichevsky advances what he considers comics' inherently subversive nature (part of the medium's appeal among the underground since the 1960s, for figures such as Slava Sysoev). This subversion is aesthetic as well as content driven. His scratchy, "crude" style[9] recalls the handmade nature of many lubki—though in a way different from the works of Alexei Kapninsky, who more faithfully reproduces the look itself. Litichevsky, however, atavistically suggests the *"ghost"* of the lubok, in a way not dissimilar to how Eddie Campbell's style recalls Victorian-era engravings in the graphic novel *From Hell* (2000).[10]

Finally, Litichevsky follows a "quintessentially Russian" muse in his approach to comics themselves (as opposed to their elaborate "framing") by first and foremost treating them as a narrative, text-based medium. As he told an interviewer in 2006: "I'm interested in uniting intellectualism with brutal aesthetics and a representational/narratival structure" (Miskarian: 89). In other words, Litichevsky embraces Russian *literaturnost'*; he in fact was initially attracted to comics precisely because they allowed him to tell stories, however nonsensical. "All the best Russian artists share the same addiction to literaturnost', from Repin and Surikov to the Moscow Conceptualists," he said in 1988. "A word should share its rights with things, signs and images. Putting them together you can achieve in some instances a magical effect where the word becomes flesh" (Litichevsky and Royter).

Comics for him always retain an ironic edge,[11] but unlike in full-blown Sots-Art—which would only quote established iconography so as to show up its hollowness—Litichevsky resists the "empty referent" reading of his work. As he told me in 1996:

I have to allude to Russian art, with lots of visual and literary history inter-twined. Russia is the land of literature, of Tolstoy, Dostoyevsky. [Word and image] often meet in Moscow artists' works, like those of the Conceptualists, but if conceptualism in America uses texts that have no meaning, in Russia the text does have some sort of meaning. This is not simply some sort of composition of words or citations deprived of any sense, taken at random from a diction-ary, like in the work of Joseph Kosuth. In Russia the text retains its link to something concrete, or to something depicted in a literary work. Therefore, when I make use of literary texts, this is very much in the tradition of Moscow Conceptualism. But insofar as I understand the general world situation and in particular the role of comics in it, and since, in my opinion, the role of comics is growing in the art world, I think that it is completely natural, this unification of image and text. This unification leads to comics. And I speak not only of myself, although I find it hard to think of someone else doing precisely what I'm doing. (my emphasis)

Through recurring personages such as meditating policemen, psychopathic ants, anthropomorphized crossword puzzles, and prostitutes, Litichevsky is a fount of storytelling. Through frequent, erudite allusions to Russian literature, art, history, and culture, his is a specifically Russian brand of storytelling in the classical, nine-teenth-century tradition. Though parodic and "silly," his works often treat tradi-tional Russian themes: the Slavic soul versus European rationality; the healing power of art; the "little man" versus the state; and a Russian attribute usually asso-ciated with the works of Nikolai Gogol: a tragicomic "laughter through tears."

Furthermore, we can think of Litichevsky's work—for all its visual "contami-nation" of a "pure" textual culture—as very much in line with the Russian literary tradition of experimenting with form. (This is how we should read such utter-ances as "A word should share its rights with things, signs, and images. Putting them together you can achieve in some instances a magical effect where the word becomes flesh.")

The subject of literary form consumed the founders of modern Russian litera-ture in the early nineteenth century as they struggled to define themselves apart from their Western European counterparts.[12] By midcentury, Gogol would fa-mously write an "epic poem" in prose, *Dead Souls* (1842), in the form of a novel, while Alexander Pushkin would produce a novel, *Yevgeny Onegin* (1823–1831), written in verse. To the Russians these were never just questions of literary experi-mentation and identity formation; rather, this was often a subtle form of subver-sion, which in some cases might help get one's manuscript past the czarist censors.

5.3. *Roman Scribbles*, by Litichevsky, features a Russian version of Tintin and "Stalkerzan" (1990s).

We can see here, then, how Litichevsky could perceive a visual/verbal mix such as comics primarily as an attractively literary *and* an appealingly subversive practice.

As in *Lecture on the Spider*, Litichevsky's ArtKomiks evince an awareness of comics history and its rich store of international characters to celebrate and mock. These works are syntheses of the local and global, a "comicspace" where figures of the most disparate periods and sensibilities interact and merge. This is clear even in the title of the 1990s story "Roman Scribbles" (Rimskie karakuli), a pun on the 1953 William Wyler film *Roman Holiday* (in Russian, *Rimskie kanikuly*). But this only begins to unravel its many delirious and wide-ranging references: its hero is a crude Russian version of Tintin (cowlick again), prone to vandalism. He is saved from arrest by "Stalkerzan" (a blend of Tarzan and the Stalker, antihero of the Strugatskys' *Roadside Picnic* and Andrei Tarkovsky's film), who swoops through the air like Superman but dresses like the lord of the jungle. Tintin winds up in Rome, site of many other classical and literary references.[13]

But Litichevsky's komiks are at their most Russian, of course, when he evokes his native history and literary tradition. Without being a straight adaptation, "Russian Women" adapts the work of the nineteenth-century poet Nikolai Nekrasov, on the devotion of Maria Volkhonskaya to her husband, Sergei Volkhonsky (leader of the Decembrists, a group of army officers who failed to overthrow the czar in 1825). "Dance of the Sabres" treats the interactions of several 1920s cultural lights: Anatoly Lunacharsky, Soviet commissar of education; the dancer Isadora Duncan; her husband, the poet Sergei Esenin; and his lover, the Armenian dancer Shagane—celebrated in his 1924 poem "Shagane, you are mine, Shagane!"—who turns out to also be Scheherazade, the weaver of tales from *1,001 Nights*. Among Litichevsky's most delirious "remixes" of Russian cultural history with a comics sensibility is "The Choice of Levitantan," which posits the nineteenth-century landscape painter Isaac Levitan as a middle-aged Tintin with a beard. The story is set in some bizarre parallel nineteenth century in which Levitantan is the "leading komiksist of our era"; accompanied by his faithful dog Milasha, he advocates creating comics out in the open, even at the risk of rain. His theory of "pleine air" comics, he argues, "will secure authentic communication." The story mocks crank theories of the sort often imported from the West, as well as the lovable crank himself.

More than the aforementioned, Litichevsky's short story "Café of the Poets,"[14] with its poignant allusions to major Russian cultural icons, transcends what he himself describes as the "limiting, comic" nature of the medium (1996). Another fictionalized account of the poet Esenin and his American wife, Duncan, the story unfolds in an oneiric, alogical play of words and images that echo the anxieties of this famously troubled relationship.

The primitivist style of drawing, with thicker lines, harkens back more insistently to the lubok, while the page layout contains many borderless panels, for a more dreamlike mood. Esenin, frustrated over Isadora's celebrity in Russia, suffers nightmares in which she flies away from him, shattering panel borders. Wakened by Isadora and a boisterous crowd of friends, Esenin complains to his wife, but she only answers, "Ah, Esenin, in your country everybody loves me so much. It's so difficult not to return their love" (77). She nods off to sleep, leaving Esenin to go for a walk in resentment. He crosses a Russian birch forest in the nineteenth-century landscape tradition (Esenin makes an explicit reference to the painter Nikolai Ovchinnikov), where he encounters several peasants, among them his mother. Esenin, the "peasant poet" from the provinces, reunites with his roots.

Meanwhile, Isadora wakes from her own nightmare: the death of her children in a 1913 Parisian car accident, when they drowned in the Seine. "If they came to life again and one climbed on the shoulders of the other, and if Esenin were also here, they would be exactly the same height," she says. The story concludes with Duncan, rendered in the thick-lined "lubok" style, comparing the heights of her children on one side and Esenin on the other, their figures depicted in thinner lines (79). Since both her children and Esenin preceded Duncan in death, the final panel's visual contrast suggests a missed connection, a thwarted attempt at intimacy; Isadora at last wants to give Esenin the wifely attention he craves, but he's already gone.

5.4. *Café of the Poets*, by Litichevsky, 1997.

Litichevsky's most sustained and allusive work in a Russian literary vein is his 1997 story "She Is Anna" (Ona—Anna). This recounts the story of the middle-aged Count Leo Tolstoy, sometime in the 1860s, running into a mysterious woman at the theater. He recalls her face from his earliest infancy, when, he remembers, she swooped out of the sky to save him, still in his baby carriage, from wild animals. Now, leaving his own wife at the theater, obsessed with discovering the woman's identity, he follows home the alluring, black-tressed, black-attired stranger. Surprise: Leo Nikolayevich is invited into the strange lady's home by her aged husband. We discover that her name is Anna, that her husband's family name is Karenin, that the dashing officer escorting her, who is obviously her lover, is called Vronsky. In short, this is *the* Anna Karenina, the woman destined to become the author's heroine, to flee her stifling married life and take up residence with Vronsky in Italy, to die heartbroken by suicide at the end of one of the most beloved novels of all time.

But here and now in this house, Karenin turns out to be a willing cuckold. Karenin gets rid of the meddlesome writer, sees Anna off on her nightly flight through the ether above the city (reminiscent of the witches in Mikhail Bulgakov's *The Master and Margarita*), and talks Vronsky into immediately spiriting his wife out of Russia—to Italy. "You see," he says, "how this scribbling count has taken an interest in Anna. Just wait a bit, and the whole world will know what we've all been up to here." The rest of the story deals with Anna and Vronsky's flight from a persistent Tolstoy, always in hot pursuit—an author in search of two

5.5. *She is Anna*, by Litichevsky, a rewriting of Tolstoy's *Anna Karenina*, 1997.

characters. Finally, to throw him off their trail once and for all, Karenin instructs Anna to fake her own suicide, by seeming to fall under a train. This she does, just as the count is running up along the platform to catch her. But her "death" only results in the reunion that Tolstoy has longed for, as they meet at last in the sky in a sort of bizarre nirvana.[15]

Litichevsky is playing several games at once here. First, he is obviously inverting the plot, characters, and motivations of the novel *Anna Karenina*, among the most sacred of sacred cows in Russian culture, as well as world literature. He doesn't really change anything, however, since all the characters essentially do the same things, only for different reasons.[16] Second, he participates in a time-honored Russian literary tradition: rewriting the lives of historical figures and authors, blurring the line between reality and fiction. For example, the formalist Yuri Tynianov composed a grotesque semi-fictional biography of Peter the Great, *The Wax Figure* (1932); Vladimir Nabokov produced a very unflattering life of the nineteenth-century Soviet darling Nikolai Chernyshevsky in his 1937–1938 novel *The Gift*; while more recently Tatyana Tolstaya, in her 1996 short story "A Plot," muses on what might have happened had Russia's greatest poet Alexander Pushkin survived the duel that actually killed him in 1837: among other things, he grows to a ripe old age, living long enough to kick Vladimir Ilyich Ulyanov (Lenin) in the head. Other post-Soviet authors, like Pyotr Aleshkovsky, Viktor Pelevin, and Vladimir Sorokin, delight in writing alternate histories, including of well-known cultural figures.[17]

By humorously injecting Tolstoy into a komiks version of his own famous story, as well as conflating the supernaturally beautiful Anna Karenina with a Slavic pagan witch, Litichevsky in "She Is Anna" blurs the divisions between high and low culture, literary and folkloric registers, text and image,[18] modern comics and traditional lubok. At the same time, he gently pokes fun at the great writer's pretensions, and at his unblemished, messianic reputation among cultured Russians. Moreover, the count's heavenly reunion with his muse at the end recalls Yakov Protazanov's 1912 film *Departure of a Great Old Man*, which depicts the last days of Tolstoy in a highly sentimentalized fashion. (At the movie's conclusion, the long-tormented author is personally welcomed into paradise by Jesus Christ himself.) Litichevsky's text captures some of that same campy absurdity, in a more self-conscious vein.[19]

In the fraught milieu of Russian comics, which lacks an industry and remains largely Internet based, Litichevsky's accomplishments in the form—as well as his longevity—are unique. Ten years before KOM released its first publications, Litichevsky was scribbling his student works and projecting his "slide comics," albeit for restricted audiences. Also rare among komiksisty is his feat of appealing to serious art connoisseurs who nonetheless regard him, first and foremost, as the practitioner of a pseudo-art form they would despise and dismiss in any other context:

Everyone knows I'm a comics artist, but also a painter, someone who uses lots of other forms, too. They see me through the prism of Lichtenstein, or of other people who have already used comics for other purposes, with irony. But if I have irony, it's not because of the comics. I sense it differently. Through my exhibition projects, I try to show that comics are a normal art, a regular means of self-expression. In Russia, comics are usually considered something less serious or childish. By working in this medium in Russia, you show that comics can be used in a museum exhibit, they work as art. Also, you can try to just show that comics exist. *That's why my exhibits don't just use some comics that happened to make it into a larger format or a painting—these are actual comics in large form, with a beginning and an end. People will go through one of my large-format works and by the end they realize that in order to understand it they have to have accepted the comics in there* as comics. *These are not fragments of comics, as in Lichtenstein; these are complete comics. (1996, emphasis in original)[20]*

In a general climate where komiksisty tend to adopt foreign styles, iconography, and narrative content all too readily, Litichevsky stands as the most vivid exemplar of the principle that komiks should on some overt level reflect—indeed celebrate—their very deep Russian roots.

GOSHA OSTRETSOV AND THE "NEW GOVERNMENT"

The multimedia artist Georgy "Gosha" Ostretsov (born 1967) graduated from the Theater Art School at the Bolshoi Theater in 1984. In the mid-1980s he joined Moscow's art "New Wave," which advanced an avant-garde sensibility and critique under the cover of popular iconography: fashion, comics, rock and roll. He promoted the so-called man style (chelovek-stil') of avant-garde fashion and participated in projects of the Kindergarten (Detsky Sad) group.[21] From 1988 to 1998 Ostretsov lived in Paris, working for the fashion designer Jean-Charles de Castelbajac. He also took part in projects by Jean Paul Gautier, *L'officiel*, and *Vogue*. While in France his interest in latex masks, comics, and the representation of power led to the conception of his large-scale multimedia project *The New Government* (Novoe pravitel'stvo). Upon his return to Moscow, Ostretsov resumed a creative partnership with Litichevsky under the *nomme de guerre* "George and George."[22] Through the 2000s they exhibited together and assisted in each other's projects.

While rather dissimilar, the two artists' sensibilities are complementary and united by their frequent use of comics and comics iconography. Where Litichevsky's works have a handmade quality, orient themselves toward different narrative uses and seem avant-garde more in their unorthodox, "monumental" presentation, Ostretsov's comics follow a strategy closer to Sots-Art, whereby they appropriate existing imagery (often from American superhero comics), consequently sport a more polished look, and form only part of a vast, unified vision—an enormous narrative unfolding on a "global" level.

In his *New Government* (NG) project (which he has been working on since the late 1990s but synthesizes themes and iconography present throughout his oeuvre), Ostretsov uses conceptualist irony as a pivot for a parodic *gesamkunstwerk* on the nature of power and despotism in post-Soviet Russia. Recalling the 1980s NSK project in Slovenia, NG combines masks, painting, sports, hymn, graffiti, text, fashion, advertising, photography, performance art, video, komiks, ROSTA windows, propaganda posters, and other media to create a parallel world in which "masked aliens" have taken over Russia and—aided by a compliant communications industry—rule it with an iron fist (at least, this seems the case; power by its nature is ambiguous and totalizing, like the New Government itself). Ostretsov plays various personages in the project, both masked and unmasked, including the leader of the new regime, its propaganda minister, and even a dissident. In one of many press dispatches, Russia's new rulers proclaim:

As the acting organ of power, the New Government must demonstrate its operative status; closely watch over the mass media, so that the reality of historical events does not undergo distortion; react quickly to disasters; carry out a policy of scientific-technological progress; provide for the evacuation of the globe's

5.6. *Freedom at the State Barricades* (parody of Eugène DelaCroix's 1830 *Liberty Leading the People*), by Georgy "Gosha" Ostretsov (2002), part of the artist's New Government project.

population in the event of planetary catastrophe; vigilantly ensure general adherence to the Constitution; act as a punitive power; give some attention to the development and support of cultural-educational activities; and engage as much as possible the intellectual potential of man. (Ostretsov 2002)

Providing, in the artists' words, a "wonderful and safe opportunity to realize a social utopia," the NG program (brought to life through Ostretsov's exhibits, installations, publications, and performances) has everything one would expect of a totalitarian regime: visits to factories and electricity plants by state bureaucrats, national monuments, politburo meetings, sporting matches (e.g., wrestling), propaganda posters, torture of political dissidents, and much else, all executed by soulless figures in bizarre latex masks whose shapes conform to ranks within the new society. Everything is based on efficiency, spectacle, and "remaking" oneself into an anonymous consumer. As the leaders tell their citizens: "We don't need to see your face, and you don't get to see ours" (Ostretsov 2002). The New Government has even spawned its own antithesis: antigovernment demonstrations by the émigré community, held safely in London.

Ostretsov plays a knowing game with the post-Soviet reader/viewer, in a polished and derivative style. The artist uses the language and syntax of the PR industry to create a shimmering, gonzo dystopian reality that looks equal parts Darth Vader and Madison Avenue (the photos of the masked "leaders" visiting factories seem to come from some demented industrial brochure). Ostretsov designed his deranged vision to circulate virally throughout the culture; it therefore makes for a funny—if disconcerting—experience to see an NG slogan or caricature on a Moscow fence, hear the NG hymn or catch sight of an illustrated spread, "From the Field of the Fantastic," featuring masked NG figures in the fashion magazine *NRG*.

While the project's cutting questions—Does power have a face? Do people have a predilection for tyranny? Is the modern way of life oriented toward

5.7. *Blast* (2001) from Ostretsov's *Heroica* series.

conformity and authoritarianism?—could apply globally,[23] NG has several features that identify it as particularly neo-Soviet, and in ways which resonate quite strikingly with the rising authoritarianism of Putin's Russia. Most obviously, its masked autocrats dress in contemporary Western fashion, speak frankly about world domination, and have learned the PR industry trick of slick presentations, impressive monumental statistics, and efficient management. But other props and culturemes denote specifically Soviet nostalgia, such as propaganda placards, billboards, vaguely military uniforms, an emphasis on physical fitness and the color red. Other illustrations mockingly convey xenophobia, conspiracist paranoia and the total domination of existing human power structures. Lastly, NG boasts the ultimate validation for its continued existence: a costly imperialist war (the subject of the cycle *Heroica*), whose dead and mutilated soldiers are rendered with the clean sleekness of advertising graphics.[24]

Litichevsky[25] describes Ostretsov's "New Government" as

a radical realization of the categorically artistic imperative to visualize the unseen. The artist, stepping into the unusual role of the partner/antagonist, foists upon the invisible state power his own rules of the game, compelling the latter to reveal and manifest itself in the traditional form of a high-ranking person. Although, of course, the rank, the person and in general the face—is only a guessed-at, desired, potential result. The reality or, if you will, the artistic truth which the artist manages to impart, assumes the shape of masks, which are both frightening and alluring at the same time. (Ostretsov 2002)

ПЕНСИИ
ЭКОНОМИКА
БЕЗРАБОТИЦА

5.8. Ostretsov as a masked
New Government official
touting good economic
news, 2004.

And, I would add, pathetic—since, in one performance piece, Ostretsov shows the NG autocrats brought low by traditional Russian vices such as anomie, alcoholism, and stagnation, absolutely corrupted by their own power-mad pretensions. The paradoxical impotence of these usurpers, like that of all leaders to most people most of the time, is signaled by the presence of Lenin (played by an impersonator) at the table, uselessly pontificating to his benumbed political successors.

Ostretsov continues to develop NG iconography and personae in different projects, including works in the permanent "novel trends" department at the New Tretyakov Gallery. Often the NG bureaucrats come into conflict with other "alien" signifying systems, like American superheroes. Among these are Spyder-Girl, a three-armed, mohawked female version of Spiderman, and the "original" Spiderman himself. Similar to the "Ronald Reagan" figure in Dmitry Prigov's verse, these embody American cultural imperialism, rendered mockingly ghoulish. The artist recognizes in the superhero a like form of fascistic will to power veiled by clever, colorful masks. (Ostretsov also undermines the superhero's "playful" appeal by, in part, brutally exposing its homoerotic subtext, as in his 2005 animated short film *Pedy-2*.)

If, as Ostretsov writes, "The main thing is to free man from any encroachment on his individuality. His work duties shouldn't influence his individuality, because man changes, while the mask remains the same," then a 2005 collaboration with Litichevsky serves as a dark reminder of the mask's totalizing menace. *In Process* took up a second-floor wing of the Moscow Center for Contemporary Art, with Ostretsov and Litichevsky's large wall paintings covering opposite sides of the room (the two halves met and "overlapped" in the middle, through the catalyst of a projected looping film starring "George and George" characters).

Ostretsov's Pop-Art-like canvases have been compared to the East German Sigmar Polke, though the works of Alexander Kosolapov seem a more direct influence. *In Process* featured large panels with blow-ups of 1970s Marvel and DC superhero comics—Superman, Batman, Spiderman[26]—reworked into collages that incorporate NG iconography. One depicts Superman with an NG mask, making explicit the link between the corporate superhero and Ostretsov's own power-mad creations. More darkly, the "people" in these panels literally have no words, or even thoughts, of their own: their speech bubbles have been "colonized" by alien imagery, such as Looney Toons and Disney characters. The artist uses a similar strategy in his 2004 contribution to the *Bubble* exhibit, *Gun*: armed men in black suits and tuxedos appear to set off for a confrontation; one of them "says" something, though his speech balloon is filled only with pages from *Spiderman* comics. (The only "word" in the work is the NG stamp at lower right.) Text, which might have served as an escape of sorts, through its link to something beyond the image (as it potentially does in Lichtenstein's canvases) is here absent, foreclosed.[27] Like mirrors turned toward each other, mass culture has no referent or greater "reality" other than itself.

Only as Ostretsov's comics "transformed" into Litichevsky's in the middle of the room did words appear; the slick if "realistic" superhero collages morphed into the plainly caricaturistic Primeval Forest, a continuation of Litichevsky's "psychopathic ants" storyline. These riotous panels, which convey a nonsensical but coherent narrative, are filled with text—offering hope of some mode of agency or quasi-independent thought, even if absurd. This perhaps does not refute Viktor Erofeyev's Marcusian warning of comics as the merry pictures to our own decomposition, but it does point the way to something in the medium beyond "eternally ironic," empty referents.

I do not argue for a return to some logocentric savior, but *In Process* clearly figured a progression, left to right, from a vision of the totalizing, image-based, infantilizing mind control of Ostretsov's American corporate pop culture to Litichevsky's text-driven, narratival, Kharmsian classic-comix approach of fairy tales and—at least a kind of—relative freedom. ArtKomiks syntax and grammar possess sufficient versatility to figure both the homogenization of thought and an alternative to such dystopias. This explains its appeal for Ostretsov; comics—a dismissed and "alien" signifying practice—served as an ideal means to explicitly critique (and mock) the authoritarian turn of life in Putin's Russia.

NEW KOMIKS FOR THE NEW RUSSIANS

A New Russian comes in to buy a car. He tells the salesman
he wants a gray Mercedes. The salesman finds for him exactly
the car he wants, and the man pays for it right out of his pock-
et. As he is about to leave, the salesman asks him, "Didn't you
buy a car just like this from us last week?"

"Oh, yes, I did," replies the New Russian, "but the ashtray
got full."

As described by Anna Krylova in a 1999 essay on Russian subversion, laughter, and jokes, New Russians (novie russkie) are "a post-Soviet sociocultural
category widely used in contemporary Russia to refer, usually unflatteringly,
to the group of people who have 'made it' under the new market-economy
conditions" (261). Recent critical discussions of the New Russians have highlighted both their "mythical" status and their precipitous slide (at least in
their original form) into the dustbin of history.

   Mark Lipovetsky's essay, in a 2003 issue of *Russian Review* devoted to the
subject, begins by asking, "Are Those New Russians Real?" before ceding the
question of their flesh-and-blood ontology to the social scientists and analyz-
ing their very real presence in literary and cultural texts.[1] Harley Balzer's essay
in the same issue turns to their representation in ironic *palekh* boxes sold in
New Russians' World stores (owned by Grigory Baltser, who also produced
the parodic comics version of *Anna Karenina*, discussed below), and emphasizes the fact that "New Russians are very much a product of the state of mind
of Russians who perceive themselves as losers in the [economic] transition"
(19)—a role played by many in the intelligentsia. The thuggish, uncouth arrivistes therefore act as negative-attribute projections of those who sought
to uphold humanist Russian values in the Soviet era, only to lose out economically to the barbarians with the collapse of the USSR. Emil Draitser's
sociological studies of the post-Soviet *anekdot* or joke take up this thread:

"The New Russians of the jokelore are really constructs of the popular wish that all of them were undeservedly wealthy in folkloric terms: stupid, ignorant, greedy, and immoral. These jokes give voice to popular resentment of the new economic realities of post-Soviet Russia. In them, the whole enterprise system is portrayed as criminal, exploitative, and humiliating for workers" (2001). And as Krylova adds: "New Russians are ridiculed for being illiterate, ignorant, and rude. The post-Soviet [joke-teller] implicitly counterpoises his/her civilized behavior, moderate spending habits, and erudition in history, geography, literature, theater, and music to the new beneficiaries of the post-Soviet economy, [who are seen as] narrow-minded and boorish" (261). What all these accounts (and others like them) have in common is the role *desire* plays for the producers and consumers of humor lobbed in the direction of the "New Russians." The thinking seems to go like this: "In a criminal new world, only thieves and morons will succeed, while the genuine Russian soul will languish; therefore if I have not flourished in these new circumstances, it is only because I am too good for this world, while those other monsters in their Mercedes and Lear jets are, of course, corrupt." It is the age-old Russian "little man," helpless before all-powerful social forces and thus making a virtue of that helplessness.[2]

But this only tells part of the story; the snide jokes and sneering dismissals reveal more than mere contempt. For the desire expressed in humor about the New Russians reflects not only ill wishes *toward* them, but positive wishes to *be* them: the masses and "cultured" intelligentsia (categories no less amorphous) see the brutish newcomers and feel a bloodcurdling rage—as well as envy. In a country where the average monthly salary hovers around $550[3] they, too, presumably, would like to wear $10,000 suits; travel first-class to vacation spots all over the world; drive a Mercedes; keep a platoon of bodyguards; spend ten times the per capita yearly income on a bottle of wine; spend a fortune in a casino or over dinner in a Japanese restaurant; cavort with $5,000 prostitutes; build enormous *kottedzhi* (country mansions) or live in a Rublyovka estate with its own helicopter pad[4]—in other words, live the stereotype.

In contrast to the politically minded popular humor of the Soviet era, Krylova writes, "Jokes about the New Russians do not attempt to subvert the new post-Soviet symbolic order grounded on free-market and 'independent individual' . . . values. They suggest no alternatives to the current state of affairs, which is characterized by dramatic social polarization and inversion of social status. On the contrary, post-Soviet jokes demonstrate an enormous fascination with the lives of the 'rich and ignorant'" (261). This fascination overcomes even what the anthropologist Caroline Humphrey calls the extraordinary success of Soviet propaganda against speculators, or people who profit by buying and selling commodities at a mark-up, without adding any value through their own labor. (This is the popular presumption of how the New Russians accumulate wealth, at least those who are not full-fledged mafiosi, thieves, and embezzlers.) In spite of such beliefs, and probably because of them, ordinary post-Soviet Russians insatiably fill their television screens, scandal sheets, and gossip talks with the lives of the idle rich.[5]

To sum up, humor about the New Russians invents and perpetuates a social type, an Other, despised for its success and "foreignness" to "Old Russian" values. This type serves as a psychological defense mechanism, an ego-salve, for those who have "failed" in the new economy and who prefer disparagement of the new group to open admission that they themselves want, desire, covet what the new group has.

As one would expect, all these traits manifest themselves in the depiction of New Russians in post-Soviet Russian comics. But what I find striking is how many of those knee-jerk assumptions about the novie russkie (they are uncultured, vaguely "foreign," and Other, lacking in a proper respect for tradition, crude, undeserving of a place in Russian life) also apply to Russian cultural perceptions of comics themselves.

ARE KOMIKS "FUNNY"?

As in other national comics cultures, the very term "komiks" brings up unwanted connotations of humor and light-heartedness that get in the way of promoting it as a serious art form.[6] Languages such as French (la bande dessinée), Spanish (historieta, tebeo), Japanese (manga), and Italian (fumetti) sidestep this issue by applying their own terms to the medium, but the Russian word's derivation from the English "comics" brought along with it the same old "funny" cultural baggage,[7] as noted in chapter 4.

However, the peculiar *modus operandi* of komiks does have distinct ideological consequences for its portrayal of the "mythic" New Russian—revealing it quite self-consciously, precisely and in ways no other medium can, *as* myth. Thus, komiks serve as a valuable tool for unveiling the phantasmatic desire at the heart of humor aimed at/for New Russians.

In his semiotic approach to comics, Ole Frahm seeks to cut the Gordian knot of its "humorous" linguistic lineage, arguing for a double-entendre hermeneutics of the form: "Perhaps we have to take 'comics' literal [*sic*] and they really are comic, *komisch*, funny and strange, entertaining and weird. In German *komisch* has both these meanings. If something is *komisch* you can laugh at it and be puzzled by it at the same time." (This semantic shade of the word "comic," as a synonym of "funny," of course, also applies in English, and would carry its germ into the Russian term "komiks" as well.) Furthermore, the two-headed nature of the medium has its parallel in the collusion of text and image to produce a unique kind of signification; the "flattening" equalization of the visual and verbal, Frahm contends, serves to destabilize any and all authoritative speech: "In comics the signs are *exposed* as signs. The images are *exposed* as panels in small frames. The words are *exposed* in speech balloons, in captions, as sound [effect]s. We have to read the words but at the same time they are elements of the image" (my emphasis). Critically, this referential/formal duality has the effect of making meaning in comics fundamentally *ironic*. "Truth" in this medium is always conditional, negotiated, in dialogue between what we read/see and see/read.

Frahm brilliantly illustrates his point through a reading of the Jack Davis story "Bats in My Belfry!" (*Tales from the Crypt*, no. 24, EC Comics, 1951), which involves the delightfully ludicrous transformation of the protagonist into a man-sized blood-sucking fiend. In the climactic panel, the hero (looking like a hairy Max Schreck with grotesque fangs and claws) widens his eyes at the reader and proclaims: "I'm a *vampire bat!*" (emphasis in original).

"What could be more ridiculous," Frahm opines, "than showing a figure with pointed ears and teeth telling us that he is a vampire bat? We see it. We read it. It is banal. And yet, something else is happening in this simple repetition. To show the obvious twice is to produce a certain *unheimlichkeit*, a certain uncanniness. At first glance this appears as just an explanation for people who do not know vampire bats. But in fact it stresses the unbelievable: *the existence of vampire bats*" (my emphasis). As with man-sized vampire bats, so with New Russians. Comics, Frahm notes, "mock the notion of *an* origin, of *an* original, that were to be signified by the heterogeneous signs. They mock such notions by twice confirming the improbable" (emphasis in original). The power to "confirm the improbable," furthermore, stems from the comic artist's ability (like the caricaturist) to produce not strict adherence to what the "real world" looks like, but, paradoxically, to render a gross exaggeration or reworking of it that is still viscerally recognizable.[8] Comics avoid utter referentiality (like live-action film and photography never can) and add the heteroglossic attribute of textuality, making for a complex signifying system of juxtaposition that simultaneously creates and critiques stable meaning. We should bear this in mind as we examine the forcefully, often outrageously, "twice-confirmed" New Russians in the komiks representations to which we now turn.

ANNA KARENINA BY LEO TOLSTOY

And furthermore. Comics must not be confused with literature. It is not only inaccurate, but completely false to consider comics an abridged retelling of a literary work. Yes, there are comics based on famous literary texts, including *Anna Karenina*, *War and Peace*, "The Queen of Spades," etc. At first I was annoyed by such things, but then I realized: "It's humor!" When an artist takes a world masterpiece and transplants it in a comic, he is in effect

creating a parody of the masterpiece. It should not be consideered
a translation or a transposition, but an entirely new work, created
by the artist using a universally-known literary model. The cover
should bear the name not of the author of the literary text, but the
name of the artist. And civilized readers and viewers will recognize the literary heroes, they will recognize them and laugh. So
such things should be approached with a healthy sense of humor.
I would not include them in a required school curriculum, however,
and not because they are insulting to the great writers, but because
of the limited time allotted to literature in the educational system.
—IRINA ARZAMSTSEVA (QUOTED IN MAKSIMOVA: 79)

On the other hand, there does indeed exist a means by which to
kill off a great literary heritage, and it is this: beastly seriousness.
That cheerless, sullen veneration with which the jubilees of classics
are celebrated, in which the classics are discussed, and through
which the classics are taught in schools. This is where the real blas-
phemy takes place—in schools, where not only the desire to reread
Tolstoy's novel, but even to ponder doing so, is fatally stamped out.
—VAIL

The truth is, we just didn't have the money for a film, so we made
a comic book.
—METELITSA (QUOTED IN BOLTIANSKAIA)

Anna Karenina by Leo Tolstoy, a graphic-novel adaptation of the nineteenth-century classic, appeared in 2000 to considerable scandal. Written by Katya Metelitsa, with art by Valery Kachayev and Igor Sapozhkov, and produced by Baltser of
New Russians' World, the ninety-page hardcover (priced in the $25 range, out of
reach to average Russians) restages the well-known plot in Moscow circa 2000,
complete with cell phones, coke snorted from atop credit cards, Mercedes, sushi
bars, strip clubs, Bart Simpson, and a heroine the *Guardian* newspaper called a
morphine-addicted Russian version of Lara Croft. This Anna was New Russian
down to her crudely rendered Versace suits and Victoria's Secret lingerie.[9]
    Critical discussions of *Anna Karenina by Leo Tolstoy* focused on its "shocking"
komiks format. Some, like Tolstoy's great-grandsons, berated the medium itself as
inherently "beneath" consideration as true literature. "I was shocked. Then I tried
but failed to see the funny side," said Vladimir Tolstoy. "I can't believe that this is a
serious project. I hope that our children will not start studying literature using this
kind of material," said Ilya Tolstoy (Yablokova).[10]

Such a reaction in the wider culture was not surprising. But the book also met with disdain among many in the Russian komiks scene, which saw it first and foremost as a crass publicity stunt and not a "serious" work of real comics (which of course would not exclude a humorous treatment). As Zaslavsky told me: "The whole thing was calculated to produce a scandal. . . . It was hard for me to support this venture, the *Anna Karenina* book, since one could call it the most commercial of comics work. It was made for cynically commercial reasons: it was a very expensive book by Russian standards, and only a few people who could afford it bought it. . . . But the mass media is always looking for a story, and this was a good story: is it right to make comics out of Tolstoy?" (Zaslavsky 2004). Metelitsa did nothing to change such perceptions. Appearing on a radio talk show in January 2001, she declared, "We just wanted to make money. We made a beautiful, striking commercial publication, that looks like a slide film" (Boltianskaia). The book's publication, and that of its follow-up (*Pikovaia Dama by Alex Pushkin*, 2002), were thus quite blatantly calculated as *épatage*. Metelitsa's own lack of previous experience with comic art,[11] her well-publicized denigrations of the medium, and the perceived "crudeness" of the product (despite its French album-style package) endeared the book's creators to neither the literary elite nor the komiks subculture.

And yet *Anna* functions very much along the lines of Frahm's "double entendre" visual/verbal hermeneutics of comics to deconstruct both the "sacrosanct" status of Russian novelistic high culture as well the "New Russian" myth. It does this through a relentless aesthetics of parodic "contamination"; as with Kujundzic's McDonald's menu, the virus of Western pop culture "infects," "degrades," and overwhelms the linguistic registers of Tolstoy's text, turning it into the prose equivalent of "Dvoinoi Mak." The visual layer, meanwhile, is a colorful pastiche of late twentieth-century Pop signifiers, including logos, brands, films, fashion, dishes, and much else.

The book's cover, rendered in "metallic" blue with faux rivet holes, echoes that of Madonna's 1992 softcore porn book, *Sex*. The title, in "glistening" red, white, and blue, appears in the "exciting" font of a movie blockbuster or superhero comic. It pictures Anna's face as she, in a dream, flees the train that will destroy her. The whole magazine-size ensemble, together with the New Russians' World "winged bull" logo, resembles a high school student's cheap spiral notebook, complete with "weathered" look and nubile model.

From the first page, *Anna Karenina by Leo Tolstoy* subverts the original text not only by "dumbing it down"—setting only short snippets of description in captions or dialogue in balloons—but by inserting an immediate English translation as well (approximating the Soviet experience of watching a foreign film with annoying "synchronous translation" voiceover). Metelitsa makes reading the komiks even more "crude" and irritating than need be; space is scarce on the comics panel,

6.1. Levin marvels at the excesses of post-Soviet Russia in *Anna Karenina* by Leo Tolstoy.

so having to say everything *twice* forces the writer into even more of a staccato-like style than would otherwise be necessary (this effect, of course, is precisely what she is trying to achieve: anglicizing the all-but-paraphrased lines of Tolstoy will only further aggravate the "serious-minded" lover of Russian classics).

To make things worse, those English translations are often inaccurate, occasionally missing, stylistically infelicitous, and/or intentionally misspelled. Just one of many instances: when Anna forlornly calls out her son's name, *"Seryozha! Miliy!"* ("Seryozha! Sweety!") the English counterpart reads, "Seryozha! Sweaty!" [*sic*] (47). In addition, Metelitsa casually breaks the rules for comics grammar: a line of Stiva's is followed by the attribution, "declared Stepan Arkad'evich" (16), even though with word balloons no attribution is needed (since the balloon's tail is supposed to point to the character delivering the dialogue, as this one does). The English equivalent does not carry the attribution.

Metelitsa does violence even to Tolstoy's epigraph. The well-known biblical quote "Vengeance is mine, I will repay" is here, in the Russian text, credited to Alexander Pushkin! The English translation accurately attributes it to Romans 12:19 (though one can trace the verse back to the Old Testament, in Deuteronomy 32:35). This cavalier stance toward the quotation is meant to provoke an appalled

6.2. "John Travolta" as Vronsky, a stuffed bunny as Anna's son in *Anna Karenina* by Leo Tolstoy.

double-take in "serious" readers, a shrug in the ignorant who may not know or care about scripture, and a knowing wink in those inclined to appreciate the joke (not unlike Quentin Tarantino's epigraph to *Kill Bill Vol. 1:* "Revenge is a dish best served cold."—Old Klingon Proverb).[12]

Finally, the style of lettering in *Anna Karenina by Leo Tolstoy* itself bears an oddly "dual" quality. Like many mainstream comics works of the computer age, its lettering is done with software, not by hand, giving the speech balloons a "mechanical" quality.[13] But the font was clearly produced by scanning in letters that *had* been written by hand; they therefore look both amateurish *and* consistent. Furthermore, the font does not provide bold versions of the letters, so particular words do not receive emphasis; this further gives the text a dully repetitive, uninteresting look. (In cases where characters are shouting—"Bravo, Vronsky!"—the letters are simply reproduced at a larger font size.) To complicate things further, Kachayev/Sapozhkov do make use of hand-drawn sound effects (also very crude looking): "driiing!" for a cell phone; "tr-r-r" for Karenin cracking his knuckles; *"bakh"* for various pistols going off; "brrrooom" for an automobile. But these too seem pro forma, evincing none of the text/image dynamism of, say, Soviet propaganda posters of the 1920s. Someone interested in making graphically striking, "good" comics lettering would have used the art form's full arsenal of techniques (elaborated over centuries) to do so. Metelitsa and her collaborators obviously were not; they intentionally wanted to make a "bad-looking" comics work.

The artwork in *Anna* involves even more of a cut-and-paste job: garish computer coloring is used to "cover up" the artists' mediocre pen-and-ink drawings. In Frahm's terms, "the signs are exposed as signs"; everything is a muddled quotation, making for a grand collage of mostly Western visual cues: Karenin's decrepit "Soviet apparatchik" look (dark trench coat, thick glasses, fedora); Kitty's "Generation Y" appearance and dress; Levin's bearded, turtleneck-wearing "intellectual"; Anna's ball gowns and emoting, straight out of Mexican soap operas (Vail); John Travolta as Vronsky (flowing black locks, dance poses lifted from *Pulp Fiction*); the monster from *Alien* as the train.

Anna and Vronsky's escape to Italy (57), rendered in a splash page, an example of what Makoveeva calls the novel's "collage" technique, situates the lovers amid an ocean of traditional and Pop signifiers (themselves included). A billboard in the background proclaims "Farewell, 19th century," while beneath it another sign stares back with female eyes and the inscription, "All you need is love." A smaller billboard contains a Warhol-like portrait of Leonardo Di Caprio, while a smaller sign in front of that points to Italy—even though it is located in what appears to be a provincial Russian hamlet (a sign hawks "bird dung wholesale"). The couple is pictured in a red convertible, in the classic pose from the film poster of *Titanic*. Their reckless driving is causing havoc—a several-car smash-up is taking place immediately behind—to which they remain oblivious.[14] A barking dog chases them out of Russia. This page, perhaps more than any other in the novel, exemplifies its "television ad" sensibility: the dynamism and crazy quilt of references shows a mastery of the late 1990s Russian mediascape. Here we see most clearly that *Anna Karenina by Leo Tolstoy's* medium is, defiantly, its message.

Metelitsa and her collaborators also add more subtle touches: drawing on comics' capacity to caricature, the "faces" of trains and automobiles are rendered "menacing" throughout the work, graphically foreshadowing Anna's demise; the art at times ironically contradicts the text, as when a caption reads, "She loved him for himself . . ." while Anna stares desirously not at Vronsky, exactly, but at his Charles-Atlas-like muscles (58), or when Levin gawks in disbelief at his dinner bill (in a strip club), but his dialogue somewhat incongruously reads, "Why should I know Vronksy?" (13); elsewhere the art and text complement each other precisely, as in the panels where a gossip mutters, "This is becoming . . . indecent," while Anna's face is split by the distorting visual effect of a filled martini glass (24); finally, an odd but expressive piece of surrealism renders Anna's son, for all but one panel, as a stuffed bunny (this sort of thing would draw attention to itself even in a Luis Buñuel film, but it functions smoothly in comics to convey Anna's subjective mental state).

In short, *Anna Karenina by Leo Tolstoy* is a work of comic art that insistently utilizes the form's capacities to dialogize between the visual and verbal so as to satirize, critique, celebrate, and subvert the myth of the New Russians. All the same, for many a commentator who defended Russian literature as the sole repository of truth through various repressive historical eras, the miscegenation of a nineteenth-century classic with the *novie russkie*, the perceived antithesis of high culture, proved intolerable. That it was presented in a banal "comics" form only added insult to injury.

Metelitsa, knowing this, writes as much "miscegenation" into her adaptation as possible, even when such passages seem gratuitous (the entire project, one could maintain, seems gratuitous). Thus, when Dolly comes to visit Anna and Vronsky in their stylish Italian home, she cries out, "New European luxery!" [*sic*] / *"O, u vas evroremont!"* (62)—in this way both playing up the image of the New Russians as superficial, but also visually displaying their wealth, the sort of place no impoverished Russian reader could ever hope to live in (but wishes to).

The author also recrafts the stereotype of the invented New Russian type (primitive, infantilized, imbecilic) into the driving metaphor of her work. As she explained to me:

New Russians are a special object for ironic treatment. Not so much for mockery. In the first place, they don't exist. This is a myth, after all. The term "New Russian" was invented by Newsweek ... *What interested me was their language, this whole stratum of speech that they embody ... It was a game. With the [New Russian] Primer, it was as if I had taught the New Russians how to read—P is for "pager," etc.—and now that they could read, this was to be their first book,* Anna Karenina *as a comic, since comics have few words and lots of action. (Metelitsa 2002)*[15]

Several details scattered throughout the novel drive home this "New Russian as child learning to read" theme: Vronsky's car has a license plate that reads "07-FR-FR 99 RUS" in homage to his horse Frou Frou from the racing scene (29); as Karenin strolls in a bizarre "zoo," animals freely wander about on the sidewalks, including a man-sized giraffe wearing a suit (45), as in a children's book. The low-reading-level text and colorful art also foster the appearance of "literature" for those of a tender age.

And in no sense does *Anna Karenina by Leo Tolstoy* seem more "puerile" than in its "bratty" relationship with its source, Leo Tolstoy, Inc. A telling episode occurs late in the novel, when in one of Anna's fevered dreams, her friends and loved ones stand at a "great wall" to mourn her passing. The brick structure is covered in English and Russian scrawls, from the banal—*"Anna, you're alive!"*; *"Anna forever"*; *"Anna, I'll love you forever"*; *"Karenina's the best"*—to the specifically

6.3. The "screaming" graffiti wall in *Anna Karenina by Leo Tolstoy.*

referential—*"Tsoi lives! He's living in the Crimea, and Anna lives!"* (referring to the untimely deceased Perestroika-era singer Viktor Tsoi); "Kurt & Anna are alive" (alluding to the Nirvana lead singer and suicide Kurt Cobain)—to the openly accusatory—*"Leo Tolstoy's bloody killer / Karenina is the Best!"* (80).

These messages, delivered in the "low" literary genre of graffiti,[16] underscore the equivalence in the popular mind between fictional heroines like Anna and real-life folk heroes, as well as the necrophilic impulse to keep them alive forever. But more than that: they cast hatred and abuse on the figure most associated with Anna's demise: not Vronsky, but Tolstoy himself, the "killer" (this ties in with the sentiments of generations of readers who have felt the author "unfairly" murdered his heroine).[17] The stolid brick edifice (with its evocation of the Berlin Wall) stands in for the Tolstoy industry, the "beastly seriousness" of the classics which Vail so decries in this chapter's epigraph, while the graffiti conveys the anarchic, unrestrained license with which readers receive any "grand" literary text and make it personally meaningful. Almost by definition, those personal responses and interpretations will be "vulgar," go counter to the "official message" of the author, and reflect contemporary, "local" perceptions, their own "language."

Anna Karenina by Leo Tolstoy is of course one of those responses, but its comics format opens another line of interpretation: the stylish "graffiti" above the crowd could also be read as sound effects, the crowd's cries and yells. (A bold-type "Anna!" immediately over a grieving Vronsky strongly suggests such a reading.) The people, in other words, have gone beyond the dead, frozen text of the novel *Anna Karenina* which the wall symbolizes; they talk back to it, they have a *voice.* Only comics' Janus-faced duality—the text can be referential (graffiti) or textual (the crowd's voice) *or both at once*—allows such an interpretation. Only by stubbornly worshiping the dead wall will one feel offense at the living adornment that obscures it; only as one takes the ludic *Anna Karenina by Leo Tolstoy* "seriously" could one come to believe in New Russians. As children believe in fairies.

"NOVY KOMIKS" AND MEN'S HUMOR

The early 2000s comics journal *Novy Komiks* stands out as a realization of everything the Soviet authorities—and later the anti-comics crusader Natalya Markova—most feared about "decadent" Western comics: "The badly executed drawings foster bad taste and with its elements of militarism and adventure the primitive content produces a defective system of values, ideals and conceptions" (Mansurov: 145). Lewd, crude, and slickly produced, *Novy Komiks* unapologetically aimed at an adult readership, its distribution restricted mainly to nightclubs, strip bars, casinos, and other stereotypical New Russian haunts. An antithesis to the hardcover, ironically "graphic novelesque" *Anna Karenina by Leo Tolstoy*,[18] the disposable, chapbook-sized *Novy Komiks* would feel right at home next to such Moscow nightlife publications as *Ne Spat'!* (Don't Sleep!), *Medved'* (The Bear), Russian *Playboy*, or *Andrei*; it emphatically—and transgressively, given Russians' persistent association of comics with children's literature—asserts the post-Soviet prevailing ideology of virile male power. It does this through debauched comics depictions of sadistic violence and sexual perversions, in short vignettes between raunchy ads for Moscow nightlife establishments.[19]

The men in these three- to four-page stories by the artists Vladimir Volegov and "Shamil & Co." uniformly appear as violent Mafiosi, sex-starved troglodytes, or both, while the women without fail are scantily clad hookers, strippers, molls, or "ugly" old hags. Off-color Russian jokes, erotic situations, and much misogynistic humor get played out in endless variations.

Novy Komiks represents a baldly chauvinist strand of New Russian male self-fashioning: the scorned comics medium serves to conveniently bridge the gap between his (presumed) unwillingness to read some long boring screed in between blackjack or craps sessions at the casino, and his desire for titillating, accessible entertainment before the next round of drinks or blow. Foreign fashions, cars, guns, drugs, women, all serve as mere status markers; he can consume them freely without in the least compromising his identity as a true Russian. Similarly, the comics form has been "Russianized," its crude pen-and-ink drawings "tarted up" with computer coloring effects similar to those in *Anna Karenina by Leo Tolstoy*, but if anything even more garish and made to do harder duty to cover up the mediocre art.

Much of the sexually driven material operates according to the logic of what Linda Williams calls "pornotopia" in hardcore porn films, and what Emil Draitser

6.4. *Novy Komiks* used imagery from American B-movies to promote its vision of Russian hypermasculinity.

(following Gershon Legman) terms "the primacy of coitus" in the Russian male anekdot. This sometimes leads to the threat of male inadequacy in the face of a "frightening" feminine sexuality, as in Volegov's "The Tie" (2001): a balding mafioso guns down his moll when she questions his "gay" fashion sense.

But other brands of Russian dirty humor portray women using their sexual powers to put men in their thrall. Dianne Farrell and Natalia Pushkaryova, in their studies of the bawdy lubok, find some examples that show women getting the upper hand in their romps with men. Both scholars conclude, however, that these pseudo-pornographic lubki do largely advance misogynistic themes. Pushkaryova notes they reflect a marked "gender asymmetry": "The representation of nude women with a precise designation of their sexual characteristics, while not a common phenomenon, was widespread all the same. It was not possible, on even a single lubok print, to encounter a nude male body" (47).

More directly, *Novy Komiks'* hypersexualized content recall American "Tijuana Bibles," also known as "eight-pagers": small collections of pornographic comics popular among the cognoscenti as far back as the early twentieth century. (They too often depicted recognizable cartoon characters and celebrities in graphic sex scenes.) *Novy Komiks'* stories thus promiscuously access Russian jokelore, the lubok, the *chastushka*, or humorous rhyme, Western pop culture, "dirty" comics, and other genres for a cynical, pornotopic view of post-Soviet, specifically New

6.5. A New Russian mafioso guns down his moll for suggesting he is gay in Volegov's "The Tie."

Russian, life. Sex-themed comics had appeared in the popular press even in the first Perestroika-era *komiks* collections, but compared to the "New Russians" in *Novy Komiks*, they radiated "innocent" fun (even as they, too, exercise a flagrant misogyny).

Much more common in *Novy Komiks*, however, are stories that simply humiliate or punish women. Issue no. 0's "The Refueling" (Zapravka 2001) by Volegov makes for an arresting blend of old and new. Two nubile New Russian women in tight clothes are driving in the countryside. One of them is running late to catch a train, but the car needs to refuel. The two push the vehicle to an isolated quarry, where, sitting before a dingy trailer home, a lone "muzhik" (cigarette, unshaven, bottle of Stolichnaya, prominent forehead) sits reading an issue of *Novy Komiks*. The brunette asks if the train station lies far off, and he replies with an ambiguous smile. She then offers him fifty dollars to fill up her car, but he'll agree only if he can "fill her up" first. After some coaxing from her blonde friend, the brunette agrees, and for three panels the reader is treated to the pot-bellied, brutish muzhik eagerly—he literally leaps out of his pants—ravishing the buxom maid (8). Meanwhile, the blonde has filled up the car and drives off, extending her middle finger to her stunned friend. As the naked, sweaty muzhik cackles and slobbers uncontrollably, the brunette angrily points to a nearby sign that says, "Train station—200 meters" (9). This panel markedly recalls Pushkaryova's description of

6.6. The "punchline" to the incestuous joke-tale "The Lift," by Volegov.

the pornographic lubok's "gender asymmetry": the shocked, humiliated brunette is shown at the doorway, in full frontal nudity, while next to her the laughing "mu-zhik" (a fellow reader of *Novy Komiks*, let us not forget) remembers to cover his genitals. Every cue tells the reader at whom to snigger and with whom to relate.

Many of these elements—women as sexually insatiable, even perverse; men as opportunistic rapists; the new Russia as dangerous and crime ridden—come together in "The Lift: For Those Who've Heard, But Haven't Seen" (2001), another Volegov anekdot/story. A voluptuous girl in pigtails, spilling out of her flimsy attire, enters a dark elevator whose lamp is broken. The menacing silhouette of a man in a trench coat and hat rides with her, staying in shadow even as the girl's body remains available to our gaze. The girl begins to worry he might be a "maniac," but then, in close-up, her eyes fill with desire and she offers herself to the stranger ("Khochesh' menia?") (the element of danger seems to arouse the girl—she "wants to get raped").

The entire next page shows the two having sex, with the girl's Jessica Rabbit-like body somehow always illuminated in the "dark" lift (her computer-colored flesh tones evoke an airbrushed three-dimensionality, while the stranger's hands are rendered in more crude pen and ink). We see only the black outline of the man's body, still in the hat and coat, and only a hint of his face as they tryst. On the final page, the girl offers him a post-coital cigarette, and as they light up, the "stranger" is revealed as . . . her father ("Masha!??" "Papa!??"). The last panel delivers the punchline: a stunned "papa" stares in horror at his daughter's cigarette: "Masha-a! You smoke??????" (28). Masha only smiles seductively.

Draitser notes that incest is "widely represented" in bawdy *chastushki* and other oral folklore, including jokes. "The Lift" unites that transgressive tradition with the "urban legend" plausibility of mistaken father/daughter relations in the dark. The story thus occurs in a timeless, mythological space. At the same time, the visual markers identify the setting as post-Soviet: Masha's lift is located in a large *khrushchevka*-type apartment building, but her barely there garb would have been considered much too provocative in the Soviet era. Comics' duality, its capacity to *simultaneously* render the specific and abstract—like the disparate visual registers of the "illuminated" half-nude daughter and her obscured rapist-father—serves to *graphically* bridge the Russian past with its present (something an oral genre like the anekdot cannot do).

With X-rated material appearing in a slick, all-color comics edition, distributed free in establishments that were off-limits or nonexistent before 1991, with both Western and Soviet-era pop culture iconography, *Novy Komiks* serves as a candy-hued "primer" of New Russians—especially New Russian males—at their most primal. Interestingly, the journal's creators consciously figured their work as a response to imported Western comics, which, they claimed, Russians find "strange" and "alien." During my 2002 conversation with the (all-male) editors and writing staff of *Novy Komiks* in their southwest Moscow offices, they repeatedly underscored their dedication to an image of the real Russian man as prone to sadistic humor, casual sex, drinking, head-bashing, coarse badinage—the simple things in life. As the chief editor, Mikhail Terent'ev, explained: "Russian humor is different; we have a lot of satire. Americans like to laugh at their president, like when he choked on a pretzel and lost consciousness, and there were all sorts of articles and discussion about that. But in Russia we don't care about the government. We prefer to laugh at what's happening all around us, right before our eyes" (2002). With content reflecting an imaginary world of easy sex, endless booze and the occasional high-caliber *razborka* or gang fight, Terent'ev noted, these are comics *for us* (dlia nas). But notice again: *Novy Komiks* is not just a primer in what New Russian males *are*, it's also an instruction manual in Metelitsa's sense, in how to *be* a New Russian: the stories show one how to dress, what to say, where to go, when to lash out. For those who despise the New Russians, *Novy Komiks* confirms the worst. For those who aspire—desire—to become New Russian, it tells you all you need *to play the role.*

In *Novy Komiks* as well as *Anna Karenina by Leo Tolstoy*, New Russianness stands exposed as performance—in the Butlerian sense, as drag.

CONCLUSION

During Metelitsa's talk-show appearance on *Ekho Moskvy* in early 2001, listeners were asked to call in and vote their opinion on comics adaptations of the classics. Sixty-two percent proved in favor of the proposition that "Great literature in pictures is a mockery" of the classics, while 38 percent considered it "a different art form." Even accounting for the radio station's more erudite audience, the latter figure strikes me as reassuring, given the vexed history of comics in Russia throughout the twentieth century, especially among the intelligentsia.

But whatever komiks' fate on its home soil, the medium had already proven quite adept—perhaps ideally suited—for attacking the viability of the New Russian myth in the twenty-first century. In an essay on the folklore about the New Russians, Seth Graham insightfully points out, regarding the Soviet *anekdot*, that "many or even most of the best-known cycles are based not on unmediated, abstract socio-political and historical concepts, or on real-life personalities or groups, but on the *representations* of these phenomena in mass culture" (44, emphasis in original). The New Russians in komiks are, in this sense, doubly mediated: represented representations, "illustrated" jokes, urban legends brought to visual life. In the process they are rendered exponentially absurd and unreal: Metelitsa and Volegov's "New Russians" become like Davis's "I'm a *vampire bat!*" The dance between text, image, and sequence that is comics' peculiar gift, induces the irony under whose withering gaze no myth can long remain unpunctured. As also noted, comics uniquely—at least uniquely effectively—uses the reader/viewer's desire against him, giving him exactly what he wants only to show the flatness and flimsiness of that longed-for object. (Comics giveth, comics taketh away.)

Though she developed a new respect for comics as a "labor-intensive" medium, Metelitsa in *Anna Karenina by Leo Tolstoy* exploited its perception in Russian culture as a kind of "literary popcorn or bubblegum" to introduce the New Russians as an (ironically) valid subject for a "novel."[20] Despite her snide dismissal of the medium as inferior to film, she mobilizes it quite adroitly to construct a "living" stereotype (myth-making) so as to have it collapse in on itself all the more comically (myth-breaking).[21]

Novy Komiks, while more coarse and less self-conscious than *Anna Karenina by Leo Tolstoy*, shares a vision of its post-Soviet subject that still conforms to (and also actively constructs) the popular preconceptions of the New Russians in all their Yeltsin-era glory. But it is this very over-the-top, grossly exaggerated quality of the material—all those blazing barrels; Barbie-shaped molls; grunting rapists; crashing cars—that makes it a cartoon, not the medium.

Komiks works about the New Russians are doubly uncanny, in Freud's understanding of that which should have remained hidden but has been brought to light. Insistently exposing themselves as what they are (signs, marks on paper), comics always threatens to produce coherent, impossible meaning. Comics is an art form that continually, coincidentally does and dismisses, makes and mars: funny pictures, long outgrown, ever haunting.

AUTOBIOGRAPHY IN POST-SOVIET RUSSIAN COMICS

THE CASE OF NIKOLAI MASLOV

God have mercy on us all. How agonizingly difficult it is being Russian.
—MAXIM GORKY

The genre of autobiography, a staple of Western comics—especially of the underground and alternative persuasion—has been slow to develop in post-Soviet Russia. This chapter will explore some of the reasons for why this is the case, through a reading of Nikolai Maslov's comics memoir work and the scandal it provoked among komiksisty upon its publication in 2004 France. The scandal did not register among the Russian public at large, which had never heard of Maslov, nor in the Russian literary scene, as the work has to this day not been published in Maslov's own country. The contretemps erupted instead within Russia's tiny, fledgling, highly marginalized comics subculture. The indifference to the Maslov case among the general public only confirms the longstanding Russian bias against comics as a legitimate medium for adult themes—nothing new there. But the uniformly vehement—even virulent—antagonism against Maslov on the part of his fellow komiksisty says much not only about that group's preconceptions regarding komiks; about the "right" way to get published; and the "proper" approach to depicting contemporary Russia in comics form. There was more at stake here. The Maslov case revealed how Russian self-conceptions—what it means to be a Russian—have splintered and changed since the collapse of Communism.

AUTOBIOGRAPHY

Literary critics, at least since the deconstructionist Paul de Man's influential essay "Autobiography as Defacement," have read the genre less as a referential document of "true-life" events, and more as a rhetorical mode of illusionistic auto-creation. As de Man puts it in an oft-quoted passage:

But are we so certain that autobiography depends on reference, as a photograph depends on its subject or a (realistic) picture on its model? We assume that life produces the autobiography as an act produces its consequences, but can we not suggest, with equal justice, that the autobiographical project may itself produce and determine the life and that whatever the writer does is in fact governed by the technical demands of self-portraiture and thus determined, in all its aspects, by the resources of his medium? (69, emphasis in original)

The autobiographer/self-inventor presents, through an elaborate linguistic scheme, a unified "face" (or prosopon) to the reader, who plays along with the charade by accepting the story as referentially valid, clear, and delimitable. In prose autobiography, both writer and reader rely on ready-made cultural types, settings, and narrative logic to round out a coherent, decipherable version of reality.

For Charles Hatfield, autobiography in comics poses unique challenges and opportunities to identity and truth, since by their hybrid visual-verbal nature comics problematize the very idea of "non-fiction" in ways neither prose nor the visual arts can manage. In *Alternative Comics: An Emerging Literature*, Hatfield writes: "If autobiography has much to do with the way one's self-image rubs up against the coarse facts of the outer world, then comics make this contact immediate, and graphic. We see how the cartoonist envisions him or herself; the inward vision takes an outward form. This graphic self-representation literalizes a process already implicit in prose autobiography, for . . . the genre consists less in faithfulness to outward appearances, more in the encounter between 'successive self-images' and the world" (114).[1] "The cartoon self-image, then," Hatfield concludes, "seems to offer a unique way for the artist to recognize and externalize his or her subjectivity" (115).[2]

MASLOV

Nikolai Maslov (born 1954) hails from a working-class family (his father was a telephone lineman), in rural Russia near Novosibirsk, Siberia. Shy and unassuming, he lost his father at the age of ten. As a young man Maslov worked various jobs, including construction, did his military service in Mongolia, attended a local art institute for one year, and eventually moved to Moscow in the 1970s to work in a bakery and a gallery, delivering Lenin portraits. Following the death of his brother Oleg, and in response to numerous personal setbacks and spiritual malaise, he fell into alcoholism and severe depression before winding up in a mental

7.1. A nonidealized depiction of the Stagnation-era USSR in *Siberia*, by Nikolai Maslov, 2004.

hospital. He recovered, with his wife raised two daughters, and for several years has worked as a night watchman in a Moscow warehouse.

In 1996, Maslov approached Emmanuel Durand, a French expatriate who had published the Russian version of *Asterix*, at Pangloss, his foreign language bookshop in Moscow. The nervous Maslov produced three pages of a memoir in comics form he was working on, executed in pencil, in a naïve style. Haltingly, he made Durand an offer: pay him an advance so that he could quit his job and work on the memoir, and he could have the publishing rights once it was done. Durand agreed and three years later Maslov completed the work, which was released by the French Denoel Press in 2004 under the title *Une Jeunesse Sovietique*. (A second volume of comics stories, *Les Fils d'Octobre*, appeared in 2005.)[3]

In his work the poor, provincial, mostly self-taught komiksist Maslov addressed—through what many Russians still consider an "imbecilic" medium—such mature topics as alcoholism, rural squalor, and the taboo subject of hazing in the Red army. Against bleak landscapes strewn with garbage—both industrial and human—Maslov's portrait of the mindless banality, brutality, and despair of ordinary Soviet life in the Stagnation-era 1970s makes the comics of Harvey Pekar look like *Tintin* in comparison.

Suffused with a profound sorrow, Maslov's vision of his Siberian hometown and its environs owes much to classic literary treatments of the Russian masses (Dostoyevsky, Saltykov-Shchedrin, Bunin, the Village Prose school), while his

... EVERYTHING ABOUT MAN SHOULD BE BEAUTIFUL...

7.2. Maslov often presents late-Soviet citizens as grotesque figures.

drawings (in their delicate, primitivist pencil) hauntingly recall the more naive iterations of lubok. By any fair-minded standard, Maslov's work deserves at least some credit for broaching such mature, weighty, even depressing themes, demonstrating decisively that Russian comics need not be funny, light-hearted, fanciful, or flashy—that indeed they yield nothing to other media in depicting serious material with an economy of style and seriousness of purpose. Whatever its shortcomings, *Siberia* is clearly the work of someone who needed to tell this story and found in comics the only honest means *to* tell it.

As Jon Fasman wrote in his *Moscow Times* review, "In its narrative's honesty and the deceptively simple vibrancy of its draftsmanship, it testifies to the worth of any single examined life."

THE SCANDAL

Yet both Maslov's subject matter *and* his execution earned him the scorn of established Russian comics artists, who charged him with pandering to a stereotypical "foreigner's view" of a benighted Russia—and through naïve, "ugly" drawings, to boot. In this, the scandal revived Perestroika-era discourse on *chernukha* ("gloomy realism") in cinema.[4]

In an era when many komiksisty—who hold day jobs in advertising and other commercial ventures—opt for slick, garish work produced on computer, Maslov's art seemed pathetically crude. Some said he couldn't draw at all. Only someone who was giving the French a vision of a weak Russia that they wanted, they reasoned, could have scored such a lucrative publishing coup. Maslov, as they saw it, had sold out the motherland. As the cofounder of the KomMissia comics festival, Khikhus, explained it to me:

They're angry. Here a lot of them have been trying for years to break into the foreign markets, especially France, and they were always turned down. But now this nobody from the sticks shows up, this old guy, and he can't draw and his comics look like shit, and he's just showing all these poor, dumb Russians who drink and do all kinds of depressing stuff and we're all so sick of that old shit. There's been like a million stories just like that. But the French, they eat that shit up; they love to see this Russia where there's still bears walking the streets of Moscow, and everybody's an alcoholic. It just confirms all these outdated stereotypes that they have about us. Foreigners just want to read things that make Russia look bad. And this guy with no talent gives it to them, and he gets paid thousands of Euros. So, yeah, they're pissed. (2006)

Maslov was ostracized by the comics community (though he had never really been a part of it) and barred from the 2006 KomMissia Festival—even though at that point he was probably the most famous Russian comics artist in the world. Khikhus, a practicing Buddhist, felt some pangs of conscience over that decision, but, he explained to me, he really had no choice, given the widespread enmity against Maslov. A tireless promoter of a marginal art in a hostile cultural environment, the last thing he needed was a rift in the nascent industry. By 2007 the controversy had cooled, and his conscience had reasserted itself enough to where Khikhus agreed to advertise a presentation and book signing by Maslov during the KomMissia festival—but offsite, at the French Cultural Center. He also allowed Maslov to sell books onsite. (The situation with the French had turned awkward, especially since the Russians were eager to expand their contacts abroad; it simply made no sense to keep alienating the Russian artist best known in Europe from the largest festival in his own country. But Maslov was not allowed to display any of his work, and he received no awards or recognition.)

For their part the French publisher Durand and Maslov insisted he had not gotten rich off his publications, despite healthy sales, and had in fact experienced delays in payment. Durand expressed to me his exasperation with what he considered a smear and rumor campaign on the part of the Russian comics scene against him and Maslov (2006).⁵ For someone who had supposedly "made it" abroad, Maslov did not live like a rich man when I met him in 2006. He still maintained his old job as a warehouse night watchman and said he lives very modestly. It should be said, however, that the scandal took a heavy toll on Maslov, a very sensitive, soft-spoken, and emotionally fragile man; he admitted to me that the rejection by his fellow artists, and the many venomous rumors swirling around him (none of which he had ever expected) almost drove him back to depression (Maslov 2006).

I should also mention one other thing: to a person, all the Russian artists I spoke to who condemned Maslov and dismissed his work—every one—had not actually read it. In this chapter's remaining pages, therefore, I will do Maslov the decency of actually examining his work in some detail before pronouncing any sort of judgment on it.

THE THEME OF PROVINCIAL SQUALOR

The theme of the backwardness and suffering of the common people—what Khikhus calls "that old shit"—does indeed have a long pedigree in Russian literary culture. All the great masters addressed it. Anton Chekhov, for example, describes peasants this way in his short story "Peasants": "[T]hey were coarse, dishonest, filthy, and drunken; they did not live in harmony, but quarreled continually, because they distrusted and feared and did not respect one another. . . . Yes, to live with them was terrible; but, they were human beings, they suffered and wept like human beings, and there was nothing in their lives for which one could not find an excuse" (350). Nor has Russian autobiography avoided the issue. In *My Childhood*, his memoir of a brutal upbringing in a poor provincial family, Maxim Gorky noted: "I am not telling about myself, but about that close, stifling circle of horrible impressions in which the ordinary Russian lived and continues to live" (Scherr: 338). The critic Helen Muchnic adds, "Gorky's child is not the focus of attention at all, but an instrument used to record the habits of brutal people in a barbarous society" (Scherr: 338).

As with Gorky, Maslov's subject is the disfigurement—bodily and spiritual—brought about by living in a time and place where hope has all but disappeared, and where self-consumption through drink, violence, and blind cruelty are simply a fact of existence. The official Soviet propaganda, which proclaims a utopia on earth, only makes the reality more appallingly hellish.

Maslov's treatment of this theme is no worse or better than many who have come before him. His innovation is the visual strategies for conveying the grisly irreality of life in the dying USSR (such as the grotesque caricatures through which he portrays drunkards, party hacks, brutal soldiers), within an overall mood of bland psychological realism. His often-pedestrian layouts echo the sheer banality and monotony of his subjects' lives, while their cackling, gargoyle-like features mirror their corrupted souls. These do not appear without humor: a teacher who tells his students, "Everything about man should be beautiful . . ." looks like some Sysoev-like homunculus with bad teeth, a squinting eye, and a huge ear (59).

7.3. A tractor accident "intercut" with a wedding by Maslov.

Also like Gorky, Maslov contrasts the fallen, polluted city with a nature of stark, enduring beauty, itself being progressively and thoughtlessly destroyed. Kolya's experiences take him back and forth between land and city, and it's made clear where his loyalties lie. Maslov is tapping into an old cliché about the heartland as restorative and evocative of the true Russian soul—though again, his treatment of it through comics techniques such as page design yields fresh insights.

FORM

The theme of the suffering masses boasts a long and proud tradition in art as well. Maslov's protagonist, the Francophile Kolya, mentions Monet and Cezanne as his heroes, but Maslov's style also somewhat recalls that of the Franco-Dutch painter Van Gogh's canvases of the working class and criminals. The Russian neo-Primitivists, themselves influenced by the lubok, come to mind as well. It's more productive to view Maslov's naïve style as extending from and in dialogue with those old movements and artists, it seems to me, than to simply dispense with him as a "bad artist," whatever one's tastes.

In the course of discussing art with some fellow students in college, Kolya declares: "A healthy imagination always discovers a way to express itself in simple forms, forms that are accessible to all. Esotericism, coded messages, all that, only ambitious, ignorant people need that, and so they're a menace to society" (52). Maslov's own meta-poetic declaration is simply the age-old bromide about "clarity" and accessibility, the stodgy realist's hammer and sickle (so to speak), but it amounts to a medium-is-the-message artistic credo, an ethics justifying his comics style, not just making excuses for it. Though not to everyone's liking, there is nothing accidental or "crude" about Maslov's art when one approaches it on its own terms, and in light of the rich traditions it references.

Moreover, Maslov's soft, delicate pencils find a correlative in the protean, hazily unreliable nature of memory—without which the genre of autobiography would not exist. Like all memoirists, Maslov rearranges, condenses, and substitutes past events to maximize narrative effects—as in his recounting of the episode where a man dies in a tractor accident at the same time that a wedding party is taking place. (The panels "crosscut" between the two locations.) Moreover, Maslov often inserts odd "cutaways": nonlinear or aspect-to-aspect panel progressions, which for at least one reviewer highlight the arbitrariness of memory. As Jeremy Estes writes, "Memoir and autobiography are subject to these sorts of strange shifts. Memory isn't linear because our brains will drag up any number of thoughts and feelings to a single event whether they're actually relevant or not." Rather than a pure re-experiencing of the past via some Proustian time machine, Maslov's art emphasizes the contingencies, reimaginings, and lacunae that honeycomb history, especially personal history.

No vignette better illustrates this than when Kolya says that, try as he might, he cannot recall the look of his father on a special day shortly before his untimely death. (Similarly, the evocative silhouette of a lone horse rider, rather than a crisp image, is how Kolya chooses to remember his time as a serviceman in Mongolia; emotions, possibilities, matter more than acuity of vision.) As Estes put it, "Maslov steps away from the story he's telling and acknowledges the failure of memory. Instead, there's only a gray pencil shadow of his father, an impression. This is how

7.4. The honeycomb of memory: Kolya cannot remember his father's appearance.

memory works—it's haze and shadows, with a definite feeling of how things were, even if the details aren't there. *Siberia* is filled with these images, snapshots of the monumental and the trivial."

This is why, in the words of another critic, Maslov's pencil drawings "seem to shift as you look at them"[7]; one can imagine that a more defined, sharper, ink-based style would shatter the "memory fog" effect. Not naïve at all, this is a setting down in visual terms of a beloved gossamer past on the cusp of dissolution. In *The Language of Drawing*, Edward Hill notes, "Drawing diagrams experience.

SOMETIMES WE WENT ON TRIPS TO PAINT OUTDOORS.

THOSE WERE THE HIGH POINTS OF MY TIME AT SCHOOL.

OUT OF THE ACADEMY WINDOWS, ON THE OTHER HAND, WHAT YOU SAW WERE SMOKESTACKS OF WEAPONS FACTORIES, FACTORIES HIDDEN BEHIND HUGE SIGNS THAT SAID THINGS LIKE "CHILDREN'S TOY PLANT #7" OR "WHEELCHAIR FACORY #8."

ONE DAY AFTER CLASS, MY FRIENDS DECIDED TO CELEBRATE MY BIRTHDAY.

7.5. Siberia's "dichotomizing" page design: pure nature versus urban desolation.

7.6. Maslov's contemplative landscapes of the Russian countryside forego narrative flow.

It is a transposition and solidification of the mind's perceptions. From this we see drawing not simply as a gesture, but as mediator, as a visual thought process which enables the artist to transform into an ordered consequence what he perceives in common (or visionary) experience" (8). Or a disordered, irresolved consequence, as it were. On the other hand, Maslov's page compositions often serve

7.7. Kolya learns about his brother's death by telegram.

that organizing, dichotomizing, "ideological" function: he splits pages in half, with panels depicting the natural world contrasting with those below it that show factories, urban desolation. Other pages slow down the narrative flow with panel after panel of polluted landscapes, as when Kolya goes on foot to seek help for his truck, stuck in the mud. Occasionally, though, Maslov's page designs break the memoir's customary tranquility with jagged and unconventional panel shapes, as when Kolya learns about his brother's death.

HOPE IN THE MUCK

If Maslov's art is not so "naïve" as it might seem, neither is his autobiographical practice quite so gloomily "hopeless" and negative as those who derogate him assert. It is not chernukha, but again a familiar pattern in Russian literary and philosophical culture that yields redemption after a via dolorosa of sufferings and horrors. The catalyst of salvation, predictably, is found in time-honored, premodern Russian culture, represented here by traditional Russian peasants' clay stoves. Kolya and his art school friends cross a contaminated landscape in search of the real color "ultramarine." It lies in "grandmother's" folksy cottage, on her stove, along with an old Russian emblem of twin peacocks. (The work's black-and-white presentation compels the reader to imagine the "perfect" color.) These stoves appear in force later on, as part of Kolya's hallucinations in the mental institution. Taking the place of tanks, they roll in military formation, parade-style, on Red Square: Russian tradition is stronger than the modern usurpers of the state.

The autobiography ends with the "resurrection" of Kolya's dead father, from wispy pencil smudge to full-on portrait, dispensing home-spun wisdom to his sons. Like much recent Russian literature and film, the return and rehabilitation of the father (after a long absence) grounds the work in a continuity with the past as a sort of strength and hope, in the face of life's horrors.[6]

THE "RIGHT" KIND OF RUSSIAN COMICS

Returning to Hatfield's point on the cartoon self-image's capacities to "externalize" the artist's subjectivity, the question in the case of post-Soviet Russian autobiographical comics is what kind of "externalizations" gain purchase and which are ignored, even vilified. Elena Uzhinova and Khikhus, two of the rare komiksisty who, with Maslov, work in the genre, have the markers for popular acceptance: ironic, urban, apolitical, nonrealist, and sardonic in approach.

Khikhus's "Once Upon a Time I Had a Muse" (2006), for example, expounds on his relationship with a girlfriend (KomMissia festival cofounder Natalia Monastyrova) through a surreal, Chagalesque approach in which the author's muse

7.8. Kolya's dream: traditional clay stoves replace tanks in a Red Square parade.

7.9. Khikhus's "Once Upon a Time I Had a Muse," 2006.

flies through the air, consumes bits of his soul, and helps him become fabulously rich. The narration is casual and "up-front" with its revelations:

> *She was an easy talk. Cool. I enjoyed hearing her chat while I was drawing.*
> *And . . . strictly between us . . . She was a great fuck.*
> *Best sex in my life, to be honest. (34)*

This is autobiography comfortable with its self-image and the confessional mode (even when discussing childhood trauma, as in Uzhinova's "Story about My Eye," discussed in the next chapter). This, I maintain, to some extent echoes the resurgent strength and swagger of the New Russia, which under Putin has recovered its footing, and (at least until the financial crisis of late 2008) arrogantly eschewed the need for self-examination beyond its surface image.

The reaction against Maslov, even among a population like the progressive comic subculture, then, reflects the new compulsion to project confidence and power, not the outdated weakness and self-flagellation of past generations—the new Russia, not "that old shit." Maslov's work contradicts the currently fashionable, forward-leaning self-presentation of Russia as a great nation: tech-savvy, urban, Westernized but still retaining its own Eurasian identity. In such a climate, self-reflective genres like autobiography and the political tract are relatively rare and, when they appear, largely ignored—all the more so if they don't uphold the new ideology. Fantasy, escapism, sensualist pleasures are the coin of the realm in Putin's modern authoritarian neo-Soviet capitalist kleptocracy; we see this duplicated in the sphere of even such marginal phenomena as comics.

In such a world, artists like Maslov, who don't play along, get no seat at the table.

8

"I WANT"

WOMEN IN POST-SOVIET RUSSIAN COMICS

In her essay "The Visual Turn and Gender History," Almira Ustinova posits the gender split in Russian culture as largely falling along a verbal versus visual dynamic. In a familiar move, she associates the masculine with language, the Law of the Father, history, while the feminine—that historically repressed element forever "looking in from the outside"—she relates to the visual register. Ustinova's argument is more subtle than this description of a simple gender dichotomy might suggest (for one thing it recalls *l'ecriture feminine* and the critic Julia Kristeva's notion of the pre-verbal "semiotic"), while its attention to the role played by the visual turn in late/post-modernity to resolve and refute that dichotomy seems to me crucial in an increasingly image-saturated world: "The question is not one of the 'canceling out' (if such a thing could be contemplated) of written history, nor of refusing verbal language as a means of communication or the transmission of historical knowledge, but of the combination and synthesis of the verbal and visual fields in more active forms" (158). Ustinova partly bases her argument on Mikhail Ryklin's concept of "speech vision," which relates to the ways the discursive determines perception. Ryklin's essay "Bodies of Terror: Theses toward a Logic of Violence" describes how the sociohistorically/verbally determined visual field (which Ustinova sees as gendered male) actively constructs its subjects, but also how it hands over the tools of deconstruction, to see between the lines.[1] Ustinova posits postmodernity's turn from the verbal to the visual as an opportunity to subvert age-old Russian, masculinist, logocentric culture: "The logos regulates (kontroliruet) the image, appropriates its sense, fixes and secures its referents behind it, thus foisting onto the image its own truth. Is the emancipation of a visual 'language' from a verbal language possible? Is there a truth of painting or photographic representation outside the truth of the discursive? Can one overcome the attraction (pritiazhenie) of the dominant field of speech culture and liberate vision from the power of the word . . . ?" (153).² At the same time, for Ustinova and Visual Studies scholars like W. J. T. Mitchell, the visual/verbal split is itself a false dichotomy in need of exposure. The image's dual, protean nature underscores its power to open up meaning, including subversive meaning. In his 1986 essay "What Is an Image?" Mitchell writes:

The picture of an eagle in Northwest Indian petroglyphs may be a signature of a warrior, an emblem of a tribe, a symbol of courage, or—just a picture of an eagle. The meaning of the picture does not declare itself by a simple and direct reference to the object it depicts. . . . In order to know how to read it, we must know how it speaks, what is proper to say about it and on its behalf. The idea of the "speaking picture" which is often invoked to describe certain kinds of poetic presence or vividness on the one hand, and pictorial eloquence on the other hand, is not merely a figure for certain special effects in the arts, but lies at the common origin of writing and painting. (28)

And further:

The image of an eagle may depict a feathered predator, but it expresses the idea of wisdom, and thus works as a hieroglyph. Or we may understand expression in dramatic, oratorical terms, as did the Renaissance humanists who formulated a rhetoric of history painting complete with a language of facial expression and gesture, a language precise enough to let us verbalize what depicted figures are thinking, feeling, or saying. And expression need not be limited to predicates we can attach to pictured objects: the setting, compositional arrangement, and color scheme may all carry expressive charge, so that we can speak of moods and emotional atmospheres on the order of a lyric poem. (41)

This last point is crucial: the look—colors, composition, style, "mise-en-scene," and so on; in short, *design*—carries its own particular charge which can complement or conflict with the verbal or textual register. This is especially important for comics, which taps precisely such textual/visual tensions to open up meanings not contained or containable by either register on its own, allowing for uniquely subversive readings—an explicit dramatization and transcendence of the conflict, in Ustinova's terms, between the "masculine" verbal and the "feminine" visual.³

This chapter examines the work of several contemporary Russian women comics artists—komiksistky—especially their use of such design strategies for (re)fashioning feminine identity in the post-Soviet era. What possibilities do the comics medium offer women authors? What genres do they gravitate toward, and how do these choices reflect current economic, literary, nationalist, and gender realities? What cultural burdens borne by komiks affect the sorts of expressions komiksistky can, cannot, do not, or will not produce?

WOMEN'S KOMIKS

Perhaps due precisely to their marginality and disdain in mainstream Russian culture, komiks have attracted artists of diverse creeds, backgrounds, and generations, from the older "First Wavers" of the Perestroika era to the younger "Second Wavers" of the Internet age. Some of the most interesting and challenging work today is being produced by women, a situation which mirrors that in other media such as literature (e.g., Tatyana Tolstaya, Lyudmilla Ulitskaya) and film (Kira Muratova, Renata Litvinova, Anna Melikyan).

As a venue for opposition and subversive expression, however, Russian women's komiks are a mixed bag. In some ways, they present a uniformly post-feminist vision: there is no doubt over gender equality, or the absolute freedom to do and be what one chooses in the post-Soviet idea-scape. This in and of itself is revolutionary when compared even to the late-Soviet era,[4] while some komiksistky go even further: assaulting and belittling traditional women's roles; frankly addressing body-image issues and the beauty industry; freely and aggressively expressing their power as sexual beings. But in other ways, these komiks tend to conform all too readily to the new Russia's circumscribed fields of action, be they ideological, sexual or, especially, economic.

In this necessarily schematic excursus, we will examine three important areas—aesthetic, ideational, and generic—pertaining to the work of modern komiksistky, for what insights Ustinova's notion of a gendered "visual turn" in late-Russian modernity may yield when applied to komiks by and about women.

THE VISUAL AND THE VERBAL

We can see a variation of Ustinova's gendered verbal/visual tension in a 2004 issue of the comics journal for young girls, *Yula* (Whirligig).[5] This features the ongoing adventures of two child characters, the hyperfeminine blonde Mania (who enjoys such traditional "womanly" activities as ironing, taking care of the home, tea parties, wearing Barbie-like dresses) and the rebellious, spiky-haired tom-boy Kira (who hates dresses but enjoys skateboarding, rough-housing, and the like).

In the story "A Terrifying Force" (Strashnaia sila 2004), Kira receives instructions from an unseen narrator (via the text-driven captions) on how to transform herself into a pretty starlet like one she sees in an ad. "There is a special . . . means," the caption tells her seductively as she stares at a vanity mirror stocked with cosmetics (30, panel 6). But, despite repeated attempts over six symmetrical panels

8.1. "A Terrifying Force" (*Whirligig,* 2004).

along the next page, Kira never quite gets the idea behind making herself up, instead resisting and subverting the logocentric narrator's intent: her crude stabs at maquillage produce a war-paint-like effect ("What are you, playing Indian?" the caption sarcastically asks) and billowing clouds of powder (31, panels 2 and 4).

Kira's final results, a kabuki-type face, scares even her own reflection, which stares tentatively from the mirror as she turns away. "Yes, beauty is a terrifying force," the caption concludes in the old cliché, "but not that darn terrifying . . ." (panel 6). Kira's humorous incompetence at the traditional feminine task of applying make-up frustrates the befuddled, unseen, text-based narrator, which in Ustinova's "verbal vs. visual" paradigm is gendered male. And indeed it is clearly conformity, traditional culture, and conventional standards of pulchritude which the "voice" represents, and which Kira obliviously mocks. In so doing, she reorients and redefines the meaning of the phrase "beauty is a terrifying force" to allow for alternate ways to be beautiful—albeit for grotesquely comedic ends. At the same time, it must be said, and precisely because of the humorous tone, "A Terrifying Force" upholds the old standards of beauty by counterexample.[6]

8.2. "Clouds," by Namida, 2006.

The gendered verbal/visual antagonism toyed with in "A Terrifying Beauty" appears in much more radical form in the St. Petersburg komiksistka Namida's[7] 2006 short story "Clouds" (Oblaka). Unfolding over nine pages, most of which contain only one panel, the black-and-white story depicts a female figure against a stark white background. She is overwhelmed by "clumps of disconnected thoughts" graphically illustrated by word balloons stuffed with random-sounding text ("What the heck is happiness?"; "There's a lot of snow this winter"), all bumping against each other and looming over her like giant air balloons.

Caught in a predicament which recalls the "monkey mind" of Zen Buddhist meditative practice, thoughts overflowing their banks, the woman is tortured to the point of madness by the storm clouds of raging thoughts, which proliferate and come to dominate the panel space, crowding into and overlapping each other like grotesque dirigibles, threatening to collapse and crush her. The balloons' thin tails seem to burrow into her skull; in agony, she holds her hands up to her head as if trying to keep out the thought-balloons, which expand over a two-page spread (82–83).

At last, the word storm breaks (the balloons all pop); the woman achieves a Zen-like state of freedom from oppressive, text-based thought, ushering in a new regime of tranquil white space. But soon, a single stray balloon, reading, "All the same . . . all the same . . . it's such happiness to just think . . ." floats along; she eagerly seizes it (86–87, ellipses in original). The young woman decides she cannot live without *some* thoughts, and starts another cycle, gathering word clouds to ground her once more in a coherent, rational, *verbal* identity.

Both "A Terrifying Force" and "Clouds" exercise Ustinova's reading of the feminine as operating along a visual register and struggling against its other: an oppressive, implied masculine, textual dimension. At the same time, both reinscribe that conflict (the false dichotomy between word and image), by utilizing comics' syntactic strategies of narratival progression (pictures as language) and in Namida's case displaying text as a graphic element. We observe this latter strategy in several of the following works, made by young Russian women (in their twenties) who have all had art school training to varying degrees, and who exhibit the new possibilities for feminine identity formation in an increasingly consumerist Russia.

ALISA IN CONSUMERLAND

Writing on the new Russian women's prose in the late Soviet/early post-Soviet era, Helena Goscilo describes change in spatial terms: women's space—long thought of as domestic, constrained, predetermined, and fixed by patriarchal culture—was moving into new, free, and open spaces. She traces this move—likened to Mikhail Bakhtin's chronotope of adventure and exploration—in the fiction of Tatyana Tolstaya, Lyudmilla Petrushevskaya, Valeria Narbikova, and other authors, writing: "One might say that when women 'knew their place,' they occupied a circumscribed, convention-bound space; contemporary women's fiction has remapped that territory along imperialistic lines, so as to encompass a broader range of possibilities for women's being" (Dehexing Sex 1996: 132). Movement, dynamism, and overcoming barriers are emphasized in this new "imperialist" women's prose, as is the possibility of reinventing oneself into multiple selves and the world into multiple—often untethered—realities. She in fact compares these flights of fancy—both stylistic and plot driven—to Lewis Carroll's *The Adventures of Alice in Wonderland*.

We can take as emblematic of this new women's prose the work of Tolstaya, a writer who, incidentally, vociferously rejects the very label "women's prose," and whose ecstatic metaphors, Mark Lipovetsky notes, "simply supplant reality and subordinate it to themselves" (quoted in Givens: 268). In the 1986 story "The Poet and the Muse," for example, Tolstaya's grotesque literalization of metaphors yields a surreal lyricism: "Nina kicked Agniya out, lifted her bag from her shoulder, and hung it on a nail, carefully took her heart from Grishunya's hands and nailed it to the bedstead" (281). And further: "Destroying Lizaveta turned out to be as hard as cutting a tough apple worm in half. When they came to fine her for violating the residence permit in her residence passport, she was already holed up in a different place, and Nina sent troops over there. Lizaveta hid out in basements and Nina flooded basements; she spent the night in sheds and Nina tore them down; finally, Lizaveta evaporated to a mere shadow" (286). We can see a visual/verbal version of these gendered, ecstatic, transformative flights of fantasy in the comics work of several young komisistky—with an additional element that does not appear in the late-Soviet or early post-Soviet work: the traces of a new consumerist mentality in Russia. These works marry Tolstaya's boundary-bursting aesthetic with the class privilege so much on display in the stories of (to take one example) the young writer and Internet phenomenon Irina Denezhkina.[8]

Natalya Bronnikova's[9] 2004 story "Angel, Don't Be Sad" (Angel, ne grusti), for example, unfolds with little dialogue or sound effects (except for the beep of a cell phone). Its mise-en-abyme structure first shows a colorful, painted street scene of a girl meeting up with an angel, then flying off with him. Back in her apartment, the girl longs for a reunion, as different panels show her sleeping (or dreaming) in bed; staring out an upper-story window; tearing up among a crowd of strangers. The eye catches a cell phone, drawn in a different pen-and-ink style, lying "on top of" the painted portions, like a real object; the screen says, "subscriber temporarily not available." On the next page the style changes radically, as now we see Lukeria or Lu, the artist of the painted "angel" portions, staring angrily at the same cell phone, waiting for a call from her boyfriend (we can now tell that the phone does indeed lie on top of the same page we had been immersed in before; the scowling Lu leans over it, pen in hand).

The page's design prolongs this split-identity motif: three small panels stacked one on top of the other show the impatient artist washing her hair, staring at her weepy self in the mirror, and staring forlornly at her lover's picture. Juxtaposed with those panels, at a canted angle, Bronnikova paints the continuation of the "angel" girl's story in a single long panel—she now stands on the windowsill, about to jump. (A pen, a key, and a hairpin lie on top of the objectified artwork, casting shadows over it, enhancing its two-dimensional look.) In the concluding page, the boyfriend finally calls, Lu sets up a date and in the last panel she joyfully leaps into his arms. In stark contrast, the fictional "angel" girl leaps to her death in another long, canted panel, her downward motion emphasized by several sharp-ended pencils left by the artist on top of her painted image. Yet this suicide is also a reunion: plunging to her death, the girl is met by the angel and the friendly ghost of her cat.

"Angel, Don't Be Sad" testifies both to the "Alisa" and the "consumerland" aspects of "imperialist" women's comics. The star-crossed story of the girl longing for love, to the point of giving up her life, recalls the romantic tragedies of ages past, all the way back to Nikolai Karamzin's 1792 *Poor Liza*.[10] But these panels' kaleidoscopic, "classical" painted look diverges sharply from the modern "real" world of the artist, who knowingly promulgates the same old clichés of the romance genre while herself pining for love's reward. *Her* story, however, does not end tragically—after all, such denouements belong to a different age and visual register; Lu has her cake and eats it, too.

The modern world (depicted in pen and ink with sharp angles and colored on computer) does not entirely clash with the softer, borderless Chagallesque reality of the doomed angel girl; rather, the two dimensions coexist side by side, like a house of mirrors. Each story contains aspects, refractions, of the other. Both heroines find the kind of love they need. But the "framing" story, the world of

Lu, is clearly the preferred reality: the artist's immaculate studio apartment is a consumer paradise of modern conveniences: manga comics on the shelves, stylish Ikea-type furniture, a well-appointed bathroom. The model-thin Lu keeps up with the latest young ladies' fashion (certainly more revealing than the modest pastel-color dresses worn by the angel girl). Money is therefore the true "reality" that structures both "worlds"; it presupposes and secures the free-flow of identities between wispy heroine and modern girl about town. Bronnikova's different-but-not-too-different styles for each story, married seamlessly through page design, effect a simultaneity and equivalence of disparate (though appealing) selves, across suspended ontological borders.

A younger komiksistka, Re-I (real name Liudmilla Steblianko),[11] advances a similarly unbounded figuration of feminine identity, with an Internet-age twist, in her 2004 story "Menia.net."[12] Like "Angel, Don't Be Sad," Re-I's story proceeds without dialogue as a red-haired young woman tries to connect online (the only text is her computer's status updates—"Dialing number," "Connection attempt failed"—which float, disembodied in white against the dark background). The author casts her world in a murky, highly expressionistic style that makes everything appear as if underwater; the red-haired woman's impossibly long tresses (made to seem even longer by a red plaid skirt) wave and defy gravity as she stares gloomily at the monitor, through several failed connections. She in fact stares blindly, as if dreaming: all the figures have half-closed or slitted eyes rendered in solid black. Ghostly electric lines shoot and crisscross through the ether, emblems of other e-messages sent, virtual connections made.

Like Bronnikova's "tragic" heroine, the red-haired woman leaps from her upper-floor window—curious cats, with antennae tails, track her progress—but she lands safely on her feet, on the sidewalk below. Earphones on, trailing cables behind her, like a sleepwalker, the woman traverses an expressionistic cityscape as the e-lines and computer messages proliferate ("Error," "Calling again"). She at last runs into her intended, an impossibly long-haired, androgynous young man wearing earphones, red plaid pants, and a white shirt with a sewn-on red heart, just like the woman's (he in fact seems a slightly more masculine version of her). The two lock hands and at last connect, eyes shut: the ghostly text reads, "Dialing number . . . Verifying name and password" . . . Registering computer on the net . . . Verification complete . . . Hi :)_ " (63). In the final panel, man and woman hold hands together in the distance, on the street, while other red-haired, plaid-wearing people wander about, looking for connection.

"Menia.net" offers some radical insights on feminine identity in a post-Soviet cyber-milieu of online chats and virtual romance, to say nothing of flesh-and-blood alienation. All the characters, whether human or feline, evince a marked lack of affect, as if wandering aimlessly, zombie-like, through a dreamscape, with only the vague impulse to hook up driving them on. Both people and cats also bear the signs of full-blown cyborg-hood: their body/minds waft freely along in a universe of pixels and bytes, trailing wires and hardware—in fact, what we may be witnessing here are not body/minds at all, but mere avatars, fantasy selves. The mechanistic mood is enhanced by Re-I's page design: it squeezes between six and eight panels per page, each with a thick black border which only the electric "ghost-lines" pass through.

The story enacts (critiques?) the reduction of human interaction—human love, even—to the artificial, the solipsistic, the virtual. The object of "affection," the man, is merely a projection or mirror image of the woman. To the extent that love is the operative emotion in this universe of automatons, she essentially loves only a slight variation herself.[13] Furthermore, Re-I has inverted the usual "rules of the game": it is the woman who is the active, seeking force, while the man merely waits to be found, conquered, plugged into. (This is confirmed by the other anonymous figures in the final panel: the women actively hustle about, while the one man only stands there, available.)

All of this makes "Menia.net"—its very title an abnegation of the story's "reality"—a "colonizing" narrative in Goscilo's sense of women's literature that respects no temporal-spatial limitations on the self, that swallows up territory previously unavailable to the feminine subject, including virtual territory. That this act of emancipation and conquest is based on ready access to modern telecommunications technology (however slow), and thus presumes a certain economic status— and moreover that this new unfettered identity is explicitly identified with an urban, tech-savvy, narcissistic impulse to remake the world in one's own image—all demonstrate the possible drawbacks of this "new" mode of being. Bronnikova and Re-I's heroines may float through the clouds and explore ethereal worlds of possibility, but they are fundamentally, first and foremost grounded in an ethos of consumption.

Such, too, is the case for another komiksistka with a major Web presence, Lumbricus Terrestris (Anna Suchkova).[14] I will have more to say about her self-inventions and -reinventions via her blog in the next section; here I want to examine her story "Comics for Nike," a particularly apt allegory for feminine identity-formation through consumer products in the new Russia.[15]

In the story, a green goblin plush toy inhabits a woman's purse. He does not get along, however, with the other objects in the purse: a stick of lipstick, a mirror, mascara applicator, and other typically feminine possessions. "Oh, look how unglamourous you've gotten," they tell the goblin. "Unhappy again?" The other denizens of the bag drive him to literally tie his ears in knots with their endless chatter. But, unexpectedly, the goblin gets his chance at escape: he spies a boy's backpack with the Nike swoosh logo (it belongs to the son of the purse's owner). In a single bound, the goblin covers the distance, landing in the backpack's maw, open as if to receive him. Inside, a gaggle of new, gender-appropriate items happily welcomes him: a ball, a portable CD player, basketball shoes, a water bottle. "This dude's one of us," they proclaim. "He's a real bagman! A real jumper!" In the final panel, the goblin gives the "thumbs up" sign and tells the reader, "Now this is the life! The main thing is, you have to jump at the right time and into the right place!"

The story's "just do it," liberatory ethos promises an easy switch in identity, figured as a leap to freedom. Gender—or rather its subversion—seems at the heart of the transformation in this "ugly duckling" scenario: the goblin just needs to find his niche and drum up the courage to claim the right identity for himself. But this simple message is belied both by the piece's form and content. For this "transformation" is entirely premised on acquiring the right consumer products (the story even takes place inside the containers for those products); the only "choice" involves putting yourself in one box or another. The "leap to freedom" is actually a leap to buy more name brands. (Not surprising, given the project's promotional nature.) The slapdash, near-minimalist quality of the story's line-work underscores the message's artificiality and cheapness: as in much contemporary komiks, the art relies on garish computer coloring to compensate for missing backgrounds, the lack of shadows and little variety in the thickness of the lines. (This commercial ad job contrasts sharply with Lumbricus's much more meticulous creative work.) Even its one unusual design element, the tiling of gutterless panels as if they were lying one on top of the other, only produces a jumbled effect (are we to read the panels as separate items thrown together, like the objects in the bags?).

In short, the ad self-consciously declares it cannot rise above its own hollowness as shoddy corporate propaganda. Its promise of gender-switching transgression is merely a product-placement chimera crowned with a cliché. Trapped, not liberated, by the object-fetishes of consumer desire, we find no "right time and place" that isn't predetermined by the market. Lumbricus and Bronnikova, perhaps unconsciously, take as a given the paradoxical space of freedom and unfreedom that is the structuring base for feminine identity in twenty-first-century Russian capitalism. Only Re-I, with her darker vision of emotionless automatons stumbling into each other in cyberspace, offers an explicit critique of that base, even as she too celebrates it in the name of love.

The trends in post-Soviet Russian women's comics already discussed—visual/textual tensions; the opening-up of time/space to an "imperialist" poetics, often expressed through formal experimentation; and the turn to an identity grounded in consumerist practice—find perhaps their fullest expression in the multifaceted genre of autobiography. In tapping this means for self-knowledge, self-invention, and self-expression, two komiksistky both uphold and challenge the market values of the new Russia.

WOMEN AND POST-SOVIET COMICS AUTOBIOGRAPHY

The American comics scholar Trina Robbins notes that autobiography became a staple of American women's underground comics in the 1960s (91), and the genre is well represented by women comics artists in European and North American alternative comics today (e.g., Julie Doucet, Lynda Barry, Phoebe Gloeckner, Marjane Satrapi). As noted in chapter 7, however, the genre remains relatively rare in Russian comics. Yet two post-Soviet komiksistky have produced significant autobiographical works.

In her blog *The Queen of Worms* (Koroleva chervei) and through prolific output—comics, advertising, storyboards, sketches, an illustrated dog encyclopedia, children's book and magazine illustrations, painting, flash animation, fridge magnets, buttons, and other applied art—the aforementioned Lumbricus celebrates divergent, disparate, and self-contradictory selves, further demonstrating the opportunities and pitfalls for feminine identity formation in the new Russia.

Lumbricus's copious blog entries meticulously recount the artist's daily life, discoveries, and tastes, often down to minutiae. In one of many threads, for example, she reports her driving woes on Moscow roads; car trouble; getting stuck in the snow; the nightmare of public transportation; frustrations registering her car in crowded government offices; road trips; and wishes to someday acquire her dream car. These are accompanied by photos, sketches, animation, links to various brands, and so on.

Another thread is devoted to her interest and activity in the Russian Goth scene; she publishes an occasional newsletter, *Accessible Goths*, in which she comments on and ridicules other would-be Goths' Web pages and utterances. She is also a DJ at various Moscow clubs and does not hesitate to play the role of fashion police, railing against what she considers the decline of Moscow's Goth couture (in an accompanying photo, she uses arrows to comment in detail on various sartorial faux pas).[16] The blog also amounts to an ongoing shrine to Lumbricus's beloved chihuaha Gotik, whose walks, meals, bowel movements, illnesses, and foibles are affectionately detailed in portraits, comics stories, sketches, photos, and other media.

As with any personal blog or diary, much of *Queen of Worms*'s fascination stems from its at times brutally frank depiction of a psyche confronted with an uncooperative world, and the many (often paradoxical or hypocritical) ways—denial, courage, deflection, remorse, blame, sanctimony, rationalization, sincerity, sputterings of rage and bile—in which it reacts, all the time seeking to maintain its "preferred" persona.[17]

One such central paradox structures the blog's Lumbricus persona. On the one hand, the artist deploys her wide diversity of styles and techniques to portray herself as not one identity but many: wide-eyed manga-like innocent; cartoony horned demon; screaming harridan; half-dressed slut (the "evil pornographer" persona); sweet-faced picnicker; or "normal" mohawked shopper.[18] These drawn images compete with her many photo self-portraits, which themselves depict Lumbricus in various guises, from Goth royalty to artist at work to lazy-afternoon couch potato.

All the same, and despite that awesome heterogeneity, Lumbricus consistently returns to what one might term a more classically "femmy" mode of expression, in which she laments her plus-size body; demands special indulgences for her emotional outbursts; upholds gender double standards; and gives in to flights of narcissism. Often these switches in register occur within the same discourse, paragraph, or sentence.

An entry for November 18, 2004, for example, notes Lumbricus's likes and dislikes: "I like to blurt out some profanity once in a while, [but] I don't like when people use profanity around me too much (strange, huh?)." On March 8, 2005 (Women's Day), Lumbricus complains, "I don't like when they give me flowers on the street . . . and then I have to drag them around everywhere, feeling sorry for them and seeing how the leaves and petals are wilting." This leads to a long disquisition on the types of flowers she prefers, before the sighing conclusion, "But nobody gives me flowers."[19]

The blogger's personal insecurities—over such things as getting "defriended"— make occasional appearances, usually as a result of some confrontation or crisis. For example, an entry from May 20, 2005, finds the writer at her most dramatically self-flagellating, casting her personal mishaps into a taught courtroom psychodrama:

The defendant Lumbricus stands accused of thinking that she can explain everything to everybody; she also stands accused of excessive openness and desire to socialize, which some take to be coming on to them; she also stands accused of making personal assumptions, which provoke responses by people of the type "stupid neurotic girl, what's she going on about"; she's also accused of worrying about this; and that despite the given preliminary program of perestroika, she is lazy, scared and pities herself; she is also accused of just doing things with an eye to what others think, and that she's afraid, afraid, afraid. It is the opinion of this Lum-judge that the accused Lumbricus is found guilty of all the crimes she has committed against her own tranquility of life; she is hereby condemned to punishment in the form of isolation for a time, without the right of correspondence. The sentence has been declared and is not open to appeals.

But it is when Lumbricus asserts and illustrates her divergent opinions on body image (particularly as they pertain to her own body) that the blog most explicitly speaks to the competing pressures on young women in Russia to conform to predetermined standards of beauty. So from singing the praises of Dita Von Teese—and sketching herself in the guise of the world-famous burlesque artist—on October 10, 2006, Lumbricus two weeks later can excoriate the wedding industry and, in all caps, question why a wedding day should have to be the happiest of a woman's life. While earlier in that month, on October 4, the artist finds herself in St. Petersburg, self-conscious about her dress and capacity to carry herself among what seems like a crowd of supermodels: "Even though it was cold, the girls in St. Petersburg walked around basically naked . . . totally naked . . . Totally letting their naked stomachs and waists stick out . . . Where can I fit in . . . ?" (Kuda mne uzh . . . , ellipses in original). An accompanying sketch (colored on computer) shows a diminutive, rotund Lumbricus with a furrowed brow, dragging her backpack in t-shirt and jeans through a forest of women's bare legs in mini-skirts and stilettos, towering over her.

In a March 10, 2005, diatribe, Lumbricus discusses most heatedly and at length her attitude toward "fat" and its discontents:

Sometimes I see how people react to or speak out about physical appearance or the weight category that someone is in. I'll say for myself—of course I cop to the fact of my distinct deviation from the average . . . but personally, I wouldn't tell another person that. To say nothing about judging them by their weight, I would never do that . . . Some asshole wrote me too one time, that I'm fat, that I should run to the gym . . . uh-huh, right . . . Like I'll run to the gym and kill myself so some asshole will sing my praises . . . And when I read the things some "ladies" say about other women, I'm totally shocked—where the fuck do they get this shit into their heads? . . . But I'm gonna be a fat girl. I won't be conforming to some fucking fashion, I'm going to shave my head, tie up my fake hair, get myself pierced and tattooed. Maybe I can't feel proud of my ass because it won't fit into a size 2. But I will feel proud that hundreds of people see my comics and they like them!

I find it instructive to compare these impassioned jeremiads on creativity and the myriad ways of being feminine to the drawings of many different women's bodies in Lumbricus's blog. One particularly compelling example appears in a parody of a Gillette razor ad, posted on May 29, 2007. The text reads, "In every woman a goddess is hidden. Release her with the Gillette Venus." The gruesome image complementing the copy shows a naked, Barbie-doll-figured beauty holding a long straight razor, dripping with blood. She stands over—or rather out of—the greenish, obese corpse of Lumbricus, with a large gash along its back. The "goddess" has fulfilled the text's injunction to literal absurdity: she has used the Gillette to slash her way out of an ordinary woman's body and shed it like a cocoon, beaming triumphantly over the remains.

8.2. "In every woman a goddess is hidden.
Release her with the Gillette Venus," by
Lumbricus, 2007.

And yet, lest the reader think that lacerating parody Lumbricus's final word on the body image issue, within a week of that ad's posting, the artist reports (on June 4) that the Russian edition of *GQ* has just published one of her illustrations—of a thin, buxom, scantily clad blonde with a come-hither look, draped over an office desk, with an anthropomorphicized cheetah in a business suit sitting by her, like a pimp.

Lumbricus's flouting of contemporary Russia's feminine models of pulchritude in her blog posts belied by the (to some) disappointing reaffirmation of those same standards in her professional illustration work and comics, returns us once more to the realities of the market. Like Bronnikova, Re-I, and the producers of *Yula,*[20] Lumbricus's occasional resistance to the gender mainstream and new consumerist ethos never truly posits a tenable alternative vision or sustained critique. These komiksistky all seem too busy enjoying the new possibilities for identity-formation through purchases to mount a vigorous dissent.

In a January 29, 2007, post, for example, Lumbricus offers the following ditty:

Here I am, pretty me, with my doggie
I'm waiting for them to give me lots of work
and I do it for a lot of money
for which I've already prepared
a big red bag.

The accompanying portrait shows Lumbricus in yet another aspect: wearing a tasteful green shirt, jeans, glasses, and lipstick; her dreadlock-like hair under control; Gotik in her right hand like an accessory; and the red bag in her left. A far cry from the Gothic dark goddess or corpulent cadaver of the "Gillette Venus" ad, here the artist assumes her persona as radiantly happy shopper. In post after post, the author lauds the market economy's cornucopia of choices: a new Ikea divan for Gotik; favorite brands of Japanese car (with, at one point, an actual prayer for a Suzuki-Samurai); American romantic comedies and action flicks; and, in an echo of her "Comics for Nike," a thorough description of the items in her purse.[21]

Yet stirrings of discontent do surface on occasion. A undated sketch comics story, "Shopping Day," shows the "domesticated Lumbricus" figure trying on clothing before a mirror and coming home with stuffed bags. Later, over a cup of tea, a worried-looking Lumbricus contemplates the receipts spread out before her. The text reads, "A day of shopping ends with somber thoughts about our daily bread—we have nothing to spread on it after all those purchases!"

ELENA UZHINOVA

Where Lumbricus and most of the other artists mentioned demonstrate enduring ties to modern consumerism in their work, to the extent of basing their heroines' identities on recognizable products and purchases, Elena Uzhinova's[22] komiks are remarkable, among other things, for how they largely avoid the new Russian commodity fetishism. Her short autobiographical pieces (many only a page long) instead focus unsparingly on inner realities. While beautifully drawn or painted, the stories' content at first glance seems slight, easy to overlook. But their quiet power builds to devastating, often humorous, effect. In Uzhinova's autobiographical komiks the grief, wonder, and horror of childhood—dead pets, monstrous parents, the terror of one's own body—provoke laughter through shudders. That Uzhinova describes this material as a kind of therapy only lends it a more disconcerting allure. She explains, "I drew these comics about childhood . . . out of my own social withdrawal and introversion as a child, out of a lack of understanding of who I was then. I put it down on paper so that I myself could see what had happened to me. . . . In Russia we don't go to psychiatrists, we're not used to expressing our grief. And I've only been to confession once—and decided I'd never go again! So I suppose this is what was left . . ." (2007, personal interview). Uzhinova cites such disparate influences as Anton Chekhov, the absurdist Daniil Kharms, and the Russian/Ukrainian filmmaker Kira Muratova; their sensibility certainly informs such works as the 1995 "Birds" (Ptitsy), an allegorical autobiography recounting a failed love affair, in which the heroine shaves her head to mark the separation from her hairdresser lover—and the hair refuses to grow back after six months. Eventually, like others before her, she leaps to her death, though her spirit grows wings and flies off with the birds. This simple retelling belies Uzhinova's subtle drawing style and twelve-panel page design, in which the top six "masculine" panels feature explanatory textual captions, while the bottom six—which detail the woman's death and release into the heavens—are entirely "silent."

As seen in "Birds," love as mutilation forms a common theme in Uzhinova's work. In the 2004 story "Geography" (Geografia), everything the child heroine loves dies, especially pets: a hamster, turtles, fish, bugs, chicks—all literally loved to death. Only a boyfriend who runs from her affections manages to survive—causing her to shave her head. In the final panel, a grown-up Uzhinova sitting over a glass of vodka declares flatly to the reader, "So you should thank me, that my love passed you by" (4). The stylistic representation of these Uzhinova-selves recalls Hatfield's point about the strategies of comics autobiographies for representing "externalized subjectivities." In this and other stories, Uzhinova draws herself as portly, awkward, ungainly, and "unfeminine," all visual evocations of her attempt to, as she puts it, "see what had happened to me," of understanding "who I was then."

The threats to the child-Elena are not all internal. Parents, and by extension, the Soviet state, figure as foreboding, inscrutable presences with violent power over weak children in the 1999 "Story about My Eye" (Pro glaz).²³ This tells of young Elena's experiences in Paris in the early 1970s (her family lived a severely restricted existence in the Soviet embassy complex, with monitored access to the French). In a horrible nighttime accident, Elena's mother nearly blinds her—the people one trusts prove the most dangerous, scheming, and unresponsive. Despite her protests, Elena must wear dark glasses she clearly doesn't need, so that any French citizens they might come across "won't see the protruding eye of a happy Soviet child. Who, by the way, wanted for nothing . . ." In the inverted world of adults, pleasures must confusingly be avoided: Elena has to throw away an apple given to her through the complex gate by a French lady ("It's poisoned . . ." her sister tells her).

"To Be a Boy" (Byt malchikom, 1998), perhaps Uzhinova's most body-obsessed (and gynocentric) work, presents a sardonic fable of female empowerment and penis envy. In the first tier, Uzhinova lounges on a rug on a featureless beach (not unlike the desolate backgrounds in George Herriman's *Krazy Kat*), while, in the following panel, a bald naked man with his back turned—presumably a lover—urinates into a campfire. Uzhinova's body is a parody of Reubenesque nudes: corpulent, with bulbous breasts, hair-covered shins, tiny feet, and a mound-like backside. She scratches—"skr-skr"—her bulging belly, as she stares off toward the man (from whom she is separated by the panel gutter), saying, "Once, when I was a kid, I really wanted to learn how to be a boy . . ."

The next two tiers consist of eight small panels recounting the young Elena's struggles and humiliations in her attempts to become a boy: adults make her wear uncomfortable dresses (a subway grate blows up her skirt in a parody of Marilyn Monroe, from *The Seven Year Itch*); she must endure the taunts and spitballs of real boys; she pees all over herself when emulating a masculine stance at the toilet. Tellingly, Elena tries to redefine her female identity through

8.4. "To Be a Boy," by
Elena Uzhinova, 1998.

boys' consumer products—Chapaev toy soldiers, a toy pistol, a slingshot, boys' clothes—but it doesn't work; she keeps running into the anatomical barrier of not having a penis.

Finally, in the last large panel (the solo, grown-up Uzhinova always inhabits the largest panels, denoting both the weight and irrefutability of the present, as well as her aloneness), the author decides to do things her way: she confidently squats over the campfire, peeing on it as steam rises up to the heavens—"pshshshshsh . . ." "I never did learn how to be a boy," she smirks, "but someday I'll learn how to do *this*" (my emphasis).

"To Be a Boy" exercises a feminine will to phallic power, tragicomically beached on the shores of biology. (In a subtly humorous turn, all the male figures in the story have bald heads, accentuating the narrator's penis fixation.) Still, Uzhinova's ultimate response to the quandary of not being a boy makes for an empowering vision of women: she will find her own, better way to "put out the fire." This solution, which admirably strains against traditional gender categories, is not without pitfalls, even dangers: as she crouches over the campfire, Uzhinova displays a backside covered in pustules and bandages—evidence of the burns received from her "method." Moreover, her ridiculous posture over the flames, with clouds of steam rising, recalls the conventional image in much scatological underground comix of farting, to say nothing of the ancient Russian superstition whereby women jump over fire as a fertility rite.

For Lumbricus and Uzhinova, such contradictions and Procrustean concessions vis-à-vis the gender order form the crux of their comics practice.

CONCLUSION: SHINY BAUBLES

Indeed, contemporary Russian women's comics are suffused with these sorts of compromises: ideological, sexual, and especially, socioeconomic. The fact that most komiksistky are producing work in a near-vacuum—publishing almost exclusively on the Web, in festival catalogs, or small-circulation children's journals and anthologies (something applicable to male comics artists, too)—only makes their general acquiescence to the gender status quo all the more poignant. That in many cases their exhilarating formal experiments (the text/visual aspects of which Ustinova would applaud) are not matched by more exigent oppositional politics in their stories (which she would not) is, lamentably, also a feature of Russian comics as a whole. Rather than, say, lesbians, transsexuals, and female presidents in these comics, we tend to get lovelorn, good-looking, fabulously dressed heterosexual young people on shopping sprees. This is all increasingly, and regrettably, par for the course in Putin's Russia—even in such marginal subculture practices as comics.

All of which leads me to conclude this chapter with a reading of Uzhinova's 2007 story "I Want" (Khochu), an example of what Russian women's comics could be and too rarely are: both formally and ideologically sophisticated; eyes-open balanced in their treatment of fantasy's Siren allures (and perils); and always—even down to the title—desiring, demanding something better.

The first notable feature of "I Want" is the art, an amalgam of the cutting-edge and the infantile: Uzhinova sets down the most rudimentary, scratchy drawings, then scans them into computer and colors them, making for a disorienting effect. (The stylish hues, dominated by red—"the color of love"—form an integral part of the work; they are not there to cover up or compensate for less-than-sterling line art, as in many modern komiks.) Secondly, the story and anonymous heroine amount to another parodic refutation of the egocentric fulfillment-through-consumption ethos advanced by many of the komiksistky we have surveyed.

The anonymous narrator, at first a young student, begins an affair with her teacher,[24] who warns her, "Thoughts can materialize. Think before you think" (30). The heroine takes that message to heart as, during a separation from her lover, she resorts to "SMS-love," obsessively typing in "I want" (khochu) as a cell-phone text message. In an echo of Namida's "Clouds," the embubbled word "khochu," repeated ad nauseum, grows into a graphic element; hundreds of pro-liferating pink "khochu's" come to float about the panels in clumps and galaxies, even getting tangled in her hair. In a modern re-telling of Genesis, the heroine's compulsive desire creates a whole new world over the course of a week: first a win-dow (day one), then a chestnut and sea beyond (day two), and so on, until she has brought into being an ideal realm of sun, surf, and her own "beautiful reflection in the mirror" (31)—all through the agency of language.

Up to this point, "I Want" would seem to have lived up to the highest aspira-tions of many women's komiks: the supremely attractive heroine has love (albeit long distance), possessions, rich surroundings, men for the picking (one, unseen, propositions her on the beach). All of which makes Uzhinova's resolution doubly devastating: the heroine discovers her much-ballyhooed desire is impotent—her lover never materializes—her perfect realm a mere shiny bauble. What's more, it's all rather boring. In the final panel, the heroine elects, with hardly a shrug, to abandon her utopian world: Uzhinova shows her older, with a jaded look, smok-ing a cigarette, dragging a wheeled suitcase, walking away from the pretty house and beach, three "khochu's" still clinging to her hair. The block-text caption reads, "I'm a bad pupil, but I will forever miss this world created by our love" (32). But this melodramatic, clichéd soundbite is undermined by the heroine's seen-it-all expression; she now longs for reality's higher stakes. (All the same, her eyes do gaze back to the house, with a twinge of longing. Besides, she still holds the cell-phone.)

A final element of "I Want" crystallizes its complex meaning-making strategies, in a way which recalls Ustinova's visual/verbal tension. Throughout the story, in addition to the regular text captions, Uzhinova embeds directly into the art a run-ning commentary in cursive; this stylish text is almost unnoticeable upon a first reading—it easily dissolves into waves on the beach, ridges on the ground, strands of hair. We can take these as the heroine's random thoughts ("the pleasure of the sea," "a round lamp reflected in my cup of tea") or, more radically, as a meta-poetic triple-voicedness—a "Third Party" negotiating text and image. In "I Want"—and mirroring the willed reunion of the separated lovers—the art strives for the sim-plicity and consistency of text, while the text twists and contorts itself in yearning for the expressiveness of art. Uzhinova, recalling Goncharova's early twentieth-century experiments mixing text and image, melts the difference between the two to almost nothing.

The last of these embedded, "artish" texts reads, "And so, the question is asked, when the still-young God was creating the world, what was really on his mind?" (32). It is tempting to redirect this question to today's komiksistky, heirs to a lit-erary and artistic tradition much-neglected in Russia, but—precisely for that ne-glect—one bursting all the more with potential. In creating what I have argued are mere shiny baubles (formally inventive but politically conformist works), what visions do these artists unconsciously desire? What Tolstayan worlds of possibility would they really rather create?

Uzhinova's heroine renounces her nice little dream world as barren; like the child-Elena in "To Be a Boy," she literally turns her back on its established values, going off in search of her own way. The message is clear: desire's rewards, however beguiling, will not suffice as Russian women comics artists construct novel identities. Something more is needed to attain true happiness.

It's not just that, for all the new possibilities of post-Soviet Russia, such myths as "having it all" are not possible or not finalizable. More crucially, as seen in "I Want," they are simply a case of aiming much too low.

CONCLUSION

IMPOLITIC THOUGHTS

The power in the heirarchized surveillance of the disciplines
is not possessed as a thing, or transferred as a property; it
functions like a piece of machinery. And, although it is true
that its pyramidal organization gives it a "head," it is the ap-
paratus as a whole that produces "power" and distributes
individuals in this permanent and continuous field.
—FOUCAULT (177)

As KomMissia 2005 was taking place, across town, Moscow's imposing
House of the Artist played host to the annual Art Moskva art fair, with displays from over forty-five Russian and European galleries. Many of the works
on display made use of comics iconography—showing yet again that in Russia, comics were everywhere and nowhere; only the rich would be purchasing
such canvases.

Television crews and reporters covering the show converged on one display in particular: that of the artist Pavel Shevelev and his exhibit of courtroom sketches from the trial of oil tycoon Mikhail Khodorkovsky. The former
chair of the petroleum giant Yukos and Russia's richest man, the oligarch had
been laid low in 2003 by what many agreed was a bogus arrest on corruption
charges, meant to punish him for financing Putin's political enemies. Khodorkovsky's over-zealous prosecution (the 2005 trial's outcome was a foregone
conclusion)[1] had raised fears about Russia turning back to its old authoritarian ways. Shevelev's sketches, at once disturbing, funny, and banal, captured
the kangaroo court in real time: the beak-nosed ex-billionaire, as always exhibiting a Zen-like calm, stares out from behind bars[2] like some rare bird; guards
asleep, sprawled in their chairs; bored lawyers' faces; fat judges slumped over
the verdict (which, farcically, took days and days to read). Shevelev's quick

portraits had managed to effect a visual equivalent of Nikolai Gogol's prose: hilarious and horrid—just like Khodorkovsky's modern-day show trial.

It was the sort of work that is getting harder to find—especially in komiks—in a twenty-first-century Russia which each day tosses aside little nuggets of its hard-won freedoms. I close this book on a solemn note, then, with my own quick sketches of the political apathy, hegemony and outright censorship that has come to characterize the rare attempts at sociopolitical critique in modern Russian comic art. (And as the komiks go, so goes the country.)

At the 2008 KomMissia (held in April–May), Xatchett told me a story, perhaps apocryphal, which took place at the first festival in 2002. A man no one knew came in off the street and, without speaking to anyone, taped up a poster on the wall, next to the competition works. The poster depicted a "very violent" comics story dealing with the second post-Soviet war in Chechnya, then in its third year. He left it there and walked away. I have never seen this piece or pictures of it, and I do not know if it even survived to the present. But the episode illustrates a key, sobering fact: by and large, it's primarily the "nobodies"—their works taken down as soon they go up, their names forgotten or never known—who are using comics as a means of protest in Russia.

For all Khikhus's exhortations to expand the scope, generic diversity, and "seriousness" of komiks, the area he rarely pushes (or makes mention of) is the political. In fact, he—like so many others in Russia—shied away from the topic completely at least until recently. In 2006 I asked him about the paucity of "politkomiks," and why more artists didn't use their work to speak out about the many problems in their society. Surely with his love of American underground comix, he could see that this made for a rather conspicuous gap in Russian comic art. He hemmed and hawed. "Look, I care about that stuff," he said. "But I don't—nobody wants to deal with the repercussions. I make some critical comic about Putin, and next thing they're auditing me. Or they're calling the publisher, and I can't print with them anymore. Or suddenly there's a problem with all my clients, they don't want to work with me anymore . . . That's what happens.[3] And I'm already happy doing what I'm doing. Why bother? It's not worth it—it's not like it'll change anything anyway."[4] And so on, in this vein. We had been discussing the work of Nikolai Maslov, and the komiks' community's revulsion over it. And yet it is Maslov who comes closest—as an integral part of his komiks—to a full-blown attack on the warped values and enduring "backwardness" of so much Russian culture—part of the reason, along with his French publisher's contract, why his peers hated it. ("But you can't sell that," Xatchett had sighed, meaning the mystery man's Chechnya piece. "Those stories. No one's going to buy them.")

All this is happening, I remind my reader, in the general context of growing intolerance, chauvinism, and xenophobia in twenty-first century Russia, less than two decades out from the collapse of the Soviet Union. Khikhus himself has been repeatedly attacked by Moscow skinheads, who accosted him on the street, zeroing in on his dreadlocks, or else recognizing him from a TV appearance. Once they told him, "We're going to kill you," before beating him to a pulp. (In July 2008 he proudly posted a portrait of himself, head in bandages, on his *zhzh* page.)

And it's not just political content that gets marginalized, if and when it appears. Anything perceived as transgressive risks a clamp-down. The hentai artist Grif saw his pornographic *Diary of a Laboratory Bunny* removed from the walls of the 2003 KomMissia due to visitor complaints, then rehung with the "offensive" portions obscured, then removed again, for good. In 2004 the police were called, apparently by an elderly woman who had brought her grandson to the festival, and caught sight of another X-rated adventure of Grif's bunny. The policemen hauled the poster away (Grif). After a similar complaint at the 2009 KomMissia, the organizers hung a warning at the entrance.

It's not that political or critical commentary is completely absent; but it seems largely confined to the Internet and political cartoons in the newspapers, especially provincial newspapers. Konstantin Yavorsky's satirical caricatures and strips on Putin appeared in the magazine *Vedomosti*; Alexei Merinov produced a series of humorous illustrations to choice Putin utterances; while the revived *Krokodil'* assayed some political commentary.

Yet another KomMissia censorship "mini-scandal" arose in 2008, involving the caricaturist Denis Lopatin of Kamchatka. His *My Voting Booth* (Moia izbiratel'naia kabinka) portrays the seething anger (or is it benumbed apathy?) of an alienated electorate in five panels. A pair of hands crumple up a voting ballot, use it as toilet paper (we see a close-up of the buttocks), and fling it into the bowl; the "voting booth" is the shitter. This quite boldly comments on the presidential elections of March 2, 2008, which most observers considered only pro forma. "Outgoing" president Putin had fingered his protégé Dmitry Medvedev, a choice the vast majority of Russians obediently rubber-stamped. What few opposition figures dared challenge Medvedev were muzzled, harassed, and banned from the airwaves by the authorities.

My Voting Booth did not last long at KomMissia's wall display. According to published reports, confirmed by Khikhus, the directorship of M'ars (and every other potential display space in the city) refused to exhibit the work, threatening never to collaborate with Khikhus again if he pushed the matter (Smirnova). The work, along with other critical pieces by Lopatin, did remain in the festival catalog and Web site, but the incident once more demonstrated the extreme lack of desire to tempt the Kremlin's ire. There was no indication that the state itself had complained; it didn't need to. Everybody knew—or imagined they knew—what the limits were, particularly when Medvedev was being inaugurated right in

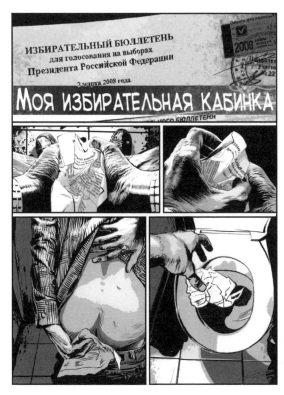

9.1 *My Voting Booth*, by Denis Lopatin, removed from display at the 2008 KomMissia Festival.

the middle of the festival, on May 7. Besides, why bother? It's not like it'll change anything anyway.

I happened to serve on the prize jury of KomMissia that year. When I proposed a new category, Best Politically Themed Comics, to honor Lopatin and encourage this type of work, I was rebuffed. One of my fellow jurors (a Russian) said, in so many words, "I don't do politics." One hears this often today in Moscow, where in certain circles political apathy has become a mark of sophistication.[6]

An irony: komiksisty may, by and large, care little for politics, but Russian politicians have, historically, cared quite a bit about comics and cartoons. They even made them. In their book *Piggy Foxy and the Sword of Revolution*, Alexander Vatlin and Larisa Malashenko delve into the predilection for sadistic, obscene doodlings and caricature of such Bolshevik luminaries as Nikolai Bukharin, Stalin himself, and a less well-known official, Valery Mezhlauk (made chairman of the State Planning Committee in 1934). At Politburo meetings and planning sessions in the 1920s and 1930s, bored Soviet leaders put forth on pads and document margins an endless stream of satirical portraits, usually of one another, showing them masturbating, urinating, castrated, or otherwise sexually humiliated; hanging from lamp posts by their testicles; or recast as devils and cockatrices. Some even dared poke fun at Stalin's Georgian accent. Far beyond the pale of what was allowed in the official press,[7] these scribblings evoke the illicit notes and drawings passed around in classrooms, or perhaps the male posturings of some Bolshevik boys' locker room; the cartoons were exchanged, commented upon, retaliated against through "revenge" portraits, snickered over.

Long locked away in archives, to be rediscovered in the post-Soviet era, these doodles formed a trace, as Mikhail Ryklin might say, of the violence underway in the society during the Great Terror, violence which these men had directed—and which eventually consumed many of them as well. (Mezhlauk was purged in December 1937; Bukharin, once among the most powerful figures in the country, did not survive the decade either.)

With present-day Russia receding more and more from its democratic hopes of the Perestroika era and the early 1990s, one may idly wonder: will we some day discover Putin's doodles in an archive? What traces will they reveal? Will they seem all that different from Shevelev's grotesque portraits of Khodorkovsky, his judges, the sprawled guards?

As this book was nearing completion, on August 7, 2008, Russia launched an invasion on the southern Caucasus nation of Georgia, with which it had skirmished—verbally and militarily—over the last several years. The nominal reason was Georgian president Mikheil Saakashvili's ill-considered, possibly criminal, attack on a separatist province, South Ossetia, in what appears to have been a clumsy attempt to subdue it back into the fold. Russia, which may have in part provoked the Georgians, was in any case ready, and leapt at the opportunity for its "peacekeeping troops" to reclaim South Ossetia—as well as to occupy a swathe of sovereign Georgian territory. The killings, ethnic cleansing, and atrocities (on both sides) that followed showed, tragically, that the peoples of Georgia, South Ossetia, and Russia had all been tragically ill-served by their leaders.

This is not the forum to enter into the sociopolitical and ideological fallout of this event, except to say that the "peacekeeping operation" reinforced a familiar pattern of post-Soviet Russia (under now prime minister Putin) as a resurgent quasi-imperialist state intent on asserting its old influence (by force, if necessary) on its weaker neighbors in the so-called Near Abroad.

Even more disheartening was the swift response of many komiksisty on *zhzh*; as in the rest of the state-controlled media, patriotic jingoism, demonization of the Georgians, and scorn of the West proved the order of the day. Igor Kolgarev portrayed a stereotypical image of an unshaven Georgian soldier atop some rubble, bloody body parts strewn about. Repyov drew a hand holding a blood-splattered dagger, with a button on its sleeve that read, "I am a Georgian." Daniil Kuzmichov, true to form, blogged incessantly about the rightness of the war and ranted about

Russia as a "fortress under siege" by its many enemies (though as always with him, it could be hard to tell how much of this was meant in half-jest). From television and radio, to newspapers and the komiks subculture, everyone was on message: Russia was in the right; indeed its actions were beyond reproach.

Not everyone. Not all komiksisty felt this way, and heated arguments flared up in the forums. Yet I saw no one post or publish an antiwar cartoon. After all, why bother? It's not like it'll change anything anyway.

Apart from my best wishes for Russia—a cruel mistress I adore—it is my sincere hope that the Russians—komiksisty first and foremost—will stop underestimating the power of this medium, this legacy they have been blessed with, and exploit it to its fullest expressive potential—and this includes its viability as an implement for political action. They have great examples to follow. They need simply look to those set down by their predecessors: Slava Sysoev, Konstantin Rotov, Efrosinia Kersnovskaia, Vladimir Mayakovsky. That man off the street, with the Chechnya comics poster.

They bothered.

NOTES

INTRODUCTION

1. A 2004 essay devoted to comics in *Sinii Divan* (Blue Couch), a journal of cultural criticism, was titled "The Paper Opera." As we will observe throughout this book, many Russians who advance comics as an independent art form nonetheless tend to refer to it as "cinema on paper" or similar terms, partly in a bid for legitimacy.

2. Siloviki: the term most often designated for those members of the "power" ministries, military and security establishment who have held so much sway in Putin's Russia. It literally means "men of power/force."

3. On the problematic application to the Russian context of Clement Greenberg's approach to mass culture, see Barker. On its relation to the problem of kitsch, see Boym 1994: 15–16.

4. Coined so by Barker. See Barker: 14.

5. Though, again, this is far from a book on Russian caricature, a tremendously rich area explored by, among others, Mikhail Zlatkovsky (2006). Such important figures as Zlatkovsky, Andrei Bilzho, Boris Efimov, and Denis Lopatin (and these are just the ones still living or recently deceased!) receive only passing references, except for the latter in our conclusion.

CHAPTER 1

1. The Kievan Rus prince Vladimir adopted Christianity as the state religion in 988 C.E., after which the religion was enforced upon a vast pagan population. The emergence of what would become the Russian nation dates to this event.

2. James Billington adds, "Of all the methods of depicting the feasts and mysteries of the faith, the painting of wooden icons soon came to predominate Muscovy" (29).

3. "[The icon's] truth could be immediately apprehended even by those incapable of reading or reflection. It offered not a message for thought but an illustration for reassurance of God's power in and over history . . ." (Billington: 35).

4. As seen, for example, in its use as late as the fourteenth century of inverse perspective, "(where lines seem to converge on a point in front of the picture) to draw the viewer into the picture space and to symbolize the fact in the words of Russia's greatest icon scholar Leonid Ouspensky that 'the action taking place before our eyes is outside the laws of earthly existence'" (Figes: 299–300). See also Billington: 31.

5. As noted by Bonnell, "The centrality of visual images and rituals in old regime pageantry and especially the Russian Orthodox Church made for a highly visual traditional culture" (4). Leonid Ouspensky adds, "It can be said that if Byzantium was preeminent in giving the world theology expressed in words, theology expressed in the image was given preeminently by Russia" (quoted

in Bonnel, 4). Billington, for his part, called the early Christian era in Russia a "sea of pictures," in which "thought tended to crystallize in images rather than ideas" (35). This fixation on the visual went beyond the "upper echelons" of society, to permeate every Russian's apprehension of the world, writes Catriona Kelly: "An important distinguishing feature of Russian popular culture was its saturation with visual imagery" (1998: 49).

6. See, for example, the icon of St. George, twelfth century (Rice: 66).

7. As described by Likhacheva: "Here all the episodes, beginning with the birth of the saint and ending with his death, unfold along the margins, gathering in separate, independent scenes. But each individual border panel does not give a complete impression of the saint. It is only a part of the whole, supplementing and explaining it" (29).

8. So identified by Rice and Hamilton.

9. It is worth briefly mentioning two other Russian Orthodox pictorial traditions, not unrelated to the icon, which too evince a proto-comics sensibility combining text and image, and shared a similar concern with the conventional depiction of time, space, and the sacred: the illuminated chronicle and the iconostasis. The former has its roots in the illuminated manuscripts dating to Kievan Rus (tenth and eleventh centuries), and saw its most spectacular example in the thirteenth-century Radzivill Chronicle, covering eight hundred years of Russian history and boasting over six hundred colorful, naïve illustrations. The iconostasis, a kind of "pictorial encyclopedia of Christian belief" (Billington: 33), deployed dozens of icons in up to six rows in strict "rankings" along a high wall at church altars. This provided, notes Billington, "a model for the hierarchical order of Russian society. Each figure occupied a prescribed position in a prescribed way, but all were united by their common distance from the God of the sanctuary, and by their dependent relationship to the central panel of Christ enthroned" (35). The iconostasis, to some degree, explodes the "multi-incident" icon to a monumental scale. For another discussion on the icons' devices compared to modern comics, see Uspensky.

10. In 1810, the memoirist N. I. Strakhov called lubki a kind of "common people's library": the wealthier peasants would cover their walls with them and hang some up on their gates and exteriors of the home. In the evenings illiterate peasants would gather around these prints, which a literate person would "read and interpret." Writing in 1914, the ethnographer V. Petrov reported that even poor peasants in Ryazan province felt it incumbent upon them to buy "a few" (neskol'ko) prints with which to decorate their huts for Easter (both quoted in Rovinsky: 11).

11. Norris argues that the wartime lubki, starting with those devoted to the conflict with Napoleon and in every war since then up to WWI, contributed to the consolidation of a patriotic and national identity through its visualization of Russianness and "otherness."

12. Despite their low status as "people's pictures," the traditional lubki blazed the trail, both commercially and educationally, for the massive popularity after 1860 of *lubochnaia literatura*, Russia's first type of popular literature. As with its predecessor, this "low" form appealed to public taste with its often lurid adventure tales, folklore-derived stories, and rewritten versions of foreign and domestic classics. With such fare as *Ivan the Knight* and *The English Milord*, the literatura resembled traditional lubki with its colorful covers and subject matter, and was sold by the same ofeni, who kept abreast of demand by consulting with the public "in a language it could understand" (Reitblat 1991: 154). This public input is crucial to an understanding of Lubochnaia literatura; it was not subject to the whims of critics or cultural prognosticators, but rather reflected only what its readership demanded according to sales. For this purpose, an entire "underclass" of writers, themselves largely of peasant origin, rose up to fill that demand, often borrowing or plagiarizing from high-brow culture. See especially Brooks, chapter 3, and Reitblat 1991, chapter 9.

13. Even though, as E. A. Mishina shows, a virtual "struggle over terms" (borba terminov) raged among lubok scholars in the nineteenth and twentieth centuries, adding to the confusion. Today (at least to specialists) the adjective *lubochnyi* connotes something much more positive, indeed opposite, to what it meant pre-1820: iarkii ("colorful") and narodnyi ("folk") (quoted in Reitblat 2000). On the name controversy, see Reitblat 2001, Brooks: 63; Sokolov: 10; and Snegirov: 223–24.

14. See Sokolov's examples of intentionally "distorted" and "mistaken" texts, including an 1887 citation of Pushkin's *Evgeny Onegin*—"Eyes as blue as the sky . . ."—accompanying an image of a brown-eyed woman (141). We see an extreme example of such disjuncts for humorous purposes in the modus operandi of the raeshniki, who in the course of commenting on their "funny panoramas" would take pride in contradicting the image and successfully fooling the viewer about what she was seeing (161). Writing in 1873, I. E. Zabelin noted, "The raek pictures, in large measure, mean nothing in and of themselves, but they receive completely unexpected colorings as a result of the lively, sharp, at times extremely witty explanations" (quoted in Lotman: 484).

15. As in an unknown artist's circa 1812 "Napoleon's Winter Quarters": the doomed French invaders, sinking in deep Russian snow, have speech balloons with decidedly long and wispy tails, underscoring their helplessness.

16. In this regard, technological change and its base of production affected the lubok's poetics, sometimes drastically. The widespread use of copper plates in Russia, starting in the mid-eighteenth century, meant better printing and, according to Sakovich, the expansion of the textual captions so that this "wordiness" comes to dominate the image—which "reacts" by heightening its "theatricality" (quoted in Sokolov: 18).

17. As does Boris Sokolov, who relates the work of Zhora Litichevsky (the subject of chapter 5), Leonid Pirugin and other modern komiksisty to the lubok (195).

18. Mikhail Zaslavsky mentioned to me in 2004: "People say comics are alien to Russians, that they will never accept them, that there's something about Russians that sees comics as alien. I do not understand such sentiments." Vladimir Sakov, head of the Tema comics and animation studio, also noted that "Russians don't know how to read comics" (Sakov interview, 1997). Their forefathers certainly had no trouble reading comics in the form of the lubok, and delighting in the activity!

19. Years later, when the narrator passes through again, the pictures still hang on the wall, though much else in the domicile has changed. The lubok, incidentally, appears in such works of nineteenth-century Russian literature as Nikolai Gogol's "The Nose" (1833) and "The Portrait" (1835), and Mikhail Zagoskin's 1831 novel *Roslavlev, or the Russians in 1812*. Moreover, A. G. Sakovich notes that important Golden Age writers, including Pushkin, Gogol, Nikolai Leskov, and Fyodor Dostoyevsky grew up reading lubok chapbooks (131).

20. "Specifically, lubok narrativity is reflected in the creation of lubok chapbooks, constructed along the principle of comics and genetically tied to icon border panels" (Lotman: 491).

21. Though by then the business of lubok had largely left the villages and "the people," a process accelerated by the widespread introduction of a superior technology, lithography, at about the time of the 1851 law's drafting. For a useful summary, see Norris, chapter 3.

22. Rovinsky's reading influenced generations of scholars, but some have resisted his reasoning, and question whether these works are actually about Peter at all; see, for example, Farrell 1993 on the traces of shamanic culture in "Baba Yaga . . . Crocodile."

23. Pushkin's allusion to this print in his 1836 novella *The Captain's Daughter* (22) thus represents a slyly subversive commentary on the then-current czar, Nicholas I.

24. Mainly a phenomenon of the Russian far north (to where many of these communities had fled), the drawn lubok of the Old Believers represents its own separate category, in that the works were hand-painted on wood and often very subtly colored. They were one of the last examples of the people's picture as a true folk form, often employing children (such as the ten-year-old Sophia Kalinkina of the village Gavrilovskaia) as artists. See Itkina: 22–24.

25. Cofounder Benois's pronouncement in his book *Art Treasures of Russia* (1901) isolates the neo-nationalist/cosmopolitan philosophy of World of Art in its mature form: "We believe that those forms which once upon a time grew naturally from the Russian soil are closer to the Russian heart. We believe that the Russian artist, in finding inspiration in them, will find himself, will find the expression of his own, still obscure ideal. Better he do that than examine foreign models of art and imitate them. However, the reform of Peter the Great even for art did not pass completely without trace. To cease being European now, to shelter from the West behind a wall would be very strange, even absurd . . . That is why, alongside works of our own national art we will not fear to present everything foreign and

European that is preserved within the borders of Russia. That is why we focus equal attention on what was created both *before* and *after* Peter" (quoted in Bowlt: 186, emphasis in original). On World of Art, see Bowlt; Lincoln: ch. 13.

26. Bilibin himself noted of his engraving-like work: "The style is old Russian—derived from traditional art and the old popular print, but *ennobled*" (quoted in Golynets: 10, my emphasis). On Bilibin, see Bowlt: ch. 13; Golynets; Petrova; and Klimov.

27. Moreover, a series of illustrations for Pushkin's *The Tale of Tsar Sultan* (1905) betrays another influence: a drawing of a barrel adrift at sea strongly recalls Hokusai's *The Great Wave Off Kanagawa* (1832). The work of another Japanese master of the print, Hiroshige, is evoked in an unpublished 1927 Bilibin aquarelle, *The Falcon*. See Verizhnikova: 36–37.

28. "In drawing public attention to the Russian icon, to the lubok, peasant embroidery and woodcarving, Bilibin prepared the ground for the Neo-Primitivists and the Futurists," notes Bowlt, and even contends that he may have been the direct precursor to the much more radical Natalia Goncharova (234). Other book illustrators, such as Mstislav Dobuzhinsky, Elena Polenova, and Konstantin Somov also played important roles in "legitimizing" (some might say "housebreaking") lubok for a middle-class audience, though Bilibin remains by far the best known to generations of Russian children who cannot imagine some fairy tales without his drawings. Bowlt also credits Bilibin with providing an "important source of ideas and motifs" for Christmas cards, menus, and other ephemera both in Russia and the West (233), putting him in the same league as the Czech father of Art Nouveau, Alfons Mucha.

29. Larionov and Goncharova presented their primitivist and lubok-inspired works in 1909 at the Third Golden Fleece exhibition. Larionov's painting *Soldiers* (1909), for example, depicts its crudely rendered figures with text streaming from their mouths (Gray: 96–97), while his *Katsap Venus* (1912) depicts the famous lubok image "The Cat of Kazan" on a wall. Artists such as Vasily Kandinsky and Kazimir Malevich, later known for abstract and suprematist works, also took inspiration from the lubok; in addition, the latter made anti-German WW I *lubki*. The early twentieth century was a heady time, when the Russian avant garde rediscovered its indigenous roots: the Moscow artist Nikolai Vinogradov organized an important, first-of-its-kind exhibit of lubki in February 1913, whose catalog praised Rovinsky and the ancient peasant masters. See Norris: 164–66 for a useful summary.

30. As Susan Compton noted, Russian Futurists strove not to co-opt these old forms as some sort of ironic cant, but rather to resurrect them; they "recreated past styles in the original spirit of their invention, whether folk broadsheet (in Russia named lubok), sign painting, folk song, Byzantine painting or even cave-painting. Each was explored for what it had to give to provide a renewed direct form for painting or poetry" (13).

31. In his 1790 critique of Russian society, *Journey From St. Petersburg to Moscow*, Alexander Radishchev wrote: "If a Hogarth was born among us, he would find an abundant field for caricature" (quoted in Zlatkovsky: 7). Much of this brief sketch on Russian caricature leans in part on Zlatkovsky's 2006 study.

32. We should also consider imported caricature (particularly from France) that made its way into Russian publications in the last third of the nineteenth century, such as Ovod and Eugene's work. A translation of George Colomb's (a.k.a. Christophe's) 1889–1893 saga *La Famille Fenouillard* appeared in the journal *Rodnik* (Wellspring).

33. In Kunzle's opinion, such illustrations mostly aped those in European gazettes, rarely rising above the "facetious anecdote."

34. Bowlt argues that extreme focus on the "necrological" in these works had a profound influence on the first generation of Soviet caricaturists in their anticapitalist works of the 1920s and 1930s (115).

35. Another branch of comics-related art that debuted in Russia in the late nineteenth century deserves mention: the movie poster or kinoplakat. Almost from its beginnings in about 1896, the kinoplakat differed from its Western counterpart; rather than adopt the nature-derived "organicity" of Art Nouveau, Russian artists—in keeping with prerevolutionary avant-garde trends such as Constructivism—emphasized machine-like forms, geometrical shapes, primary colors, and purity of line. They also highlighted the dynamism of the moving image by capturing the critical moment of

a scene, as in Pol' Assaturov's poster for the first Russian feature film, Vladimir Romashkov's *Stenka Razin* (1908), which depicts the Cossack rebel tossing his "unfaithful" princess overboard. This work plainly shows the folkloristic influence of the lubok.

CHAPTER 2

1. The Bolshevik Revolution has received much scholarly scrutiny; see, in particular, Figes 1996 and Freeze 1997. On early Bolshevik culture, the reader will find Stites 1989 and 1992, and Gleason et al. the most cogent.

2. As described by Daniel Orlovsky: "The Bolsheviks were cultural revolutionaries, particularly in their feverish attempt to construct a new symbolic world—with new icons, new language, new monuments, new festivals—to bestow legitimacy on the new order" (262).

3. Stephen Norris argues that in this and other posters Moor (himself a Don Cossack from the southern city of Novocherkassk) is transforming a Cossack soldier (his ethnicity marked in part by his mustache) into a Red citizen, catalyzing the change from nationalist hold-out to Soviet patriot, an important goal in early Soviet culture. Cossacks, who fought for both the Reds and the Whites, were a divided ethnic group which the Bolsheviks sought to win over (Norris, forthcoming). If so, this represents yet another combination of old and new in Moor's poster!

4. Led by Alexander Bogdanov, this troubled (and trouble-making) group sought to build a true proletarian culture, despite those—like Lenin—who criticized its extremism. See Gleason et al.: 11–13.

5. Stepanova designed unisex and other functional clothing; Lyubov Popova made plane-flattening sets for the "biomechanics" theater productions of Vsevolod Meyerhold; Mikhail Mokh created Constructivist dishware and other applied art. No area was left unexplored in the movement's drive to bring art and life together, from the recrafting of mundane objects like spoons to projects of the most grandiose ambition, such as Tatlin's never-built, multistory Monument to the Third International. On Constructivism, see Gray and Lavrentiev.

6. NEP, launched in 1921 by Lenin, reintroduced limited free enterprise to the floundering centralized economy of the USSR. Some welcomed its boost to economic growth, while others viewed it as a betrayal of the revolution.

7. As pointed out by Figes, "In artistic matters [Lenin] was as conservative as any other 19th-century bourgeois" (1996: 742), preferring classics to proletarian art.

8. "The campaign against illiteracy became the cause célèbre of the early stages of cultural revolution. In the first twenty years of the Soviet period there grew up a generation for whom the ability to read, and in particular to read 'well,' was an important mark of social distinction" (Lovell 2000: 21). Note that early Soviet efforts led by Lenin's wife, Nadezhda Krupskaia, even attacked fairy tales as detrimental to proper learning. See Kelly 2005 on state criticism of the fairy tale spinner Kornei Chukovsky. Reading had become a political act.

9. Stephen Lovell depicts the situation thus: "In Western countries, even those apparently dominated by the 'culture industry,' middlebrow culture is supplemented by a range of other cultures (or subcultures) which are by and large granted public representation, even if they are economically deprived (examples include hippies and academics). In Soviet Russia, on the other hand, subcultures were forced out of public view and social consciousness. In particular, the autonomous intellectual field characteristic of 'bourgeois' society was removed and replaced by a new legitimizing authority" (2000: 17).

10. This seems to have applied elsewhere in Europe. The Czech comics historian and journalist Tomáš Prokůpek has written on the early twentieth-century resistance to word balloons in his country as based in part on anti-Americanism.

11. As noted by Bonnell, there were also more pragmatic reasons for the troubled young state to turn to posters rather than newspapers as a primary information delivery system: paper shortages, disruptions in transportation, and high rates of illiteracy among the peasantry (5). Waschik and Baburina, for example, report an illiteracy rate of 56 percent at the time of the revolution, particularly outside the cities and among women (84). Other estimates range as high as two-thirds of the population. Posters varied in size from the smaller (62 x 38 cm) to quite large (over 200 x 140 cm for the multipaneled ROSTA windows).

12. These groups, too, had ideological sympathies with the Communists. Figes writes, "All these artists were involved in their own revolutions against 'bourgeois' art, and they were convinced that they could train the human mind to see the world in a more socialistic way through their new art forms" (2002: 447).

13. In 1925 Viacheslav Polonsky, head of Litizdatotdel (publishing arm of the Red army and Revolutionary Military Council) during the Civil War, praised the poster as a means of "organizing the collective psychology" (Waschik and Baburina: 14). Through changing fortunes and political ups and downs, the poster remained a part of Russian visual culture through seventy-four years of Communism. Over 400,000 individual posters were produced in twentieth-century Russia, according to Waschik and Baburina (84).

14. And in any case GIZ was only one of several entities responsible for publishing and poster production, which was not centralized until 1931.

15. We can thus read Alexander Apsit's 1918 allegorical print *Internatsional* as a parody of the "pyramid" motif. It depicts the pyramid crumbling as workers scramble to the top and murder the revolting, crowned worm ("capital") with sledgehammers and their bare hands.

16. Writing in 1932, Klutsis advocated for the use of photography in posters as a more "authentic" and indexical means of portraying the Soviet society now coming into being, which accorded with the soon-to-be-adopted state policy of Socialist Realism: "Photomontage for the first time introduced new social elements into the composition—the masses, the new man, building a socialist state, the workers of new kinds of production . . . undistorted by aesthetic additives (pridatki), but through real people" (quoted in Waschik and Baburina: 142). It goes without saying that Klutsis's photomontage works were staged, allegorical, and by definition "unrealistic" depictions of Soviet Russia. See, for example, his many works showing industrial workers or party leaders towering over factories and crowds, as in *Toward the Battle for Fuel, for Metal* (1933). Compare this image to Vertov's double-exposed shot of the "gigantic" cameraman standing over the masses in *Man with a Movie Camera* (1929). In the eyes of some, photography brought the plakat one step closer to cinema.

17. Bonnell identifies this print as the first to represent Bolshevik leaders in a "larger than life" vein, a common device of many plakaty, which she links to the symbolic perspective of the lubok and icon (143).

18. We may be observing in these "odd" Russian examples a vestige of the inverse perspective native to the icon, and theorized by, among others, Pavel Florensky (1882–1937). I thank Mark Konecny for this insight.

19. The penchant for dichotomies in Russian thought is explored in the influential essay by Yurii Lotman and Boris Uspensky, "Binary Models in the Dynamics of Russian Culture (to the End of the 18th century)."

20. It is also "cinematic" in the most direct sense. The technique of ratcheting up anticipation for the "pay-off" of some technical feat or grand appearance was a staple of the Soviet silent cinema; see for example the tractor's arrival to the village in Alexander Dovzhenko's *Earth* (1930) and Lenin's Finland Station appearance (after much build-up) in Sergei Eisenstein's *October* (1927).

21. The use of posters for "shaming" undesired social types—drunks, shirkers, in some cases even the disabled—was not uncommon. Compare this to the cruelly sadistic cartoons made by politburo members (and even by Stalin himself!), examined in this study's conclusion.

22. Compare this to the conservative icon-making practice of using pattern originals (*ikonnopisnie podlinniki*) with traceable patterns (*prorisi*) to transfer designs with minimal variation to new works.

23. Less inclined to avoid the term, Stephen White compares the multiframe approach to a comic book (67), while Waschik and Baburina note, "Having emerged almost simultaneously with the Soviet political animated film, [the windows] seem the forerunner of comics" (175).

24. Kovtun adds: "[The windows] have the same compositional narrativity seen in the lubok or the hagiographic icon with its 'life scenes' (kleima): although each separate frame is not resolved at all through narrative means—it is monumental, laconic and representationally graphic; but taken together, they yield the development of an action or a graphic story" (1968: 6).

25. On Communism as a religion, see Stites 1989: ch. 5.

26. Kenez describes agitki, introduced in the first years of the revolution: "These were short films, five to thirty minutes long, with extremely didactic content, aimed at an uneducated audience.... The simplest of the agitki had no plot at all, but were called *living posters*" (34, my emphasis). See also Kenez's discussion of the 1919 agit-film *Children—The Flower of Life*, which unfolds in a "split" plot showing two families: one which does not follow Soviet rules of hygiene and perishes, and another which does and prospers (35). This strategy closely mirrors the aforementioned either/or multipanel design of many posters; compare this, for example, to Radakov's *The Life of an Illiterate / The Life of a Literate*.

27. The schematic nature of a survey prevents me from pausing long on the rich discourse comparing the poster with early Soviet silent cinema—usually to demonstrate the superiority of the latter. For example, Kozhin and Abramov favorably compare cinema to Moor's 1920 poster *Labor* (whose action unfolds in five sequential panels), arguing that in the latter the "story" concludes in a more "static" final image: a worker and peasant standing by the fruits of their just efforts: "Here we cannot speak of a resurgence of that which we see in the 19th century; the narrativity (povestvovatel'nost') of the modern lubok is related to the tendencies of our own time, which demands new forms and a new expression of the narratival principle. These new forms of narrativity recall the cinema: the cine-film (kino-fil'm) shows a picture made up of dialectically coordinated scenes (the frames) unfolding without interruption, dynamically—more fully resolving the problem posed by some modern lubok pictures" (33). As Richard Taylor describes: "Like machinery, the cinema was perceived to be a dynamic form, unlike, for example, the poster, which, even in the modified form of the ROSTA window, remained predominantly static" (Stites et al.: 191). Yet film directors such as Sergei Eisenstein and Alexander Dovzhenko valued caricature, and duplicated its iconography; see especially the former's *Strike* (1924). Figures such as Rodchenko and Mayakovsky worked in both media. The interactions and antagonisms between the Soviet comics language and cinema deserve further study.

28. Compare the acceptance of even critical ROSTA windows to the party's furor over Yevgeny Zamiatin's satirical dystopian novel *We* (1920), which it banned.

29. As we will see, this more "refined" approach would make the Petrograd windows artists vulnerable to charges of "formalism." As occurred throughout the arts, their ties to the avant-garde would damn them in the 1930s, with the advent of Socialist Realism. Chistiakova and Kovtun wrote for a poster exhibit in 1968, at a safe distance from the excesses of the Stalinist thirties.

30. Although, as Bonnell notes, the average print run for a poster in 1932 was 30,000 (43), the state confiscated, rejected, or censored sizable portions of the works, citing bad quality or politically impermissible depictions; this was complicated by the sharply shifting political winds, which made it difficult for artists to anticipate what expressions were allowable, virtually from month to month. See Waschik and Baburina: 250.

31. A series of posters modeled on the windows method of sequential panels, the IZOGIZ windows, did appear intermittently in the 1930s. In these color lithographs, artist such as Yulii Ganf and Konstantin Rotov elucidated the intricacies of the first five-year plan (Waschik and Baburina: 208). IZOGIZ stood, rather cumbersomely, for the Publishing House of the Union of State Book and Journal Publishers.

32. In 1920 Commissar of Education Lunacharsky praised the power of caricature, as did Nikita Khrushchev in the post–WW II era. Trotsky, once the leader-in-waiting of the Soviet Union (Stalin later exiled him), even wrote the preface to a 1924 collection of the caricaturist Boris Efimov's cartoons.

33. Soviet attempts to ignite a satirical press during the Civil War included the journals *Solovei* (The Nightingale, 1917), *Krasnyi d'iavol* (The Red Devil, 1918), and *Gil'otina* (The Guillotine, 1918). All these publications, however, had production problems and/or failed to win a following, and closed down relatively quickly. The most renowned, then and since, was *VOV* (an acronym which stood for Voennyi otriad' vesel'chakov, "Military Detachment of Merry-makers"). Led by Mayakovsky, it saw release in 1921, and shut down after one issue. (See Stykalin and Kremenskaia: 13–16 and 58–63.) In many ways *VOV* proved a direct precursor to *Krokodil*.

34. *Tonkie zhurnaly:* so called to distinguish them from the "thick journals" of the nineteenth- and twentieth-century intelligentsia.

35. Having founded their new state on "scientific" Marxist principles, the Bolsheviks saw religion as a ripe target for vituperation and ridicule. Moor, cofounder of *Bezbozhnik*, produced some of his best, most scathing satire for the journal.

36. In this, the satirists were merely following the lead of the resolution "On the Party and Soviet Press," penned by Lenin: "One of the most important tasks of the Party-Soviet press is the exposure of crimes committed by various types of public functionaries and institutions, the pointing out of mistakes and deficiencies of the Soviet and Party organizations" (Stykalin and Kremenskaia: 15).

37. Sometimes they took the rayok-style linguistic hijinks so far as to upend the goals of the government literacy campaigns, as happened in *Lapot'* (The Bast Shoe): "In its striving to please the reader, the journal itself at times becomes less than literate, and instead of aiding in the struggle to establish a culture of proper speech, it expresses itself in a broken pseudo-peasant 'dialect'" (Skorokhodov: 452).

38. We should take note that many cartoons, such as this one, had captions written not by the artists but by *temisty* ("theme-makers"). In addition to writing captions, they in many cases came up with the ideas for the drawings, which the artists would execute. The main temisty at *Krokodil* in this era were Mikhail Glushkov and Boris Samsonov, who wrote the bureaucrat's famous line in Eliseev's cartoon.

39. In 1923 it even established the "Krokodil Award" for most inept, dyed-in-the-wool bureaucrat. It was still permissible in the early 1920s to use satire for *samokritika* (the hard-nosed exposure of social problems so as to address them), but later material like this would open the journals to attack.

40. One device not used by Rotov (nor, apparently, by any other Soviet caricaturist) is the sound effect, which remains rare in Russia even to the present day (with the exception of manga). I have found it difficult so far to establish definite connections, beyond the aesthetic, between Soviet and Western cartoonists in the pre–WW II era. Clearly the Soviets were heirs to the European tradition of caricature, at least until 1917. All reflected this, some more strongly than others. Intriguingly, Eliseev's pagelong "When the Sleeper Awakes . . ." (*Krokodil* no. 15, April 1927, 9) presents a dream story about a venal bureaucrat much in the manner of Winsor McCay's *Little Nemo in Slumberland*. The official even wakes up in the final, bottom right-hand panel, following the *Little Nemo* formula.

41. Coined by Trotsky, the term Fellow Traveler (*poputchik*) identified those artists and cultural figures who broadly supported the Communist government but did not join the party or strictly follow its aesthetic guidelines. As the 1920s wore on, their position grew increasingly untenable. Eventually, they were eliminated by the totalitarian state. See Robert MacGuire's *Red Virgin Soil* (Princeton, N.J.: Princeton University Press, 1968) for an account.

42. As the only humor journal for most of the Soviet Union's history, *Krokodil* enjoyed a huge circulation: 300,000 in 1953; 1,700,000 in 1963, when it received 6,000–7,000 readers' letters *a week* (Stykalin and Kremenskaia: 212).

43. Apart from his many titles, accolades and fervent support of the party, Koltsov was also the brother of the renowned caricaturist Boris Efimov. As if to underscore the grotesque, byzantine nature of Soviet culture, Efimov suffered hardly at all during the purges, but was showered with prizes, befriended Stalin, basked in praise from far and wide (even outside the Soviet Union), and at 108 was still regarded the grand old man of Soviet caricature, a living legend. (He died in 2008.)

44. See Rosenfeld 1999 for a good survey of the period's great diversity in this sphere.

45. Railing: 3. As she explains: "El Lissitzky's story-in-language, the word and its typographical presentation, was conceived to live with the story-in-images. Neither one is an understudy for the other. Both derive meaning and vitality from the other. The word and letter have visual form as does the image; separate and together they create movement and space. . . . Lissitzky is exploring exactly where these media meet; discovering how the laws of movement, space, form, sound and color find expression in the different media of his book. Image and graphic letter and word are a creative whole" (ibid.).

46. He adds: "The book invites us to thumb its pages—like the doodles sketched during a boring lecture in students' notebooks, which, when rapidly leafed through, are transformed into an *animated cartoon*. In this way the book is presented as a metaphor for the filmic . . . . But it also denounces the optical illusion of cinematic continuity" (119, emphasis in original).

47. Lissitzky also dabbled in what he called the "perfect non-hierarchical unity" of figure and letter through cartoon work. In 1919, while in Vitebsk (a major center for Russian modern art, in Belarus), he even produced ROSTA windows and caricature portraits. See Shatskikh: 62–63.

48. Also, one could add this Soviet renaissance man's film and theater acting, as well as collaborative works in Soviet advertising with Rodchenko.

49. Klutsis experimented with sequentiality, e.g., by repeating images within works to suggest motion. See his postcards for the 1928 Spartakiad proletarian games.

50. Turovskaia calls the children's journals *Chizh* and *Yozh* part of the "mico-institutions" that enjoyed relative autonomy below the radar of the totalitarian state longer than other cultural producers (36). There were, however, criticisms of other children's journals in the 1920s, including the first *Merry Pictures*, which was shut down. In any case, both founder Nikolai Oleinikov and major writer Daniil Kharms perished in the purges of the 1930s. More auspiciously, the 1937 publication of the children's book *Stories in Pictures* with art by Nikolai Radlov showcased extensive comics techniques.

51. Boris Groys launched a storm of debate with his controversial thesis that Socialist Realism in fact represented not the disruption but the extension of the Russian modernist project: "With respect to the main ambition of the avant-garde, which was to overcome the museum and bring art directly into life, socialist realism both reflected and consummated avant-garde demiurgism" (72). Those who have argued against his thesis include Matthew Cullerne Brown, Svetlana Boym, and Thomas Lahusen.

52. The 1932 party resolution "On the Activities of Publishing Houses" criticized formalism in book design and illustration. On this and other relevant party edicts, see Mansurov: 148–49.

53. Though the vagueness of this definition led to much anxiety, confusion, and debate. See Struve: ch. 20.

54. In one of the more bitter ironies noted in this book, the writer Maxim Gorky, who played an instrumental role in implementing Socialist Realism, was a longtime supporter of Russian caricature. In 1932 he wrote: "Caricature is a socially significant and most useful art for representing the various deformities (not always visible to the naked eye) in the esteemed visages of modern heroes or those aspiring to heroism" (Kukryniksy: 211). Gorky impressed on Soviet caricaturists the need to emphasize the differences between the USSR and the West, fueling the "us/them" device (Stykalin and Kremenskaia: 193). Yet his support of Socialist Realism contributed to policies that turned Soviet caricature—for all the talent of its practitioners—into little more than an attack dog for the state, muzzled by formulaic conventions and restricted targets.

55. With the collapse of the USSR, there has emerged an extended scholarly debate on the uniformity of Socialist Realism and Soviet culture in general. If Andrei Sinyavsky, the dissident and writer, could characterize it this way: "There is one science: Marxism; one eminent Marxist: Stalin; one 'creative method' in art and literature: Socialist Realism; one basic history book; and so on. All originality is dangerous and suspect. Conspicuous stylistic deviations are forbidden. The fight against 'formalism' is a fight for the party standard, for a strict, ecclesiastical form in art and literature" (112), by 1994 Svetlana Boym and other critics are complicating that picture: "The unified Socialist Realist culture did not have a unity of grand style. It was rather a kind of monstrous hybrid of various inconsistent elements from right and left: aristocratic and proletarian culture; radical avant garde rhetoric and chaste Victorian morals of 19th-century realism; happy endings and stormy weather from popular fiction of the turn of the century; and 'positive heroes' from the Russian classics and Slavic hagiographies" (106). In fine art, Cullerne Brown and Taylor have argued, Socialist Realism evinced much variety through five decades as the official style (11–12).

56. These 1930s works' descriptions don't require qualifiers like "comics-like"; they are fully fledged, even slavish, versions of Western—especially American—adventure strips (serialized narratives, word balloons, occasional sound effects, purple prose). Their style can be observed in much Serb and indeed East European mainstream adventure titles to this day.

57. These examples come from Dragincic and Zupan: 53, 59. Kuznetsov also produced adaptations of Pushkin's fairy tales.

58. Nabokov's English pun on *poshlost'*.

59. One reads an appreciation for the "tiny magic" of comics in *Speak, Memory*, when the author describes his childhood scrutiny of an American strip: "If one looked closely, one could see that the color was really a mass of dense red dots" (69–70).

60. Elsewhere Nabokov derides "rosy-cheeked comic strip fans" (1959: 62), while the villain in his 1932 novel *Camera Obscura* works as a cartoonist. In the novel's translation to English (as *Laughter in the*

Dark), the character's occupation was changed to art critic; Jane Grayson speculated that cartooning made the villain too sympathetic!

61. Note again the implication of the speech/thought balloon, in particular, as "alien" to Russian culture. Pnin's response relates to the *literaturnost'* ("literariness") of Russian culture, discussed in the Kabakov section and elsewhere below.

62. Tufts: 35. She reports Krassousky, who emigrated from Kiev, lost family members during the Civil War and was himself wounded. His alleged epilepsy and unhinged passions may have resulted from his war experiences.

63. On the war and its toll on the Russians, see Fuller.

64. This was the Soviet Union's news service until 1991. It had replaced ROSTA in 1935.

65. See her discussion of Viktor Ivanov's *How the Peasant Women Took a Fascist Prisoner* (1941), which tells its story in four brisk panels of Socialist Realist art accompanied by text. She compares it to Cheremnykh's 1920 poster *Story of the Bagel and the Peasant Woman* (223).

66. The Soviets produced over eight hundred posters (in a total of 34 million copies) during the war. On WW II and the poster's contribution to Russian nationalism, see Norris: 179–85.

67. The attacks appeared in the party's "Resolution on the Magazines *Zvezda* and *Leningrad*" of August 14, 1946. One gets a sense of Zhdanov's comments from the excerpt: "Does it become our advanced Soviet literature, the most revolutionary literature in the world, to bow low before the narrow philistine-bourgeois literature of the West?" (27).

68. Nelson reminds that the Soviet caricaturists had inadvertent help from Western political cartoonists. Critical cartoons were reprinted not only from the Communist foreign press, but from the Western press as well, including the *Washington Post*, *New York Herald Tribune*, and European newspapers (119).

69. Longana is part of Vanuatu, in the south Pacific. The Soviets supported its resistance to the Western colonial powers.

70. See also Mark Abramov's anti-Korean War cartoon from 1950, in which a "businessman" holds open a moneybag to catch bomb fragments "magically" transformed across the gutter into coins; "The more bombs, the more profit," says the caption (Abramov and Mikhalkov).

71. I have yet to discover whether this drawing was published. It belongs to a private collection I viewed in Prague, whose owner did not know either.

72. Nelson describes cartoons of contrast as often showing the Soviets or "struggling colonial peoples" in brighter panels, with the other side "usually dark, with more cluttered lines presenting Western figures as on a much smaller scale, weak, deformed, repulsive and sinister" (119). The same light/dark technique appears in posters, as shown in the Koretskii example.

73. See Nelson: 7–8 and Buzek: 49–50.

74. Despite the criticisms, the poster and caricature were celebrated even at the highest reaches of Soviet power. Chairman of the Presidium of the Supreme Soviet Mikhail Kalinin published "On the Art of the Poster" in 1943, while in 1961, Soviet premier Nikita Krushchev joined Gorky, Trotsky, Lunacharsky and others in the long line of eminent Bolsheviks who had praised the caricature: "Satire is like a sharp razor: it displays the outgrowths (narosty) of a man, and quickly, like a good surgeon, cuts them off" (Stykalin and Kremenskaia: 31).

75. Alexei Dvoriankin of BigAnt Comics, quoted in Droitcour, curated an exhibit of these works at the 2006 KomMissia Comics Festival in Moscow.

76. Semenov worked with Yurii Postnikov, V. Belotserkovskii, and other writers on the Petia series.

77. Petia's last name, Ryzhik, derives from *ryzhyi* ("red-haired").

78. To some extent, we can also compare them to the Czech Jaroslav Foglar's boys series *Swift Arrows* (Rychlé Šípy), published in this era.

79. Though a Pavel Morozov did exist, and did die as a child, almost every aspect of the Soviet mythology about Morozov has been disputed. See Catriona Kelly, *Comrade Pavlik: The Rise and Fall of a Soviet Boy Hero* (London: Granta, 2005).

80. A bizarre footnote in the East/West hostility reflected in comics is the strange case of Petr Sadecký, a pathological liar who defected from his native Czechoslovakia to West Germany in 1967, absconding

with the sketches and comics artwork of Zdenek Burian, Bohumil Konečný, and Miloš Novák. He had tricked these artists into creating an eroticized female character, which he altered into Oktiabrina, a "devil woman" and vengeful spirit of Communism allegedly created by a Ukrainian underground sect, Progressive Political Pornography. To read more of Sadecky's hoax, the international incident it spawned, and how far the lie went, see Tomáš Pospiszyl's *Octobriana and the Russian Underground: The Incredible Story of Petr Sadecky* (Octobriana a Ruský Underground: Neuvěřitelný Příběh Petra Sadeckého) (Prague: Labyrint, 2004). Needless to say, this episode did comics in Russia no favors.

81. These two journals proved major sources of knowledge on Western comics for the underground cartoonists Zhora Litichevsky and Ilya Kitup. Also, the komiksist Andrei Snegirov noted magazines smuggled from abroad in diplomatic pouches as a source; this is how he saw manga during the Soviet era (Snegirov 2004).

82. Which had begun during World War II as the anti-fascist periodical *Le Jeune Patriote*. The Soviets also let in collections of Jean Effel's *The Creation of the World* series in 1951–1953.

83. His work also appeared in *Krokodil*. As the komiksist Khikhus told me in 2004, "The Danish artist, Herluf Bidstrup, we all grew up on him. He's extremely funny. Every fucking family in Communist times had a book of Bidstrup. But when I emigrated to Denmark, I found out that nobody knows who Bidstrup is. Only one teacher of Danish told me, 'Oh, you know Bidstrup! He was from our Communist party!' He was so excited. Bidstrup was a Danish cartoonist, but nobody knew him there."

84. As noted by Lovell: "The Soviet publishing system was generally very hostile to the genres of 'mass' and entertainment fiction. "Mass culture" was regarded as the morally corrupting product of late capitalist Western societies. As a result, Soviet popular print culture neglected or ignored completely genres that are a staple of popular literature in the West: detective novels, violent thrillers, romantic fiction, comics" (2000: 52).

85. As Nelson comments on Russians commenting on America during the cold war: to them, "the sensationalism of our literature and films are further evidence of our 'barbarity'" (55). His book reprints a 1949 Kukryniksy cartoon showing "sensationalist" American literature characters—including one wearing a Ku Klux Klan costume—taking over a library (57). Swearingen reprints an (undated, unattributed) Boris Leo cartoon of an American boy literally drowning in a sea of pulp books, their actual covers reproduced in the work (135). "Save our souls!" screams the caption. This comes from *Krokodil* no. 18 (1959).

86. Lapitsky recounts the plot of the Superman animated cartoon *Electric Earthquake* (d. Max Fleischer, 1942)—but no comics story—to "prove" his point. This cartoon deals with a Native American mad scientist who demands that Manhattan be returned to the Indians.

87. Kukarkin nonetheless marveled (no pun intended) at the ubiquity of superhero iconography in American consumer culture: "Labels with Superman, Batman and other heroes from the comics decorated even the food products, and manufactured goods, and book covers, boxes of bubble bath. Their representations have appeared on television programs, store window displays, on posters, in picture galleries and museums. Comics even more recently have filled so many areas of economic and cultural life, that they've started calling Pop Art 'the culture of comics'" (1985: 233).

88. Kukarkin quotes at length from other writers in his essay "Comics: The Case For and Against," including the Spanish author Alberto Rocca and an article from the Italian magazine *Espresso*, from which most of his non-superhero examples are taken. He also seems to be drawing much information from Nedelin's 1965 *Inostrannaia Literatura* article, which remorselessly pursues the "comics as imperialist propaganda" meme.

89. Nonetheless, penetration there was. A curious relic of the Soviets' fixation on taboo foreign mass culture is the recurring vogue for Tarzan, peaking in the 1920s with translations of Edgar Rice Burroughs's pulp classic and the 1950s with Johnny Weismuller films based on the character. On this see Leblanc; Stites 1992: 125–26; and Clark: 104. As Yurii Bogomolov noted in the Glasnost era: "Authorities lamented for years that our children did not want to play Chapaev, Maxim, or Chkalov, the legendary heroes of the first Soviet myths. Now we can open up the secret why they played Tarzan

and Fantomas, a French comics character, instead. Both Tarzan and Fantomas presented the patterns for primitive individualism" (22).

90. It bears repeating that these are ingrained Russian cultural ideas, not exclusively Soviet ones. See, for example, the uber-dissident Alexander Solzhenitsyn's Harvard commencement address (1976), in which he attacks Western mass culture along very similar lines.

91. This may relate to Soviet pedagogical principles which linked "aberrant reading" in children to recalcitrance and intellectual deficiencies. See Kelly 2005: 727.

92. Children's publications weren't the only ones subject to such balancing acts. Party resolutions in the 1950s castigated the weekly *Ogonyok* for inappropriate illustrations and other newspapers for devoting too much space to pictures relative to text. See Lovell 2000: 46.

93. Similarly, Weaver reports in her 1970s study of children's pedagogy in the Soviet Union: "Horror tales about witches, fire-breathing dragons, and monsters are considered harmful, and parents are advised not to allow them" (204).

94. For background, see Douglas Weiner, *A Little Corner of Freedom: Russian Nature Protection from Stalin to Gorbachev* (Berkeley and Los Angeles: University of California Press, 1999).

95. Rosenfeld describes the categories of "unacceptable art" as Political, Religious, Erotic, and "Formalist" (1995: 37).

96. This list could go on indefinitely; we await a fully researched analysis of comics techniques in Non-Conformist art. For now I would add one more work, Georgi Kizevalter's *A Blind Man Asks a Parrot for Alms* (1988), in which tiny figures with the aid of word balloons utter such self-reflexive comments as, "I don't understand what the author's trying to say!" and "Here we can clearly see the decadence of postmodernism."

97. Wallach comes closest: ". . . Kabakov's albums descend directly from Russian stock, from the narrative icons of the medieval church, forerunner of the story board and comic book . . ." (55).

98. Brown 1989: 78 and Groys 1998: 35.

99. In her discussion of Kabakov's *Kitchen* series (1981–1982), Degot notes the artists' disembodied dialogue accompanying the objects turns speech into "monumental 'verbal clouds,' into clusters which have forever solidified in the air" (1995: 62). Though she does not intend it this way, she is describing the (perversely concretized) dialogue captions in Kabakov's experimental comics-like works.

100. Another faction of the Russian avant-garde, led by Malevich and Kandinsky, rejected this "linguistic intrusion" or *literaturnost* in favor of transcendent, nonobjective forms. Groys refers to this in the next note below. Literaturnost overlaps with the Russian cultural predilection for visual forms discussed in chapter 1.

101. He was not alone. As noted by Groys, "In the formal respect, the Soviet postutopian art of the 1970s is characterized above all by a renewed narrativity that runs counter to the avant-garde rejection of literariness and instead continues the narrativity of Socialist Realism" (1992: 94).

102. Though as discussed in chapter 1, Epstein's characterization of the lubok's text and image maintaining a supplementary relationship in which one "corresponds" to the other is, strictly speaking, naively mistaken. The subversion of such correspondences was a common lubok trait.

103. Examples abound of sequential (anti-) narrative in Kabakov's oeuvre. See his *Shower: A Comedy* (1970s); The *Kitchen* Series (1987); *In Strict Order* (1967); *Small Gallery* (1968), to name but a few.

104. The poem and illustrations close the anthology, with the image of a man and woman running free. For more on the *Metropol* affair, see Porter: 26–30.

105. For an account of Sysoev's case, see Alaniz 2006.

106. Certainly throughout the Soviet era ordinary Russians who were active enthusiasts of the form simply kept their work to restricted circles. The head of the Tema studio Vladimir Sakov told me, "Many boys would draw these little comics since they were very young; it was a way of expressing the imagination. Of course, you could draw them, but you couldn't publish. You might not get in trouble for making them, but a publisher would sit in jail for putting them in print" (Sakov 1996). These comics expressions mostly stayed in the margins of school notebooks, he said.

CHAPTER 3

1. Though Westerners tended to romanticize these gains beyond what the reality would bear. The USSR until its disintegration was a totalitarian society, with widespread forces that resisted these changes and sought to restore the country to its "rightful" Brezhnevite path. Mikhail Fedotov, a Supreme Soviet legislator, noted: "Naturally, the glasnost' that was proclaimed to let off steam amounted to merely an ersatz freedom of speech and the press. The powers-that-be simply relaxed their grip on the reins, they did not let them go" (Vachnadze: 8–9).

2. Lovell 2000: 81. See especially chapter 4's useful summary of Perestroika print culture and economics.

3. Kapranov had attended the state film school, VGIK, and worked at the animation studio Soiuzmultfilm before landing at the youth-oriented magazine *Moskovskii Komsomolets* in 1986, where he produced adult-oriented strips. A change in editorship led to the cancellation of his comics work, and he departed for *VM* (Kapranov 2006).

4. When he read the announcement, recalled Akishin, a graduate of the 1905 Art College and a devotee of genre fiction and comics, he leaped at the opportunity. He had long desired to work making comics like *Pif*, but had never seriously considered it a possibility in the USSR. "It was great, getting together on Thursdays, at 5–6, after work, to chat, to show what we had drawn," he told me (Akishin 2006). Andrei Aeshin, a journalist and comics enthusiast, heard about the Klub through his grandmother, who alerted him to the ad (Aeshin 2008).

5. Kolgarev, a former colleague of Kapranov's at *Moskovskii Komsomolets*, had drawn a strip series based on the experiences of Afghan war vets for *VM* in 1986. He and Zaslavsky played a key role in establishing the club, with Kapranov.

6. In all thirty artists, writers, and other staff joined what would become the KOM comics studio by 1990 (Ananov, *Vecherniaia Moska*, 1990).

7. The general plot and the name Vadim for the privileged boy would leap out to Soviet readers as allusions to Yury Trifonov's *The House on the Embankment* (1976), the first official novel to broach class inequalities and the legacy of Stalinism in the USSR.

8. Fotofilm had an interest in developing photocomics, and managed to interest the actor Oleg Shklovsky, the director Alexander Pankratov, and other filmmakers to its projects. One of its more notable releases was a photocomics adaptation of Abraham Merritt's *Burn Witch Burn!* (1992), with drawings by Akishin and Belov.

9. The program included the rock group Mister Tvister, video excerpts from superhero films, and a screening of the 1968 Roger Vadim film *Barbarella*, based on the Jean-Claude Forest comics series.

10. *Breakthrough*, the first sbornik, had been released in July 1990 (Zaslavsky 2003).

11. For the Soviet view on horror, see Woll 2004.

12. While based at Fotofilm, KOM's comics collections were published by various presses and through different financing schemes. These first volumes were partly financed by the commercial association ABEKS, Interbuk Press, and the Soviet Fund for Culture.

13. The studio proposed a prize of 10,000 rubles for readers who could prove they had a complete set of the first ten KOM publications, plus answer some difficult questions on comics history. Kapranov meant this as an educational tool, though it also seems to have served as a sales generator. The collective made the "offer" a running gag, addressing it in self-parodic comics.

14. The KOM artists—almost all of which were men, and almost none tee-totalers—bonded as well in vodka-soaked social events. Several pictures (and photocomics) show them enjoying each other's company in the age-old milieu of the Russian woods, over refreshments. Some participated in the "military historical" club RKKA. Similar to American Civil War reenactors, this organization celebrates the history of the Red army with authentic uniforms and outdoor activities.

15. The jokes didn't stop there. The back cover of *KOM-paniia* features no less than two parodies of Lenin. One mocks the famous line (attributed to him): "Cinema is for us the most important of the arts," changing it to "Comics is for the us the most important of the arts!" Another shows a drawing of the father of Russian Communism reading a KOM publication, declaring, "A very necessary and extremely timely book!" This alludes to one of Lenin's oft-quoted phrases, "extremely timely" (arkhisvoevremennoe). The times were indeed changing.

16. Akishin's *Nekropolis* (1990) daringly portrays a copy of *Pravda* blowing by in a postapocalyptic cityscape.

17. Perhaps because of comics' associations with the United States, these early KOM works seem to shy away from overly "American" content or culturemes. However, the cover of *KOM O.K.* does show padded and helmeted football players against a field of comics. And, of course, the collection's name itself contains an Americanism.

18. Other early to mid-1990s comics adaptations of Russian classics include *History of a Town* by Mikhail Saltykov-Shchedrin (Kapninsky 1993); Mikhail Bulgakov's *The Fatal Eggs* (Dmitry Tkachev, *Mukha* no. 11, [1993]: 20–31) and Bulgakov's *The Master and Margarita* (R. Tanaev 1996). The more "conceptualist" of these comics homages include *Kharmsiada* by Alexei Nikitin (1998) and various works by Zhora Litichevsky.

19. A pen name for Kapninsky.

20. Other artists adopted similarly "retro" styles for individual works. Egorov draws "The Town in a Snuffbox" in a quasi-lithograph format, while Zhigunov turns to nineteenth-century realist painting and graphic art for "The Soldier's School." Both stories appear in *Ofenia* no. 2 (1992).

21. *Georgy Zhukov* (script by Yury Kamenetsky and Ezhen Shchedrin, 1991) does show the revered military leader criticizing—mostly to himself—the commander-in-chief, Stalin, and touches on the Purges's devastation of the military ranks. It was published by Progress Press in Moscow.

22. A few of Akishin's stories have appeared in English translation: "Snow" in *The Mammoth Book of Best War Comics* (2007); "The Zombie," "The Corpse," and "Ship of the Dead" in *The Mammoth Book of Zombie Comics* (2008), both from Running Press. I translated the stories in the latter volume. *A Chronicle of Military Actions* remains unpublished, save for in the online journal *Komiksolet*, discussed in the next chapter.

23. Recall this was the name for the peddlers of lubki in the eighteenth and nineteenth centuries.

24. For example, "Belgian school" artists like Zhigunov and Snegirov, whose style and delicate colors depended on quality reproduction, had experienced considerable frustration with Fotofilm's facilities from the beginning (Zaslavsky 2003). Soviet printing equipment in general suffered in comparison with that of Western publishers.

25. Tema also had more success attracting foreign financing; e.g., from Spain through Rovina Andorra Press.

26. The title is a play on the Soviet disaster film *The Crew* (d. Alexander Mitta, 1980).

27. This also recalls the climax of Sergei Eisenstein's *Ivan the Terrible, Pt. II* (1946, released 1958), which contrasts color and black-and-white shots.

CHAPTER 4

1. The *Kapitan Donki* books appeared in Spanish, English, German, French, Slovak, and Polish editions, while Sakov's character was featured in brief stories published in *Stolitsa* magazine well into the decade. Tema artists, including Lukyanchikov, received recognition at comics festivals abroad, including Saló del Cómic de Barcelona. But since those successes and contacts in the early 1990s, foreign interest in Russian work plummeted drastically. Tema saw comics contracts with foreign clients annulled after 1991, while general instability in the country made Russia unattractive for many foreign investors.

2. During the putsch a group of KOM artists rushed to man the barricades; Kapranov rallied them, claiming that if the revanchist forces won out, they would close down comics studios (Velitov 2008). He was surely right.

3. An impressionistic but not unrecognizable "highlights reel" of the 1990s, an era many Russians would rather forget.

4. According to Lovell, in 1991 Russian product comprised only 54.3 percent of book titles published, and 40.6 percent of the overall print run; in 1992 the numbers were 36.9 and 22.0, respectively, with Russian titles as low as 15.1 percent of overall print runs in the last quarter of 1992 (2000: 134).

5. These were indeed the darkest days for the Russian cinema industry since just after the 1917 revolution. By 1996, film production had contracted to fewer than thirty, and by some accounts fewer than ten, features per year. Pirated films on cassette and cheap overseas product dumped on the Russian market

sapped the attention of consumers away from their domestic cinema. See Larsen: 192–93 and Beumers. Some movie theaters in the 1990s took to renting out their lobbies as office space and car dealerships, something I observed while living in Moscow in 1993–1994.

6. In short, as Menzel noted, "culture was exposed almost overnight to the laws of the market" (41), a radical shift for a society (especially its intelligentsia) that had long tried to keep these spheres separate. For generations, Russia's authoritarian state had made artists (particularly writers) into the conscience of the people. Speaking truth to power, they were moral because they were artists and artists because they were moral. Now, in freer times, the public's literary appetites had shifted, often to the sensational.

7. Borenstein gave the name "overkill" to the representational excess of the 1990s, during which the mass media privileged extreme, cold-blooded violence and rampant sexuality. Across the media, Russians in this era ingested one unrelenting master narrative: that they were living in a sort of Hell on earth.

8. Among the epithets that adhered to 1990s Russia: kleptocracy; the "Wild East"; *dermokratiia* ("crapocracy"); "predatory capitalism"; oligarchy.

9. Akishin went through a bout of depression at this time, until his wife told him, "'You're an artist. You have skills. Go and make a living.'" Thinking back on it, he said, "'She was right'" (2007).

10. "We should have started with regular journals instead of sborniki (anthologies)," Kapranov told me in 2006. "We would have had a more consistent publication schedule, a readership could have been built up more easily. Maybe then by 1991 we could have had enough of a base of support to weather the changes." So much for the "author-based" model; 1990s Russia was not France.

11. Early entries into the Russian market included *Tom and Jerry* from Makhaon Press. By the early 2000s publishers like Praim-Evroznak and Rovesnik imported *Spiderman, Fantastic Four, Star Wars, X-Men, Scooby Doo, Jurassic Park,* and *Gen*13, among other titles. More "substantial" Western comics and graphic novel works did appear in Russian translation in the post-Soviet era, but they were rare. In the 1990s the magazine *Pinoler* published a chapter from Art Spiegelman's *Maus*; Konstantin Yavorsky and Zaslavsky published a newspaper version of works by Hugo Pratt in 1996–1997; in 2005 Amfora Press published the first volume of Frank Miller's series *Sin City*; David Zane Mairowitz and Robert Crumb's *Introducing Kafka* appeared from Popuri Press in 2004; Amfora Press published Alan Moore and David Lloyd's *V for Vendetta* as a tie-in with the film version's 2006 release.

12. A 1993 poster for Democratic Choice Movement (reproduced in Schleifman: 52) mocked what it considered the obstructionist congress during the ongoing constitutional crisis. In twelve panels, the unknown artist shows Lenin seated in the lap of (Supreme Soviet speaker) Ruslan Khasbulatov and revanchist Communists retaking control of the society. The poster's dark warning, "The congress is pushing Russia to Civil War" foresaw the violence of October 3–4, 1993, when Yeltsin bombed the White House building in response to riots and the lawmakers' revolt.

13. The works, many photocopied and without translations, were displayed against a background of old packing paper and corrugated cardboard, to "represent contemporary Russian life" (Snoodjik).

14. A watershed moment: the appearance of the goateed Conceptualist author Vladimir Sorokin on the cover of the youth magazine *Ptyutch* (No. 4, 1997), dressed as Batman.

15. We could add a fourth: Russian comics artists working or publishing abroad. Among the better known: Andrei Feldstein (United States), Svetlana Chmakova (Canada), Yuri Zhigunov (Belgium), Konstantin Kryssov (Berlin), Yevgeny Zhilinsky (Canada), Andrei Arinuchkin, Polina Petrushina and Nikolai Maslov (France).

16. Ufa is the capital of the Republic of Bashkortostan, some 1,000 kilometers southeast of Moscow.

17. A play on the Soviet institution of the *medvytrezvitel'*, or "Medical Sobering Station," the detox centers or drunk tanks found in many cities.

18. Similarly, another series by A. Tkachev features a foolish policeman, Modest Porfirievich, and is set in the prerevolutionary era. It mocks the czarist authorities as well as Communist plotters and anarchists.

19. *Mukha* published some thirty issues in all. Mukhametzyanov went on to a successful career in music videos, designing the animated avatar for the pop star Glyuk'oza, and directed films. Rubtsov won the Art Prix at the 2006 KomMissia Comics Festival for his continuing *School of Mages*.

20. The story ends with a note: "The author of this strip is a skew-eyed person! BEWARE!" Kitup is indeed cross-eyed, making this one of the few komiks to touch on disability from a subject position "on the inside."

21. Not to be confused with the recent Capitalist Realism art movement, represented by such painters as Konstantin Latyshev.

22. The editor, Boris Kostin, confirmed this to me. He had faith, he explained, that readers in Russia had enough experience with comics to appreciate the journal's ironic nuances (1999). Apparently not enough to save the journal, which appeared at a very inopportune time, soon after the ruble crash of late 1998.

23. *Brother* (d. Alexei Balabanov, 1997), the enormously popular crime film.

24. The name of the late actor who played Danila Bagrov, hero of the *Brother* films, was Sergei Bodrov Jr.

25. In the story they are called Ella Pervacheva (the last name suggestive of the word "to fart") and Tulup Purpurov ("Purple Sheepskin Coat"). The real duo, an obsession of the tabloid press, were married from 1994 to 2005.

26. However graphic and sexualized Russian media representations have become, there remains a taboo on profanity, especially in literature. Its blatant use in comic books, therefore, is bound to make some wince. On scatology in post-Soviet Russian culture, see Erofeyev: 2003.

27. These issues were published about six and two months, respectively, after the attacks of September 11, 2001.

28. For all that, Erofeyev did also have a reputation as a bête noire who reveled in attacking the hypocrisies of the intelligentsia in such novels as the pornographic *Russian Beauty* (1990) and scatological short stories like "Life with an Idiot" (1980s).

29. The reader can see what I think of Erofeyev's comics scholarship in the notes to my translation of the essay.

30. "So when I hear that serious subjects are not appropriate for comics, I can't help but be surprised," he elaborated. "Where does this idea come from? None of the reviewers, as a rule, has read more than twenty or thirty comics, maximum. Yet there are millions of comics. Russian critics are not familiar with the classics of the genre because they have simply not been published here" (Maksimova: 87).

31. This refers to Trofim Lysenko (1898–1976), the Soviet agronomist and director of the Institute of Genetics, whose pseudoscientific experiments to improve agricultural yields included plant grafts of the sort Markova describes.

32. Personal correspondence, August 2008.

33. Their ambit included sexual minorities; a gay newsletter, *Triangle*, occasionally published gay-themed comics at a time of rampant homophobia in post-Soviet Russia (Essig: 211).

34. The latter two published mostly Western work: contemporary superhero series such as *Ultimate Spiderman* (*Ded Moroz*), classic comic strips such as *Charlie Brown* (*Klassnyi Zhurnal*).

35. The solicitations feature appeared in June 2000, the forum opened in July 2001.

36. The site does have problems. The limitations of Ayoshin's equipment led to the presentation of works in an inconvenient "strip" or "diafilm" format of at most two or three panels at a time. Any sense of page composition is lost. Those works that do appear as complete pages are hard to read. Also, *Komiksolyot* does not allow for downloads.

37. The net has revolutionized social and cultural life in Russia. A September 2006 bulletin from Yandex.ru, the Russian search engine, noted the exponential growth of the Russian blogosphere. *Zhivoi Zhurnal* (the Russian version of Live Journal) was the most popular blog-hosting site, with over 45 percent. Over 80 percent of users resided in Moscow or St. Petersburg. Many in the komiks community communicate and post work via *Zhivoi Zhurnal* or *zhzh*, as it is popularly called. In 2009, Russia had approximately 38 million Internet users, or about a quarter of the population, according to Internet World Stats (http://www.internetworldstats.com/stats4.htm).

38. Kunin and his collaborators also launched major Internet comics databases such as *Komiks Katalog* (http://comics-catalog.ru/dir/) and *Ruskokomiks* (http://ruscomics.com/) in the mid-2000s; the latter seeks to document every Russian-language comics publication dating back to 1900. Several Web

sites, such as *Komiks Katalog*, provide links to Russian translations of new foreign comics titles, often concurrently or soon after their publication abroad.

39. Lamentably, GIK stumbled soon after. Unable to resolve the deep systemic problems outlined in this chapter, it dissolved after about a year.

40. The word combines "komiks" and "missiia" (mission), and also means simply "commission." The festival takes place annually in Moscow in late May or June and runs as long as two weeks.

41. GIK president Bessmertny served on the festival organizing committee.

42. Monastyrova died of cancer in November 2006. Her role was taken over by Nadya Imra and later Nastya Galashina. The festival was officially renamed "The Natasha Monastyrova Moscow Festival of Drawn Stories KomMissia" and a special festival prize for lifetime achievement was created in her name.

43. This included Alim Velitov, Konstantin Komardin, Alexei Lipatov, Lumbricus (Anna Suchkova), Alexei "Xatchett" Baranov, Alexei Rubtsov, Daniil Kuzmichov, and Bogdan. According to Khikhus, the name came from the realization that (sufficiently stylized) the English word "comics," to the Russian eye, "looks like a dead fish." The group's logo is thus the English "Comics" in distorted Latin letters made to accentuate that visual coincidence. Incidentally, the French zine publisher Philippe Morin saw another coincidence; he was reminded of a 1993 Julie Doucet comic, "Leve ta jambe, mon poisson est mort" (Lift Your Leg, My Fish Is Dead). Since its inception, the acronym LMR has been repeatedly "rebranded" with humorous phrases to fit the Russian letters: "People of the Mythological Revolution," "Left Little Finger of the Hand," "The Lama Washed the Frame." This running gag recalls Oleinikov's "explanation" for the acronymic titles of his early Soviet journals *Chizh* and *Yozh*.

44. Khikhus asked the human rights campaigner Elena Bonner (Andrei Sakharov's widow) for permission. "Why do you want to exhibit comics in the Sakharov center?" she asked. Khikhus answered, "Well, I guess because we are dissidents of art. It's still forbidden here. And she said okay." Khikhus added that "many Russian intellectuals" secretly love comics but feel they cannot say so publicly. He named the film producer Konstantin Ernst and *Ekho Moskvy* cofounder Sergei Buntman as two of the biggest comics collectors in Russia (2004).

45. Brought with the cooperation of TomatoFarm, an Italian agency that represents several Russian komiksisty, including Nikolai Maslov, Re-I, Vadim Rubtsov, and Namida.

46. No original art is displayed at KomMissia, only blown-up reproductions on posters with artists' biographies and other information.

47. The list of lecturers at KomMissia includes myself. Since 2005 I have given illustrated talks on American fan culture, women in American comics, Chris Ware, Charles Burns, superheroes, and comics theory.

48. Ukraine, a former Soviet republic, has close historical and cultural ties to Russia. The festival was founded by Alexei Olin, editor of the comics journal *K-9* (which published many Russian komiksisty). Despite its promising start, the festival fell apart after its first year, due to organizational and financial problems. It reorganized and took place again in late 2008.

49. I use the term advisedly; these "master classes" or lectures" routinely descended into free-for-alls of about ten people talking over one another at high volume.

50. As Khikhus explained to me, "We made a Russian calque for the festival, 'graficheskaia novella' (graphic novel), but many people said it was pathetic. But some publishers have taken up the term seriously. . . . We don't want to call it 'comics,' because then people expect something funny, or *Superman*" (2004). Khikhus has said similar things in several interviews, adding that for him "comics" refers to American product, bande dessinée designates French, Manga Japanese. See, for example, Fedorova. "Neo-lubok," another term vetted for the Russian market, did not take, and now only describes a style of komiks which references prerevolutionary prints.

51. Khikhus wrote this after the Fabrique de Fanzine demonstration and workshops at that year's festival.

52. As I have written in my festival reviews for *IJOCA*. From 2006: "For starters, there was KomMissia's merchandise area. While bigger than last year, it still basically amounted to a small horseshoe of tables. The commercial imperative, so overwhelming in American cons, hasn't really taken hold here. And there's no collector or back-issue market to speak of. Most of the books on sale were French, along

with small press stuff, past year's programs, etc. . . . Of course, you had to have enough money to afford these volumes, which most visitors did not. So most copies stayed on the tables. That's another problem" (450–51).

From 2008: "Again this year, the majority of works on sale were (untranslated) French and Italian books from Pangloss, with only a precious few native publications—though all at such high prices that average Russians could not begin to afford them. Case in point: Oleg Tishchenkov's lovely and weighty tome *The Cat*, going for a whopping 1,450 rubles ($60). Most copies stayed on the table. A handful of self-published artists like Alvena Rekk (*Strawberries*), Sergei Repyov (*Knights of the Turnip*), Artyom Trakhanov, Mad Blade, and the hentai komiksist Grif were again ghettoized in the least auspicious hall, away from the 'real' publications. Once more, KomMissia reeked, to my nose, of opportunities missed" (2008: 843).

53. U.E.: *Uslovnaia edinitsa* ("conditional unit"), an artificial measure to fix prices to a particular ruble rate of exchange. In practice, it is usually pegged to the dollar.

54. Although as observed by Fedorova, the link between anime and manga does not always hold in Russia. According to her, no manga was on sale at the 2007 Animatrix festival in Moscow, the largest of its kind, which has existed since 2003.

55. Dubkov was much more sanguine than Repyov about self-publishing, saying conditions weren't that bad in Russia: "You just have to work at it," he told me. "I've done my own stuff, worked it out on computer, printed it, self-published it. I have 8 booklets, I sell it to bookstores, and if they don't want it I move on. It's very time-consuming; you spend 30 percent of the time on the work, and the rest trying to sell it and distribute it" (2005).

56. Personal conversation, 2005.

57. The second volume's publication had originally been planned for 2003, and long delayed.

58. For that matter, the Russian comics community splits on some questions, such as whether manga must be drawn by actual Japanese people in order to be considered "real" manga (Xatchett 2008).

59. Personal conversation, 2005.

60. Dubkov 2005, Snegirov 2004: 100, and Sakov 1997: 104.

61. Like Berlin, Zaslavsky sees this as a dominant trait in Russian cultural expressions going back centuries: "Russian literature, too, takes a lot from other world traditions, especially European. For example, Dostoyevsky was attracted to the English 'documentary' realist novels, and this influenced his work. But then everything gets reworked, so that Dostoyevsky ends up producing something very original and fresh" (Zaslavsky interview 2004).

62. Such thinking goes beyond Russia. For a discussion of French comics' ties to literary culture, and comics artists' challenge to that model, see Beaty 2007, especially chapter 2.

63. Personal conversation, 2005. Kolgaryov's Protestantism complicates this picture, as the Russian Orthodox Church has actively sought to marginalize other Christian denominations in the post-Soviet era.

64. This recalls the komiksmen Andrei Ayoshin's comment to me in Moscow, "Comics is good when a person who reads it can understand 70 percent of it without understanding the language" (2004), which on its face seems anathema to Russian literary "norms."

65. Though this is changing, as the roundtable scholars also acknowledged, to a more visually oriented cultural forms, such as video games and cinema. And in any case, the "text-based" culture model is problematic, as discussed in chapter 1.

66. One of my KomMissia 2008 lectures got embroiled in long discussions of whether the definition of comics necessitated the inclusion of text and narrative. To the extent that definitions are useful, I submit it does not, as argued in my introduction.

67. This is another very common Khikhus utterance; he often describes komiks as "film in pictures" (kino v kartinkakh) or "film on paper" (kino na bumage).

68. Fedorova. Although those working in a manga style produce longer stories, according to Bogdan (2005).

69. The retrenchment of quasi-Soviet values and political culture in Russia occupied Slavists at least since President Vladimir Putin's 2004 reelection. The orchestrated "election" of Dmitry Medvedev to the

presidency and Putin's near-simultaneous ascension to prime minister in 2008, followed months later by the conflict in Georgia over its separatist regions, cemented the perception of a new cold war between Russia and the West.

70. Egmont also published Russian children's series: *Smeshariki* (tie-in with an animated TV series); *Tosh and Company*; *Prostokvashino* (Curdled Milk) and *Cheburashka*, the latter two canceled within a year (Styshneva).

71. This inevitably affects komiksisty's work choices as well. As explained by Khikhus: "An artist will draw a comics page in one to four days. Clearly, such a job will cost a lot more than foreign publication rights. That's why we're not in a condition to compete with foreign translated works. Advertising pays a whole lot better: up to $300 a page. Besides that, the glossy magazines pay reasonable fees for strips, short stories on one page" (Styshneva). Although according to Ayoshin, the Russian comics market remains so anarchic some clients will pay over $1,000 per page, "because they don't know any better and they have the money" (2008).

72. He did, on a smaller scale, representing artists for advertising jobs, among other ventures. In 2008, he launched the comics journal *Evgenios* in Odessa.

73. Konstantin Kostyuk, director for development of DirectMEDIA, which bought up some of Nitusov's unsold stock, repackaged it with other material, and put it back on the market—with only moderate success (Styshneva). In its own tie-in strategy, DirectMEDIA also released a flash animation version of *Site-o-Polis* on DVD in 2005, as well as DVD versions of the Internet phenomena *Masiania* and *The Little Store Bo*. On the link between komiks, lubok, and flash animation, see Strukov.

74. Events like KomMissia, the popularity of Western films and the Westernization of Russia in general have mostly put to rest the old Soviet prejudice in its most virulent forms (the full-on Markova position is an outlier, though as mentioned her government position and social capital should not be ignored).

75. Zaslavsky, personal correspondence, August 2008. Some accounts peg the cost as high as 30,000 euros. Anubis comics reported being charged a $20,000 "placement fee" (Kulikov). This racket has led to the reality that many Russian news vendors make their money not from sales but from "entry fees"—and they have every incentive to maintain the status quo.

76. Both launched in 2004. *Yula* went to reprints in 2008, heralding cancellation.

77. "I'm the son of a physicist. I come from a scientific family," he told me (his late father was George Zaslavsky, a physics professor at NYU specializing in chaos theory). "I look at things from a rational perspective. So statements like 'Russia will never embrace comic books because they are foreign to the Russian soul' make no sense to me. This is an industry which we're trying to build, and we are taking steps toward that. It is very hard, slow work, but ultimately it will be mainstream publications like ours that build the broad-based foundation for a full-fledged Russian comics industry" (2005). Few are better placed to make such an attempt. Zaslavsky lived in New York for several years, knows the ins and outs of the American industry (he translated Will Eisner's *To the Heart of the Storm* into Russian), and is a KOM veteran. He serves an important function for the medium as its leading historian and as a link between Russia and the West.

78. Started by Emmanuel Durand, who "discovered" the komiksist Nikolai Maslov, Pangloss also published some French works in Russian translation, including *Asterix and the Goths* in 2001.

79. Led by Alim Velitov and Mikhail Khachaturov, the klub organized lectures, workshops and comics jams, and in general sought to keep interest in komiks alive between festivals.

80. Some of these concerns, as we've learned, serve as nothing more than a refuge for illicit funds, as apparently so in the cases of RKK and *Novy Komiks*.

81. Such comments are easily found in the online forums. In June 2008, for example, "a vata ra" advanced the *tusovka* thesis on *zhzh*: "KomMissia . . . was created basically just for these artists. So we wind up with a very strange 'con': artists come to the festival to look at the works of other artists, and get sloshed. Kinda doubtful as a fan base" (Alaniz 2008: 861).

82. In 2008 Khikhus declared KomMissia "one of the five major comics festivals in Europe," a problematic statement, to say the least.

83. As happened after the 2005 and 2008 festivals. See Alaniz: 2008 for my account of, and involvement in, the latter. The rifts in the Russian comics community were especially apparent at KomMissia 2009, with many former participants no longer attending the final ceremony. Held again at Klub Bilingua on May 10, the ceremony was notable for the fact that the hall was only about two-thirds full. Andrei Tkalenko and Elena Voronovich reiterated to me that KomMissia was irrelevant to their careers, while Mikhail Zaslavsky and Khikhus had broken off ties completely.

84. Ayoshin softened his comments to me in 2008, praising Khikhus's important role in keeping komiks in the public eye.

85. Ayoshin, one of the few to make a living off komiks work, confirmed: "There are no potential clients at KomMissia, only media and fans. So far KomMissia is not a serious venue for attracting serious people. I have lots of work and clients, and they all came to me through venues other than KomMissia" (2008).

86. As Tkalenko told me: "Since we're doing it for free, we could put our soul into it. Everything else we'd done was material someone had ordered and paid for. When we saw the anthology was coming out, we decided to do a project on something we like, something closer to us. Something without humorous content. We got tired of having to come up with jokes and gags all the time, so we took advantage of the opportunity. In Russia comics are perceived primarily as funny, or jokey, as 'merry pictures.' We wanted to show that comics are their own genre, through which you can communicate all moods and emotions" (2007). A Polish translation of the graphic novel appeared in 2008 from Timof i cisi wspólnicy Press. The story's conclusion was published in the 2009 LMR anthology.

87. In 2006 Surzhenko produced a well-regarded adaptation of the 1995 cult "Slavic fantasy" novel *Wolfhound* (Volkodav) by Maria Semenova (it was also adapted as a film in 2007).

88. The graphic novel comes bundled with a DVD containing the 1948 Alexander Stolper film adaptation of Polevoi's book, along with the 2005 Alexander Slavin documentary *Fate of a Real Man*.

89. Subsequently the festival established a separate category for comics—then rescinded it in 2007 for lack of quality entries (Yusupova: 2). The ad firm Man'iako uses comics especially often in its campaigns.

90. One should not, however, confuse Kuzmichov's "underground" tastes with his vision for Russian comics in general (as shown by his 2005 KomMissia master class, which I attended and wrote about; see further in this chapter). He fully supports the idea of building an industry, including a mainstream. In a response to my characterization of him as a "somewhat tongue-in-cheek" extreme Russian nationalist and ardent promoter of an anti-commercialist model for komiks (Alaniz 2008: 845), Kuzmichev corrected me: "Komiks have to get sold. THEY HAVE TO. Only then will people be able to produce them on a serious basis, instead of on their lunch breaks. And then they'll fall into other people's field of vision. As for all this crap about 'this will sell,' 'this won't sell,' 'people won't get it,' 'they won't appreciate it in the provinces,' 'children will see this,' I don't want to hear it. Komiks don't need 'managers' to decide what to draw for the sake of sales, and what not to draw. Komiks need komiks! Everything else will work itself out—including the moolah (bablosy)" (Kuzmichov 2009). As for his "extreme nationalism" I would emphasize the qualifier "tongue-in-cheek" (to which I would add ironicized, performative, over the top) and offer Mr. Kuzmichov an apology for my overly simplistic description of him.

91. The works of KomMissia 2008 Art Prize winner Apolinarias also exhibit a recognizable "St. Petersburg style." He too hails from there.

92. The initials, which when pronounced sound like *chepukha* ("rubbish"), actually stand for something more scatological: *Chisto Piterskaia khuynia* or "Pure Petersburg Shit"—a common Muscovite phrase denoting pretentious or excessively abstract proclamations from denizens of Russia's second city.

93. One could elect to buy it with a case, which would raise the price to 14,000 rubles ($583). Zlatkovsky's elite publisher WAM produces many such extravagant and beautiful editions for a select readership.

94. On Preved, an Internet phenomenon dealing with humorous alternate word spellings, see Sonkin and Idov.

95. Falkovsky's comment on comics' "lower level of personal involvement" deserves some refutation as well; readers through the ages might not agree. Its capacities in this area yield nothing to other media.

96. See Erofeyev's "Soviet Literature: In Memoriam" (1990) in which he argues for a new model of Russian literature unburdened by the need to moralize.

CHAPTER 5

1. Comics art and caricature also found its way from the page to the galleries (e.g., a 2007 Krokin Gallery exhibit of the *Kommersant* and *Izvestia* cartoonist Andrei Bilzho). KomMissia, the first comics festival in Russia, has been held at the respected M'ars Gallery in Moscow since 2004, and displayed works at the trendy Vinzavod Contemporary Art Center in the southeast of the city since 2008.
2. It must also be said that even Russian critics who welcome comics imagery do not always seem to understand some of the form's basic premises and history. Worse, they seem hazy on what *constitutes* comics. Writing on the 2006 Litichevsky and Ostretsov exhibit "Physicists and Lyricists, or Sex in the Big City" at the Guelman Gallery, Valentin Dyakonov notes: "As in the case of Lichtenstein, Ostretsov and Litichevsky's works are far from being comics not because they contain a certain well-made quality, concreteness or insane avant garde sensibility which are not characteristic to the genre. Rather, they become art because they lack a most important feature of the genre: literary narrative and, of course, bubbles with text (D'iakonov)."
3. He earned a degree in ancient Roman history from Moscow State University (MGU).
4. The long list of top-name Moscow venues where Litichevsky has exhibited include the XL Gallery, the M'ars Gallery, and the Tretyakov Gallery, where he shares a permanent installation. He also acts in films and writes cultural/art criticism, and remains one of Russia's most active and exhibited artist/installationists. Since the late 1990s, he has lived in Berlin and Moscow.
5. Like many komiksisty of the Soviet era, Litichevsky cited *Pif* and the journal *Science and Life* as an early source of information on Western comics. He later read the French satirical magazine *Hara-Kiri*, where he found the work of the scatological Dutch artist Willem, whom he considers an influence. Though devoted to the underground comix he read while abroad, he shies away from any overt political content in his stories. As he told me: "I am from a different generation than those who seriously participated in [Soviet-era] political protests. In the 1970s I was too young, and I came into my own only in the late 70s/early 80s, when the dissidents were older people, while I belonged to the more cynical, disappointed generation, more disposed to the absurd. That's why, as a result, in my work there is no direct appeal to politics, but a tendency to turn all serious themes into nonsense" (1996).
6. My reader will recognize this as a throwback to the lubok, which sometimes appeared as calendars and almanacs.
7. As discussed in chapter 2, such "demotic" and integrative strivings formed a major aspect of Constructivist art. But comics' accessibility makes it especially suited to the task and belies what the artist considers its "inherently subversive" nature. "[Komiks] is obvious and democratic," said Litichevsky in 1995, "and despite the fact that few people in Moscow have any experience of comic art, its simplicity makes it understandable to everyone" (Graeme). In 2006, he mused in an interview whether comics had had so little success because they were "too democratic for Russia" (Miskarian: 88).
8. Litichevsky has often worked in collaboration with other artists. In the 1990s he formed (with Farid Bogdalov) the two-man group BOLI, while his later joint exhibits with Georgy "Gosha" Ostretsov predominated in his later 1990s and 2000s practice. They work together under the group name "George and George," as discussed below.
9. At the 2004 International Comic Arts Festival, the comics scholar Joseph "Rusty" Witek mentioned that Litichevsky's style somewhat reminded him of Dame Darcy's work.
10. For some projects Litichevsky does make the lubok influence explicit, as in his contributions to the 2003 exhibition *Apocalypse Now*, in which several Russian artists produced versions of the Book of Revelations in a primitive, lubok-like comics form (see introduction).
11. Max Fry describes Litichevsky's ArtKomiks as "a mockery of the reader and at the same time an act of reconciliation with him."
12. As Figes notes: "In the last three-quarters of the 18th century some 500 works of literature were published in Russia. But only seven were of Russian origin" (2002: 49). In looking abroad (and chiefly to

the West) for literary-artistic models to emulate, as well as in seeking to eschew native alternatives, the modern-day "Second Wave" komiksmeny are reliving an old cultural pattern. Litichevsky is an important exception.

13. Other Litichevsky works in this vein have included a life of the ancient Greek philosopher Heraclitus. More recent explorations of the global "comicspace" concept appear in his comics painting *Muhammad Ali in the Russian Forest* (2005), in which the American boxer, in a fairy tale setting, encounters a Russian bear (actually a maiden in disguise).

14. Appearing in the 1997 *Stripburek* anthology, this was one of Litichevsky's first comics publications in the West.

15. A woman soaring up to the sky, trailing an elongated body made of railroad tracks, is a recurring image in Litichevsky's comics and paintings. It appears in "Dance of the Sabres" as well.

16. A comparison with Katya Metelitsa and colleagues' equally intertext-driven *Anna Karenina by Leo Tolstoy* (2000) is instructive here: Litichevsky's work plays with the Master's original characters and settings in a humorous but light-hearted vein; he never resorts to the mockery and disparagement, the willful attempt to shock, which Metelitsa's work gleefully traffics in: Vronsky in a strip club, well-known characters snorting coke. Litichevsky's "She Is Anna" operates more as a sort of literary variation on a well-known theme; like Tom Stoppard's 1966 play *Rosenkrantz and Guildenstern Are Dead*, its enjoyment derives from knowing the source material and how the author is dancing with it, not from seeing cultural icons dragged through the mud. (Not that there's anything wrong with the latter.)

17. See Aleshkovsky's *Vladimir Chigrintsev* (1995), Pelevin's *Chapaev i Pustota* (translated as Buddha's Little Finger, 1996) and Sorokin's notorious *Sky-Blue Lard* (Goluboe Salo 1999), in which clones of Nikita Khrushchev and Joseph Stalin engage in homosexual sex.

18. The title in Russian, "Ona—Anna," carries an internal rhyme, and appears on the first page as railroad tracks and rails forming the letters. In addition, the homophonic near-coincidence of "Ona" and "Anna" relates to the tale's "doubling" of identity.

19. Quasi-conceptualist comics homages to the Russian classics made for a small cottage industry in the post-Soviet era. Vladimir Leftov and Alexei Nikitin's *Kharmsiada* (1998) adapts Daniil Kharms's absurdist anecdotes about Russian authors such as Tolstoy, Pushkin and Gogol into comics form, while Andrei Bilzho's "One Hundred" (Sto 2005) adapts other Kharms texts to commemorate the one hundredth anniversary of the poet's birth. We can best compare Litichevsky's classics-themed work, however, to Metelitsa's follow-up to their Anna Karenina book, *The Queen of Spades by Alex Pushkin* (2002). This sets the poet's "horror story" in a modern world of virtual reality and gaming, with much fewer "shock tactics" than are employed in its predecessor.

20. Eleven years after that expression, Litichevsky maintained his stance—and stature. The Russian comics world had been transformed by the Internet and the KomMissia festival, though it remained a largely marginal practice in Russian culture. He told me: "I exist on a liminal level between comics and art. I am an artist and a komiksmen. I don't think of myself as an artist who uses or exploits comics aesthetics, I think of myself as doing real comics, just in a different format, an exhibit format" (2007). Notably, however, while Litichevsky and Ostretsov have attended KomMissia, they have not exhibited their works or competed in the festival, upholding the ArtKomiks/commercial komiks divide—though as discussed in chapter 4, KomMissia falls short as a commercial venture anyway.

21. Andre Solomon describes an aspect of Ostretsov's art practice in this period: "I met Gosha Ostretsov, who was at that time causing a stir in Moscow, wearing absurd outfits and surrealist hats, leaving his hair so long it fell to his waist, sometimes piling it on top of his head in a mass of paint. He claimed that his art was the art of pure communism; if you live in a communist country, he said, you must act like a communist. He maintained that his pose was not an ironic one, and took Lenin at his word with a bizarre self-dramatizing seriousness. Gosha designed tablecloths, wall hangings, clothing, and other items that were decorated to remind those who used them of communism in every aspect of daily life" (54–55).

22. In 1998 Ostretsov also coedited *Russian Jungles* (Russkie dzhungli), an anthology of graphic works published by Moscow's Institute of Contemporary Art.

23. As the example of American corporate advertising shows; imagine a United States taken over, say, by figures from the Jack in the Box hamburger chains' television/print campaigns.

24. This clearly references the two wars Russia fought in Chechnya since the collapse of the Soviet Union and hauntingly prefigures its conflict with Georgia. Ostretsov explains in his artist's statement: "By launching military missions, [the state] creates the illusion of itself as peacemaker . . . By sanctifying its victims, the state presents its actions as the fulfillment of its sacred duty before the people. For its part, the people deify their heroes, fashioning a historical epic about the victorious state. . . . As an artist living through this war taking place in my country, I tried, by turning to the plastic language of comics as a popular and easily understandable aesthetic form, to bring the attention of my contemporaries to this subject."

25. Litichevsky appears in the project as an NG torture victim. Photographs show him bloody and beaten, a flashlight shining in his face, as the masks press their interrogations.

26. Most of Ostretsov's source material comes from the Bronze age, with works by artists such as Neal Adams, John Buscema, John Romita Sr., and Joe Sinnott. When I mentioned these names to him in 2005, they seemed a discovery to him. The episode underscores the blithe perception—even among Russians involved in comics practice—of mainstream American comics as "pure" mass-culture objects, produced not by artists but by faceless drones or machines somewhere.

27. Ostretsov has pointed out that his interest in comics iconography in part reflects his experience with dyslexia, which makes it difficult for him to read printed text.

CHAPTER 6

1. Lipovetsky finds fascinating the many mutually contradictory conceptual modes for apprehending the New Russians: "They are titans and monsters, greedy gangsters and selfless knights of the market economy, tasteless thieves and visionaries . . . . [T]he New Russians rapidly became ideal material for intensive cultural mythologization. In fact, the mythology of the New Russians is one of the most quickly evolving elements of post-Communist culture . . ." (55).

2. Draitser 1999 and others interpret the virulent misogyny in many Russian jokes in a way similar to this reading of the New Russian humor; essentially they express the thought, "I may be pathetic and weak, but at least I'm not a woman."

3. Nikolaeva and Shapovalov. This figure pertains to 2007, during the Russian oil boom. Salaries were much lower in the late 1990s and early 2000s.

4. A 2005 homebuilder advertisement on the Rublyovka Highway outside Moscow stated, "Any house, helicopter as a bonus" (Murphy).

5. As confirmed by the 2005 success of Oksana Robski's best-seller *Casual*, about the "real lives" of the Rublyovka wealthy.

6. Publisher William Gaines did not help when he named the first comic book *Famous Funnies* in 1933.

7. The term causes other sorts of confusion. A call for proposals for a 2005 AAASS panel on "Comics in Russia" yielded an abstract for a paper on Russian stand-up comics.

8. We can here make a fruitful comparison with Alexander Alexeyev-Svinkin's 1998 painting *The New Russians*. This depicts a group of portly, debauched but oddly saint-like arrivistes in the throes of a swank Moscow party, the Kremlin in the background. The founder of "fairy tale realism," Svinkin reproduces Russian presuppositions about the subject—so insistently, in fact, that these are "short-circuited," shown up as projections of a contemptuous desire to "understand" the new Russians, to put them in their place. Svinkin's painting is therefore quite explicitly about the desire-borne limits of representation, of realism *as* fairy tale.

9. Kachaev and Sapozhkov borrow the style of Italian *fumettista* Milo Manara, but without the latter's graceful lines and mastery of female anatomy.

10. This language echoes the 1950s American reception of the first *Classics Illustrated* comics versions of Western literature, which also characterized such adaptations as harmful to student learning. See Bart Beatty's essay, "Featuring Stories by the World's Greatest Authors: Classics Illustrated and the 'Middlebrow Problem' in the Post-war Era," in *IJOCA*1, no. 1 (Summer–Spring 1999): 122–39. Many negative reactions took on quasi-religious overtones. Zaslavsky notes, "Film director Stanislav

Govorukhin, upon hearing of the publication of a graphic-novel adaptation of *Anna Karenina*, went into shock: 'It's disgraceful. Is nothing sacred anymore?'" (Maksimova: 87). Valentin Osipov, in an article bemoaning the general state of classic Russian literature in the post-Soviet period, even refuses to accept *Anna Karenina by Leo Tolstoy* as comics at all, citing a scene in which Anna dreams of living in a *ménage à trois* with Vronsky and Karenin. Osipov seems unable to countenance comics as anything other than a "children's medium."

11. Though she had previously released, with the artist Viktoria Fomina, two hilarious parodies of children's activity books, *The New Russian Primer* (Novy Russkii Bukvar') and *New Russian Leisure* (Novy Russkii Dosug) in 1999. Both were also published by New Russians' World.

12. As pointed out by Makoveeva, the work's title itself figures as a parody of modern-day marketing of style over substance in the culture industry. Films such as *Bram Stoker's Dracula* (1992), *William Shakespeare's Romeo + Juliet* (1996), and *Mary Shelley's Frankenstein* (1994) include the name of the source material's author as a marker of authenticity.

13. I do not mean to imply that the practice only began with desktop publishing. Many comics, like the famous 1950s EC horror line that led to congressional sanction, and its successor *Mad* magazine, had machine-type lettering.

14. Metelitsa here could be making a comment on post-Soviet Moscow's dangerous road conditions.

15. To *Ekho Moskvy* she added, "This is, by the way, in the Tolstoyan tradition; he made Russian books for elementary reading [*knigi dlia chteniia*]" (Boltianskaia).

16. On the significance of graffiti in late/post-Soviet culture, see Bushnell.

17. In another of Anna's dreams, the monstrous train barreling down the rails toward her even bears the name *"Lev Tolstoi"* (75).

18. Though *Novy Komiks* also traffics in the "contamination" of Russia by Western pop culture. The covers routinely featured caricatures of American movie stars such as Angelina Jolie in her *Tomb Raider* outfit (reworked as a Russian maid complete with long braid, secured with a bullet), Pamela Anderson, and a reimagined poster for the comedy *The Naked Gun 33½: The Final Insult*, with the actor Leslie Nielsen wearing a giant condom on his head and the Swedish actress Victoria Silvstedt sporting live snakes in her hair. Crude references (visual and verbal) to Britney Spears were a staple.

19. Kanton-Flesh, Ltd. owned *Novy Komiks*; the journal's publication history apparently lasted until 2002. Its publishers envisioned it as a complement to their advertising business, whose clientele was reflected in the journal's pages.

20. Makoveeva writes that the transposition of Tolstoy's classic text to the "frivolous" genre of comics leads to a "legitimization of the New Russians' identity vis-à-vis not only traditional Russian but also Soviet culture" (43). I would argue the opposite: in these texts the myth of the New Russians is rendered so over the top as to reflect badly on those who would actually *believe* it, take it seriously. Could this be why both the Soviets and the Orthodox Church so chastised the form: its myth-breaking power?

21. Metelitsa's patchwork of quotations to build her "mythical" space recall's Viktor Pelevin's similar strategy in his "New Russian" novel *Generation "TT"* (translated into English as "Homo Zapiens," 1999). Metelitsa has contended that *Anna Karenina by Leo Tolstoy* is in fact *not* a "New Russian" novel, reflected in the fact that its look is rather timeless: a mixture of historical periods and fashions, prerevolutionary orthography and clichés, which, like myths, also exist outside time. As Metelitsa explained to me, "I wanted it to belong to an uncertain time, not to reflect a particular time" (2002)—a statement difficult to credit.

CHAPTER 7

1. Hatfield here makes reference to the work of the literature scholar Stephen Shapiro.

2. Joseph Witek makes a similar point in discussing Harvey Pekar's *American Splendor*, an autobiographical series in which the hero is routinely drawn by different artists, each of which captures a different "aspect" of his personality (137).

3. Soft Skull Press released an English translation, titled *Siberia*, in 2006, while Alet Edizioni released an Italian version in 2007. Each of these books has slightly different contents; the Italian edition, *Siberia*, combines Maslov's autobiographical comics with his later short stories, while the English-language *Siberia* provides only the autobiographical material.

4. On chernukha, see Graham 2000.

5. Maslov broke from Durand sometime in 2007. I don't know why.

6. On the return of the father in post-Soviet Russian cinema, see Goscilo and Hashamova, eds., *Fathers and Sons Onscreen*, forthcoming.

7. From the *Publisher's Weekly* review (2005).

CHAPTER 8

1. On Ryklin's "speech vision" concept applied to comics, see Alaniz 2007.

2. This recalls the early twentieth-century Russian avant garde's experiments examined in chapter 1.

3. The American comics theorist Scott McCloud calls this the interdependent aspect of word/picture combinations in comics. He too describes (and illustrates) such combinations in gendered terms: in a panel depicting a man and woman dancing, the text reads, "Words and pictures are like partners in a dance, and each one takes turns leading" (156).

4. See Goscilo 1996: 9, for an assessment of women's hurdles to full equality in late Soviet culture.

5. *Yula* was launched in 2004 by Moscow's Edvans Press, which pursued a brand strategy to compete with foreign comics imports. *Yula* attained a circulation of about 20,000 at its peak, capitalizing on the popularity of the Japanese manga style in Russian comics. In 2008 it switched formats and reduced its circulation drastically, a step toward cancellation.

6. *Yula* was produced by a collective of young women, who see their mission as providing fun but edifying stories for girls—in many cases reinforcing "comfortably" traditional gender roles. For every minor transgression of the gender order by the mannish Kira, the super-femmy Mania reinscribes and reconstitutes the familiar image of girlhood.

7. Namida (real name Anastasia Vasileva, born 1981), whose pseudonym means "teardrop(s)" in Japanese, graduated from the St. Petersburg University of Technology and Design. She has won several awards at the KomMissia festival. "Clouds" represents her ongoing interest in the possibilities for formal experimentation in manga-influenced comics. Like Re-I, discussed below, she is a founding member of SPb. Nouvelles Graphiques.

8. Author of the 2000 short story collection *Give Me!* (*Tales for Lovers*). The new Russian femininity defined by the Putin era's free flow of goods, money, and pleasures also appears in such recent literature as Oksana Robski's 2005 *Casual* and Katia Metelitsa's 2005 *The Diary of Louisa Lozhkina*, as well as in the ubiquitous person of television host and celebrity Ksenia Sobchak.

9. Bronnikova (born 1973), a graduate of the Magnitogorsk Graphic Arts Pedagogical Institute, hails from Miass in the southern Urals. She has achieved considerable fame for her comics devoted to the pop star Glyuk'oza (another post-feminist "girl power" figure) and work on MTV campaigns to raise AIDS awareness. Her comics work has earned recognition and prizes at the KomMissia festival since 2003. In 2006 Anigo Press released her first collection of comics stories, *Lu, Goga and K.*

10. This influential story, which Victor Terras called "a wholly derivative and insipid literary exercise" (158), imported the theme of dying for love from the German *Sturm und Drang* movement.

11. A graduate of St. Petersburg's Rerikh Art School, where she studied design, Re-I (born 1980) works as an animator at the Melnitsa studio. She has won several prizes at KomMissia since 2002.

12. The title is an untranslatable, multilinguistic pun. *Menia* (first-person pronoun in genitive case indicating negation) is joined to the Internet domain suffix ".net" (i.e., *nyet* or "no") to suggest the phrase "*menia nyet*"—"I do not exist," "I am not here."

13. The boyfriend in Bronnikova's "Angel, Don't Be Sad" also appears as an androgyne, having more physical characteristics in common with Lu than distinct from her.

14. Suchkova (born 1977) graduated from the Moscow Pedagogical State University with training in fine arts and design. She is a founding member of Khikhus's studio "People of the Dead Fish" (LMR).

15. This story formed part of a 2001 Nike ad campaign (discussed in chapter 4) produced by LMR.

16. In addition, several comics works deal with "gothic" themes, such as her *Gothcomics* series (derivative of her idol, Tim Burton) and the 2006 vampire story "Temptation."

17. As when, on June 17, 2005, she forbids her friends from telling her about their wonderful vacation trips abroad.

18. The multiple-persona approach is familiar to readers of American underground comics, that most confessional of genres, e.g., the works of Robert Crumb and Aline Kominsky-Crumb.

19. This flower section, incidentally, follows a consideration by the author on the merits of breakfast in bed vs. coprophilia and "golden showers" on vinyl-covered water beds. These switches in register can come at a dizzying pace!

20. Namida's story "Clouds"—due to its minimalist, formally experimental approach—largely avoids the consumerism issue, and I want to tie it to the same tradition as Uzhinova's work, discussed below.

21. In regard to the potential and pay-off of Lumbricus's work, I echo, mutatis mutandis, Hector L'Hoeste-Fernández's "so near and yet so far" opinion of the Argentine female comics artist Maitena Burundarena: "In a naïve way, what I find disenchanting is the awareness of the lack of problematization and the disregard for a critical engagement or identity, contemplating all forms of capital, in the path to mindful entertainment" (360).

22. A 1987 graduate of the 1905 Art College, the Moscow-based Uzhinova (born 1967) began making comics in the early 1990s. The oldest komiksistka surveyed in this essay, she belongs to the "First Wave" of komiks, despite her late start. Her style bears a passing resemblance to that of the Canadian Julie Doucet, but we might also compare her morbid take on kids to Lynda Barry's. Among the most honored komiks artists, she has won awards at KomMissia and Boomfest.

23. This was published in the first (and last) issue of the anthology Komikser.

24. Rather than give us another banal image of lovebirds embracing, Uzhinova draws a self-referential black panel with the mocking text, "There is no picture here, because any representation would only debase our love" (30). Malevich meets romance fiction.

CONCLUSION

1. On May 31, 2005, Khodorkovsky was found guilty of tax evasion and fraud and sentenced to nine years. He is serving his time in a remote prison, in the Russian Far East. To some, he is a political victim of Putin's administration, while to the majority of Russians—who always despised the oligarchs—he was a criminal and symbol of the 1990s' excesses.

2. Defendants in Russian trials often sit in cages in the courtroom.

3. Worse than that can happen to the state's enemies. While Khikhus and I were speaking in November 2006, the world was abuzz with the story of Alexander Litvinenko, a former KGB agent, later a Putin critic, who had been mysteriously poisoned with a radioactive isotope, Polonium-210. He was slowly dying in a London hospital. Rumors swirled that the FSB (the Russian Secret Service) had performed the assassination. In Russia itself, reporting (especially news broadcasts) on the matter was light and tended to intimate that the British had done the deed, to "embarrass" Russia.

4. Xatchett gave another reason: most komiksisty are young, and have little knowledge of the country's political situation. "We don't have a lot to be dissidents about right now," he told me. "To be a dissident, you need to have not just social courage, but you also need to know what you're talking about" (2008).

5. After a hiatus during the 1990s, the venerable satire journal returned to print in a new version in 2006.

6. Though "politicized" komiks do make it into the news. A recent case: the 2007 Russian translation of 1950s anti-Russian comics by Leonid Perfetsky, Ukraine at War, dealing with the World War II–era Ukrainian Insurgent Army, a nationalist group of partisans which skirmished with the Red army. See "Komiksy pro 'moskal' skikh dushegubov' . . ."

7. Montefiore notes of the sketches: "They express a sense of humor that differs from both the official optimism of censor-approved satire and the alternative subculture of jokes and ditties" (2).

BIBLIOGRAPHY

Abramov, Mark, and Sergei Mikhalkov. *Politicheskaia satira.* Moscow: Izobrazitel'noe iskusstvo, 1973.

Adorno, Theodor, and Max Horkheimer. "The Culture Industry: Enlightenment as Mass Deception." *The Cultural Studies Reader*, edited by Simon During, 29–43. London: Routledge, 1993.

Adzhamov, A. "Nukusskii musei: Kladovaia iskusstva v epitsentre dolgoi bedy." *Fergana.ru*, July 5, 2007. http://www.ferghana.ru/article.php?id'5215.

Aeshin, Andrei. Personal interview conducted by José Alaniz, Moscow, June 2008.

———. Personal interview conducted by José Alaniz, Moscow, June 2006.

———. Interview with author. Moscow, August 2004.

———. "Podruzhki." *Komikser* 1 (1999): 24–25.

Akishin, Askold. Personal interview conducted by José Alaniz, Moscow, May 2007.

———. "R.I.P." *Al'manakh risovannyikh istorii* 4 (2006): 21–23.

———. *A Chronicle of Military Actions.*1990. http://www.comics.aha.ru/rus/hronica/.

Alaniz, José. "Caricature and Incarceration: The Case of Slava Sysoev." *International Journal of Comic Art* 8, no. 1 (Spring–Summer 2006): 145–59.

———. "Review of KomMissia 2006." *International Journal of Comic Art* 8, No. 2 (Fall 2006): 447–53.

———. "'Nice, Instructive Stories Their Psychologies Can Grasp': How to Read Post-Soviet Russian Children's Comics." *Russian Children's Literature and Culture*, ed. Marina Balin and Larissa Rudova, 193–214. New York: Routledge, 2007.

———. "Notes from the Inside: KomMissia 2008." *International Journal of Comic Art* 10, no. 2 (Fall 2008): 849–61.

———, ed. "Post-Soviet Russian Komiks: A Symposium." *International Journal of Comic Art* 7, no. 1 (Spring 2005): 5–125.

———. "Supercrip: Disability and the Silver Age Superhero." *International Journal of Comic Art* 6, no. 2, 2004): 304–24.

Ananov, G. *Vecherniaia Moskva* 274 (November 29, 1990).

———. "Znakomtes'—eto 'KOM!'" *Moskovskaia pravda*, (November 6, 1990).

Androsenko, T. (ed.). *Murzilka* 6 (1996). Moscow: Molodaya Gvardiya.

Arkhangel'skii, Andrei. "Ataka komiksov." *Ogonek* 46 (December 15–21, 2003): 46–49.

Avramskii, Isaak. *Vragi i druz'ia v zerkale Krokodila: 1922–1972.* Moscow: Pravda, 1972.

Bakhtin, Mikhail. 1984 [1965]. *Rabelais and His World.* Trans. Hélène Iswolsky. Bloomington: Indiana University Press.

Balina, Marina, Nancy Condee, and Evgeny Dobrenko. *End-Quote: Sots-Art Literature and the Soviet Grand Style.* Evanston, Ill.: Northwestern University Press, 2000.

Balzer, Harley. "Routinization of the New Russians?" *Russian Review* 62 (January 2003): 15–36.

Barker, Adele Marie. "The Culture Factory." *Consuming Culture: Popular Culture, Sex and Society since Gorbachev,* ed. Barker, 12–45. Durham, N.C.: Duke University Press, 1999.

Barmina, Natal'ia. "Polovina schast'ia." *Sobesednik* 29 (June 1989): 14.

Beaty, Bart. *Unpopular Culture: Transforming the European Comic Book in the 1990s.* Toronto: University of Toronto Press, 2007.

Belaia, G. A., and G. A. Skorokhodov. "Zhurnaly 'Krasnaia Niva,' 'Prozhektor,' 'Ogonek.'" *Ocherki istorii russkoi sovetskoi zhurnalistiki.* Ed. A. G. Dementiev, 441–62. Moscow: Nauka, 1966.

Beaudoin, Luc. "Masculine Utopia in Russian Pornography." In *Eros and Pornography in Russian Culture,* ed. M. Levitt and A. Toporkov, 622–38. Moscow: Lodomir, 1999.

Berlin, Isaiah. *Russian Thinkers.* Ed. Henry Hardy and Aileen Kelly. New York: Viking Press, 1978.

Beronä, David. "Breaking Taboos: Sexuality in the Work of Will Eisner and the Early Wordless Novels." *International Journal of Comic Art* 1, no. 1 (Spring–Summer 1999): 90–103.

Billington, James H. *The Icon and the Axe: An Interpretive History of Russian Culture.* New York: Vintage, 1970.

Bogdan. *Nika 1–2: Drakon zhelaniia.* Moscow: Pangloss, 2008.

Bogdan and Xatchett. *Skunts i Oselot.* Self-published. 2008.

Bogomolov, Yurii. "Cinema for Everyday." *Russian Critics on the Cinema of Glasnost.* Ed. Michael Brashinsky and Andrew Horton, 18–24. Cambridge: Cambridge University Press, 1994.

Bois, Yve-Alain and Christian Hubert. "El Lissitzky: Reading Lessons." *October,* Vol. 1: *Essays in Honor of Jay Leda* (Winter 1979): 113–28.

Bokhorov, Konstantin. "Aktual'nyi balagan: Festival' 'KomMissiia v Tsentre 'M'ars.'" *Kul'tura* 17 (March 3–17, 2007). http://www.kultura-portal.ru/tree_new/cultpaper/article.jsp?number'710&crubric_id'100421&rubric_id'205&pub_id'838245.

Boltianskaia, Natella (radio talk-show host). "Bolshaia literatura v kartinkakh: nasmeshka ili dan' vremeni?" *Ekho Moskvy,* January 25, 2001, accessible at http://echo.msk.ru/guests/2367/.

Bonnell, Victoria E. *Iconography of Power: Soviet Political Posters Under Lenin and Stalin.* Berkeley and Los Angeles: University of California Press, 1997.

Borenstein, Eliot. *Overkill: Sex and Violence in Contemporary Russian Popular Culture.* Ithaca, N.Y.: Cornell University Press, 2008.

———. *Men without Women: Masculinity and Revolution in Russian Fiction, 1917–1929.* Durham, N.C.: Duke University Press, 2000.

Borokhov, Konstantin. "Aktual'nyi balagan." Kul'tura 17–18 (March 3–16, 2007). http://www.kultura-portal.ru/tree_new/cultpaper/article.jsp?number=710&crubric_id=100421&rubric_id=205&pub_id=838245.

Borovskii, Aleksandr. *Tsep' romanov: russkoe iskusstvo proshedshego veka.* St. Petersburg: ERVI, 2001.

Bowlt, John E. *The Silver Age: Russian Art of the Early Twentieth Century and the 'World of Art' Group.* Newtonville, Mass.: Oriental Research Partners, 1979.

Boykewich, Stephen. "Strip Show." *Moscow Times,* December 24, 2004 http://www.moscowtimes.ru/arts/2008/06/06/364845.htm.

Boym, Svetlana. *Common Places: Mythologies of Everyday Life in Russia.* Cambridge, Mass.: Harvard University Press, 1994.

Brik, Osip. "Mayakovsky—khudozhnik." *Vladimir Mayakovsky.* Ed. V. Katan'ian. Moscow: Gosudarstvennoe izdatel'stvo izobrazitel'nykh iskusstv, 1932.

Bronnikova, Natalia. *Lu Goga i K.* Miass, Russia: Anigo, 2006.

Brooks, Jeffrey. 1985. *When Russia Learned to Read: Literacy and Popular Culture 1861–1917.* Princeton, N.J.: Princeton University Press.

Brouns, Jesse. "Review of Russsian Comics Exhibit at The Belgian Comics Strip Center." *The Bulletin* (March 16, 1995): 10.

Brown, Clarence. "Krazy, Ignatz and Vladimir: Nabokov and the Comic Strip." *Nabokov at Cornell.* Ed. Gavriel Shapiro, 251–63. Ithaca, N.Y. : Cornell University Press, 2003.

Brown, Matthew Cullerne. *Art under Stalin.* Oxford: Phaidon, 1991.

———. *Contemporary Russian Art.* Oxford: Phaidon, 1989.

———, and Brandon Taylor. "Introduction." *Art of the Soviets: Painting, Sculpture and Architecture in a One-Party State, 1917–1992.* Ed. Brown and Taylor, 1–15. Manchester, UK: Manchester University Press, 1993.

Brzhezinskaia, Karina. "Zdes' zhivut liudi." *Peterburgskii teatral'nyi zhurnal* 39 (2005). http://ptzh.theatre.ru/2005/39/144/.

Bukatman, Scott. *Matters of Gravity: Special Effects and Supermen in the Twentieth Century.* Durham, N.C.: Duke University Press, 2003.

Bum komiksov. Festival Catalog. 2007.

Bunkin, Nikolai. "Obrazovana gil'diia izdatelei komiksov rossii." Press release. October 8, 2001. http://www.comics.aha.ru/rus/articles/17.html.

Burko, Pavel. Personal interview, conducted by José Alaniz, Moscow, January 2002.

Buzek, Antony. *How the Communist Press Works.* New York: Frederick A. Praeger, 1964.

Chistiakova, A. "Petrogradskie 'okna' ROSTA." *Petrogradski okna ROSTA* (exhibit catalog). Leningrad: State Russian Museum, 1968. 7–10.

Clements, Barbara Evans. *Russian Masculinities in History and Culture,* ed. Clements, Rebecca Friedman, and Dan Healey. New York: Palgrave, 2001.

Colebrook, Claire. *Irony.* London: Routledge, 2004.

Compton, Susan. *The World Backwards: Russian Futurist Books, 1912–16.* London: British Library, 1978.

Conquest, Robert. *The Harvest of Sorrow: Soviet Collectivization and the Terror-Famine.* New York: Oxford University Press, 1986.

Constantine, Mildred, and Alan Fern. *Revolutionary Soviet Film Posters,* 1974.

Crary, Jonathan. *Suspensions of Perception: Attention, Spectacle and Modern Culture.* Cambridge, Mass.: MIT Press, 1999.

Danilova, I. E., ed. *Mir narodnoi kartinki.* Moscow: Progress, 1997.

Davydova, Mariamne. *Memoirs of a Russian Lady: Drawings and Tales of Life before the Revolution.* Ed. Olga Davidoff Dax. New York: Harry N. Abrams, 1986.

Degot, Ekaterina. *Contemporary Painting in Russia.* Roseville East, NSW: Craftsman House, 2001.

———. *Russkoe iskusstvo XX veka.* Moscow: Trilistnik, 2000.

de Man, Paul. *The Rhetoric of Romanticism.* New York: Columbia University Press, 1984.

Dergachov, Oleg. "Leonid Tishkov's Dabloids: Russian Myth in Comics." *IJOCA* 2, no. 1 (Spring 2000): 109–16.

D'iakonov, Valentin. "Bez puzyrei." *Khudozhestvennyi zhurnal* 61/62 (2006). http://xz.gif.ru/numbers/61-62/bez-puzyrei/.

Dmitrenko, Sergei. "Eto Rotov!" *Literatura* 13 (2002). http://lit.1september.ru/article.php?ID=200201308.

Dorfman, Ariel, and Armand Mattelart. *How to Read Donald Duck.* Trans. David Kunzle. New York: International General, 1975.

Dostoyevsky, Fyodor. *The Brothers Karamazov.* Trans. David Magarshak. New York: Penguin, 1958 [1880].

Dragincic, Slavko, and Zdravko Zupan. *Istorija jugoslovenskog stripa.* Novi Sad: FORUM, 1986.

Draitser, Demokratizatsiya. Summer 2001. http://findarticles.com/p/articles/mi_qa3996/is_200107/ai_n8959347/.

Draitser, Emil. "The New Russians' Jokelore: Genesis and Sociological Interpretations." *Demokratizatsia* (Summer 2001). http://findarticles.com/p/articles/mi_qa3996/is_200107/ai_n8959347/.

———. *Making War, Not Love: Gender and Sexuality in Russian Humor.* New York: St. Martin's Press, 1999.

Droitcour, Brian. "Slick Images: The fifth annual KomMissiya festival illustrates the growing professionalism of Russian comics." *Moscow Times,* May 5, 2006, accessible at http://context.themoscowtimes.com/story/167799/.

Dubkov, Konstantin. Personal interview conducted by José Alaniz, Moscow, June 2005.

Efimov, Boris. *Na moi vzgliad . . .* Moscow: Iskusstvo, 1987.

Egorov, Sasha. Personal interview conducted by José Alaniz, Moscow, June 2007.

———. "Spok nochi malyshi: Druzhba druzhboi" (Good Night, Kiddies: Friendship is Friendship). *Komikser* 1 (1999): 40.

Eisenstein, Sergei. *Selected Works, Vol. II: Towards a Theory of Montage.* Ed. Michael Glenny and Richard Taylor. Trans. Michael Glenny. London: BFI Publishing, 1991.

Elliot, David. 1986. *New Worlds: Russian Art and Society 1900–1937.* New York: Rizzoli.

Epstein, Mikhail. *Cries in the New Wilderness: From the Files of the Moscow Institute of Atheism.* Trans. Eve Adler. Philadelphia: Paul Dry Books, 2002.

———. "Emptiness as Technique: Word and Image in Ilya Kabakov." *Russian Postmodernism: New Perspectives on Post-Soviet Culture.* Ed. Mikhail Epstein, Aleksandr Genis, and Slobodanka Vladiv-Glover, 299–342. New York: Berghahn Books, 1999.

———. "The Origins and Meaning of Russian Postmodernism." *Re-Entering the Sign: Articulating New Russian Culture.* Ed. Ellen Berry and Anesa Miller-Pogacar, 25–47. Ann Arbor: University of Michigan Press, 1995.

Erofeyev, Viktor. "Dirty Words." *New Yorker,* September 15, 2003, 42–48.

———. "Comics and the Comics Disease." Trans. José Alaniz. *International Journal of Comic Art* 7, no. 1 (Spring–Summer 2005): 22–38.

———. "Soviet Literature: In Memoriam." Trans. Andrew Meier. *Glas* 1 (1991): 226–34 [1990].

Essig, Laurie. "Publicly Queer: Representations of Queer Subjects and Subjectivities in the Absence of Identity." In *Consuming Culture: Popular Culture, Sex and Society since Gorbachev,* ed. Adele Marie Barker, 281–302. Durham, N.C.: Duke University Press, 1999.

———. *Queer in Russia: A Story of Sex, Self and the Other.* Durham, N.C.: Duke University Press, 1999.

Estes, Jeremy. "Siberia." *Popmatters,* October 20, 2006. http://www.popmatters.com/pm/review/6509/siberia/.

Falkovsky, Ilya. "Ataka komiksov." *Ogonyok* 46 (December 15–21, 2003): 46–49.

Farrell, Diane Ecklund. "The Bawdy Lubok: Sexual and Scatological Content in Eighteenth-Century Russian Popular Prints." In *Eros and Pornography in Russian Culture,* ed. Marcus Levitt and Andrei Toporkov, 16–41. Moscow: Ladomir, 1999.

———. "Shamanic Elements in Some Early Eighteenth-Century Russian Woodcuts." *Slavic Review* 52, no. 4 (Winter 1993): 725–44.

Fedorova, Dar'ia. "Komiks: Khikhus i liudi mertvoi ryby." *Render.ru,* February 2007. http://www.render.ru/books/show_book.php?book_id =506.

Fernández-L'Hoeste, Héctor. "Beyond Just Gender: On the World of Maitena Burundarena." *International Journal of Comic Art* 8, no. 1 (Spring–Summer 2006): 346–61.

Figes, Orlando. *Natasha's Dance: A Cultural History of Russia.* New York: Henry Holt & Co., 2002.

———. *A People's Tragedy: The Russian Revolution, 1981–1924.* New York: Penguin, 1996.

Filippov, Daniil. Personal interview conducted by José Alaniz, Moscow, January 1996.

———. "Research of Text No. 2." *Kitup's Own Propeller Comics Monthly* 3–4 (February–March, 1994).

Fischer, Craig. 2003. "Fantastic Fascism? Jack Kirby, Nazi Aesthetics, and Klaus Theweleit's *Male Fantasies.*" *International Journal of Comic Art* 5, no. 1 (2003)334–54.

Foucault, Michel. *Discipline and Punish: The Birth of the Prison.* Trans. Alan Sheridan. New York: Vintage Books, 1979 [1975].

Frahm, Ole. "Too Much is Too Much: The Never-Innocent Laughter of the Comics." *Image [and] Narrative: Online Magazine of theVisual Narrtive,* October 2003, accessible at http://www.imageandnarrative.be/graphicnovel/olefrahm.htm.

Franchetti, Mark. "Stalin Drew Cartoons of His victims' Fate." Sunday Times, July 8, 2001. http://www.timesonline.co.uk/tol/news/pages/Sunday-Times/stifgnruso2002.html.

Freud, Sigmund. "Thoughts for the Times on War and Death" [1915]. *Standard Edition of the Complete Psychological Works of Sigmund Freud,* ed. James Strachey, 275–300. London: Hogarth Press, 1957. Vol. 17.

Fry, Max. "K: Komiks." *Art-Azbuka*. Ed. Fry, 2000–2007. http://azbuka.gif.ru/alfabet/k/comic-strip.

Fuller, William. "The Great Fatherland War and Late Stalinism: 1941–1953." *Russia: A History*. Ed. Gregory Freeze, 319–46. Oxford: Oxford University Press, 1997.

Gagina, Ekaterina. "Pod mukhoi." *Ufimskoe vremia* 3 (December 2006) http://animasfera.narod.ru/article/muha.html.

Gamburger, L. *Ai da ia!* Moscow: Detskii mir, 1961.

Gentleman, Amelia. "Sushi and Coke: The New World of Anna Karenina." *Guardian*, January 30, 2001, accessible at http://books.guardian.co.uk/news/articles/0,,430695,00.html.

Givens, John. "Reflections, Crooked Mirrors, Magic Theatres: Tatiana Tolstaia's 'Peters.'" *Fruits of Her Plume: Essays in Contemporary Russian Women's Culture*. Ed. Helena Goscilo, 251–70. Armonk, N.Y.: M. E. Sharpe, 1993.

Gleason, Abbot, Peter Kenez, and Richard Stites, eds. *Bolshevik Culture: Experiment and Order in the Russian Revolution*. Bloomington: Indiana University Press, 1985.

Goldschmidt, Paul. "Pornography in Russia." In *Consuming Russia: Popular Culture, Sex and Society Since Gorbachev*, ed. Adele Marie Barker, 138–60. Durham, N.C.: Duke University Press, 1999.

Golomshtok, Igor. *Totalitarian Art in the Soviet Union, the Third Reich, Fascist Italy and the People's Republic of China*. Trans. by Robert Chandler. London: Collins Harvill, 1990.

Golynets, Sergei. *Ivan Bilibin*. Leningrad: Aurora Arts, 1981.

Goscilo, Helena. *Dehexing Sex: Russian Womanhood During and After Glasnost*. Ann Arbor: University of Michigan Press, 1996.

———. *The Explosive World of Tatyana N. Tolstaya's Fiction*. Armonk, N.Y.: M. E. Sharpe, 1996.

Graeme, Chris. "Gallery Exhibits Comic Art with Erotic Twist." *Moscow Tribune*, December 21, 1995, 7.

Graham, Seth. "The Wages of Syncretism: Folkloric New Russians and Post-Soviet Popular Culture." *The Russian Review* 62 (January 2003): 37–53.

———. "Chernukha and Russian Film." *Studies in Slavic Cultures* 1 (2000): 9–27.

Gray, Camilla. *The Russian Experiment in Art: 1863–1922*. New York: Harry N. Abrams, 1962.

Grif. Personal correspondence. August 20, 2008.

Groensteen, Thierry. *The System of Comics*. Trans. Bart Beaty Nick and Nguyen. Jackson: University Press of Mississippi, 2007.

Groys, Boris. "Survey: The Movable Cave, or Kabakov's Self-memorials." *Ilya Kabakov*. Ed. David Ross and Iwona Blazwik, 30–79. London: Phaidon, 1998.

———. *The Total Art of Stalinism: Avant-Garde, Aesthetic Dictatorship, and Beyond*. Trans. by Charles Rougle. Princeton, N.J.: Princeton University Press, 1992 [1988].

Gruntovsky, A. *Russky Kulachniy Boi: Istoriya, Etnografiya, Tekhnika*, TOO Tekhnologiya Avtomatizirovannikh System, St. Petersburg, 1998.

Gubarev, V., and R. Stoliarov. *Pavlik Morozov*. Moscow: Diafilm Studio, 1959.

Guliaev, Dmitrii. "Komiks protiv manga." Fabrika komiksov website. Janaury 1, 2000. http://comics factory.ru/?p=110.

Gurianova, Nina. "A New Aesthetic: Word and Image in Russian Futurist Books." In *Defining Russian Graphic Arts from Diaghilev to Stalin: 1893–1934*, ed. Alla Rosenfeld, 97–120. New Brunswick, N.J.: Rutgers University Press.

Gurov, Evgenii. *Krokodil*, 1990. http://community.livejournal.com/old_crocodile/25869.html#cutid1.

Harvey, Robert C. *The Art of the Comic Book: An Aesthetic History*. Jackson: University Press of Mississippi, 1996.

Hatfield, Charles. *Alternative Comics: An Emerging Literature*, Jackson: University Press of Mississippi, 2005.

Hatty, Susan. *Masculinities, Violence, Culture*. London: Sage, 2000.

Herausgegeben, von Alphons Silberman, and H. D. Dryoff, eds. *Comics and Visual Culture: Research Studies from Ten Countries*. New York: K. G. Saur, 1986.

Humphrey, Caroline. *The Unmaking of Soviet Life: Everyday Economies after Socialism*. Ithaca, N.Y.: Cornell University Press, 2002.

Iarskaia-Smirnova, Elena. *Odezhda dlia Adama i Evy: ocherki gendernykh issledovaniy.* Moscow: Center for Socio-political and Gender Studies, 2001.

Idov, Michael. "What a Bear Says When He Sees a Couple Making Love in the Forest." *Russia!* (Spring 2007). http://www.readrussia.com/magazine/spring-2007/00014/.

Itkina, E. I. *Russkii risovannyi lubok.* Moscow: Russkaia kniga, 1992.

Ivanova, V. "Komu priz KOMa?" *Vecherniaia Moskva* 280 (December 6, 1990).

Iversen, Breuk. "Sex, Violence and Catholicism." *Umelec International* 3 (2004). http://www.divus.cz/umelec/en/pages/umelec.php?id=373&roc=2004&cis=3.

Jahn, Hubertus. *Patriotic Culture in Russia during World War I.* Ithaca, N.Y.: Cornell University Press, 1995.

Julius, Anthony. *Transgressions: The Offenses of Art.* Chicago: University of Chicago Press, 2002.

Kai, Sato (Alexandra Tyuleneva). "Metro." KomMissiia 2005 catalog: 72–73.

Kamensky, Yury, Ezhen Shchedrin, and Askold Akishin. *Georgy Zhukov.* Moscow: Progress, 1991.

Kapninsky, Aleksei. Personal interview conducted by José Alaniz, Moscow, May 2005.

Kapranov, Sergei. Personal interview conducted by José Alaniz, Moscow, November 2006.

Kataev, Valentin. *Time Forward!* Trans. by Charles Malamuth. Evanston, Ill.: Northwestern University Press, 1995 [1932].

Kelly, Catriona. "Thank you for the Wonderful Book: Soviet Child Readers and the Management of Children's Reading, 1950–75." *Kritika: Explorations in Russian and Eurasian History* 6, no. 4 (Fall 2005): 717–53.

———. "Territories of the Eye: The Russian Peep Show (Raek) and Pre-Revolutionary Visual Culture." *Journal of Popular Culture* 31, no. 4 (Spring 1998): 49–74.

Kenez, Peter. *Cinema and Soviet Society, 1917–1953.* Cambridge: Cambridge University Press, 1992.

Kersnovskaia, Evrosiniia. *Skol'ko stoit chelovek?* Moscow: Rosspen, 2006.

———. *Naskhal'naia zhivopis'.* Moscow: Kvadrat, 1991.

Kerzhentsev, Petr. "Okna Satiry ROSTA". *Okna satiry ROSTA* (exhibit catalog). Moscow: Tretiakovsky Gallery, 1929.

Khidekel, Regina. *It's the Real Thing: Soviet and Post-Soviet Sots-Art and American Pop Art.* Minneapolis: University of Minnesota Press, 1998.

Khikhus (Pavel Sukhikh). Personal interview conducted by José Alaniz, Moscow, June 2005.

———. Personal interview conducted by José Alaniz, Moscow, August 2004.

———. Press release after KomMissia 2004. 2004.

———. "Moskovskii festival komiksov." KomMissia 2002 Catalog, 1.

———. "Krasnaya Shapochka: A Christmas Tale." In *Almanakh: Volshebnie Komiksy* [KomMissia 2003 publication], ed. Lyudi Mertvoi Ryby, 42–43. Moscow, 2003.

Khmelnitskii, Dmitrii. "Especially Dangerous Little Pictures." *Terraincognita.spb.ru* 8/18 (August 2003), accessible at http://terraincognita.spb.ru/n18/index2.htm.

Kincaid, James. *Child-Loving: The Erotic Child in Victorian Literature.* New York: Routledge, 1992.

King, David, and Cathy Porter. *Images of Revolution: Graphic Art from 1905 Russia.* New York: Pantheon, 1983.

Kitup, Il'ia. "The Only True Guide to Russia: Hidden Secrets Revealed, Fact 3." *Kitup's Own Propeller Comics Monthly* 16 (September 1998).

———. "Skew Power: A Novel." Unpublished comics work. 1997.

———. "Dostoyevsky Forever: Comic Culture in Russia." *Stripburek: Comics from behind the Rusty Iron Curtain.* Ed. Katrina Mirovic, 66–67. Ljubljana: Forum Ljubljana, 1997.

———. Personal interview conducted by José Alaniz, Moscow, June 1997.

Klimov, G. *Ivan Bilibin: po materialam sobraniia E. P. Klimova.* Moscow: Terra, 1999.

Kolgarev, Igor. Personal interview conducted by José Alaniz, Moscow, November 2006.

———. *The War with the Snowmen.* Moscow: KOM, 1992.

Komarev, Vladimir. Personal interview conducted by José Alaniz, Moscow, January 2002.

Komarev, Vladimir et al. "Dimych and Timych Rescue Pritney Poops." *Dimych and Timych* 4 (2002): 1–12.

——— et al. "Dimych and Timych Save the World." *Dimych and Timych* 1 (2001): 2–19.

"Komiksy pro 'moskal'skikh duwegubov' pereveli na russkii." *Lenta.ru*, December 12, 2007. http://www .lenta.ru/news/2007/12/12/comics.

Komolov, Anton, and Ol'ga Shelest. "Khudozhnik Khikhus." *Radio Maiak* (April 21, 2008). http://www .radiomayak.ru/tvp.html?id=139835&cid=.

Kon, Igor. "Muzhkiye Issledovaniya: Menyayushchiyesya Muzhchiny v Izmenyayushchemsya Mire." *Vvedeniye v Genderniye Issledovaniya, Chast' I*, ed. Irina Zherebkina. Kharkov: Aleteiya, 2001.

Kondrat'ev, Vasilii. "Bumazhnaia opera." *Sinii divan* 4 (2004): 221–37.

Kostin, Boris. Personal interview conducted by José Alaniz, Moscow, January 2000.

Kovtun, E. F. *Russkaya Futuristicheskaya Kniga* (The Russian Futurist Book). Moscow: Kniga, 1989.

———. Introduction. *Petrogradskii okna ROSTA* (exhibit catalog). Leningrad: State Russian Museum, 1968.

Kozhin, N. A. and I. S. Abramov. *Narodnyi lubok.* Leningrad: Izdanie muzeia obshchestva pooshreniia khudozhestv, 1929.

Kravtsova, Maria. "Marginal'nyi zhanr?" *Artkhronika* 8 (2006): 90–93.

Krylova, Anna. "Saying 'Lenin' and Meaning 'Party': Subversion and Laughter in Soviet and Post-Soviet Society." In *Consuming Russia: Popular Culture, Sex and Society since Gorbachev*, ed. Adele Marie Baker, 243–65. Durham, N.C.: Duke University Press, 1999.

Kubeeva, Polina. "Zhelteiushchie mal'chiki v glazakh." *Izvestia* (July 24, 2002), http://main.izvestia.ru/ print/?id=21508 (accessed June 21, 2006).

Kujundzic, Dragan. "Can the Other Be Eaten: Live from Moscow or Royal with Cheese?" *ArtMargins* (1999), accessible at xx.

Kukarkin, Alexander. *Burzhuaznaia massovaia kul'tura: teorii, idei, raznovidnosti, obraztsy, tekhnika, biznes*, 2nd ed. Moscow: Izdatel'stvo politicheskoi literatury, 1985.

———. *The Passing Age: The Ideology and Culture of the Late Bourgeois Epoch.* Trans. Keith Hammond. Moscow: Progress, 1979.

———. *Po tu storonu rastsveta. Burzhuaznoe obshchestvo: kul'tura i ideologiia*, 2nd ed. Moscow: Politizdat, 1977.

Kukryniksy. *Vtroem.* Moscow: Sovetskii khudozhnik, 1975.

Kulikov, Ivan. "Nenuzhnye kartinki." *Ezhenedel'nyi zhurnal* 64 (April 8, 2003). http://supernew.ej.ru/ 064/life/art/03/.

———. "Ze Best Komik of ze Best Atist." *Nezavisimaya Gazeta*, January 8, 2002, accessible at http://ex libris.ng.ru/printed/comics/2002-08-01/4_comic.html.

———. "A vot my—priparilis." *Exlibris* (supplement to *Nezavisimaia gazeta*), November 15, 2001. http:// exlibris.ng.ru/masscult/2001-11-15/4_komarov.html.

Kunzle, David. *History of the Comic Strip. Vol I: The Early Comic Strip: Narrative Strips and Picture Stories in the European Broadsheet from c. 1450 to 1825.* Berkeley and Los Angeles: University of California Press, 1973.

Kurguzov, Oleg, Andrei Snegirov, and Natalia Snegirova. "Kot-poliglot." *Keshka* (1993): 3–10.

———. "Kot-poliglot." *Nu, pogodi!* 1 (2004): 27–34.

Kuzmichev, Daniil. "Khose, esli vy menia schas chitajte, snajte." *Lichnyi blog D. A. Kuzmicheva*, June 9, 2009. http://blog.dahr.ru/.

———. Online forum post transcript. Live Journal. September 25, 2002.

Kuz'mina, Natalia. "Chtivo dlia malen'kikh detei," *Niania* 8 (2004), http://nanya.ru/opit/9341 (accessed August 20, 2009).

Lamm, Leonid. *Birth of an Image.* Durham, N.C.: Duke University Museum of Art, 1998.

Lapitskii, Isaak. *V teni neboskrebov.* Moscow: Molodaia gvardia, 1958.

Larina, Antonina. Personal interview conducted by José Alaniz, Moscow, August 2004.

Larsen, Susan. "In Search of an Audience: The New Russian Cinema of Reconciliation." *Consuming Russia: Popular Culture, Sex, and Society since Gorbachev*, ed. Adele Marie Barker, 192–216. Durham, N.C.: Duke University Press, 1999.

Lavrentev, Alexander. *Laboratoriia konstruktivizma: opyty graficheskogo modelirovaniia.* Moscow: Grant, 2000.

LeBlanc, Ronald. "Feeding a Poor Dog a Bone: The Quest for Nourishment in Bulgakov's *Sobach'e serdtse.*" *Russian Review* 52 (January 1993): 58–78.

———. "A Russian Tarzan, or 'Aping' Jocko?" *Slavic Review* 46, no. 1 (Spring 1987): 70–86.

Levinson, Nan. *Outspoken: Free Speech Studies.* Berkeley and Los Angeles: University of California Press, 2003.

Likhacheva, Vera, and Dmitrii Likhachev. *Khudozhestvennoe nasledie drevnei rusi i sovremennost'.* Leningrad: Nauka, 1971.

Lincoln, W. Bruce. *Between Heaven and Hell: The Story of a Thousand Years of Artistic Life in Russia.* New York: Viking, 1998.

Lipatov, Alexei. "Stalin vs. Gitler." Komiksolyot, 2000, accessible at http://www.comics.aha.ru/rus/stalin/1.html.

Lipovetsky, Mark. "Vsekh lyubliu na svete ya!" *Iskusstvo Kino* 11 (2000): 55–59.

———. "New Russians as a Cultural Myth." *Russian Review* 62 (January 2003): 54–71.

Lisin, Alexander. "Mif o komiksakh." *KOM O.K.* Ed. Sergei Kapranov. Moscow: ABEKS, 1990. Inside cover.

Litichevskii, Georgii, and Andrei Royter. "From Moscow." *Flash Art* 10 (1988): 101.

Litichevsky, Georgy. Personal interview conducted by Jose Alaniz, Moscow, January 1996.

———. Personal interview conducted by José Alaniz, Moscow, June 2007.

———. "Isadora." *Striburek.* Ljublana: Forum, 1997, 74–79.

———. Personal conversation, 1997.

———, interview with Jose Alaniz, Moscow, March 1999.

———. "Ona—Anna." *Mesto Pechati* 10 (1997). http://www.geocities.com/SoHo/Exhibit/6196/mp10-12.htm.

———. "The Troekurov Style" (Stil' Troekurova). *Mesto Pechati* 9 (1997), accessible at http://www.geocities.com/SoHo/Exhibit/6196/mp9-4.htm.

———. Personal interview in Moscow, Russia, January 1996.

———. Personal interview conducted by José Alaniz, Moscow, June 2007.

———. "Russkie zhenshchiny." Unpublished. Ca. 2000.

———. "Tanets s sabliami." Unpublished. Ca. 2000.

———. "Vybor Levitantana." Unpublished. Ca. 2000.

———. "Rimskie karakuli." *Ptyutch.* Ca. 1995.

———. "The Café of the Poets."

———. *Stripburek: Comics from behind the Rusty Iron Curtain.* Ljubljana: Forum Ljubljana, 1997: 74–79.

Litichevsky, Georgy, and Georgy Ostretsov. "Georgii Ostretsov i Georgii Litichevskii o vystavke." *Gif.ru,* December 20, 2004. http://www.gif.ru/themes/culture/bubble-gg/int/.

Litichevsky, Georgy, and Gosha Ostretsov. "O vystavke" (interview) in *Gif.ru,* December 12, 2004, accessible at http://www.gif.ru/themes/culture/bubble-gg/int/.

Lopatin, Denis. *Moia izbiratel'naia kabinka.* KomMissia 2008 Festival Catalog: 183.

Lotman, Iurii. *Ob iskusstve.* St. Petersburg: Iskusstvo SPB, 1998.

Lovell, Stephen, and Birgit Menzel, eds. *Reading for Entertainment in Contemporary Russia.* Munich: Verlag Otto Sagner, 2005.

Lukyanchikov, Alexei. Interview with Jose Alaniz, Moscow, June 1996.

———. *The Crew* (Ekipazh). Moscow: Tema, 1992.

Lumbricus. "Comics for Nike." Accessible at http://www.lumb.ru/comics/commer/NIKE/9094.html. [2005].

MacFadyen, David. "Night Watch" (film review) in *Kinokultura,* October, 2004, accessible at http://www.kinokultura.com/reviews/R104dozor.html.

Makoveeva, Irina. "Revisualizing Anna Karenina." *Tolstoy Studies Journal* 16 (2004): 43–54.

Maksimova, Svetlana, ed. "Komiks v obrazovanii: est' li pol'za dlia dela?," *Narodnoe obrazovanie* 9/1322 (2002): 131–42.

Malpas, Anna. "Brushing Up on the Apocalypse, One Cartoon Frame at a Time." *Moscow Times,* December 30, 2003. http://context.themoscowtimes.com/stories/2003/12/30/103.html.

Mansurov, N. S. "Children's Publications in the Soviet Union." In *Comics and Visual Culture: Research Studies from Ten Countries.* New York: K. G. Saur, 1986. 134–48.

Manuil'sky, M. Z., and B. M. Nikiforov. "Introduction." *Karrikatura na sluzhbe sotsialisticheskogo stroitel'stva* (Exhibit Catalog). Moscow: Pravda, 1932.

Marcus, Laura. *Auto/biographical Discourses: Theory, Criticism, Practice.* Manchester: Manchester University Press, 1994.

Mar'esev, Viktor. Personal interview conducted by José Alaniz, Moscow, November 2006.

Margolin, Victor . "Constructivism and the Modern Poster." *Art Journal* 44, no.1 (Spring 1984): 28–32.

Markova, Natalia. "Komiks." 2002. http://r-komitet.narod.ru/smi/smi-p-017.htm.

Maslov, Nikolai. Siberia. Trans. Blake Ferris. Brooklyn, N.Y.: Soft Skull Press, 2006 [2004].

Mayakovsky, Vladimir. *Vladimir Mayakovsky.* Ed. V. Katan'ian. Moscow: Gosudarstvennoe izdatel'stvo izobrazitel'nykh iskusstv, 1932.

McCloud, Scott. *Understanding Comics.* Northampton: Kitchen Sink Press, 1993.

Merino, Ana. *El Cómic Hispánico.* Madrid: Ediciones Cátedra, 2003.

Merrill, Megan. "Artist's Work is Fixed in Flights of Fancy." *Moscow Times*, April 2003. http://www.krokin gallery.com/english/prissue_43/issue_96.html.

Messner, Michael. *Politics of Masculinities: Men in Movements.* Thousand Oaks, Calif.: Sage, 1997.

Metelitsa, Katya. Personal interview with author. Moscow, July 2002.

———, and Viktoria Fomina. *Novy russkii bukvar'.* Mir Novykh Russkykh, Moscow, 1999.

———, Valery Kachaev, and Igor Sapozhkov. *Anna Karenina by Leo Tolstoy.* Mir Novykh Russkykh, Moscow, 2000.

Miskarian, Kara. "TV—glavnyi konkurent komiksov v Rossii." *Artkhronika* 8 (2006): 84–89.

Misler, Nicoletta. "A Public Art: Caricatures and Posters of Vladimir Lebedev." *Journal of Decorative and Propaganda Arts* 5 (Summer 1987):60–75.

Mitrevski, Ivan. "Russian Comics and the Internet Underground." *International Journal of Comic Art* 7 no. 1 (Spring–Summer 2005): 67–74.

Moist, Velimir. "A Sandpiper for Curious Old Ladies." *Gazeta.ru*, November 14, 2003, accessible at http://www.gif.ru/podval/kulik.

Montefiore, Simon Sebag. "Foreword." *Piggy Foxy and the Sword of Revolution: Bolshevik Self-Portraits.* Trans. Vadim Staklo. New Haven, Conn.: Yale University Press, 2006.

Moskin, Dmitry. "Detskaia illiustratsiia." *Kratkaia entsiklopedia karikatury.* Accessible at http://fairytale .by.ru/Press/Caricature.htm.

Mukhametzyanov, Vitaly, ed. *Mukha* 9, 10, 11, 12, 13 and 14 (1991–1993). Ufa: Bashkorstan.

Murphy, Kim. "In This Part of Russia, The Rich Live Very Large." *Los Angeles Times*, April 24, 2005, accessible at http://www.boston.com/news/world/europe/articles/2005/04/24/in_this_part_of_russia_the_rich_live_very_large/?rss_id=Boston+Globe+--+World+News9#X.

Museum.ru. "Komiks v sovremennom iskusstve," Dec. 2004, accessible at http://www.museum.ru/N20332.

Nabokov, Vladimir. *Speak, Memory: an Autobiography Revisited.* New York: Vintage, 1989 [1967].

———. *Nikolai Gogol.* New York: New Directions, 1959.

———. *Pnin.* New York: Vintage Books, 1989 [1957].

Namida (Anastasia Vasil'eva). "Clouds." *Napoleon is Always Happy* [Napoleon vsegda schastliv]. St. Petersburg: SPb Nouvelle Graphiques, 2006: 78–87.

Nedelin, V. "Barbarella i letchiki s napalmom." *Inostrannaia literatura* 9 (September 1965): 252–60.

Nekrylova, A. "Istinno patrioticheskii podvig." In Dimitrii Rovinsky, *Russkie narodnie kartinki* St. Petersburg: Tropa Troianova, 2002. 3–16.

Nelson, William. *Out of the Crocodile's Mouth: Russian Cartoons about the United States from 'Krokodil,' Moscow's Humor Magazine.* Washington, D.C.: Public Affairs Press, 1949.

Nesbitt, Lois E. *Brodsky and Utkin: The Complete Works.* New York: Princeton Architectural Press, 2003.

Neuberger, Joan. *Hooliganism: Crime, Culture and Power in St. Petersburg, 1900–1914.* Berkeley and Los Angeles: University of California Press, 1993.

Nikanorov, Aleksei. "Klash and the Vices." *Komiksolet*, 2001.

http://zabeich.borda.ru/?1-1-0-00000230-000-0-0-1214985763.

———. "Pobrali." *Mukha* 11 (1993): 13–18.

Nikiforov, B. M. "Za proletarskii tvorcheskii metod v sovetskoi karikature." *Karrikatura na sluzhbe sotstroitel'stva* (exhibit catalog). Ed. M. Z. Manuilsky and Nikiforov. Moscow: Pravda, 1932.

Nikolaeva, Daria, and Aleksei Shapovalov. "Average Monthly Salary Averages $550 in 2007." *Kommersant*, January 30, 2008.

http://www.kommersant.com/page.asp?id=847117.

Norris, Stephen M. *A War of Images: Russian Popular Prints, Wartime Culture, and National Identity, 1812–1945.* Dekalb: Northern Illinois University Press, 2006.

O'Dell, Felicity Ann. *Socialization through Children's Literature: The Soviet Example.* Cambridge, Mass.: Cambridge University Press, 1978.

Orlova, Milena. "Georgii Litichevskii." *Segodnia*, September 11, 1993.

http://www.art-data.ru/artists/litichevsky,htm.

Orlovsky, Daniel. "Russia in War and Revolution: 1914–1921." In *Russia: A History*, ed. Gregory Freeze, 231–62. Oxford: Oxford University Press, 1997.

Osipov, Valentin. "Klassika v obrabotke dlia rynka." *Literaturnaia Gazeta* 47 (5857), (November 21–27, 2001), accessible at http://www.lgz.ru/archives/html_arch/lg472001/Polosy/art5_1.htm.

Ostretsov, Georgii. Personal interview conducted by José Alaniz, Moscow, June 2006.

———. *Novoe Pravitel'stvo* (Exhibit Publication). Moscow: Velta Gallery, 2002.

———. "Iz oblasti fantastiki." *NRG* 15 (March–April 1999).

Pelevin, Viktor. *Omon Ra.* Trans. Andrew Bromfield. New York: New Directions, 1992.

Penzin, Viktor. *Grafika, monumental'noe iskusstvo* (exhibit catalog). Moscow: Sovetskii khudozhnik, 1989.

Petrova, Evgeniia, and Jean-Claude Markade, eds. *Avangard do i posle.* Moscow and Brussels: Palace Editions, 2005.

Pomerantsev, Igor'. "An Artist in the Zone" (radio talk-show transcript), July 31, 1998, accessible at http://www.svoboda.org/programs/OTB/1998/OBP.09.asp.

Porter, Robert. *Russia's Alternative Prose.* Oxford: Berg, 1994.

Pushkaryova, Natalya. "Russkie lubochnie kartiniki XVIII–XX vv.: nachalo pornografii ili otrazhenie narodnykh eroticheskikh vozzreniy?" In *Eros and Pornography in Russian Culture*, 42–53. Moscow: Ladomir, 1999.

Pushkin, Alexander. *The Captain's Daughter and Other Stories.* Trans. Natalie Duddington and T. Keane. New York: Vintage, 1936.

Railing, Patricia. *More About 2 Squares.* Cambridge, Mass.: MIT Press, 1991.

Re-I (Lyudmilla Steblyanko). "Menia.net." KomMissia Festival 2004 Catalog. Moscow, 2004: 60–63.

Reitblat, Avram. "Shto nes s bazara russkii narod: lubok v issledovaniiakh poslednikh let." *Novoe literaturnoe obozrenie* 44 (April 2000): 317–26.

———. *Ot Bovy k Bal'montu.* Moscow: MPI, 1991.

Reynolds, Richard. *Super Heroes: A Modern Mythology.* Jackson: University Press of Mississippi, 1992.

Rice, Tamara Talbot. *A Concise History of Russian Art.* New York: Frederick A. Praeger, 1963.

Robbins, Trina. *From Girls to Grrrlz: A History of Women's Comics from Teens to Zines.* San Francisco: Chronicle Books, 1999.

Robinson, Sally. *Marked Men: White Masculinity in Crisis.* New York: Columbia University Press, 2000.

Rosenfeld, Alla, ed. *Defining Russian Graphic Arts from Diaghilev to Stalin: 1893–1934.* New Brunswick, N.J.: Rutgers University Press, 1999.

———. "Figuration Versus Abstraction in Soviet Illustrated Children's Books: 1920–1930." In *Defining Russian Graphic Arts from Diaghilev to Stalin: 1898–1934*, ed. Rosenfeld, 166–97. New Brunswick, N.J.: Rutgers University Press, 1999.

Rovinsky, Dmitrii. *Russkie narodnie kartinki.* St. Petersburg: Tropa Troianova, 2002 [1881].

Ruban, Anna. "KomMissionye istorii." *Kul'tpokhod* 11 (2007). http://kult-pohod.ru/themes/kultprosvet/kommisionieistorii.phtml.

Ryklin, Mikhail K. "Bodies of Terror: Theses Toward a Logic of Violence." Trans. Molly Williams Wesling and Donald Wesling. *New Literary History* 24, no. 1 (1993): 51–74.

Sadecky, Petr. *Octobriana and the Russian Underground*. New York: Harper and Row, 1971.

Sadreyev, Igor. "Isderzhki vospitaniia." *Aktsiia* 55 (April 10–May 21, 2006): 4.

Safarov, Roman. "Chelovek-litoi: Kak on stal sovershenno litym." *Pegas* 3 (2008): 36–40.

Sakov, Vladimir. Interview with Jose Alaniz, Moscow, July 1997.

——. Interview with Jose Alaniz, Moscow, June 1996.

——. *Priklucheniye Kapitana Donki: Kapitan Donki Ishchet Pravdu, Pt. 1 _ Ad*. Moscow: Ufleky, 1990.

——. *Priklucheniye Kapitana Donki: Kapitan Donki Ishchet Pravdu, pt. 2 _ Rai*. Moscow: Ufleky, 1991.

Sakovich, A. G. "Narodnie gravirovannie knigi v Rossii XVII–XIX vekov: repertuar i bytovanie." *Mir narodnoi kartinki*. Moscow: Progress, 1997: 112–31.

Sapgir, Genrikh, and Anatoly Brusilovsky. "Puty." *Metropol'*. Ed. Viktor Erofeev et al. Moscow: Zebra-E, 2001, 822–26. [1979].

Savchenkov, Ilya. "Red Army Men and Comics." *Proryv*. Moscow: KOM, 1990.

Schleifman, Nurit. *Russia at a Crossroads: History, Memory and Political Practice*. New York: Routledge, 1998.

Schmid, Ulrich. "Flowers of Evil: The Poetics of Monstrosity in Contemporary Russian Literature (Erofeyev, Mamleyev, Sokolov, Sorokin)." *Russian Literature* 49 (August 15, 2000): 205–22.

Semenov, Ivan. *Konstantin Rotov: karikatury*. Moscow: Pravda, 1966.

——, and Yurii Postnikov. *Heobyknovennie prikliucheniia Peti Ryzhika i ego vernykh druzei Mika i Muka*. Moscow: Malysh, 1964.

Semenyuk, Oleg. "Comics Art in the USSR: A Short Overview (1917–1985)." Trans. by José Alaniz. *International Journal of Comic Art* 7, no. 1 (Spring–Summer 2005): 56–63.

——. Personal interview conducted by José Alaniz, Moscow, January 2002.

Sfinktr, A. [Aleksei Kapninsky]. "Shutka." *KOM-positsia*, ed. Sergei Kapranov, 7–8. Moscow: Interbuk, 1990.

Shamil & Co. "Vot shto byvaet s temi, kto p'yot moloko vmesto piva!" *Novy Komiks* 1, no. 3, (November 20–December 20, 2001): 22.

Shatskikh, Alexandra. *Vitebsk: The Life of Art*. Trans. Katherine Fokko Tsan. New Haven, Conn.: Yale University Press, 2007 [2001].

Shevelev, Igor'. "They were Waiting for the Artist Sysoev at the Lubianka." In *Nezavisimaia Gazeta*, December 12, 2003, accessible at http://exlibris.ng.ru/fakty/2003-12-04/2_sysoev.html.

"Siberia." *Publishers Weekly* 252.46 (November 21, 2005): 32(2).

Sidlin, Mikhail. "Pif i Matiss: komiks v Rossii bol'she chem komiks." *Nezavisimaia gazeta*. April 23, 2004. http://www.ng.ru/accent/2004-04-23/23_comix.html.

Silverman, Kaja. "Historical Trauma and Male Subjectivity." In *Psychoanalysis and Cinema*, ed. Ann Kaplan, 110–27. New York: Routledge, 1990.

Sinyavsky, Andrei. *Soviet Civilization: A Cultural History*. Trans. by Joanne Turnbull. New York: Little, Brown and Company, 1990.

Sjeklocha, Paul, and Igor Mead. *Unofficial Art in the Soviet Union*. Berkeley and Los Angeles: University of California Press, 1967.

Skorokhodov, A. G. *Saticheskaia zhurnalistika. Ocherki istorii russkoi sovetskoi zhurnalistiki: 1933–1945*, ed. A. G. Dementiev, 444–72. Moscow: Nauka, 1968.

Smirnov, Dmitrii. "Pribyl' ne iskliuchaetsia . . ." (interview), *Komiksolet* (2000). http://comics.aha.ru/rus/articles/7.html.

——, and Sergei Gavrish. "Lyzhnaia katavatsiia." *Velikolepnye prikliucheniia* 7 (2000): 1–24.

——, and Andrei Ross. "Kanikuly Maksa-1." *Velikolepnye prikliucheniia* 21 (2002): 1–12.

Smirnova, Anastasiia. "Ezhik kak natsional'nyi geroi." *Russkii reporter*. No. 46 (76), December 4, 2008. http://www.rus.rusrep.ru/2008/46/geroi_i_chitateli_komiksov/.

Smirnova, Inga. "Scandal na Kommissii" [*sic*]. *Argumenty i fakty* 18 (April 29, 2008). http://kamchatka.aif.ru/issues/1435/09.

Smith, Hedrick. *The Russians*. New York: Ballantine, 1976.

Snegirov, Andrei. Personal correspondence. November 1, 2005.

——. Personal interview conducted by José Alaniz, Moscow, August 2004.

Snoodijk, Martijn. "Daar komen de Russen!" *Algemeen Dagblad* (March 25, 1995).

Snopkov, Alexander, Pavel Snopkov, and Alexander Shklyaruk. *The Russian Film Poster*, 2002.

Sokolov, Boris. *Khudozhestvennyi iazik russkogo lubka*. Moscow: Rosyskii Gosudarstvennyi gumanitarnyi universitet, 1999.

Solomon, Andrew. *The Irony Tower: Soviet Artists in a Time of Glasnost*. New York: Alfred A. Knopf, 1991.

Sonkin, Viktor. "Preved." *Moscow Times*, May 12, 2006. http://www.moscowtimes.ru/ arts/2008/06/06/364054.htm.

Stites, Richard. *Russian Popular Culture: Entertainment and Soviety since 1900*. Cambridge: Cambridge University Press, 1992.

———. *Revolutionary Dreams: Utopian Vision and Experimental Life in the Russian Revolution*. Oxford: Oxford University Press, 1989.

Strebkov, Denis. "Obraz biurokrata v sovetskoi karikature." *ES Forum*. December 2007, 9–16.

Strukov, Vlad. "Video Anekdot: Auteurs and Voyeurs of Russian Flash Animation." *Animation: An Interdisciplinary Journal* 2 (2007): 129–51.

Stykalin, S., and I. Kremenskaia. *Sovetskaia satiricheskaia pechat': 1917–1963*. Moscow: Izdatel'stvo polit-icheskoi literatury, 1963.

Styshneva, Evgeniia. "Samye risovannye investitsii." *Den'gi* 30 (July 31, 2006): 26–28.

Sussman, Elizabeth. "The Third Zone: Soviet Post-Modern." In *Between Spring and Summer: Soviet Conceptual Art in the Era of Late Communism*. Boston: MIT Press, 1990. 61–72.

Sviridov, V. "'Zolotaia Lozh' in *KOM O.K.*, Komiks Klub _VM." *Vecherniaia Moskva* (1990): 14–15.

Swearingen, Rodger. *That's So Funny, Comrade!* New York: Frederick A. Praeger, 1961.

Sysoev, Viacheslav. Personal interview with the author. Berlin, Germany, 2005.

———. *Walk Softly, Talk Softly* [Khodite tikho, govorite tikho], 2nd ed. Moscow: NLO Press, 2004.

———. *That's Alright, Mama* [Vsyo khorosho, mama]. Moscow: Retro, 2003.

———. *A Duck at His Winter Dacha or, They're Following You* [Utka na zimnei dache ili za vami slediat]. London: Overseas Publications Interchange Ltd, 1992.

Tamruchi, Natalia. *Moscow Conceptualism: 1970–1990*. Roseville East, NSW: Craftsman House, 1995.

Taussig, Michael. *The Nervous System*. London: Routledge, 1992.

Terent'ev, Mikhail. Personal interview conducted by José Alaniz, Moscow, January 2002.

Terras, Victor. *A History of Russian Literature*. New Haven, Conn.: Yale University Press, 1991.

Tishchenkov, Oleg. *Kot*. Moscow: Artemy Lebedev Studio Press, 2008.

Tishkov, Leonid. "Luchezarnye ptitsy, stomaki i pervyi dabloid." Krokin Art Gallery, 2005. http://www .krokingallery.com/russian/prissue_43/issue_151.html.

———. *Creatures*. Durham, N.C.: Duke University Museum of Art, 1993.

Tkalenko, Andrei, and Elena Voronovich. Personal interview conducted by José Alaniz, Moscow, June 2007.

———. *Suka*. Warsaw: Timof i cisi wspólnicy, 2009.

Tolstaia, Tatiana. "The Poet and the Muse." Trans. Jamey Grambell. *The Penguin Book of New Russian Writing*. London: Penguin, 1995. 278–91.

———. "Okkervil River." Trans. Antonina W. Bouis. *On the Golden Porch*. New York: Vintage, 1990.

Trofimenkov, Mikhail. "Toporom po Raskol'nikovu." *Kommersant* 164 (3740), November 9, 2007. http:// www.kommersant.ru/doc.aspx?DocsID=803061&print=true.

Troshin, A. S. "Griffit komiksa, ili iazik deviatogo iskusstva (po materiialam zhurnala *Filmvilág*)." *Kinovedcheskie zapiski* 32 (1996/97): 154–60.

Tufts, Claire. "Vincent Krassousky: Nazi Collaborator or Naïve Cartoonist?" *International Journal of Comic Art* 6, no. 1 (Spring 2004): 18–36.

Tupitsyn, Margarita. "On Some Sources of Soviet Conceptualism." *Non-Conformist Art: The Soviet Experience, 1956–1986*, ed. Alla Rosenfeld and Noton T. Dodge, 303–31. New York: Thames and Hudson, 1995.

Turovskaia, Maia. "Soviet Films of the Cold War." *Stalinism and Soviet Cinema*, ed. Richard Taylor and Derek Spring, 131–41. London: Routledge, 1993.

Turovskaia, Marina, and Askol'd Akishin. "Poslednii glotok." *Nesmeiana* 2 (2002): 4–21.

Ushakin, Sergei. "Vidimost' Muzhestvennosti." In *O Muzhe(N)stvennosti: Sbornik Statei*, ed. Ushakin, 479–503. Novoe Literaturnoe Obozrenie, 2002.

Uspensky, Boris. *The Semiotics of the Russian Icon*. Ed. Stephen Rudy. Lisse: Peter de Ridder Press, 1976.

Ustinova, Almira. "'The Visual Turn' and Gender History" ["Visual'nii povorot" i gendernaia istoriia]. *Gendernye issledovaniia* 2 (2000): 149–76.

Uzhinova, Elena. Personal interview conducted by José Alaniz, Moscow, June 2007.

———. "I Want" [Khochu]. KomMissia Festival 2007 Catalog. Moscow, 2007, 30–32.

———. *The Horrors of Life* [Uzhasy zhizni]. Moscow: Self-published, 2005.

———. "Story About My Eye" [Pro glaz]. *Komikser* 1 (1999): 16–17.

Vachnadze, Georgii. *Secrets of Journalism in Russia: Mass Media under Gorbachev and Yeltsin*. Commack, N.Y.: Nova Science Publishers, 1992.

Vail, Pyotr. Review of *Anna Karenina by Leo Tolstoy* by Katya Metelitsa et al., in *Itogi*, January 12, 2001, accessible at http://www.itogi.ru/ paper2001.nsf/Article/Itogi_2001_01_12_135849.html.

Vatlin, Alexander, and Larisa Malashenko. *Piggy Foxy and the Sword of Revolution: Bolshevik Self-Portraits*. Trans. Vadim Staklo. New Haven, Conn.: Yale University Press, 2006.

Velitov, Alim. E-mail correspondence. August 2008.

———. "Batman." *Almanakh: Volshebnie Komiksy* (2003): 10.

———. "Kerdyk." *Almanakh: Volshebnie Komiksy* (2003): 11, accessible at http://xixyc.mrtech.ru/old/av-kcrdyk.htm.

———. "Comics in the Underground." *Komiksolyot*, 1999, accessible at http://www.comics.aha.ru/rus/articles/4.html.

Vergueiro, Waldomiro C. S. "Brazilian Superheroes in Search of Their Own Identities." *IJOCA* 2, no. 2 (Fall 2000): 164–77.

Verizhnikova, Tatiana. *Ivan Bilibin*. St. Petersburg: Aurora, 2001.

Viskova, I. S. *Lushchie stranitsy sovetskoi satiricheskoi grafiki, Vol. 1: 1917–1941*. Moscow: Sovetskii khudozhnik, 1988.

Volegov, Vladimir. "Wild Things." *Novy Komiks* 1, nos. 1–4 (2001): 4–9.

———. "Chernaya Zvezda." *Novy Komiks* 1, no. 3 (November 20–December 20, 2001): 6–10.

———. "Versace." *Novy Komiks* 1, no. 1 (2001): 5–9.

———. "The Lift." *Novy Komiks* 1, no. 0 (2001) 25–28.

———. "The Tie." *Novy Komiks* 1, no. 0 (2001): 10–12.

———. "The Refuelling" in *Novy Komiks* 1, no. 0 (2001): 5–9.

Wallach, Amei. *Ilya Kabakov: The Man Who Never Threw Anything Away*. New York: Harry N. Abrams, 1996.

Waschik, Klaus, and Nina Baburina. *Real'nost' utopii: Iskusstvo russkogo plakata XX veka*. Moscow: Progress-Traditsiia, 2003.

Weaver, Kitty D. *Lenin's Grandchildren: Preschool Education in the Soviet Union*. New York: Simon and Schuster, 1971.

Wheeler, Marcus, Boris Unbegaun, and Paul Falla, eds. *The Oxford Russian Dictionary*, rev. ed. New York: Oxford University Press, 1997.

Williams, Linda. *Hardcore: Power, Pleasure and the Frenzy of the Visible*, 2nd ed. Berkeley and Los Angeles: University of California Press, 1999.

Woll, Josephine. "Exorcising the Devil: Russian Cinema and Horror." *Kinokultura* 4 (April 2004), accessible at http://www.kinokultura.com/articles/apr04.html.

Xatchett and Bogdan. "Skuns i Oselot: Insektarii." *Al'manakh risovannykh istorii, graficheskikh novell i komiksov No. 3*, ed. Alim Velitov, 16–19. Moscow: Liudi Mertvoi Ryby, 2005.

Yablokova, Oksana. "A Comical Approach to Tolstoy's Heroine." *Moscow Times*, January 30, 2001, accessible at http://www.themoscowtimes.com/stories/2001/01/30/003.html.

Yandex Press Release. "Yandex Researches the Russian Blogoshere." 2006. http://company.yandex.ru/news/2006/0926/index.xml (last accessed October 27, 2007).

Yusupova, Dina. "Biznes v kartinkakh." *Piatnitsa* (supplement *to Vedomosti*) 14 (April 20, 2007): 1–2.

Zaslavskii, Mikhail. "Autsaider russkikh muz." *Aktsiia* 55 (April 10–May 21, 2006): 2–3.

————. Personal interview conducted by José Alaniz, Moscow, May 2007.

————. Personal interview conducted by José Alaniz, Moscow, August 2004.

————. "Kovcheg rossiyskogo komiksa." *Komiks.com.aha.* 2003. http://www.comics.com.ua/node/464.

————. "On the Author of Alpha and the Komiks Studio KOM." *Komiksolet*, 2003, accessible at http://www.comics.com.ua/articles/article0002.shtml.

Zelensky, Elena Kristofovich. "Popular Children's Culture in Post-Perestroika Russia: Songs of Innocence and Experience Revisited." In *Consuming Culture: Popular Culture, Sex and Society Since Gorbachev*, ed. Adele Marie Barker, 138–60. Durham, N.C.: Duke University Press, 1999.

Zemenkov, V. S. *Grafika v bytu.* Moscow: AXR, 1930.

Zhdanov, Andrei. *Essays on Literature, Philosophy and Music.* New York: International Publishers, 1950.

Zhigunov, Yuri. "The Magical Power of Art." *KOM-paniia.* Ed. Sergei Kapranov. Moscow: ABEKS, 1990.

Zlatkovsky, Mikhail. "On risoval vlast', ego obvinili v pornografii." *Novaia gazeta* 17 (March 3, 2006). http://2006.novayagazeta.ru/nomer/2006/17n/n17n-s28.shtml.

————. *Russkaia karikatura.* Moscow: Knigi WAM, 2006.

Zmeyukina. "Interview with Andrei and Natalia Snegirov." *Spidermedia* (April 2005), http://www.spidermedia.ru/.

Zupan, Zdravko. "The Golden Age of Serbian Comics: Belgrade Comic Art 1935–1941." *International Journal of Comic Art* 2, no. 1 (Spring 2000): 90–101.

http://www.ostretsov.com.

http://www.ironi.ru/lumb/ Lumbricus blog, Koroleva chervei.

"A Terrifying Force" [Strashnaia sila]. *Whirligig* [Yula] 7 (2004): 30–31.

INDEX